Law, Humans and Plants in the Andes-Amazon

Extending law beyond the human, the book probes the conceptual openings, methodological challenges and ethical conundrums of law in a time of deep socio-ecological disturbances and transitions.

How do we learn and practice law across epistemic and ontological difference? What sort of methodologies do we need? In what sense does *conjuring* other-than-human beings as sentient, cognitive and social agents—rather than mere recipients of state-sanctioned rights—transform what we mean by "law" and "rights of nature"? Legal institutions exclusively focused on human perspectives seem insufficiently capable of addressing current socio-ecological challenges in Latin America and beyond. In response, this book strives to integrate other-than-human beings within legal thinking and decision-making protocols. Weaving together various fields of knowledge and world-making practices that include—but are not limited to—Indigenous legal traditions, Earth Law and multispecies ethnography, *Law, Humans and Plants* focuses on the entanglement of law, ecology and Indigenous cosmologies in Southern Colombia. In so doing, it articulates a general post-anthropocentric legal theory which is proposed, a tool to address socio-ecological challenges such as climate change and bio-cultural loss.

This book will be of interest to scholars and students in the disciplines of environmental law, Earth Law and ecological law, legal theory and critical legal studies as well as others working in the in the fields of Indigenous studies, environmental humanities, legal anthropology and sustainability and climate change justice.

Iván Darío Vargas Roncancio is Assistant Professor in the Law & Society Program, Department of Social Sciences, Faculty of Liberal Arts & Professional Studies (LA&PS) at York University.

Part of the LAW, JUSTICE AND ECOLOGY series
series editors Anna Grear
Law School, Cardiff University, UK

A GlassHouse Book

For information about the series and details of previous and forthcoming titles, see www.routledge.com/Law-Justice-and-Ecology/book-series/LAWJUSTECO

Law, Humans and Plants in the Andes-Amazon

The Lawness of Life

Iván Darío Vargas Roncancio

Routledge
Taylor & Francis Group
a GlassHouse Book

First published 2024
by Routledge
4 Park Square, Milton Park, Abingdon, Oxon OX14 4RN

and by Routledge
605 Third Avenue, New York, NY 10158

Routledge is an imprint of the Taylor & Francis Group, an informa business

a GlassHouse book

British Library Cataloguing-in-Publication Data
A catalogue record for this book is available from the British Library

ISBN: 978-1-032-39367-4 (hbk)
ISBN: 978-1-032-39369-8 (pbk)
ISBN: 978-1-003-34942-6 (ebk)

DOI: 10.4324/9781003349426

Typeset in Sabon
by Apex CoVantage, LLC

Law, Humans and Plants in the Andes-Amazon

The Lawness of Life

Iván Darío Vargas Roncancio

Routledge
Taylor & Francis Group
a GlassHouse Book

First published 2024
by Routledge
4 Park Square, Milton Park, Abingdon, Oxon OX14 4RN

and by Routledge
605 Third Avenue, New York, NY 10158

Routledge is an imprint of the Taylor & Francis Group, an informa business

a GlassHouse book

British Library Cataloguing-in-Publication Data
A catalogue record for this book is available from the British Library

ISBN: 978-1-032-39367-4 (hbk)
ISBN: 978-1-032-39369-8 (pbk)
ISBN: 978-1-003-34942-6 (ebk)

DOI: 10.4324/9781003349426

Typeset in Sabon
by Apex CoVantage, LLC

En memoria de Juana Evarista Parra Guerrero, abuela.
Gracias por las lecciones que todavía hoy me enseñas.

A Myriam, mi madre, y Laura, mi hermana, por ser fuerza, aliento y ternura.

Contents

Tables

Preface

Over the last few years, the Colombian Amazon has been the center of a new extractivist boom as well as the recipient of large international conservation efforts. The expansion of industrial oil, large-scale mining—i.e., gold and copper—and the construction of dams, among other development projects, is concurrently happening with a rise in environmental regulations in a post-peace-agreement scenario, particularly in Indigenous territories. For example, recent norms and judicial decisions on the rights of nature (RON) place life at the center of legal discourse in this region. Nevertheless, the RON approach seems to depend on two core ontological assumptions: the law is a system of norms made by humans to regulate human conduct in relation to an externally existing natural world, thereby insisting on a separation between law and ecological processes; and second, the form of the law is primarily symbolic—linguistic and propositional—that is, only human.

Based on long-term collaborative fieldwork, textual analysis and embodied practice in the Andean-Amazonian region of Colombia, *Law, Humans and Plants* sets out to explore how plants as *persons*, on the one hand, and Indigenous practitioners, legal scholars, and sustainability scientists, on the other, are contributing to a crucial paradigm shift: from a highly regulatory environmental law approach to an epistemologically plural and systems-based Earth jurisprudence in contexts of war and dispossession.

Building on seminal works in the fields of Earth Law, ecological law and posthumanism, the book poses an ontological and methodological challenge for Western law: How do we learn and practice *law* across epistemic and ontological difference? What sort of methodologies do we need? In what sense does *conjuring* other-than-human beings as sentient, cognitive and social agents—rather than mere recipients of state-sanctioned rights—transform what we mean by *law* and *rights of nature* in Latin America and beyond? As its critical underpinning, *Law, Humans and Plants* suggests that legal institutions focused exclusively on human perspectives are not sufficiently capable of addressing the region's current socio-ecological crises. It seems plausible therefore to probe new analytical frameworks that integrate other-than-human beings and methodologies into legal thinking and practice.

Such an approach weaves together various fields of knowledge and world-making practices that include—but are not limited to—Indigenous legal traditions, multispecies ethnography and ecological economics. The book aims to illustrate how human and other-than-human persons such as medicinal and ritual plants, and what Indigenous practitioners in Southwestern Colombia call the "invisible ones" (*los invisibles)*, co-create legal protocols and institutions. In addition, it probes the conceptual openings, methodological challenges and ethical questions of this approach for legal theory.

Law, Humans and Plants aims to contribute answers to the following set of interrelated questions: What happens when we consider forms of agency beyond symbolic and multicultural frameworks in legal practice? How does a law that emerges from the relations between plants, humans and invisible peoples challenge concepts of justice, agency and value? The book combines a multi-sited ethnography and a post-humanist approach in anthropology and law to study the entangled lives of legal norms and ecological relationalities in Southern Colombia.

In conversation with biologists, Indigenous practitioners, legal scholars, and plants, particularly *Yoco* (*Paullinia Yoco*), *Yagé* (*Banisteriopsis caapi*) and coca (*Erythroxylaceae coca)*, *Law, Humans and Plants*, in brief, explores how legal institutions may emerge from the fabric of human and other-than-human forms of agency in the Andean and Amazonian regions. This relational orientation is at the core of Earth Law and similar approaches—i.e., Earth Systems law, Ecological law and Wild law—and the radical paradigm shift of these fields towards a legal theory for a finite planet.

Acknowledgments

There are many communities, individual persons and institutions that I wish to acknowledge for their support, guidance and friendship. I may lose sight of some names, for which I apologize in advance. A special thanks to Nicolas Kosoy in the Department of Natural Resource Sciences at McGill University for his relentless support, academic guidance and rich conversations: it has been a journey of great learning and friendship; to Eduardo Kohn, McGill Anthropology, for inviting me to "hold space open" for nonhumans in the law and to pay close ethnographic attention to the voice of those who do not communicate with words. To Kirsten Anker at McGill Law for her thoughtful and generous readings of several drafts of the dissertation that led to this book. My sincere gratitude to all of them for the many exciting conversations we had about law, ecology and Indigenous cosmologies in the context of the Earth Law movement.

Special thanks to Peter G. Brown, director of the Leadership for the Ecozoic (L4E) program at McGill, for his transformative vision of higher education in the Global North and his constant support and encouragement; to Dina Spigelski, L4E Associate Director, for her immense generosity and for being the best orchestra director L4E could wish for; to Deissy Perilla, L4E's project manager, for being a never-ending source of encouragement and support: I could not be more grateful for our meandarings across countries, languages, and experiences. The lessons have been many! Thanks to my colleagues and professors in the L4E and Economics for the Anthropocene programs: Mick Babcock, Tina Beigi, Sam Bliss, Emille Boulot, Matthew Burke, Megan Egler, Jon Erickson, Josh Farley, Ursula Georgeoglou, Jen Gobby, Katie Horner, Katie Kish, Joylon Larson, James Magnus-Johnston, Rigo Melgar-Melgar, Lindsay Ofrias, Nina Smolyar, Leah Temper and Liz Zahirovic. To my L4E colleagues Josh Sterlin for insightful conversations on law, anthropology and ontologies, and to Shaun Sellers for valuable dialogues on the limits of "development" and the importance of weaving encounters between the Global South and the Global North.

My sincere thanks to Carolina Campos for her support in transcribing several interviews; to Laura Gilbert for reading Chapter 1; to Geoffrey Garver for his pioneering work in the field of ecological law; for several conversations, guest lectures and webinars co-organized between ELGA (Ecological Law and Governance Association) and L4E; for his support and encouragement as we continue to learn about this transformative new legal paradigm. I wish to thank Julia Freeman, Hamish van der Ven and Nicolas Kosoy at McGill for a way teaching committed to methodological pluralism and social-ecological justice; to Danielle Lefevbre at the Bieler School of the Environment, Brian T. Driscoll, Sebastian Faucher, Susan Gregus and Simone Clamann at the Department of Natural Resource Sciences for their institutional support; to Colin Scott, Director of the Centre for Indigenous Conservation and Development Alternatives (CICADA) at McGill: his generous spirit, wisdom and the many stories he shared from his decades-long engaged work with Indigenous communities in Canada and beyond have been a tremendous source of inspiration for me; to my colleagues and friends Lucia Justo and Steven Schnoor (CICADA) for their warm presence and unceasing support. To the L4E program and COLCIENCIAS in Colombia for their institutional support, and to the Department of Social Sciences and the Law and Society Program at York University where I work as an assistant professor: I cannot imagine a better home to continue my research and teaching journey.

I would like to extend my gratitude to Herman Greene of the Center for Ecozoic Studies for enriching conversations at the intersection of Law, Earth law and philosophy, and for his generous invitation to contribute to the first volume devoted to the practice of Earth law globally. Special thanks to my friends, colleagues and intellectual accomplices Daniel Ruiz-Serna, Camilo Gómez and Kariuki Kirigia for inspiring conversations that extend far beyond academic waters. My deepest gratitude to them and their families.

This book would be unthinkable without the Inga, Cofán and Murui communities of Putumayo and Nariño, and the many Indigenous friends and interlocutors with whom I have had the privilege of learning and working over many years. My special gratitude to *taita* Dr. (*honoris causa*) Hernando Chindoy, Indigenous intellectual and traditional authority of the Inga people of Colombia, for several conversations on law and the law of origin; to artist Ursula Biemann for our continued collaboration towards the co-creation of an Inga-led Indigenous university in the Amazon: I am honored and humbled by this creative journey leading to Devenir Univesidad; to Sonia Mutumabajoy and *Iacha* Luciano Mutumbajoy: words cannot adequately express my gratitude; to Marcela Bravo, Cristina Chindoy, Waira Jacanamijoy, Alvaro Hernandez, Santiago del Hierro, Flora Macas, Giovanna Micarelli and Juliana Ramirez for working together towards the creation of the Inga university project. Special thanks to the education team of the Inga people of Colombia. I hope that this book will become an asset for the future Biocultural Indigenous University of the Amazon they lead.

A very special thanks to David Rodríguez-Mora for his complicity, academic collaboration and co-learning with the Cofán people. David is a researcher in ethnobotany and the territorial struggles of the Cofán of Colombia. I am grateful for his invitation to be part of his ethnobotanical research project in Nariño as a field assistant: the lessons have been many and on many levels. Special thanks to Monica Gagliano for our collective musings and collaborations: her work has been a source of deep inspiration for several years—Monica has been a pioneering voice in the field of plant intelligence and bioacoustics. My gratitude to Kristi Onzik for his excellent reading of one of the chapters; to Afshin Akhtar-Khavari for a creative mind connecting international law and ecology; to Alessandro Pelizzon for insightful conversations on Earth jurisprudence and his pioneering work in this field; to Saskia Vermeylen and Anna Grear for connecting law and ontology so eloquently and to Michael Cepek for his generous and challenging reading of Chapter 4 developed in collaboration with David Rodríguez.

My gratitude to Miguel Rojas-Sotelo and Miguel Rocha Vivas for our collaborations on Indigenous arts, politics and struggles in Colombia and beyond; to Luis Felipe Avella, Andrés García Trujillo, Julio César Montañez, Liliana Moreno, María Clara Pardo and Mauricio Velásquez Ospina for their friendship, generous spirit and support during my doctoral studies and much more. To Gabriel Ricardo Nemogá Soto and Farid Benavides Vanegas for their academic mentorship in Colombia: the seeds of this book were sown under their academic guidance; to Aaron Mills and Bruce Jennings for their insightful comments and brilliant questions, and for teaching that law must move beyond conventional frameworks.

Finally, I would like to give special thanks to a mentor and friend that life has so graciously placed in my path: Arturo Escobar. He is an inspiring *sentipensante* force and a weaver of worlds. My sincere gratitude to Magda Corredor for her spirit and friendship.

Last but not least, my deepest thanks go to my family: my wonderful mother, Myriam Roncancio Parra; my wonderful sister, Laura M. Vargas Roncancio; uncles, aunts and cousins for being a source of unconditional love and support.

Thanks to the *seres* of this Earth and to the Earth which is a tapestry of *seres*; to the Amazon, the Andes, their peoples, rivers, mountains, hummingbirds . . . *su gente invisible*.

Credits

Edited versions of materials previously published in:

Chapter 3: Vargas Roncancio, I.D. (2017). "Nomadic Ecologies: Plants, Embodied Knowledge and Temporality in the Colombian Amazon." In *Boletín de Antropología*, 32(53): 255–276.

Chapter 6: Vargas Roncancio, I.D. (2017). "Plants and the Law: Vegetal Ontologies and the Rights of Nature. A Perspective from Latin America." In *Australian Feminist Law Journal*, 43(1): 67–87. *Reprinted* for special edition in Gustafsson, R., Hill, R., Ngo, H. (eds) (2018). *Philosophies of Difference: Nature, Racism, and Sexuate Difference* (first edition). London—NY: Routledge.

Chapter 7: Vargas Roncancio, I.D. (2021). "Conjuring Sentient Beings and Relations in the Law: Rights of Nature and a Comparative Praxis of Legal Cosmologies." In Anker, K., Burdon, P., Garver, G., Maloney M., & Sbert, C. (eds.). *From Environmental to Ecological Law*, London—NY: Routledge.

Chapter 8: Vargas Roncancio, I.D. (2020). "Forest on Trial: Towards a relational theory of legal agency for transitions into the Ecozoic." Orr, C., Kish, K., & Jennings, B. *Liberty and the Ecological Crisis: Freedom on a Finite Planet*. London—NY: Routledge.

Permissions were secured through the Copyright Clearance Center (chapters 7, 8), PLSclear and Taylor & Francis Group (Chapter 6). Chapter 3 under creative commons.

Introduction

Law and the pluriverse

1. A story of encounters: a semiotic "warfare"?

On a foggy night in October 1536,[1] coming from an expedition through the Orinoco River, *Conquistador* Federmann's troops retreated in fear at what they saw through the mist while surveying the Andean *páramos* of *Sumapaz*.[2] From a nearby plateau veiled by slowly descending clouds, the Spaniards were able to descry what looked like thousands of men wearing friar-like gowns and feather headdresses across several acres of winding hills (Moreno 2015, 13). As the freezing wind of the Andes slipped through their bodies like hundreds of minuscule razors, a shivering soldier dropped his bayonet on the ground. A frightened captain managed to drink the last gulp of whiskey from his corroded flask, as Federmann gathered his meager cavalry giving the unavoidable order to retreat. What did Federmann's soldiers see through the fog?

The Colombian historian J.J. Borda described the state of the troops as they approached the Andean region of *Sumapaz*, located only a few miles Southeast from the newly founded city of *Santa Fe de Bogotá*:

> Two days after Hernán Pérez's return to Bogota, a couple of indigenous folks brought a message from Lazaro Fonte. The message warned Quesada about the arrival of a group of Spaniards coming from the mountains of Sumapaz. The people he sent there noticed that the Spaniards were under the command of captain Federmann. The captain came from Venezuela . . . his troop was almost naked and in the most miserable situation and followed by dozens of famished dogs.
>
> (Borda 1904, 43)

Famished and largely outnumbered, the Spaniards feared what they believed were hundreds of "merciless savages" in the distance ready to defend their land:

> Confusing *frailejones* for hundreds of Indigenous men in battle positions, the Spanish troops finally withdrew the attack and sought the way back home. Thus, began a "magical resistance" of the *paramo* [the moors].[3]

DOI: 10.4324/9781003349426-1

Did the soldiers see a human crowd as they surveyed the terrain? In the scene, the Spaniards were convinced that they were standing before hundreds of enemy lines in the distance. In fact, according to Northern Andes oral renditions of vegetal life, "the group of plants called *frailejón [Lat. espeletia]* acquired their name as a result of their perceived similarity with a friar walking partially hidden by the fog" (Zent and Zent 1999, 155). Precisely, Federmann's withdrawal occurred thanks to the perspective that rendered visible an army of humans instead of an "army" of shrubs.[4] Is such an episode a matter of representation or cultural belief *only*?

As this story of deterrence and survival in the Northern Andes suggests, the ontological boundaries between living entities can be quite blurry in conditions of exhaustion, hunger and fear of the unexpected. The possibility of vegetal deterrence, that is, plants influencing human behavior, may well be considered a literary trope to expose a productive "misperception": when reality becomes a matter of distance and proximity, humans may see members of their own species concealed as *frailejones* (plants). Despite this explanation, narratives of the "misperception of reality" or "cultural belief of local peoples" do not seem to foreclose other ways of engaging with these instances of plant-human encounters in the past and present.

The misperception solution, to be sure, rests on an anthropocentric premise whereby interpreting and creating the world is only a matter of human values, technologies and social institutions.[5] Challenging this underpinning premise of modernity, the book joins ongoing scholarly and societal efforts towards a non-anthropocentric law and politics that address crucial socio-ecological challenges such as climate change and bio-cultural loss (See Anker 2017; De la Cadena 2015; Escobar 2020; Kohn 2013; Kosoy et al. 2012; Vermeylen 2017).

Since 2007, I have enjoyed life-changing learning experiences alongside Inga, Cofán and Murui Indigenous communities of the Andean-Amazonian region of Colombia, which have fundamentally challenged and transformed my approach to political and legal thinking, and to *thinking* more broadly. Several dialogues with members of these communities have taught me a valuable lesson, which can be summarized as follows: we are facing *modern problems* for which *there are not (always) modern solutions* (Escobar 2018). The 2019 fires in much of the Amazon—particularly in Brazil—are a case in point.

The fires express an exacerbated modernity in agricultural systems: the exponential expansion of soy monocrops to feed agroindustries will not solve the (modern) problems of biodiversity loss, illegal grabbing of Indigenous lands and racialized violence against local populations. Conversely, Indigenous logics of territorial care centered on small-scale agro-ecological production seems to offer a long-standing and effective approach to protecting fragile ecologies and the strengthening of local cultures. This book is based on the general ethico-political and methodological premise that Indigenous knowledge and ways of life must be at the forefront of contemporary debates on socio-ecological challenges worldwide. A post-anthropocentric legal theory and practice is a step in this direction.

Law, Humans and Plants draws from several critical methodologies in social and legal theory and practice, which, broadly speaking, seek to reflexively explore how legal doctrines, norms and practices may perpetuate Western-centric views and ways of thinking, living and being. In addition, the book joins scholarly and activist efforts for epistemic justice and the decolonization *of* and *through* the law (Xavier et al. 2021). Such an approach is at the center of a critical legal pluralism across civil law, common law and Indigenous legal traditions globally. In so doing, *Law, Humans and Plants* brings post-anthropocentric approaches to the heart of legal analysis and practice.

A post-anthropocentric approach to law and society suggests that institutions and decisions emerge through the encounter between humans and other-than-human beings (Harris 2014; Vargas Roncancio 2017; Vermeylen 2017). For Amerindian communities in Southwestern Colombian Amazon, for instance, plants such as Yoco (*Paullinia Yoco*), coca (*Erythroxylum coca*) and those mixed in the *ayahuasca* or Yagé brew,[6] among others, play central political and normative roles within and outside their territories (UMIYAC 2000). These plants are considered sources of knowledge and authority, as well as the origin of law itself.

Returning to the opening story, the Spanish troops would have advanced in their attack had they learned that these lines of enemies in the distance were, in fact, a bunch of "harmless" plants with anthropomorphic shapes. In this case, the encounter between plants and humans was rendered impossible simply because those beings concealed under the mist were never vegetal from the perspective of the Spaniards. They were "literal" humans rather than "human-like" beings. In other words, the Spanish soldiers would have likely pursued the attack had they perceived resemblance (plants that looked like humans) instead of identity (literal humans like them).

The fear of the unknown, coupled with the environmental conditions of the moor, rendered the *frailejones* of *Sumapaz* blissfully imperceptible as plants but also eventful as human people. Could we venture to say that the Spanish became animists by default, or even that the *páramo* (the moor) was defending itself? Are we to far off to say that the Spanish almost-invaders produced humanity out of plants? In other words, perceiving "plants" was impossible (and yet not unthinkable) from the Spanish's point of view, as the troops faced countless lines of human enemies ready to attack. This eventfulness of the human across species, so to speak, is crucial for the concept/practice of the pluriverse (Escobar 2015, 2018; Kothari et al. 2019); especially when considering normative statements extending personhood to nonhumans in the context of an increasingly ecocentric legal discourse worldwide:[7] humans must relate to the páramo (the moor) and the frailejones as relatives and not as things. We are, indeed, facing a paradigm-shifting contestation of the ontological monolingualism of (legal) modernity. The notion of the pluriverse seems to capture this emergent plurality in law and society writ large.

The "modernist ontology of universalism" (Kothari et al. 2019) is based upon a dualist principle that separates human and non-human beings, body and mind, bio and geo, the living and the non-living, among other boundary-making concepts. This ontology of separation determines how people produce (legal) knowledge, how they act, experience the world, relate to one another and organize collectively. For example, the discipline of physics presupposes the separation between an objective universe and the subjective experience and cultural beliefs of an independent human observer; similarly, the discipline of economics separates markets from the socio-ecosystems where they are actually embedded (Brown and Timmerman 2015), and the same is true for almost all descriptive and normative disciplines of the modern learning/teaching apparatus including the law.

Anthropologist Eduardo Viveiros de Castro suggests that according to a modern scientific paradigm, one knows something when one is able to see it from the outside, that is, when the world is de-subjectivized and no intentions are attributed to the object of study (e.g., plants, animals, complex tropical ecologies). In contrast, for traditional medicine people (*sabedores*) in the "Americas," to know something well is to be able to attribute intentionality to this former object of study, namely when this object is rendered a subject or person (Viveiros de Castro 2013).

The modern ontology of universalism, then, is about creating a One World with humans on top of it. The "One World" is a way to highlight two core ideas (Law 2015; Escobar 2018). First, the notion that there is one single world made up of discrete and separable entities rather than interdependencies; and second, the notion that this world can be revealed only by science at the expense of other knowledge systems, or by relegating them to the status of cultural beliefs and myths of non-modern peoples (De la Cadena 2015). Conceived from the perspective of the West, the idea of the One World thus suggests the primacy of one local experience (the West) and system of knowledge (Science) as the veritable source of knowledge of an external world as observed by a particular kind of human: the Western Man. Alternatives to this paradigm are emerging everywhere. The pluriversal alternative, for example, challenges this modernist orientation in favor of a multiplicity of possible worlds or ways of knowing, doing and being (Kothari et al. 2019). Following the Zapatista dictum, the pluriverse can be best described as "a world where many worlds fit" (Enlace Zapatista 1996), namely a world where many ways of being, doing and knowing are rendered possible and are put at the service of "healing the web of life" (Escobar 2019).

The way humans represent and engage with other beings matters for the law. Drawing upon Brazilian anthropologist Eduardo Viveiros de Castro, the Spanish soldiers, in our opening story, were before an instance of "equivocation," that is,

> not only a failure to understand . . . but a failure to understand that understandings are necessarily not the same, and that they are not related to imaginary ways of seeing the world [i.e., plants] but to the real worlds that are being seen ["i.e., human beings"].
>
> (Viveiros de Castro 2014, 11)

The question here is not so much *what* a human being *is* (essence), but rather *when* a living sentient being is rendered human in inter-being encounters and for what social, political and normative ends.

In other words, can friar-like plants be considered people, for instance, in a court of law? (Hall 2011) Should they be granted "human qualities" such as intent, decision-making and/or intelligence before they can be considered purposeful legal agents in the legal arena? While ongoing efforts to grant rights to nature seem to offer a positive answer to these philosophical and political questions, contrasting interpretations on the scope of these rights may lead to divergent understandings and equivocations (and certainly different ontological choices) about terms such as "nature," "legal agency" and "justice." Does the clause of the rights of nature refer to any "natural" being? Does a microbe have the same right as a plant, an animal or a mountain? How does thinking about other-than-human beings in terms of social agencies—instead of biological and/or forces—contribute to legal theory and practice in times of socio-ecological crisis?

Anthropologist Eduardo Kohn offers an important methodological and ontological framework to reimage our relationships with other-than-humans like our *frailejón*. This framework is central to the book's empirical and theoretical argument concerning post-anthropocentric law. Kohn argues that both humans and other-than-humans use signs that are not always symbolic, that is, all living beings are sites of signification that are not limited to conventional, referential and linguistic symbols such as human language.[8] Based on Peirce's semiotics, he considers other non-symbolic modalities, namely icons and indices. An icon is a type of sign that indicates similarity to that which it represents, while an index indicates a relation of spatial or temporal contiguity with what it points to. These representational modalities "have to be brought into the anthropological [and legal] agenda . . . because icons and indexes are the signs that nonhuman organisms use to represent the world and communicate between life forms," including conquering humans and moorland-loving judges (Descola 2014, 269).

Kohn argues that "life-forms represent the world in some way or another, and these representations are intrinsic to their beings." And this means that we, humans, not only share our embodiment with other-than-human forms of life "but the fact that we all live with and through signs . . . signs make what we are." (Kohn 2013, 9). According to this approach, attributes such as cognition, memory and communication are distributed across different types of living selves, rather than being the exclusive domain of humans endowed with brains and centralized nervous systems. If "signs, make what we are" there seems to be a radical continuity and interdependence between humans and other beings beyond the mere physicality of our own bodies. This argument is of crucial importance for the way we define society, politics and the law beyond modern partitions such as nature and culture, body and mind, self and other, among others (De la Cadena 2015; Escobar 2018; Viveiros de Castro 1998, 2013).

In the initial story, the *frailejones* of *Sumapaz* were active participants in the production of an event that exceeded the idea of other-than-humans as external to a human observer in command of language, meaning and agency (see de la Cadena 2015). Both the Spanish invaders and the local frailejones co-emerged as humans as they encountered each another in a nearby plateau veiled by slowly descending clouds. From the point of view of the encounter, Spaniards and *frailejones* are not preexistent entities in space (Haraway 2007). Again, this idea of *the human as an event of co-emergence* presupposes a form of continuity across all life forms beyond the physicality of their bodies. Anthropologist Viveiros de Castro's notion of "equivocation" is an excellent conceptual tool to unravel these ideas of co-emergence and continuity of beings (Descola 2013).

As suggested earlier, the notion of equivocation defines a failure to understand that misunderstandings about the world are not the same across beings, and therefore they don't refer to contrasting human representations of a common world or reality that plants, humans and other beings share together, but to different worlds entirely. In the example, *frailejones* and the Spanish soldiers co-emerged through the encounter. They co-produced an event (the human!) through partially connected bodies as worlds (Strathern 2004; De la Cadena 2015): the *frailejon´s* and the Spaniards'. This encounter, again, presupposed a semiotic continuity—and physical discontinuity—rather than an absolute rift between the newcomers and the local *frailejones*. In fact, these *frailejones* communicated their positions or perspectives *as humans* by means of an iconic sign—a likeness with what the *frailejones* stand for from the point of view of the Spaniards, namely an army of humans ready to defend their land. In the story, the Spaniards were able to descry what looked like thousands of men wearing friar-like gowns and feather headdresses—all icons of humanity—across several acres of winding hills.

However, the "humanity of the plant," that is, what the "human" stands for as a common condition of all beings (Descola 2013), was only possible thanks to the equivocation on the part of the Spanish invaders who perceived likeness or sameness rather than difference: the Spanish soldiers literally *saw* hundreds of humans in battle positions rather than a forest of *frailejones*. This eventful co-emergence of what we may call "human vegetality," on the one hand, and "vegetal humanity," on the other, enacted a reality of sorts with the practical effect of dissuading the Spanish soldiers from attacking the mysterious army of the moor. If an equivocation is not a failure to understand what is out there, that is, a failure to understand what is *real*, but a failure to understand the possibility of different reals—the pluriverse—(Escobar 2018), then the Spanish's equivocation does not refer to a form of misperception leading to a form of misrepresentation (seeing humans rather than plants), but to *a real world* that is being enacted through practice ("human" *frailejones* ready to defend their land and "human" invaders ready to retreat).

Moreover, if the *frailejones* enacted their humanity through likeness or iconicity as they stand for humans (friar-like gowns and feather headdresses . . .), the Spanish invaders, on the other hand, enacted their own humanity by means of, with Kohn, an indexical sign: a retreat action to avoid the attack of the local friar-warriors insofar as these friar-warriors were real humans ready to defend their territory. To put it differently, the *frailejones* deceived the Spanish through a form of semiotic warfare, that is, embodying humanity by resemblance (an icon of the human), and by virtue of the Spanish's fear to be attacked (index of danger). This is co-evolution at work: the famished and outnumbered Spaniards failed to understand and therefore retreated to save their lives. Had they succeeded in participating in the planthood of the *frailejón*, the story would have been entirely different. In a way, this failure made humans out of plants. It created a world by means of embodied action rather than symbolic representation.

The notion of co-emergence of humanity as a condition of being (Descola 2013) expresses a form of continuity of sign and matter. Continuities, however, are not universal, but emplaced or place bound (Blaser 2019): neither the *frailejones* nor the Spanish humans preceded the event of their encounter but came into being by virtue of an equivocation. Thus, co-emergence through equivocation seems important to what counts as the "social" precisely because it tells us something *new* about how the human comes into being through the relationships between different life forms with their different regimes of perception (Ingold 2011). Encounters between plants and humans, or, let us say, between different kinds of "humans," can teach us something *new* about society and what makes society work (decisions, institutions, norms) in times of deep socio-ecological changes and transitions. In a certain sense, a modern humanist analysis that separates humans from the rest of life does not seem sufficient to explain this type of encounter. If humans and other-than-humans can represent the world in myriad ways through symbols, icons and indexes, can we venture to say that social norms continue the logics of life? Is the law immanent to life? How does the law come into being through encounters? What is the relationship between law and ecology? (Anker 2017; Capra and Mattei 2015; Davies 2017).

A post-anthropocentric approach to law suggests that institutions and decisions emerge through the encounter between humans and other-than-human beings. For Amerindian communities in Southwestern Colombian Amazon, for instance, plants such as the Yoco vine (*Paullinia Yoco*) and those mixed in the Yagé brew play central political and normative roles. These plants are considered persons, sources of knowledge and authority and even the origin of law itself.

2. A story of Amazonian legal concepts[9]

"*De aquí viene el derecho*" ("the law comes from *here*"), said the *iacha*[10] in the midst of an intense vertigo with the Yagé (*Banisteriopsis caapi*) brew[11] known as *chuma*.[12] Like a firefly hovering in the background of my memories, this enigmatic statement has stayed with me for quite some time.

In 2007, a friend invited me to Bajo Putumayo, located only a few miles north of the Colombian border with Ecuador. "There is a ceremony with the Cofán elders, and a group of visitors from the *Cumbal* region (Colombian Andes)" he said. "What is a *toma?*" I asked, halfway between curious and bewildered. "*Ayahuasca*! But this time it's going to be with the *mayores (elders)*. They know how to manage this plant." I had heard quite a few stories of people having some intense experiences with the "soul creeper vine" also known as *Yagé* (Schultes et al. 2001). But I had also heard one must keep a strict diet before ingesting the brew with a "person who knows it," as my friend said, and in the appropriate ritual setting. With trepidation, I accepted his invitation yet remained highly undecided about doing the *toma* itself. Such a bidding, however, had to be endorsed by a middle aged *Ingano iacha* from the Alto Putumayo region, who was summoned to lead the ritual.

The *iacha* finally accepted once he decided that I had the rightful intentions. The plant "calls upon the people needing it," he said, and I imagined a bunch of entangled systems of underground roots connected to an ancient stump somewhere in the Amazon while sending chemical signals all the way from the canopy to the Andean mountains. Soon we would set out on the road to the unexpected, yet open to dialogue with the "sacred vine" in its own terms (Schultes et al. 2001).

We met at the bus terminal. A good *Ingano* seasoned in the arts of trading plants and ritual objects all over the country, the *iacha* bargained with an office clerk to get a reduced fare on the tickets; we bought some snacks for the trip and finally set forth on the way down to the *Bajo*. After around 12 hours of paved roads and hilly sceneries, we arrived to *Mocoa*, capital of Putumayo and the urban hinge between the Andes and the Amazon.

Founded by Avendaño in the middle of the sixteenth century, this city vanished within a few decades. Refusing to abide by the sword, the cross and the bible, a group of audacious locals known as the *Andaquíes* burned the whole place down several times and then returned to the forest to never leave it again. With the specter of the *Andaquíes* quietly hiding behind the bushes, we arrived at our destination a few hours later.[13] "Light up a tobacco before getting in. It will help you to *pensar bonito* [to have beautiful thoughts]," the *iacha* said as we entered the *resguardo* (reservation). "This is an ancestral land, and we owe respect to its owners, so we pay with the tobacco plant," he continued almost putting forth the clause of a sacred contract between the human newcomers and its forest hosts.

We walked in silence for over 30 minutes along a muddy trail between all kinds of trees colored in several tones of green. Above, the branches almost embraced one another, while a potpourri of invisible birds momentarily suspended the rhythm of our conversations. At the end of the trail, we found a place with *malocas* (traditional wooden constructions). "And the elder?" the *iacha* asked—"keep on walking and you will find his house by the creek," one of the residents replied. Once we arrived to the *abuelo's maloca*, we climbed up a few steps to find a humble living room where we rested for a bit. Fleeting hens and ducks passed by under the wooden house floor, as the *abuela* handed us some *chicha de maíz* (a fermented corn drink).

Early in the morning we began our bodily preparation for the upcoming *toma* that night. We walked through a forest of *moriche* palms (*Mauritia flexuosa*), tobacco trees and plantains to find a creek about a kilometer away from the *abuelo's* residence. One of the community leaders was waiting for us with *totumas* (gourds) filled with the "tea of the Indigenous," as he jokingly named an infusion of the local Yoco plant (*Paullinia Yoco*) traditionally used early in the morning before work.

In large quantities, the plant may be used as a purgative, whereas a single cup may evince its tonic properties (see Chapter 1): "the *Yoco* gives strength to work; it purges the body, and it cures the soul," one of the community members said. Light and aligned, our bodies were slowly getting ready to endure the night of the *toma*. As I learned later that day, the ritual of the *ayahuasca* ingestion was particularly important those days, for it was offered to seal a pact of intercultural exchange and learning between two Indigenous communities, the Cofán from the lowlands and the Pastos from the Andean mountains of the Great Cumbal.

An earthly mirror of the cosmos, the *Gran Maloca*, where the *toma* was held, is an ample and sturdy wooden construction with a rich *carana* palm roof (*Mauritia carana*). It is also a boa, a tree-world and the house of spirits where we ingested the plant after a daylong preparation of bodies and minds. To the right, a forest of tobacco trees moved rhythmically with the wind, while the left side nested the *chagra* (family plot) plants wide open to the sunlight. "Don't go to the tobacco forest: the spirits live there entangled with the trees, and it can be dangerous for you," the *iacha* said at some point. That evening we started to learn about "where the Indigenous law comes from" and what plants can teach us about it. "*De Aquí viene el derecho indígena*" (Indigenous law comes from *Here*), the *iacha* said in the midst of the *chuma*.

What did he mean by this? I asked myself. Can plants be not only bearers of rights but also law-making entities? And what does such an odd place "*Aquí*" ('Here') represent for the human and other-than-human *people* I met?

***

Indigenous practices with plants wield repercussions that extent far beyond local life and into formal environmental politics in the Andean-Amazonian region. In fact, Indigenous relationships with sacred plants exceed ritual spaces to occupy the politics of the everyday and local dealings with the state law. The ingestion of *Paulina yocco* and the *Banisteriopsis caapi*, for example, plays an active role in decision-making protocols affording a compelling entry point to other legalities or forms of the law. Yet there is a long way before state-oriented legal frameworks incorporate more-than-human legalities in theory and practice (Pelizzon and Gagliano 2015; Braverman 2018; Davies 2017). Whilst this emergent law may benefit from Indigenous cosmologies and plant science alike, symbolic representation distinguishes the law from other fields of practice and experience. The law is almost exclusively conceived as a lettered practice. Can the plant speak *law*? How can we be analytically precise about different forms of legal meaning and agency beyond the human? Does the forest always need the mediation of the botanist, for example, in a court of law? Can a *law beyond the human* be used in concrete scenarios of legal learning, judiciary adjudication and socio-ecological justice? *Law, Humans and Plants* is an attempt to "stay with the trouble" these questions pose (Haraway 2016). But first, we need to reengage with legal theory in order to go beyond its pervasive anthropocentric premises.

3. The *lawness* of life? Unlearning law as usual and learning law otherwise

Discussing how ecological knowledge can imbue legal learning and practice, Alex, a North American environmentalist, asked me this question a few months ago: "So, *this* would be the law. Right? I want to understand what *exactly* you mean by law, and how one can differentiate it from ecological relationships in nature" (Alex, interview, February 2020). I have encountered this challenging question many times before at different stages of my research. My first reaction was to describe my own experience as a law student, and how my perceptions about the law have changed over time as I interacted with different peoples, places, and beings. When I began law school, I told Alex, I defined it as "justice." For me, there was no separation between social justice ideals and the law as a normative social institution. In a way, the law was a particular form of justice. As I learned about the history of legal ideas, you could say that I was an iusnaturalist without even realizing it, simply because I did not hold any conscious separation between law and ethical systems, or, better yet, the law was an ethical system of sorts.

As I learned about codes, decrees, statutes and constitutions, the word "law" became somewhat equivalent to the word "legal norms" and how they regulate social behavior as well as the relationships between humans and the so-called natural environment. I quickly became—or the law school turned me into—a "soft" positivist who hesitantly separated the law from any other sphere of life, for example, culture, morality or environmental relations. Furthermore, when I learned how the law can also be defined by whatever was in the mind of a judge, or when I learned how the law was used to oppress marginalized communities, the positivist (law as norms) became a realist, and soon after a student of critical legal theories (Harris 2014). All these legal schools of thought emphasized human agency or the all-too-human content of legal thought and practice.

Towards my last year of law school—I told Alex—I travelled to the Amazon and conducted fieldwork for a thesis on Indigenous justice systems. There, I encountered the word "law" in a totally different way. At times it seemed that law was everything I described earlier: "justice," "positive norms," "whims of an adjudicator," "power to oppress others," among other images and definitions. It seemed to me that there was a kind of imaginative space in which this word—law—had a relationship of continuity with the mountain and the river; the hummingbird, the jaguar, the beetle and the sacred liana that ethnobotanists are keen to study among the Inga, the Cofán and other communities in southern Colombia.[14] Law, then, didn't mean much without the territory of all these beings or the territory as all the relations of these beings. In fact, law did not come exclusively from the congressmen of a modern state, nor from the "cultural traditions" of local communities, nor even from a transcendental God. There was something elusive and indeed "equivocal" in this word (law) that arose in our encounters with other beings. Law, then, was closer to the idea of relations between human and nonhuman persons and seemed to flourish through these encounters as well.

Moreover, law has been defined as a system of norms (Raz 1980), and I was willing to assume that law was also a "system," I told Alex, but I was less comfortable with the assumption that law was only about "norms." Law, for me, was certainly about relationships that connected people through normative arguments and emotions (Lemaitre Ripoll 2009), as well as anything that a state sanctioned to regulate social behavior (Kelsen 1991). My interlocutor was not too concerned with this long detour. I tried to establish a definition that would assertively distinguish law from any other field of expertise (Davies 2017), but he was less satisfied with my final answer: law is a system of relations between human beings and other beings. "Isn't this closer to ecology?" he hastened to retort. My open-ended and unsatisfactory answer to his challenging question got me thinking for a while, and, in a way, this book is an attempt to grapple with an answer to this question. More than a mere analytic move, is it even possible to distinguish law and life? (Anker 2017)

In a sense, the law was all these definitions as expressions of a desire for social justice amid ongoing violence in Colombia and beyond (Lemaitre Ripoll 2009). However, the law was also about a *vision* and a *practice* of a world, or the pluriverse in *law*. *Law, Humans and Plants* proposes a definition of law with a very specific purpose in mind, namely caring for life in a territory ("*el cuidado de la vida en el territorio*") as Colombian biology professor Marcela Bravo would put it. In an interview, I learned about her ethnographic concept of "knowing how to live there" ("*saber vivir ahí*") as she studied Inga cosmologies and territorial struggles in the *Baja Bota Caucana* in Southern Colombia (Marcela Bravo, interview, June 2020).

I quickly realized how close her notion of "knowing how to live there" ("*saber vivir ahi*") was to my own learning experience about justice systems in the Bajo Putumayo region. "*De aquí viene el derecho*" ("the law comes from here") was certainly about caring for the continuity of life amid extractivism and colonial violence (Haraway 2016). Indeed, the notions of *knowing how to live there* and *the law comes from there* situate both life and law in the context of the surprising and often difficult encounters between humans and other-than-humans as they learn to live with each other. Even if we define law as a system of norms, that is, a system of symbols (Chapter 6), the concept of law as care for the territory slows down nominal propositional law so that a living concept can emerge through the material entanglements of manifold forms of life. In a certain way, law, ontologically speaking, has a certain living quality, while being, at the same time, a concrete tool to make life flourish.

However, for life to flourish, we need both the positive norm that guarantees Indigenous collective rights over their lands and specific forms of territorial governance, as well as the rights of nature. In that sense, law, as this book aims to demonstrate, comprises both the relations of life from which positive norms emerge as well as the positive norms themselves articulated as linguistic propositions backed up by the power of the state: Indigenous wills or testaments of the sixteenth and seventeenth centuries in New Granada recognized property rights to Indigenous ladinos shortly after the colonizing project unfolded in present-day Latin America (Vargas Roncancio 2008). This is an early example of how the symbolic register—written rules on paper—helps to create territories and ensure the continuity of communal life.

Moreover, in a recent conversation around the creation of an Indigenous intercultural university in the Amazon, I met O, a traditional healer from the Inga people in Southern Colombia.[15] Referring to what he called "our own laws," he said:[16]

> As always, we invoke our mother nature, who gives us our food and thank her for everything, the diversity, the world around us, calling it *alpa* = earth, *waira* = air and *iaku* = water, always innovation. As traditional

> medics, we do not have western science, but we do have our ancestral knowledge. The university . . . , we have it, and **we have our laws,** our culture and customs that may be in practice or not, but our ancestors have formed the knowledge, the laws, the rules, it is all written down. The landmarks are written on the trees and the stones; they are painted, drawn. They signify the knowledge, the law of the Inga people.[17]

The idea that "everything is written [the law] . . . (t)he landmarks are written on trees and stones," suggests that life has a kind of *lawness* to it. A legal attribute that is inscribed in life itself through co-evolution. To defend life, to "know how to live there" (Bravo 2015), one also needs a kind of law that takes care of that particular "there," a complex notion of time-space that encompasses life relations and lived experience in specific territories (Chapter 2). Therefore, to answer Alex's question, I needed to provisionally define law in at least three interrelated registers, namely (i) as an iusnaturalist concerned with social justice; (ii) as a legal positivist who encounters the law in state norms on collective land titles; and (iii) as an eco-centric scholar who encounters law in life relations. It seemed to me, then, that while law has a kind of material reality, life has a particular kind of *lawness* to it as well.

The Colombian Constitution of 1991 recognized the autonomy of Indigenous legal and justice systems, suggesting that Indigenous peoples are a kind of "state" in their territories. They create law according to their cosmologies in the same way that modern cosmologies of the state create something that we may call "state law." This is what I mean by ontologies of law: rather than a single legal reality produced by state norms, Indigenous law (and other law, such as environmental law) can also emerge through encounters with human and nonhuman-like beings (Borrows 2010).

Ultimately, this ontological or pluriversal orientation suggests that the law "becomes with" the state, but also that it becomes with other-than-humans (Despret 2004): territories seem to have their own kind of lawness beyond a system of normative propositions issued by a state. In a way, this is also a matter of stories (and concepts) and how we tell them (or methodologies).

4. Law as storytelling

There are ways to get in step with the modes of presence and action of different kinds of beings beyond modern anthropocentrisms. This is a deeply ethical and methodological challenge that involves a serious commitment to knowing (and the limits and risks of this) non-modern ways of creating worlds—the pluriverse. The Inga *Story of the Tapir* raises challenging questions in times of planetary crisis:

> It was the time when plants and animals transmitted their powers and knowledge to people while hunting and dreaming.[18] One day, *Taita Yacha*

> *Runa*,[19] a hunter and *curaca*,[20] left his home searching for the place where the tapir lives . . . the *Taita Yacha Runa* saw a lagoon and the place where the tapir roams . . . fell asleep and dreamt about the plants he had just seen . . . some of these plants are for good luck. . . . The *Taita* saw the lagoon in his dream and then two ducks swimming peacefully . . . then [he] met an elderly *curaca* and told him: "I had taken all the knowledge that was offered to me in the moors but left one [knowledge] in the place where I saw the yellow duck." The old *curaca* replied: "*Nuka kane dantakunapa suyumanda yaya* [I am the owner of the tapir, and of everything that you saw and heard]. . . . This is how *Taita Yacha Runa* . . . encountered the knowledge in the house of the tapir. Since then, the tapir is the omen of good times.
>
> (Recuperated from Jacanamijoy 2017, 37–39. Original in Spanish. Translation from author)

In a world where animals, plants and other beings have human features such as the power to communicate and transmit knowledge, words like "society," "agency," "person" and "law" seem to expand their meaning beyond the (modern) human. For communities in Southern Colombia, other-than-human beings can transmit their powers and personalities to humans in daily life and dreams, thus telling us a different story of what makes us humans too (Caicedo 2015). Can *legal* stories bring forth new possibilities beyond anthropocentric narratives of crisis, transformation and decision-making? How can a form of law and society that is not centered around the modern human help us navigate present times of socio-ecological collapse? What would happen to normative systems when we leave room for "the time when plants and animals transmitted their powers and knowledge to people in dreams"? What if we imagine a form of law beyond human-*only* modes of representation? Moreover, how does a post-anthropocentric law transform the rights of nature approach in the context of the Earth Law movement? *Law, Humans and Plants* probes these and similar questions through ethnographic encounters with Indigenous practitioners, legal scholars, biologists and plants across territories, ritual houses and legal documents in the Andean-Amazonian region of Colombia.

5. Doing law with plants and humans in Amazonia

In 2019, I had the opportunity to join an ethnobotanical research project led by Colombian biologist David Rodríguez-Mora. The project aimed at studying the diversity and classification of wild species of the *Yagé* vine (Banisteriopsis caapi)[21] among the Cofán people of the *piedemonte Andino-amazónico*,[22] Southwestern Colombia. David describes his research project as follows:

> It was very exciting for me to contemplate the possibility to carry out a project that would contribute to the recovery of Yagé, the most sacred

> plant for the Cofán, root of their cultural identity and their ancestral territory. But at the same time, I knew this was a huge responsibility, not only with the community and the Cofán nation but also with the Yagé plant itself. Widely regarded as a sacred master plant, the most important for the Amazonian people at large, I had heard numerous accounts that described the power of this plant's spirit. Additionally, I was aware that my training as an ethnobotanist had certainly not prepared me to know how to deal with plant spirits. Nevertheless, I felt reassured with the fact that this potential work was coming from the initiative of the Cofán authorities themselves and included the participation and endorsement of one of the most respected shamans in the Amazon.
>
> (Interview, June 2019)

David framed his project as a way to contribute to the protection of "the root of the Cofán territory" and "shamanic medicine," namely the Yagé vine itself. In his view, studying the plant's diversity was an important stepping stone in designing sustainable harvesting methods, facing the rapidly declining wild populations of the plant and ensuring the continuation of a world-known shamanic practice based on Yagé (Cepek 2012, 2018).[23] Although the purpose of his ethnobotanical project was straightforward and seemingly aligned with the desires and expectations of the local community, the awaited co-creation of a scientific and legal protocol to guide the project was not without, again, surprising and enriching equivocations.

As we learned earlier in the introduction, an equivocation is not only a failure to understand but "a failure to understand that understandings are necessarily not the same and that they are not related to imaginary ways of 'seeing' the world but to the real words that are being seen" (Viveiros de Castro 2014, 11). For example, during one of the numerous meetings with the community that year, an Indigenous practitioner and Yagé trainee considered that "since the territory protects itself, there is no need to do a project for that to happen."[24]

Interestingly, David's understanding of "protecting the territory" via the (scientific) study of the variability and conservation status of individual ritual plants was based upon our two initial shared assumptions: (1) protecting the territory was a human endeavor, and (2) the territory was the stage where this human decision unfolds.[25] On the contrary, for the local Indigenous trainee, any "protection of the territory" should count with the territory itself, which, far from the backdrop of human action, was an active shaping force of human institutions from the outset. In a way, the territory and the human remain in continuity and co-emergent relation with one another (Descola 2013).

This initial reaction to the research proposal and David's diplomatic skills to respond to it stimulated a series of productive (dis)agreements that eventually led to the co-creation of a research protocol—the law of the research project—which conjured up the will of the plant and the "invisible peoples of the mountain" themselves (Field Notes, Nariño, 2019. See Chapter 4).

It was apparent that establishing a research agreement with the community would require more than just the meeting of human wills through rational deliberation procedures (Blaser 2019). More than objects of research, territory, plants and the "invisible peoples" themselves appeared as their active shaping forces from the outset.

By the end of the meeting, it was clear that conducting the project was not merely about studying the classification of plants, but about learning with the plants, and not a matter of "protecting territories" and "shamanic legacies," but about learning an entirely different way of engaging with a *world* and its manifold visible and invisible beings. Finally, that any negotiation and eventual agreement with the community required calling respectful and humble attention both to the will of the community—with their internal deliberation procedures—as well as the will of other-than-human beings in what David would later conceptualize as "the will of the mountain" (Interview, February 2020).

If the territory could protect itself, we needed to learn whether it was feasible for us to "conduct research" with the set of epistemological, ontological and value operations informing our thinking and action in the world daily. Responding to the interpellation, David highlighted the "minimal needs of conservation of the vine" as a way to "protect the legacy of the Cofán medicine." Also, he insisted on how important it was to involve *all* the (human) community members in the design of this participatory endeavor. To be sure, studying the conservation status of ritual plants would, for him, contribute to the protection of the territory and culture of the community as a whole.

How can we care for a territory that governs itself? How does a plant make place? How can we participate—or not—in the modes of regulation that emerge from a willful place? After the meeting, words such as "community," "research," "territory," "agreement," "plant" and "research protocol" were subject to relentless "negotiations" and "mutual ontological equivocations." (See De la Cadena 2015 for a similar articulation of this idea.). In a word, we needed to weave together the relational protocol of the research project both with humans and other-than-humans.

6. Opening the conversation: encountering the relational protocol

In an intervention entitled *The Jaguar and the Telepatina of Yagé*, former Humboldt Institute director Brigitte Baptiste suggested something very similar when referring to the will of the "other" in the co-creation of (research) protocols and norms. Recalling a research experience with an Amazonian community, she said:

> We signed an agreement (with the community), but for this agreement to enter into force, we needed trust. There were good reasons to demand that

> this contract (between the Institute and the community) should go beyond the norm written on a piece of paper. The cultural contract then required the intake of the plant.[26]

To be sure, the participation of other-than-human wills in the making of normative claims seems to summarize the stakes of David's ethnobotanical project with the Cofán.

In another example of this frame shift during a conversation with the oil sector about possible post-COVID scenarios in Colombia, renowned environmental scholar and activist Gustavo Wilshes underscored the agentive capacities of nonhuman others and the limits of human agency through environmental protections and rights:

> The pandemic expresses a call of the Earth. The first alert was given with what today is recognized as the climate crisis . . . , and this is not a business just between humans. We need to learn how to come to terms with other actors of the territory that are not resources. These actors are soils, hydro-meteorological dynamics, volcanoes, and ecosystems. One of the big challenges then is to learn *how to consult* with those ecosystems to avoid forcing them to claim their rights by force.[27]

Wilshes' invitation urged us to rethink "rights," "responsibilities," "agreements" and other legal notions. What kind of law is this law beyond the human? (Vargas Roncancio et al. 2021). These and similar claims about the agentive capacities of other-than-humans by Indigenous practitioners, scientists, policy makers and researchers seem to have something in common, namely a normative type of language. Life, to be sure, had certain lawness to it. For example, David, the ethnobotanist, said: "I knew this was a huge responsibility, not only with the community and the Cofán nation but also with the Yagé plant itself" (Interview, 2019).[28] In turn, Brigitte Baptiste underscored how "the cultural contract required the intake of Yagé," while the Indigenous trainee from the Cofán community insisted that "we do not need a protocol, for the territory takes care of itself" (Field notes, 2019). Finally, Wilshes, the environmental scholar, talked about "coming to terms with other actors of the territory" and "consulting with those ecosystems."

What is all this telling us? Responsibilities, contracts and consultations with territories and ecologies abound in current conversations around environmental governance in Amazonia, especially after what some have called the "legal revolution" of nature's rights (Boyd 2017). Are scientists, environmental scholars, and Indigenous peoples asking for a new kind of contract that involves more than human agencies? What is agency, and how is it formed in Southern Colombia? Does the language of the rights of nature suffice in contexts of ongoing extractivism?

7. Law "othwerwise": Aims and arc of the book

7.1. *Aims*

Over the last few years, the Colombian Amazon has been the center of a new extractivist boom and the focus of important international conservation efforts. The expansion of the industrial oil, gold and copper extraction and dams' construction are concurrently happening with a rise in environmental regulations in Colombia. Legislation and court decisions recognize environmental rights while declaring the legal standing of rivers and forests. The Colombian Constitutional Court, for example, recognized the legal rights of a mercury-polluted river in the Pacific rainforest (*Corte Constitucional de Colombia*, Decision T-622/2016), and the Supreme Court issued a similar ruling for the Amazon rainforest (*Corte Suprema de Justicia*, Decision STC 4360-2018). Moreover, the 2016 Peace Agreement (PA) between the Colombian government and one guerrilla group included preserving the environment as a fundamental goal of its rural agenda. Nevertheless, the PA still pushes for the industrial development and extractivist activities described earlier. Different cycles of resource extraction have led to disastrous deforestation after the PA was signed, which triggered international conservation efforts to increase steadily in this region. In the Colombian Amazon alone, deforestation doubled in 2018, thus heavily impacting Indigenous territories and governance systems. While *Law, Humans and Plants* will not directly address the problem of extractivism in the Andean Amazon region—widely discussed in the literature (Ulloa and Coronado 2016; Svampa 2019; Gudynas 2011, among others)—it takes critical studies on extractivism and neo-extractivism as a springboard for debating subsequent socio-legal and ontological challenges.

What kind of research problem for the law does this tangled (post-)extractivist landscape pose?

Social and legal institutions focused exclusively on human perspectives seem insufficiently capable of confronting current socio-ecological challenges in the Andean-Amazonian foothills of Colombia. It is important to explore emerging analytical frameworks that integrate other-than-human beings within legal institutions and decision-making processes in this region. Such an approach requires weaving together various forms of knowledge and world-making practices that include—but are not limited to—Indigenous legalities (Mills 2019), ecological law, multispecies ethnography and law and cognition (Winter 2001). *Law, Humans and Plants* aims to probe how human and other-than-human beings, such as medicinal plants and what Indigenous peoples in Southwestern Colombia call the "invisible ones" (*los Invisibles)*, co-create legal institutions. And this requires an entirely different ontological framework for the law. Furthermore, the book aims to examine some of the onto-epistemic implications, methodological challenges and ethical conundrums of this post-anthropocentric approach for the broader Earth Law movement, particularly the rights of nature.

What happens when we consider forms of agency beyond symbolic and multicultural analytics in legal theory and practice? How does a law that emerges from plant-human-spirit entanglements challenge concepts of justice, agency and value in times of acute socio-ecological transitions? How may forests become legal agents through different territorial practices? *Law, Humans and Plants* will combine multi-sited ethnography and post-anthropocentric approaches in anthropology, law and decision-making theory to study the entangled lives of law and ecology in the regions of Nariño and Putumayo. In conversation with biologists, Indigenous practitioners from the Cofán, Inga and Murui communities, legal scholars and medicinal plants, in particular *Yoco* (Paullinia Yoco) and *Yagé* (Banisteriopsis caapi), the book looks at how legal institutions may also emerge from the fabric of human and other-than-human forms of agency. This relational approach, to be sure, is at the core of the Earth Law movement and the radical paradigm shift it suggests for legal theory and practice. My purpose, therefore, is to contribute to the legal "activation of relationality" to heal the web of life in Colombia and beyond (Escobar 2018).

In addition, current models of environmental governance exist in parallel to extractivist practices in this region. Nevertheless, recent legislation that highlights the rights of nature does not seem to address this ongoing paradox. To offer potential responses, the book studies how Indigenous, scientists and legal scholars and practitioners contribute to a legal paradigm shift for this region: from a piecemeal environmental law to a systems-based Earth Law (for similar discussions, see Zelle et al. 2021; Anker et al. 2021; Garver 2021). Environmental law generally focuses on remediating economic development's adverse side effects, restricting pollution and protecting natural resources primarily for human use. Meanwhile, Earth law, as an alternative, integrates science and traditional knowledge systems to live in harmony with the Earth. Ecological law offers space for a new legal analytic that not only recognizes other-than-human beings' inherent value but also their modes of participation in the making of the legal itself. *Law, Humans and Plants* is an ethnographic and conceptual proposal in this direction.

The book is interested in some Amazonian plants as an entry point to discuss political and legal issues in contexts of extractivism and its (legal) alternatives. One crucial element of this exploration is learning how human communities produce what we can call "normative claims" as they engage with plants, particularly with plants of ritual authority. Such plants, however, are not only vegetal living beings. They are persons, teachers, masters and guides (Gagliano 2018; Luna 1984). This language is important not only because it shows how some communities create worlds that are not amenable to modern partitions but also because modern partitions are being relentlessly redefined, for example, through the idiom of the rights of nature

(Martinez and Acosta 2017). Furthermore, these norms talk about nature as an object of protection and as a subject with rights, and so there is a significant change that is not only a change in epistemology; that is, a change in the tools we use to talk about the world and draw meaning from it. It is also about how this language offers space for other practices to make things, to make realities and to make worlds (Kothari et al. 2019). In a word, it is also an issue of ontology. The book, then, is about the ontologies of the law. Ideas and practices *about* and *with* plants as persons and meaning-making selves (Kohn 2013) seem crucial to understanding this shift in law in the Andean-Amazonian region today.

Moreover, the book discusses how particular kinds of forest beings in the Colombian Amazon, namely Yagé (Banisteriopsis caapi), Yoco (Paullinia Yoco) and the spiritual owners of these plants, seem to trouble what we mean by the law in this region. I am particularly interested in the kind of agencies that emerge in our interactions with other-than-human beings such as ritual plants. Here, there may be instances of the co-production of legal norms, protocols and procedures for environmental governance in the context of extreme violence, neo-extractivism and their alternatives. For example, the book probes an ethnographically inspired notion of ingestion as a legal methodology and the limits and possibilities that this etic concept offers for legal practice in post-extractivist transitions in the Andean-Amazonian region today. Ingesting (plants) as a method is, for the Inga and the Cofán, a necessary step in what Brigitte Baptist called the "cultural protocol" (see earlier). I prefer the notion of relational protocol as a way to emphasize other-than-human modes of participation in law-making in situated worlds.

This participation beyond the human is crucial for the co-production of the research agreement (the law of the parties involved) between David Rodriguez and the Cofán in the region of Nariño, Southwestern Colombia. Thus, more than a mode of representation of an external reality, ingesting amounts to mutual feasting—an anthropophagic act of sorts between human people and other-than-human people enabling the co-emergence between them (Viveiros de Castro 2014). To be sure, the creation of the research protocol between David and the Cofán was unthinkable without the plant's ingestion as a someone, or as a person with a perspective or a point of view (Vivieros de Castro 1998).

Finally, *Law, Humans and Plants* discusses how we reencounter ourselves as living and social selves in radical interdependence with other beings, as well as how we can reimagine and recursively ask the question of "agency" (who is the agent of this decision?) as we compose social relations and forms of law beyond the human, the state and the symbolic (Anker 2017; Davies 2017).

8. A legal herbarium and the limits and possibilities of the rights of nature

The book is divided into two parts. The first one (*I. Law and its ontological itineraries: a legal herbarium)* offers an ethnographic approach to the law and comprises four interrelated chapters on the relationship between medicinal and ritual plants and legal institutions in the Andean-Amazonian region of Colombia. These chapters illustrate why and how the interface between other-than-human beings and legal institutions matters today. Chapters 1 to 3 are named after three different plants to probe the implications of vegetal agencies for socio-legal thought in this region with potential repercussions elsewhere. To further explore these connections between other-than-humans and the law, Chapter 4 ("*Los Invisibles*") focuses on the making of an ethnobotanical research protocol with humans, plants and what members of the Cofán community in the regions of Nariño and Putumayo refer to as the "invisible people" (*los Invisibles)*. Part I can then be considered as one larger ethnographic and conceptual argument concerning the socio-legal agency of plants and non-visible peoples in Southwestern Colombia (Andes-Amazon) and their potential contributions to expand normative systems such as law and ethics beyond anthropocentric views.

After discussing the crafting of an ethnobiological research agreement in Southern Colombia in Section 1, Chapter 1—*Yoco*—tells a story of the emetic *Yoco* (*Paullinia Yoco*) and how this Amazonian vine prepares humans to learn how to live well with the forest—including how to learn an ecological form of law: the law of the place (Section 2).[29]

In Chapter 2—*Yagé*—I think with another plant teacher in the Andean-Amazonian foothills of Colombia. This plant is central to the argument about learning law where the law is not named as such. Here the focus is on the disruption of linear time as a pre-analytical premise of Western legal epistemologies. *Yagé (Banisteriopsis caapi): Moving words across worlds* is based on ethnographic encounters with the Yagé vine in Upper Putumayo (Caicedo 2015; Cepek 2018; Weiskopf 2002) and the Guamuez Valley[30] and investigates different modes of learning and *practicing time* in this region.

As discussed in Chapters 1 and 2, encountering the legal in Amazonia involves the active participation of other-than-human beings such as medicinal plants. Chapters 1 (Yoco: learning to learn) and 2 (Yagé: moving words across worlds) addressed the question of how we can learn to *learn* law with the guidance of plants such as the Amazonian Yoco (*Paullinia Yoco)* and the Yagé (*Banisteriopsis caapi*), as well as the conceptual openings, ethical dilemmas and political possibilities of this *vegetal* approach. Following a similar line of work, Chapter 3—*Coca leaf*—discusses ritual and everyday encounters with a local preparation of the coca leaf (*Erythroxylon coca)* among the Indigenous Murui of Putumayo. The chapter further describes how humans and plants meet and make decisions together in this region. Don A, an elder and medicine man from the Murui community of Puerto Leguízamo, Putumayo, calls this process of co-decision "ordering the world" *(ordenar el mundo)*.

After analyzing several aspects of the entangled lives of law and ecology in Amazonia, Chapter 4—*Los Invisibles*—attempts a rather different format: it invites ethnobotanist David Rodríguez Mora to the conversation. The chapter discusses several aspects of our year-long conversations about plants, law, the politics of naming nature, the invisible people and the ethical and conceptual dilemmas we both faced as we engaged "law" and "ecology" with the guidance of humans and plants in Southern Colombia.

Part I offers an ethnographic basis to support the theoretical claims of the second part of the book, namely *On the Rights of Nature: Limits, Possibilities and Challenges in Neo-Extractivist Worlds*. This part of the book deals with some of the conceptual limits and possibilities of the rights of nature clause in Latin America in the context of an emergent regional and global Earth Law movement. By attending to the social and legal worlds of other-than-human beings introduced in the first part of the book, Part II thus reimagines core premises of social and legal sciences: i) the law is primarily linguistic or propositional; ii) rights and responsibilities are commensurable across legal cultures and cosmologies (Chapter 6, *Plants and the law*, and 7, *Conjuring*), and iii) personhood is fundamental for legal redress (Chapter 8, "Forests on trial"). A contribution to a relational theory of legal agency, therefore, Part II critically assesses core notions of Western law such as legal personhood, standing and rights.

On the Rights of Nature starts with a detailed literature review in Chapter 5—*Sowing concepts*—organized in four axes: i) post-humanist theory and material agency; ii) plant studies and plant-human relations; iii) Earth Law and the rights of nature, and iv) Indigenous legal traditions and decoloniality. With this theoretical background, Chapter 6—*Plants and the law*—proposes two anthropological/legal readings and textual methodologies concerning the rights of nature clause in Latin American constitutionalism.

Chapter 7—*Conjuring*—continues this line of work to rethink fundamental premises of legal sciences in times of planetary crises, namely the idea that the law is primarily linguistic or propositional and the notion that rights and responsibilities are commensurable across different legal cultures and cosmologies. Drawing from legal theory, post-humanist anthropology and Amazonian ethnography, *Conjuring* proposes a new comparative methodology for legal analysis.

Chapter 8—*Forest on trial*—closes the book. It probes the notion of personhood through an ethnographic and *ius*-philosophical prism. Persons such as humans and corporations can seek redress before a court of law. This chapter claims that the notion of legal personhood seems to actualize the contested modern tension between nature and culture in most of the social and legal theory at present. Can the forest speak law? An attempt to overcome anthropocentric concepts of personhood and agency, this chapter furthers the empirical argument advanced in Part I of the book concerning Amazonian legal cosmologies. The chapter approaches law both as a particular kind of symbolic representation, that is, a text, as well as a non-symbolic form of representation that conjures up other-than-humans in legal theory and practice.

Notes

1 An earlier version of section 1 of the introduction in: Vargas-Roncancio (2017, 68–70) (Plants and the Law).
2 The Colombian mountainous region of Sumapaz was a pilgrimage site for the Muisca indigenous peoples in pre-Columbian times. Today, the people inhabiting this land depend on small-scale farming and livestock. For a political history of this region see Londoño (2011).
3 My translation. Original in Spanish: Al confundir los frailejones con hombres indígenas en posiciones de batalla y observar las filas que se repetían cientos de veces, las tropas españolas desistieron del combate y buscaron el camino de regreso que los había llevado hasta allí. Se iniciaba así una 'resistencia mágica' desde el páramo." Moreno (2015, 11).
4 On the notion of perspectivism, see Viveiros de Castro (1998).
5 For the notion of 'antropocentrismo fuerte' (hard anthropocentrism) see Mesa Cuadros (2013).
6 The chacruna plant is a perennial shrub used in the preparation of the ayahuasca brew. The Cofán will call it "Yagé." The name comes from the Quechua verb 'chaqruy' meaning 'to mix'. Also, this plant is combined with the Banisteriopsis caapi vine for the preparation of the brew also known as Yagé. The term comes from the Quechua as well, and it has been translated as the 'vine of the soul.' For further reference see: Daniel Mirante, On the Origins of Ayahuasca (online) 31 August 2008 <www.ayahuasca.com/ayahuasca-overviews/on-the-origins-of-ayahuasca/> (last accessed 24 October 2020).
7 See United Nations, *Hamony with Nature's* list of legal norms granting rights to nature at local, national and international level. <www.harmonywithnatureun.org>
8 Here Kohn uses Peirce's definition of a sign "as something that stands to somebody for something in some respect" (cited in Descola 2014, 271).
9 This short ethnographic account does not represent the positions of the people I had the opportunity to interact with in Lower Putumayo. I will use different names to protect their identities of and places.
10 Quichua name given to a traditional healer.
11 The *chacruna* is a perennial shrub used in the preparation of the ayahuasca brew. The name comes from the Quechua verb 'chaqruy' meaning 'to mix'. Also, this plant is combined with the Banisteriopsis caapi vine for the preparation of the brew also known as Yagé. The term comes from the Quechua as well, and it has been translated as the 'vine of the soul'. For further reference see Daniel Mirante, On the Origins of Ayahuasca. See: <www.ayahuasca.com/ayahuasca-overviews/on-the-origins-ofayahuasca/>
12 The chuma is the healing vertigo akin to a deep drunken sensation in the context of plant-based rituals in some regions of the Amazon.
13 Thanks to anthropologist Kristina Lyons for sharing this reference.
14 The Cofán live in the border between Colombia and Ecuador. On Cofán communites on today´s Ecuador see Cepek (2012, 2018).
15 For the notion of traditional healer and traditional medic and what it means in the context of Yagé shamanism in Colombia, see UMYAC *Pensamiento de los Mayores: Código de ética de la medicina indígena del piedemonte amazónico colombiano*, 2000.
16 While his intervention is an excellent example of the principle of radical interdependence, I would like to draw attention to the legal cues of his intervention.
17 Field notes, intervention by Taita O, Indigenous Intercultural University meeting, Putumayo 2020.

18 La Historia de la Danta (The Story of the Tapir) by the Inga Indigenous people of Colombia. Compiled by Taita (traditional authority) Inga Hernando Chindoy Chindoy who kindly shared this story with me (Personal communication, January 2020. Original in Inga and Spanish. My translation tries to capture the Spanish sintaxis of the story as communicated by taita Hernando) A condensed version in Vargas, I.D., and Chindoy, H. 2021. "Indigenous Legalities: A Vision" published as Vargas Roncancio, I.D., and Chindoy, H. 2020. "Indigenous Legalities: A Vision." In Zelle, A., Wilson, G., Adam, R., Greene, H., (eds.). *Earth Law: Emerging Ecocentric Law. A Practitioner's Guide*. New York: Aspen Coursebook Series. Wolters Kluwer. One the claims is that going beyond standard Western narratives which locate the sources of law only within the state, we should treat Indigenous origin stories as law. See Napoleon and Friedland: "We engage with Indigenous legal traditions by carefully and consciously applying adapted common law tools such as legal analysis and synthesis, to existing and often publicly available Indigenous resources: stories, narratives, and oral histories." Napoleon and Friedland ("Engaging with Indigenous Legal Traditions through Stories") 2016, 725.

19 Inga term for "wise person."

20 Inga term for "traditional healer." In Quechua, "a member of the Inca provincial nobility often acting as administrator or ruler over an ayllu or group of ayllus." See Merriam-Webster, Online www.merriam-webster.com/dictionary/curaca [Visited on Sept. 27, 2020].

21 The traditional Amazonian Yagé or ayahuasca concoction mixes the Banisteriopsis caapi with the chacruna (Psychotria viridis). The chacruna plant is a perennial shrub used in the preparation of the ayahuasca brew. The name comes from the Quechua verb 'chaqruy' meaning 'to mix'. Also, this plant is combined with the Banisteriopsis caapi vine for the preparation of the brew also known as Yagé. The term comes from the Quechua as well, and it has been translated as the 'vine of the soul'. For further reference see Daniel Mirante, On the Origins of Ayahuasca. See: <www.ayahuasca.com/ayahuasca-overviews/on-the-origins-ofayahuasca/>

22 The foothills or piedemonte andino-amazónico, is situated at the junction of the Andes mountain chain and the Amazon basin. Biogeographically, the piedemonte ranges from the southwest of Colombia in the regions of Putumayo and Caquetá, to the South of Peru and Bolivia. The forests in this region have ecological characteristics of both the Andes and the Amazon, demonstrating high levels of diversity with crucial conservation challenges.

23 Rodríguez-Mora, D. Summary of Research Project: "Integrating ecomorphology and ethnoecology to test Cofán ethnovarietal classification of Banisteriopsis caapi in southwestern Colombia" (Research proposal). Unpublished, 2019.

24 Andrés*, Indigenous practitioner, field notes, 2019. * Indicates the use of a different name to protect the identity of the interlocutor.

25 This assumption would later change as his project progressed. See chapter 4.

26 Baptiste, B. *El Jaguar y la Telepatina del Yagé*. www.youtube.com/watch?v=gK3BWngw7oI (Accessed 30 July 2020).

27 Wilshes G., Revista Semana, April 16, 2020. Original in Spanish.

28 Also based on Rodríguez, D. Summary of Research Project, Unpublished.

29 See Tropical Plants Database, Ken Fern. tropical.theferns.info, 3 October 2020. tropical.theferns.info/viewtropical.php?id=Paullinia+Yoco (Accessed 5 October 2020). On Yagé, see Weiskopf 2002.

30 My observations here are based on personal experience and interaction with some practitioners, and they do not represent a unified view of a particular community.

References

Anker, Kirsten. 2017. "Law as . . . Forest: Eco-logic, Stories and Spirits in Indigenous Jurisprudence." *Law Text Culture*, 21: 191–213.

Anker, Kirsten, Burdon, Peter, Garver, Geoffrey, Maloney, Michele, and Sbert, Carla (eds.). 2021. *From Environmental to Ecological Law*. London and New York: Routledge.

Blaser, Mario. 2019. "On the Properly Political (Disposition for the) Anthropocene." *Anthropological Theory*, 19(1): 74–94.

Borda, José Joaquín. 1904. *Compendio de Historia de Colombia*. Bogotá: Librería Americana Bogotá.

Borrows, John. 2010. *Canada's Indigeous Constitution*. Toronto: University of Toronto Press.

Boyd, David. 2017. *The Rights of Nature. A Legal Revolution That Could Save the World*. Toronto: ECW Press.

Braverman, Irus. 2018. "Law's Underdog: A Call for More-Than-Human Legalities." *Annual Reviews Law and Social Science*, 14: 127–144.

Bravo, Marcela. 2015. *Ugpachisunchi i katichisunchi kilkaikunata—llevando y trayendo la palabra: Territorio, "Saber Vivir Ahí" y Pensamiento Inga*. Tesis de Maestria en Estudios Sociales. Universidad Pedagogica Nacional, Colombia.

Brown, G., and Timmerman, Peter. 2015. *Ecological Economics for the Anthropocene*. New York: Columbia University Press.

Caicedo, Alhena. 2015. *La Alteridad Radical que Cura. Neo-chamanismos Yageceros en Colombia*. Bogotá: Universidad de los Andes.

Capra, Fritjof, and Mattei, Ugo. 2015. *The Ecology of Law: Toward a Legal System in Tune with Nature and Community*. Oakland: Berrett-Koehler Publishers, Incorporated.

Cepek, M.L. 2012. *A Future for Amazonia. Randy Borman and Cofán Environmental Politics*. Austin: University of Texas Press.

Cepek, M.L. 2018. *Life in Oil: Cofán Survival in the Petroleum Fields of Amazonia*. Austin: University of Texas Press.

Davies, Margaret. 2017. *Law Unlimited. Materialism, Pluralism, and Legal Theory*. London: Routledge.

De la Cadena, Marisol. 2015. *Earth Beings. Ecologies of Practice Across Andean Worlds*. Durham: Duke University Press.

Descola, Philippe. 2013. *Beyond Nature and Culture*. Chicago: University of Chicago Press.

Descola, Philippe. 2014. "All to Human (Still). A Comment on Eduardo Kohn' How Forest Think." *HAU: Journal of Ethnographic Theory*, 4(2): 268.

Despret, Vinciane. 2004. "The Body We Care for: Figures of Anthropo-zoo-genesis." *Body and Society*, 10(2–3): 111–134.

Enlace Zapatista. 1996. "Cuarta Declaración de la Selva Lacandona." *Enlace Zapatista*. https://enlacezapatista.ezln.org.mx/1996/01/01/cuarta-declaracion-de-la-selva-lacandona/

Escobar, Arturo. 2015. "Transiciones: A Space for Research and Design for Transitions to the Pluriverse." *Design Philosophy Papers*, 13(1): 13–23.

Escobar, Arturo. 2018. *Designs for the Pluriverse: Radical Interdependence, Autonomy and the Making of Worlds*. Durham: Duke University Press.

Ecobar, Arturo. 2019. "Healing the Web of Life: On the Meaning of Environmental and Health Equity." *International Journal of Public Health*, 64: 3–4.

Escobar, Arturo. 2020. *Pluriversal Politics. The Real and the Possible*. Durham: Duke University Press.

Gagliano, Monica. 2018. *Thus Spoke the Plant: A Remarkable Journey of Groundbreaking Scientific Discoveries and Personal Encounters with Plants*. Berkeley: North Atlantic Books.

Garver, Geoffrey. 2021. *Ecological Law and the Planetary Crisis. A Legal Guide for Harmony on Earth*. London and New York: Routledge.

Gudynas, Eduardo. 2011. "Más allá del nuevo extractivismo: transiciones sostenibles y alternativas al desarrollo." En Wanderley, Fernanda (Coord.). *El Desarrollo en Cuestión. Reflexiones desde América Latina*. La Paz: Oxfam y CIDES, pp. 379–410.

Haraway, Donna. 2007. *When Species Meet*. Minneapolis: University of Minnesota Press.

Haraway, Donna. 2016. *Staying with the Trouble. Making kin in the Chthulucene*. Durham: Duke University Press.

Harris, Angela. 2014. "Vulnerability and Power in the Age of the Anthropocene." *Washington and Lee Journal of Energy, Climate, and the Environment*, 6: 98–160.

Ingold, Tim. 2011. *Being Alive: Essays on Movement, Knowledge, and Description*. New York: Routledge.

Jacanamijoy, Benjamin. 2017. *El Chumbe Inga. Una Forma Artística de Percepción del Mundo*. Bogotá: OPIAC.

Kelsen, Hans. 1991. *General Theory of Norms* (M. Hartney, trans.). Oxford: Oxford University Press.

Kohn, Eduardo. 2013. *How Forests Think. Toward an Anthropology Beyond the Human*. Berkeley: University of California Press.

Kosoy, Nicolas, Brown, Peter, Bosselmann, Klaus, Duraiappah, Anantha, Mackey, Brendan, Alier-Martinez, Joan, Rogers, Deborah, and Thomson, Robert. 2012. "Pillars for a Flourishing Earth: Planetary Boundaries, Economic Growth Delusion and Green Economy." *Current Opinion in Environmental Sustainability*, 4: 74–79.

Kothari, Ashish, Salleh, Ariel, Escobar, Arturo, Demaria, Federico, and Acosta, Alberto. 2019. *Pluriverse. A Post-Development Dictionary*. New Delhi: Tulika Books.

Law, Jhon. 2015. "What's Wrong with a One-World World?" *Distinktion: Scandinavian Journal of Social Theory*, 16: 1–14.

Lemaitre-Ripoll, Julieta. 2009. *El derecho como conjuro. Fetichismo legal, violencia y movimientos sociales*. Bogotá: Siglo del Hombre Editores.

Londoño, Rocio. 2011. *Juan de la Cruz Varela: Sociedad y Política en la Región de Sumapaz (1902–1984)*. Bogota: National University of Colombia.

Luna, Luis Eduardo. 1984. "The Concept of Plants as Teachers Among Four Mestizo Shamans in Iquitos, Northeaster Peru." *Journal of Ethnopharmacology*, 11(2): 135–156.

Martínez, Esperanza, and Acosta, Alberto. 2017. "Los Derechos de la Naturaleza como puerta de entrada a otro mundo posible." *Revista Dereito e Práxis*, 4(8).

Matthew, Hall. 2011. *Plants as Persons. A Philosophical Botany*. New York: State University of New York.

Mesa Cuadros, Gregorio. 2013. *Derechos Ambientales en perspectiva de integralidad. Concepto y fundamentación de nuevas demandas y resistencias actuales hacia el Estado Ambiental de Derecho*. Bogotá: Universidad Nacional de Colombia.

Mills, Aaron. 2019. *Miinigowiziwin: All That Has Been Given for Living Well Together: One Vision of Anishinaabe Constitutionalism.* University of Victoria Dissertation, iii. https://dspace.library.uvic.ca/bitstream/handle/1828/10985/Mills_Aaron_PhD_2019.pdf?sequence=1&isAllowed=y.
Moreno, Nancy Paola. 2015. "Entre Sumapaz y las Sonrisas de Jaime Garzón." *El Espectador* (Bogotá), 11 October.
Pelizzon, Alessandro, and Gagliano, Monica. 2015. "The Sentience of Plants: Animal Rights and Rights of Nature Intersecting?" *Australian Animal Protection Law Journal*, 11: 5–13.
Raz, Joseph. 1980. *The Concept of a Legal System* (2nd ed.). Oxford: Oxford University Press.
Schultes, R.E., Hofmann, A., and Rätsch, C. 2001. *Plants of the Gods: Their Sacred, Healing, and Hallucinogenic Powers.* Rochester, VT: Healing Arts Press.
Strathern, Marilyn. 2004. *Partial Connections.* Waltnut-California: AltaMira Press.
Svampa, Maristella. 2019. *Las Fronteras del Neoextractivismo en America Latina.* Mexico: CALAS-Maria Sibylla Merian Center.
Ulloa, Astrid, y Coronado, Sergio. 2016. "Territorios, Estado, Actores Sociales, Derechos y Conflictos Socioambientales en Contextos Extractivistas: Aportes para el Posacuerdo." In *Extractivismos y posconflicto en Colombia: Retos para la Paz Territorial.* Bogotá: Universidad Nacional de Colombia-CINEP, pp. 23–58.
UMIYAC. 2000. *Pensamiento de los Mayores: Código de Ética de la Medicina Indígena del Piedemonte Amazónico Colombiano.* Putumayo: UMIYAC.
Vargas-Roncancio, Iván Darío. 2008. "En torno a la construcción de la identidad indígena a través del discurso jurídico colonial. Testamentos Indígenas de los siglos XVI-XVII en Santafé de Bogotá." *Pensamiento Jurídico Journal*, 22: 293–332.
Vargas-Roncancio, Ivan Dario. 2017. "Plants and the Law: A Perspective from Latin America." *Australian Feminist Law Journal*, 43(1): 76–81.
Vargas-Roncancio, Ivan Dario, and Chindoy, Hernando. 2021. "Indigenous Legalities: A Vision." Published as Vargas Roncancio, I.D., and Chindoy, H. 2020. "Indigenous Legalities: A Vision." In Zelle, A., Wilson, G., Adam, R., and Greene, H. (eds.). *Earth Law: Emerging Ecocentric Law. A Practitioner's Guide.* New York: Aspen Coursebook Series. Wolters Kluwer.
Vargas-Roncancio, Ivan Dario, Sterlin, J., Grear, A., and Boulot, E. (eds.). 2021. *Posthuman Legalities: New Materialism and Law Beyond the Human.* Cheltenham and Northampton: Edward Elgar Press.
Vermeylen, Saskia. 2017. "Materiality and the Ontological Turn in the Anthropocene: Establishing a Dialogue Between Law, Anthropology, and Eco-philosphy." In Kotzé, Louis (ed.). *Environmental Law and Governance for the Anthropocene.* Oregon: Hart Publishing.
Viveiros de Castro, Eduardo. 1998. "Cosmological Diexis and Amerindian Perspectivism." *Journal of the Royal Anthropological Institute*, 4(3): 469–489.
Viveiros de Castro, Eduardo. 2013. *La Mirada del Jaguar: Introducción al Perspectivismo Amerindio.* Buenos Aires: Tinta Limon.
Viveiros de Castro, Eduardo. 2014. *Cannibal Metaphysics.* Minneapolis: Univocal.
Weiskopf, Jimmy. 2002. *Yagé: El Nuevo Purgatorio.* Bogotá: Villegas Editores.
Winter, Steven. 2001. *A Clearing in the Forest. Law, Life, and Mind.* Chicago: University of Chicago Press.

Xavier, S., Jacobs, B., Waboose, V., Hewitt, J.G., and Bhatia, A. (eds.). 2021. *Decolonizing Law: Indigenous, Third World and Settler Perspectives* (1st ed.). New York: Routledge.
Zelle, A., Wilson, G., Adam, R., and Greene, H. (eds.). 2021. *Earth Law: Emerging Ecocentric Law. A Practitioner's Guide.* Aspen Coursebook Series. New York: Wolters Kluwer.
Zent, Eggle, and Zent, Stanford. 1999. "Is the *Frailejon* a Life Form or an Unaffiliated Generic? Examining Rank of an Endemic Paramo Plant." *Journal of Ethnobiology*, 19(2): 143–173.

Legal sources

Corte Constitucional de Colombia, Decision T-622 2016 [Colombia], 10 November 2016.
Corte Suprema de Justicia de Colombia, Decision STC 4360-2018 [Colombia], 5 April 2018.

Part I

Law and its ontological itineraries

A legal herbarium

Part I of *Law, Humans and Plants* ethnographically probes connections between humans, other-than-humans and the law and explores why these connections matter in times of profound socio-ecological challenges. *Law and its ontological itineraries* is comprised of four interconnected chapters that describe generative interfaces between other-than-human persons such as plants and legal theory: (1) Yoco (*Paullinia Yoco*): Cooling down the mind and learning law where the *law* is not named as such; (2) Yagé (*Banisteriopsis caapi*): Moving words across worlds; (3) Coca leaf (*Erythroxylum coca*): Territories in motion or learning law with the Amazonian *mambe* and (4) The making of an ethnobotanical research agreement in Southern Colombia: Yagé, invisible people and the law of the place. Part I can be considered one larger ethnographic and theoretical argument concerning the socio-legal agency of ritual and medicinal plants in Southwestern Colombia (Andes-Amazon) as well as their potential contributions to expand normative systems beyond anthropocentric narratives.

DOI: 10.4324/9781003349426-2

Chapter 1

Yoco (*Paullinia Yoco*)

Cooling down the mind and learning law where the *law* is not named as such[1]

Abstract

After discussing the crafting of an ethnobiological research agreement (ERA) in Southern Colombia in section 1, the chapter tells a story of the emetic *Yoco* (*Paullinia Yoco*) and how this Amazonian vine prepares humans to live well with the forest—including learning an ecological form of law: the law of the place (section 2). Expanding learning beyond the human, the third and last section surveys neurobiologist Francisco Varela's relational approach to cognition. His approach is crucial to understanding how normative systems such as law and ethics are grounded in the everyday experience of human and nonhuman organisms. The section studies how to expand these systems beyond disembodied norms sanctioned by the state or social convention. In doing so, the chapter lays the groundwork for a non-dualist and post-anthropocentric framework of environmental decision-making that challenges top-down and dualist conservation governance approaches at present. Both *Paullinia Yoco*—our plant teacher—and Varela provide important guidance for this kind of framework.

1. Unpacking the law of the place: Introduction

In Southwestern Colombia, the law is not exclusively a human affair.[2] To unpack this claim, the chapter proposes an ethnographic and theoretical argument in what it conceptualizes as a relational protocol, that is, a local way of dealing with the entangled lives of law and ecology in the Andean-Amazonian territories of Putumayo and Nariño.[3] The chapter follows a bundle of relations between local practitioners and the emetic and psychoactive *Yoco* vine (*Paullinia Yoco*) in Southwestern Colombia.[4] The underlying premise is that humans and plants are part and parcel of a larger meshwork of lifeways (Ingold 2011) that are crucial for the craft of the law in this region.[5] In addition, the chapter sets the stage for one such instance of law-making, namely an ethnobotanical research agreement (ERA) that involves the contested participation of different kinds of beings: an ethnobotanist, the political and spiritual authorities of the Cofán community, a legal scholar, several medicinal plants and what some Cofán interlocutors call "the invisible ones."[6]

DOI: 10.4324/9781003349426-3

While the chapter holds that Indigenous legal traditions are entangled with and emerge from territories, it is not about the legal system of a particular Indigenous community.[7] Instead, it focuses on how both humans and other-than-humans make law together *in* and *with* place.[8]

In the summer of 2019, Colombian biologist David Rodríguez-Mora began a research project with a Cofán community in the mountainous region of Nariño. The purpose of the project was to evaluate the diversity and classification of the wild Cofán varieties of the Yagé liana, *Banisteriopsis caapi*, recognized by elder healers and apprentices of a protected territory in southwestern Colombia (UMIYAC 2019; Pérez 2002).[9] After multiple meetings and negotiations, the project, requested and endorsed by the traditional authorities of the community, was formalized in a written document signed by these authorities, which, for the purposes of the chapter, is considered *local law* in a double sense. First, it is a contract between humans that governs all aspects of the research, including—but not limited to—its object and purpose, the parties involved, duration, methodology and expected benefits.[10]

In this sense, the agreement is an expression of state law simply because it is premised on standard contractual principles of a modern state, for example, the idea that a contract has the force of law between the contracting parties (*Congreso de la República de Colombia* 1887, 1993, 1995).[11] In addition, the agreement concerned principles of environmental risk such as the precautionary clause—taking preventive action in the face of uncertainty (European Parliament Think Tank 2015; *Corte Constitucional de Colombia* 2008)—;[12] the fair sharing or research benefits; the "sustainable use of components of biological diversity" (*Comisión del Acuerdo de Cartagena* 1991)[13] and the autonomy of Indigenous communities to determine their "traditional knowledge, innovations and practices associated with genetic resources and their derived products."[14]

While the ERA must comply with such principles and specific national regulations and standards on scientific research with biological material and associated traditional knowledge,[15] it goes well beyond the confines of state law to consider other configurations of socio-ecological participation,[16] community agency and decision-making in the Andean-Amazonian region. These configurations, nonetheless, are not easily recognizable, and they come into being through what I will call conjuring other-than-human people in the legal field (see Chapter 7).[17] By conjuring, I do not only mean calling upon to appear by means of ritual.[18] Conjuring here means that the caller cannot always control that which has been called upon and therefore must reckon with the intentions, prohibitions and decisions (norms!) of what she has conjured. My analogical use of the term foregrounds the quality of what exceeds[19] human control over environmental decision-making and territorial governance, thus expressing something akin to the force of law in the Western legal sense of the expression.[20] Since the contract between the researcher and the community (ERA) conjures up other-than-human beings in this specific use of the expression, it is an instance of *non*state law as well.[21]

Indeed, the scope of the ERA between David R.M. and the Cofán community was expanded to include certain plants (as people) and the "invisible ones of the mountain,"[22] as the condition of possibility for the local validity, social efficacy and ethical soundness of the research contract itself.[23] Interestingly, the ERA holds space for what former Humboldt Institute director Brigitte Baptiste has called the "cultural contract," or a way to enter into a *cultural* agreement beyond the written standard of the research contract.[24]

What happens when the law is not necessarily written on a piece of paper or proclaimed by an official state act? What happens when the law arises not as an act of representation of the human mind, but through the incorporation of another being into the human body? What sort of law is this *embodied* form of law, and how can we recognize it or engage with it? Beyond the necessary negotiations and written protocols between the human parties involved in the ERA, namely a Colombian biologist and the Cofán community, this cultural contract or protocol elicited and relied upon another kind of normative framework that I am calling the law of the place.[25]

Paraphrasing a crucial principle of adjudication in the Western legal tradition, namely the law of the case (*Allen v. Michigan Bell* 1975),[26] the law of the place is, analogically, the law underpinning the decision to design and potentially implement this agreement as well as the agreement itself. Broadly speaking, the law of the place refers to locally negotiated rules and procedures that guide collective decisions based on everyday relations between human and other-than-human beings in a territory. And these rules and procedures are tightly entangled with what the Cofán people often refer to as *los Invisibles* (see Chapter 4). Nonetheless, some of these rules and procedures are also clearly outlined in legal documents (UMIYAC 2000),[27] while others may arise through recursive situated practice and interaction between peoples and places. However, is this place-based law only locally valid? In this context, the law of the place should not be understood *only* as local (state) law but also as a set of relations arising from the emplaced constitutive arrangements that human and other-than-humans weave together (Blaser 2019). This form of law, to be sure, exceeds state-recognized environmental rights and even the rights of nature (*Constitución de la Repúbica del Ecuador* 2008; *Corte Provincial de Loja, Ecuador* 2011; *Corte Constitucional de Colombia* 2008, 2016; *Corte Suprema de Justicia de Colombia* 2018).

Paradoxically, however, while the law of the place is situated and experiential, it does not lose its generalizing qualities. On the contrary, the law of the place dictates the relations and responsibilities of the parties involved in forest decision-making (i.e., David and the community) and embodies the normative reason or legal force that guides the agreement and the resolution of potential conflicts for this and similar cases in the future. Thus, the law of the place can become precedent for similar cases by virtue of its effects, for example, when it has been breached: "When a person enters the territory, they must ask permission from their owners. Entering the territory without permission can bring unexpected consequences," said O, a member of the community, at one of multiple community meetings we held about the project.[28] To be sure, the law of the place includes both the eco-social processes leading up to the research agreement (i.e., a set of material relations between different kinds of beings) as well as its formal linguistic expressions: the ERA cannot be conducted unless the parties involved have appropriately requested and obtained permission from the invisible ones.

Therefore, the law of the place dictates the possibility, limits, procedures, risks and outcomes of the research process. Without the "cultural contract," or, as I prefer, the relational protocol,[29] both the ethnobotanical research agreement and the scientific project would have been unthinkable. In other words, ERA's legal framework is recognized by the Colombian state, and yet it is nested within a larger non*state* law—that is, relational protocol—rather than the other way around. Given that the ERA involves state and *non*state forms of the law, it requires moving beyond conventional deliberation methods between rational human decision-makers. It requires a disposition to ***learn and* learning and practicing law *differently* and with beings that are not only human,**[30] as well as a disposition to be interpellated by place and its entanglements. This disposition, to be sure, requires a method: conjuring. The chapter is then an approximation to *other* methodologies in the making of a form of law that involves nonhuman persons.

This was the underlying premise of a joint experience in which Colombian biologist David Rodriguez, my research interlocutor, on the one hand, and a legal scholar and David's assistant in ethnobotany (myself), on the other, began a process of mutual learning across territories, ritual houses and legal documents in Southwestern Colombia. Table 1.1 provides an outline of the multiple legal orders at play in the making of ERA.

With the ERA in mind, *Learning to learn with vegetal minds*, the next section tells a story of Yoco (*Paullinia Yoco*) and how this Amazonian vine prepares humans to work with and learning with the forest—including a kind of law that is not named as such by the state (Allen 2008; Grimes 2003; Perafàn 2000; Vargas-Roncancio 2017).[31] Expanding the idea of learning beyond the human, the third and last part, entitled *Learning law and ethics with mind-full bodies*, surveys a relational approach to cognition in the work of Chilean neurobiologist Francisco Varela (1999). Varela's approach is crucial to understanding how normative systems such as ethics and law are grounded in the everyday experience of an organism (Varela 1991) and whether we can expand those systems beyond abstract and disembodied sets of norms, principles and values sanctioned by a state.[32] *Learning law* considers a non-dualist and post-anthropocentric narrative of environmental governance that troubles the idea of protecting an external and universal nature with humans at the top (Anker et al. 2021; Garver 2019; Grear 2017; Gudynas 2009; Kohn 2013, 2022; Martínez and Acosta 2017).

2. Learning to learn with vegetal minds

> To learn all this you need the medicine. The medicine is with the *iachas*, the savants who have given all this knowledge. . . . You always need a fresh mind to be able to learn.
>
> *Abuelo* O Indigenous Inga and plant healer, Mocoa, Putumayo 2019

Usually harvested in the wild and sometimes cultivated in *chagras*—an Amazonian slash-and-burn cultivation system[33]—*Paullinia Yoco* is a tropical

Table 1.1 Prevalence of the *law of the place* in the co-design of an ethnobotanical research agreement in Southern Colombia

Type of law		*Relation between systems of law*
Nonstate law (NSL)	*State law (SL)*	*Nested relationship*
"Cultural contract" Relational protocol The law of the place	1. Research Agreement: *Convenio específico para el desarrollo de investigaciones académicas celebrado entre David Rodríguez y el Cabildo Cofán Ukumary Kankhe* 2. *Permiso de Estudio con Fines de Investigación Científica en Diversidad Biológica* (Study Permit for Scientific Research in Biological Diversity) and other regulating laws, decrees and resolutions. 3. Constitutional principles of the Colombian state (República de Colombia 1991).	NSL (human/other-than) 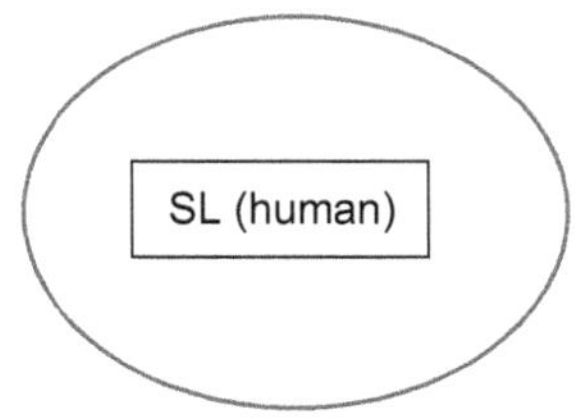
EXPRESSED AS: "The cultural contract then required the intake of the plant." (Brigitte Baptiste, Humboldt Institute ex-director 2011)	EXPRESSED AS: *"Acuerdo de personas e instituciones."/* Agreement between people and institutions (*A.A. Field Notes, Nariño, 2019*)	

climber vine that grows up to 15 meters. The stems of this plant adhere to the neighboring vegetation through tendrils that eventually become woody, and the softer tissues of the bark and stems are commonly used to extract a white or brownish sap containing caffeine and theobromine (Weiss and Kearns 2015. See Fern 2014; Vickers and Plowman 1942).[34] Conventionally used as a breakfast infusion across the Amazonian regions of Peru, Ecuador and Colombia, for example among the Cofán, Inga and Secoya communities (Belaunde and Echeverri 2008), this plant allays hunger and stimulates the muscles to endure long working hours in the forest.[35]

To prepare the Yoco beverage, one carefully rasps the phloem layer of the plant with a knife and dissolves the resulting sawdust in cold water. Besides its tonic properties, Yoco is an malarial antipyretic and remedy for the treatment of bilious disease, which is frequent in the Putumayo region.[36] Used by men and women, the Yoco plant has emetic, psychoactive, contraceptive and even abortive properties,[37] and people in Amazonia consider that it gives advice to the person who ingests it (Belaunde and Echeverri 2008; Bolívar 2009; Bolivar et al. 2004). More than a plant, however, Yoco is a person. And more than a person, it is a mode of relation: a mode of learning and participating in forest life. In what follows, I summarize the steps of this learning *with* plants and how this vegetal learning relates to normative systems such as ethics and law in Amazonia. I don't use the word "step" to suggest recipe or preestablished direction. I use this word to signal movement, activity, hesitancy, and error in the practice of learning with plants as people.

Step 1—Meeting the plant as doctor and teacher

The concept of plants as teachers is a well-established trope in Amazonian ethnology (Luna 1984), and my first encounter with the Yoco plant as people was in *Bajo Putumayo*, Southern Colombian Amazon a few years ago.[38] At that time, I had the opportunity to meet the Cofán and the vegetal beings they live and work with in this region.[39] While I didn't know it then, the purpose of this trip was to start learning about what I now conceptualize as a relational protocol or law of the place, namely a local way of dealing with the entangled lives of ecology and social norms in the *Bajo*, and with the special guidance of plants like Yoco, Yagé (*Banisteriopsis caapi*) and tobacco (*Nicotiana tabacum*).[40]

A creeping vine often referred to as the forest's sap, the Yoco plant is part of diet and ritual for several communities today.[41] For example, it is ingested as a purgative before the ritual consumption of *Yagé*[42] at night (Weiskopf 2002). The plant is also a "doctor" that treats illnesses—spiritual and otherwise—as well as a "teacher," a "mother" who transmit knowledge to their children:[43] for the Indigenous Airo-pai (Secoya), the *cuacuiyó* bird (*Lipaugus vociferans)* is the *ëjaë* or the owner of the plant because the bird "cultivates the Yoco in the forest" (Belaunde and Echeverri 2008, 87). Besides sowing the plant in her forest's plots (the forest as the birds' *chagra* or sowing plot), the *cuacuiyó* feeds her offspring by swallowing the Yoco's fruit (*guayo*), throwing the kernel and retaining the pulp for her chicks (102).[44] Much like the breeding habits of the *cuacuiyó* reflect the use of the Yoco to raise and nurture her offspring, the Secoya employ this plant to educate their human children as well.[45] Insofar as the physical properties of the plant prepare the human body to undertake different activities in the forest,[46] the Yoco, analogically, is considered a giver of advice who teaches the children to perform such activities. She is a knowledge holder. She holds medicinal and pedagogical knowledge. The plant heals and teaches.

Step 2—Learning good and beautiful thinking

I clearly remember Cofán *abuelo* (elder) O's smile as he explained how the *yoquito*, as he fondly referred to the plant, "is like the morning coffee for us, because you drink it fresh and cold very early in the morning before you go to work, and it'll give you *fuerza* (strength)."[47] And given its concentration of caffeine and theobromine,[48] a single cup is effective as a stimulant to endure long working hours in the forest.[49] More crucially, however, Yoco teaches how to start any activity with a fresh mind ("*con la mente despejada*"). In fact, after drinking two full gourds of the beverage, this relational protocol or law of the place requires developing a very important skill: the patient cultivation of what Indigenous practitioners[50] and scholars across Putumayo often describe as "*pensar bonito*" (good and beautiful thinking).

I first heard this expression from an Indigenous Inga artist and friend, Benjamin Jacanamijoy, as he recalled how his father—a reputed Yagé medic from Upper Putumayo—said during a ceremony with the plant: "*pensar bonito!*" Benjamin replied: "*caminando con el corazón contento*" [walking with a joyful and happy heart]. In my mind, "*pensar bonito*" refers to a local way of thinking with the plant to orient good action [cultivating a joyful heart] while nurturing relations of care in and with the territory.

The practice of "*pensar bonito*" is not an easy task—as common life experience teaches us. *Pensar bonito* comes with hard work and years of training. And the tonic and purgative Yoco helps to train this skill by teaching the human how "to get rid of laziness (to work and think) and purge the anger"[51] in their dealings with others, human and not. In my experience, the plant "purges anger" and "gets rid of laziness" by setting in motion a reverberating sensation of warmth in the body. This bodily sensation rises from the stomach up to the limbs and the head, then helping to expel what the body does not need. With the plant aiding to cleanse what impedes this distinct form of thought—good and beautiful thinking leading to good and beautiful action—the human body starts learning about the normative and embodied workings of the Yoco's embodied mind. In my view, the purpose of ethical principles such as "purging anger" and "getting rid of laziness" are related to the act of cleansing the body as a form of *listening* so one can "learn anything about the forest":[52]

> Wandering through tobacco plants, listening to moriche palms (Mauritia flexuosa), grateful and bewildered, the body learns to learn; travelling far, inwardly, crossing the lakes of lucid moments, and the feverish fields of dreaming, the body learns to listen, carefully.
>
> (Vargas-Roncancio 2021, 449)

This form of learning conceptualizes *learning as purging* to remove what inhibits the expression of a fresh mind to think, say, act and live well with the forest. However, contrary to Western notions of spiritual purification, which are human-centered, this is a multispecies perspective. The former aims to cleanse the body by removing all that is nonhuman in order to approach a state of purity that will help achieve clarity of mind. By this notion, detachment from the world leads to the attainment of an ideal of human self-awareness and self-realization. But for the Secoya, for example, a clear mind is attained not through separation, but human connection with other species—through engagement with the nonhuman. Like the cuacuiyó bird feeding her chicks, the plant feeds us through the embodied experience of acquiring a fresh mind by ingesting a vegetal body.

Learning with Yoco thus exceeds liberal deference toward a vegetal "other." It is about learning how to engage with the Yoco's perspective and being able to see the world from this vantage point. More than the representation of an external reality, this learning process requires the ingestion of the plant as a some*body* rather than a some*thing*. "*Chuma*," the feeling of dizziness, is both physically cleansing and a learning technique to listen to the forest. It brings about a distinct form of attunement to and unity with forest life. It is an interspecies form of communication through the material engagements of mixing bodies; a form of co-participation in the larger mind of the forest. Learning with Yoco, therefore, is quite explicitly a form of ethical training to become better partners of the forest (Kohn 2013, 2022). Through embodied engagement with Yoco, this multispecies cleanse teaches us an ethics of co-existence, co-responsibility and care for the nonhuman within and outside ourselves.

The multispecies cleansing, in fact, is—and paradoxically perhaps—akin to a mode of "contamination" (Tsing 2015) to remove whatever inhibits the expression of a fresh mind, by incorporating another into one's body thus recomposing broken relationships. The platonic cleansing concerns the individual experience of purification and detachment from the world in pursuit of a spiritual ideal of self-awareness. Relational or multispecies cleansing concerns an ethical education of care for oneself and for the other. The former produces separated bodies, while the latter creates multiplicities of relations between already entangled selves.[53]

Step 3—A mind outside of a (human) head, or mind as forest[54]

Discussing what it means to learn ethics and law with Amazonian plants is decidedly a thorny task. And this is not only because one is unable to fully grasp personal experience with plant persons (Hall 2011), but because learning and knowledge cannot always be accounted for through propositional language (Tuhiwai-Smith 2012). There is always the possibility of either saying too much or saying too little. As Indigenous Inga scholar and political leader Hernando Chindoy Chindoy put it in a recent conversation on the creation of an Indigenous Biocultural University led by the Inga people of

Colombia: "We have our own routes to access knowledge, but we ought to revitalize them."[55] And this requires the aid of vegetal minds as the root of learning (and teaching).

The idea of "plants as teachers," then, has been common currency in Amazonian epistemologies for centuries.[56] Vegetal persons like the Yoco vine seem to teach a method for re-centering corporeal experiences according to the traditional practice of knowledge creation in this region. What I have been calling the "law of the place" to understand the entangled lives of ecology and norms in this region surpasses the concept of plants as botanical objects of scientific description, market use and environmental conservation. A second ethical (and ontological) shift thus comes into being: the practice of defining former objects as persons as a form of caring for life.

This principle refers to transforming former (botanical) objects into subjects with a perspective (Viveiros de Castro 2013). And this principle was crucial for the legal development of the ERA protocol between David R.M and the Cofán people because it changed the direction of the work in an unexpected way (see Chapter 4). David's research process started off as an ethnobotanical project to evaluate the diversity and classification of the wild varieties of the Yagé liana recognized in Cofán territory while documenting the spiritually significant plants at the *resguardo*.[57] Instead of evaluating the diversity and classification of these plants and documenting their taxonomic and ecological aspects, the ERA developed into a sustained ethical-political conversation between different participants regarding whether scientific practice could help leverage Indigenous plant-based medicine in the Colombian health system. Issues of decolonial practice, participatory research design, awareness of epistemic limits and the relevance of research practice became central to the whole process. To be sure, understanding this crucial reorientation required reckoning with plants as persons through situated practice (i.e., conversations with the community, plant ceremonies, etc.) and caring for these plants and the territory they were part of, beyond scientific description.

As *abuelo* O said with clarity and precision during a long conversation in the Andean-Amazonian region of Mocoa last year concerning the Inga University—an initiative led by the Inga people of Colombia to create their own university (*Devenir Universidad* 2020): "to learn anything at all one needs a clear head (mind)." This mind, however, can be delocalized and distributed across different sentient and cognitive beings, rather than situated in a human head.[58] In this sense, the plant teaches us to relocate our learning experiences within the larger experience of a learning forest as it helps us to dislocate our all-too-human minds from our all-too-human heads that see those things as separate (Kimmerer 2013). What we often consider as the locus of thinking, decision-making and communication (a head) now emerges as one node within a larger tapestry of forest learning that involves human and other-than-human beings. What does this tell us about normative systems and how they come into being? Let us continue probing this question.

Step 4—A "minga de pensaminto"

While seated next to a *tulpa*[59] learning about the Indigenous University initiative, the idea of having a "clear head" made sense beyond my common sense. Coming from various regions, Indigenous practitioners from five different communities across the Colombian Amazon, national and international artists, academics, former Colombian state officers and friends were all invited to participate in the first *minga de pensamiento*, or collaborative conceptual work ("*pensar juntos*" or thinking together). The purpose of this four-day meeting was to imagine and begin to conceptualize an intercultural university initiative led by the Inga with the participation of other communities, including the Cofán. The purpose of the *minga* was twofold. First, to learn about a decades-long ethno-educational project of the Inga people and, second, to find new ways to leverage an ethno-educational process linked to Inga's political struggles for recognition and cultural autonomy.[60]

"To start learning anything," *abuelo* O said as he carefully ruminated on his thoughts, "one needs the clear head one gets with *yagecito*." In my mind, he was referring to a generic learning about the world that involves ingesting (and conversing with)[61] vegetal beings both in ritual and in everyday life, two continuous dimensions of experience in Amazonia. The *abuelo* was neither talking about the particularities of local botanical knowledge, nor about the cultural uses and social values associated with different plants of the forest. Most significantly, he was addressing certain plants as knowledge givers, learning partners and mind-bearing persons in their own right regardless of the human attribution of meaning.[62] The *abuelo* O, however, would not have employed any of these concepts at all. Why would he?

While drawing an invisible semicircle with his hand in the air and pointing in the direction of the canopy, he said, almost providentially: "we have our ways of *learning* about this infinite library out there . . . and our learning has always happened with the guidance of the *mayores* (elders) and the plants of the *selva*."[63] Again, "clearing the head" is, after all, learning to *learn* otherwise and with the aid of vegetal minds.[64]

Step 5—A clear head to suspend description

Having a clear head, the *abuelo* may agree, involves a particular way of opening-up to vegetal others through the momentary suspension of a university-trained predilection for description, taxonomy and certainty. In the context of the Inga initiative to create a university in their territory, the issue of "revitalizing our own ways of knowing" seemed unthinkable without the participation of other beings (plants, "invisible peoples"). And these other beings—and former objects from the point of view of Western botany—seemed to provide different principles for guiding this ambitious university project. For example, engaging with plants as teachers required a particular disposition of the body, as well as the suspension of modes of thinking and acting where the body is the passive backdrop for description, appropriation or protection, rather than an active force for the creation of social meaning, political agreement and decision-making (see Merleau-Ponty 1945). "Clearing the head" with plants defies the premise of a mind as an enclosed space where human thoughts, decisions and dreams reside. Fuzzy and erratic when not forthright and focused, this kind of mind is more than just a repository of information from an external world. To be sure, the *abuelo* was inviting the participants of the university *minga* to imagine what we may call "mind" and "learning" in a completely different way and with the help of Yoco and other plants of the forest.

Step 6—"Mente fresca" or cooling down the mind

A condition for the possibility of learning, having a clear head is a moment in a larger process that the *abuelo* O poetically called "*tener una mente fresca*" (having a fresh and cool mind). A *mente fresca* entails purging the body as a way of creating a disposition to learn, and in this sense, purging amounts to a form of pedagogy: "The university we are designing here is a place where you can go drink the plant and purge the body to be able to see" (*para poder mirar)*, as *mama* U said during an afternoon meeting in Mocoa in 2019. In other words, this learning process involves cultivating a disposition to learn with the body as a form of mind. And such a disposition is a particular quality of people that have been trained with the plant. Purging as listening and pedagogy or expelling what the body does not need as a way of tuning into the forest, is an integral part of this relational protocol.

Extending an invitation to think about the body in a different way, the *abuelo* was conceptualizing learning as a process of cooling down *(enfriar)* the human body with the help of a plant teacher. In fact, the Yoco infusion is a cold beverage one drinks in the morning before working in the *chagra* or doing any other activity in the forest (Echeverry and Kinerai 1993).[65] In a sense, the body could be imagined the other way around: as a mind taking a cold shower early in the morning. A "*mente fresca*" with the strength to endure the task of always learning something new about this "infinite library out there." To put it differently, the *abuelo* O was disrupting the famous modern division between mind and body by inviting the people at the *minga de pensamiento* to cool down their minds-as-heads by "contaminating" (Tsing 2015) their bodies-as-minds through the act of purging, thus inverting the Modern Cartesian division, if not negating it altogether:

(1) *From mind/body to*	(2) body/mind *and*	(3) body = mind
(1) "Western" university logic) to	(2) Indigenous university logic)	(3) Forest as university or "the library out-there"[66]

Indigenous artist and ethno-educator *mama* U further highlighted this reverse logic of the university with this powerful statement: "my idea of a university is where people can throw up and sweat as part of the process of learning."[67] Based on my direct experience with the Yoco and trying to go beyond my own common sense, the statement clearly captured the workings of the plant's mind:

> the bitter and earthy taste of the Yoco infusion sparks an instant sensation of warmth through the limbs and the head to then ignite a mild *chuma* (*dizziness*) making the body quiver in slow motion. The *chuma* grows stronger as the stomach folds over onto itself, while the bile and the plant are expelled with the urgency of a powerful relief. Bewildered and grateful, one can imagine the vibrant presence of a gentle song sprouting from the surrounding trees.
>
> (Vargas-Roncancio 2021, 451)

If the first step in this *learning to learn* required cleansing the body, the following steps concerned the reflexive moments of suspending the way humans usually think about these plants: we, humans, need to suspend the common sense that considers plants as sessile and mindless objects to be able to encounter them as people, namely plants full of mind rather than things for disciplinary description, market use and conservation narratives.

Step 7—Co-emergence through ingestion (and digestion)

The reflexive moment teaches us that *learning to learn from the vantage point of the plant* requires a particular form of training or "corporeal discipline" (Echeverry and Pereira 2010) involving the incorporation of the plant as *gente* (as people).[68] In other words, making the plant part of the human through ingestion and making the human part of the plant through the *chagra* labor.[69] Thus, a full cycle of propagated digestion (a metabolism of sorts) was in the making: from human sowing to multispecies mutual eating, and from nurturing to expelling to nurturing new (vegetal) life. The *minga de pensamiento* was an opportunity to reckon with this relational protocol or way of dealing with the entangled lives of meaning and ecology, and the limits and possibilities this protocol affords for Amazonian interspecies (legal) epistemologies.

In addition, learning to learn the relational protocol (law of the place) is more than the liberal deference towards an Indigenous (and vegetal) *other*. It is about the co-emergence of people, meaning and norm through ingestion, that is, learning to learn seriously, respectfully and carefully how to engage with the Yoco's perspective[70]—seeing with the Yoco's eyes—through (vegetal) anthropophagy. In this context, ingesting is an event of co-emergence rather than co-existence between two kinds of people, namely vegetal people and human people co-becoming in mutual nourishment and thought (Despret 2004; Haraway 2007, 2016). In a way, the mind of the plant and the mind of the human emerge together via ingestion.[71] In this sense, humans and plants co-emerge by virtue of exchanging their perspectives in a shared experience of matter and meaning,[72] that is, the *cuacuiyó* bird disperses the seed; the human sows the vine and prepares the beverage early in the morning; and the vine purges the human body.[73] At the same time, the *cuacuiyó* bird—the Yoco's owner for the Secoya—cultivates the plant, while the vine teaches and "gives advice" to the human who learns to work and think with the plant. This relational insight was crucial for the design of the ERA, which followed the law of the place that emerged in recursive interaction between humans, plants and the invisible peoples of Nariño, Southern Colombia (see Chapter 4: *Los Invisibles*).

Step 8—Good and beautiful action

Engaging with the world from the perspective of minds relentlessly emerging through relations between clusters of human neurons, vegetal cells, water drops, soils, clouds, invisibles ones and forests may help us to navigate good action for today's crises. This is an ethical and legal task of sorts. Plants like Yoco are an entry point into a larger constellation of interdependencies (Escobar 2018). The Yoco can help us to cool down (*enfriar*) our minds to participate in this larger world of relations. *Enfriar* requires removing (purging) whatever interrupts our ability to "*pensar bonito*" (Jamioy and Apushana 2013) or "*mirar bien bonito*" (to think and see beautifully) according to *abuelo O.*

In my experience, learning with plants is a form of ethical practice to become better partners for our wounded Earth. Thinking with plants through ingestion is then a form of ethical knowledge to align oneself with good action in today's world.[74] What happens when normative systems such as the law attend to this relational protocol? Indigenous practitioners and their vegetal partners in Amazonia are teachers in navigating the entangled realities of colonialism, extractivism and violence in this region. "Get(ting) rid of laziness and purg(ing) anger"[75] with Yoco may teach us a way to cool down the mind (and the planet) and learn to care for the forest and its mind-full dwellers.

Yoco and the law

Activated by the ingestion of Yoco as *gente* (people), the creation of the law of the place or relational protocol teaches us something about the law that goes beyond the state's monopoly over legal meaning in this region. The relational protocol with vegetal minds such as Yoco is an instance of this "excess" (De la Cadena 2015). The making of the research agreement

I followed with an ethnobotanist, the political and spiritual authorities of the Cofán community, several medicinal plants and "the invisible people" of the mountain where these plants grow required attending to this specific mode of legal learning beyond the human rationalization of conduct according to written norms sanctioned by a state. In this sense, learning law with plants complicates what we mean by this word (law) and the kind of world a law-otherwise is able to capacitate.[76] Chapter 4 deals with the making of the Ethnobotanical Research Agreement—ERA—led by David Rodriguez and the Cofán.

In this section, I've argued that learning with plants is a way of weaving law and ecology together because it situates the legal conversation beyond the realm of state's command over nature and human relations (Descola 2013), and into the realm of ecological and cosmological relationality as an expanded form of socio-legal participation (see De la Cadena 2014; De la Cadena and Blaser 2018; Escobar 2020; Strathern 2005). This means, in a way, going beyond a dualistic ontology in life and law: on the one hand, the notion that the world is divided between nature and culture and, therefore, that the human represents and shapes this world as long as she is ontologically separated from it; and, on the other hand, that the law is a subset of social norms that vary across cultures and social groups and regulate the relationships between individuals, social groups and political institutions such as the state, as well as the relationships between societies and their surrounding environments. According to this ontological premise of separation between nature and culture, the state would be part of culture and, as such, would be the most important political unit insofar as it regulates the metabolism between "nature" (i.e., natural resources) and "society" through the institutions and binding legal norms it produces.

Learning to learn with plants can therefore be an effective way of guiding action in the world. And this brings us to the third part of the chapter, *Learning law and ethics with mind-full bodies*, where I discuss an approach to cognition as emergence in the work of Chilean neurobiologist Francisco Varela, of key importance to this embodied approach to normative systems such as the law (Varela 1999). Building on Varela and others, in the following section I argue that 1) cognition is not a property of individual humans (Gagliano 2018; Gagliano et al. 2014, 2017; Mancuso and Viola 2015; Marder 2013; Wolhlleben 2016); and that 2) non-dualist approaches to the mind may allow us to encounter others (human and not) as minds in relation to other minds (Kohn 2013, 2022). This approach seems important for appreciating a different understanding of normative systems such as law and ethics in the Andean-Amazonian region, because it goes beyond narratives of environmental protection of an external and non-agentive nature.[77] A non-dualist approach to life and knowledge is also key in Chapters 2, *Yage: Moving words across worlds*; 3, *Coca leaf: Territories in motion* and 4, *Los Invisibles*.

3. Learning law and ethics with mind-full bodies

Embodied memories?

Lately, I have become aware of a curious phenomenon. When I write on a computer without intentionally focusing on the keyboard, I tend to decrease spelling mistakes. On the contrary, when I look at my hands mechanically pressing the keys, my spelling can be quite embarrassing. The recursive practice of typing without the intentional control of the event at hand made me realize that perhaps other parts of my body hold some form of "embodied memory."[78] When I try to match the movement of my fingers with the alphabet printed on the keyboard, I imagine pointing my attention to the event at hand as if telling my fingers what to do. However, when I try to remember the order of the alphabet on the said keyboard, my spelling mistakes increase. Otherwise, my hands remember the order of the alphabet on the keyboard.

It seems to me that we humans access the idea of a centralized self (Varela 1999), namely a stable "I" that is different from everything else out there, through these kinds of mundane events. This centralized "I" is in charge of retrieving information from an external and pre-given world. We seem to live under the assumption that daily experiences such as typing on the computer, eating, walking in the forest, ingesting ritual beverages, among other actions, are all expressions of an intentional commitment of the human towards an outside—what lays beyond our skin—independent and self-contained reality.

Neurobiologist Francisco Varela's ethics as practice

Do humans take for granted the existence of this self-contained *self*? Is this self or mind located somewhere in the brain? Does the brain control cognition and (ethical) behavior? Francisco Varela proposes a way to answer these questions with what he calls an enactive approach to cognition. In his book *Ethical Know-How: Action, Wisdom and Cognition* (1999), Varela intertwines two seemingly separate fields of knowledge that are of crucial interest for our argument about the making of a relational protocol in Amazonia, namely cognitive science and practical ethics. Varela himself was a neuroscientist and a practitioner of mindfulness meditation, and his suggestive piece is deeply informed by a serious commitment to the question of experience from the perspective of the neurobiology of color as well as the practice of mindfulness meditation.

The relationship between cognition and ethics is exemplified by the wise person's approach to ethical behavior: s/he is the "one who knows what is good and spontaneously does it" (Varela 1999, 4). For Varela, "(e) thics is closer to wisdom than to reason, closer to understanding what is good than to correctly adjudicating particular situations" (3). He calls this immediacy or spontaneity of experience "know-how" as opposed to the intentional adjudication of rational judgment, which he calls "know-what."

This distinction is significant: ethical expertise is akin to a practical skill rather than the actual representation of an external reality separated from the cognitive self.

As a cognitive scientist, Varela draws from the work of J. Piaget who affirms that even the highest level of cognition is situated or grounded in the concrete activity of the whole organism (a plant or a human, for example) and not only the brain (Piaget 1935). According to this approach, the world is not something given to the human mind, but "something we engage in by moving, touching, breathing and eating" (Varela 1999, 7). This means that the world emerges in recursive engagement with it and cannot be reduced to a series of discrete entities that we represent in our brains upon having the experience. With this, Varela challenges a "computationalist" approach to cognition and life based on the rift between the knowing subject who represents (and acts upon) reality by means of symbolic thought, and a pre-given world retrieved by a subject in command of a mind. This is what Varela calls an enactive approach to cognition as a way to foreground that cognitive processes do not "consist . . . in the perceptual guidance of action in a world that is inseparable from our sensory-motor capacities and (therefore) that "higher" cognition structures also emerge from recurrent patters of perceptually guided action." (17)

According to Varela's account, embodied action or enaction entails at least two associated characteristics. First, the situated character of experience or readiness to hand and, second, the individual sensory-motor capacities "that are themselves embedded in a more encompassing biological and cultural context" (12). Returning to the typing example, my memory of the order of the alphabet printed on the keyboard has less to do with a mental image or representation than with the recurrent sensory-motor coupling of my fingers and the keyboard (also Varela et al. 1992). According to this enactive approach to cognition, what do mundane events such as the one just described have to do with the attainment of "ethical expertise"? To answer this question, Varela draws from the work of Mencius, an early Confucian thinker from the fourth century BCE.

Mencius's view of ethical experience challenges the dominant Western Christian tradition of the original sin and the fall to affirm instead the fundamental goodness of the human experience. Mencius, however, does not point to an ontological *a priori*, but rather to a human capacity that can be nurtured through everyday practice and skill in what Varela himself calls the practice of transformation. "As far as what is genuinely in him is concerned (a person) is capable of becoming good. . . . As for his becoming bad, that is not the fault of his native environment." (Mencius cited in Lee Yearly 1991, 60). The question is how people may cultivate the capacities and dispositions that are necessary to attain ethical expertise as an at-hand experience rather than an external, transcendental and disembodied set of moral principles to be applied independently in any given situation.

Mencius believes that people actualize ethical behavior "when they learn to extend knowledge and feelings from situations in which a particular action is considered correct to analogous situations in which the correct action is unclear." (Varela 1999, 27). For example, when a person moved by the feeling of compassion helps another in danger, they don't act rationally by adjudicating moral or legal norms. Instead, they spontaneously extend the feelings emerging from analogous situations to the situation at hand, regardless of the formal existence of the norm yet enacting the norm through the practice.[79] In other words, Varela, following Mencius, considers ethical expertise as a matter of situated training in a body that can learn: "One starts from a simple situation we can all handle and then extends one's skills in widening circles to situations that are more complex" (27–28).

This methodology requires at least two interrelated skills: first, attention, or the capacity to identify similarities between situations, and second, awareness, or the ability to allow similar feelings to appear in a new situation.[80] For Mencius, ethical training depends on clear perception of correspondences and affinities between situations by way of cultivating attention. Thus, he is opposed to the mechanical application of transcendental rules because they disallow the training of attention to the issue at hand. Remaining attentive, then, entails recurrent sensory-motor engagement with an enacted world. It requires a body becoming attuned to the world,[81] or, in a sense, a thinking body. Varela highlights what our body already knows: cognition is not located in the brain, but distributed throughout the body, which is why it is common to all living beings. This point is crucial for a more-than-human understanding of different types of normative systems (60).[82]

Mind-full plants that teach norms and behavior

Borrowing from Varela, my goal with this part of the story was probing a simple idea: the practice of goodness (good and beautiful action) in our interactions with others (human and not) is a way to attain ethical expertise. In my experience, learning to learn with plants amounts to a form of ethical training to become better partners for our wounded and flourishing Earth, insofar as vegetal beings can be considered persons with ethical and legal standing.[83] Mind-full plants learn and teach, which means that we are not all-too-rational agents garnering knowledge from an external world, but mind-full beings that co-create this world with plants and *non*-plants full of mind. Learning ethics with plants is crucial for the craft and practice of law in Amazonia, among others, because plants are "the root of the territory . . . plants are what holds culture together."[84] What does an ethical disposition and training with vegetal beings teach us about the law in Amazonia?

Conclusions

I have argued that plant persons[85] such as the emetic Yoco vine (*Paullinia Yoco*) are not only vegetal objects of scientific description but partners of a legal herbarium, that is, vegetal beings that create law with their human partners. *Yoco: cooling down the mind and learning law where the law is not named as such* is part of a larger argument of the book concerning the entangled lives of law and ecology in Amazonia. I have focused on one main aspects of it, namely how we can learn to learn the law that emerges from relations between persons of the human and other-than-human kind ("steps"). I suggested that the ingestion of plants as persons to encounter the law of the place is one mode of the *legal* in Amazonia. However, this *non*state law exists alongside modern state law[86] in a nested relationship,[87] whereby state law can also propose viable intercultural critical environmental governance models for times of acute socio-ecological crises in this region (Philippopoulos-Mihalopoulos 2017).

In telling the story of the Amazonian Yoco as a way to encountering the law of the place, I claimed that learning with plants is central to the question of how to live well in Amazonia and beyond. What does the "recursive interaction" or "know-how" (Varela 1999) with plants tell us about how we may guide action in the world? (Kohn 2022). This issue brought us to the question of ethics. In the third section, *learning law and ethics with mind-full bodies*, I discussed the work of Chilean neurobiologist Francisco Varela and his theory of ethics, which is based on an enactive approach to cognition. Varela is primarily concerned with how people cultivate the capacities and dispositions that are necessary to attaining ethical expertise as an on-hand experience rather than a transcendental and disembodied set of top-down normative principles. As we learn to *listen* the other-than-human in normative systems, for example, by cultivating what *abuelo* O from the Inga called a *mente fresca* (cooling down the mind), this embodied approach to mind is crucial to reckoning with the law of the place, where plants are the very substance of life in Amazonia.

Notes

1 This chapter is based on 12 months of ethnographic research across the regions of Putumayo and Nariño, Southwestern Colombia, and the cyberspace (after the Covid global pandemic). When appropriate, I will use initials to protect the identity of my interlocutors.
2 Unless otherwise indicated, I use different names to protect the anonymity of my interlocutors.
3 On the relationship between law and ecology see Anker (2017), Capra and Mattei (2015), Garver (2013).
4 See Tropical Plants Database, Ken Fern. tropical.theferns.info. 3 October 2020. tropical.theferns.info/viewtropical.php?id=Paullinia+Yoco (Accessed 5 October 2020). On Yagé, see Weiskopf 2002.

5 See Winter's pioneering work (2001). *A Clearing in the Forest. Law, Life, and Mind.* Chicago: University of Chicago Press. Also, Chapter 7 ("Conjuring").
6 I first heard about "los Invisibles" in Nariño, 2019. Don O, Field Notes, 2019. "Los Invisibles" (the invisible ones) lends itself as a central emic category (and, of course, much more) in the context of ethnobiological research with the Cofán led by Colombian biologist David Rodriguez-Mora, as well as my own work around the making of an ethnobotanical research protocol as a form of law in Southwestern Colombia. This protocol included human and other-than-human practitioners. On the other hand, the idea of a "relational protocol" is a central etic category of this work. It emerged in conversation with various interlocutors including biologists, legal scholars, Indigenous practitioners and, of course, plants. For a non-anthropological audience, "emic" and "etic" refer here to two different types of field work and their ensuing perspectives. Simply put, emic, from "within" the social group or from the perspective of the "subject," and etic, from "outside" or from the perspective of the "observer." Linguist Kenneth Pike coined these terms. See Pike, K., 1967. Language in Relation to a Unified Theory of Structure of Human Behavior. The Hague, Netherlands: Mouton.
7 See Mills (2019, 2016) for a similar argument.
8 On Indigenous legal systems in the Colombian context, see the pioneering works by legal scholar and Special Jurisdiction for Peace (JEP) magistrate Dr. Gloria Amparo Rodriguez (http://gloriamparodriguez.blogspot.com/p/articulos.html). On particular Indigenous legal systems, see Perafàn, Carlos (2000) Sistemas jurídicos Tukano, Chami, Guambiano y Sikuani. Bogota: ICANH. On plant thinking and vegetal agencies, see Marder (2013), Gagliano (2018).
9 Rodriguez-Mora, David. Integrating ecomorphology and etnoecology to test Cofán etnovarietal classification of Banisteriopsiss caapi in southwestern Colombia. Description of Research project. Courtesy of author.
10 Agreement between David Rodríguez and the Resguardo Ukumary Kankhe of the Cofán People (2019), or Convenio específico para el desarrollo de investigaciones académicas celebrado entre David Rodríguez y el Cabildo Cofán Ukumary Kankhe. Courtesy of David Rodríguez (Not published).
11 Código Civil de la República de Colombia (CC), Art. 1278, and Art. 1089. The contracting parties should comply with the provisions of the contract. Art. 1089, CC indicates that obligations arise from the law, from contracts, quasi contracts, as well as illegal acts and omissions, or when there is fault or negligence. Regarding the specific case of contracts, Article 1091 CC indicates that the obligations arising from them have the force of law between the contracting parties and therefore must be fulfilled.
12 A standard definition: "The precautionary principle enables decision-makers to adopt precautionary measures when scientific evidence about an environmental or human health hazard is uncertain and the stakes are high." In European Parliament Think Tank, *The Precautionary Principle: Definitions, Applications and Governance.* www.europarl.europa.eu/thinktank/en/document.html?reference=EPRS_IDA(2015)573876 (Accessed 2 November 2020). In the Colombian context, see for example Ley 99 de 1993: "Por la cual se crea el Ministerio del Medio Ambiente, se reordena el Sector Público encargado de la gestión y conservación del medio ambiente y los recursos naturales renovables, se organiza el Sistema Nacional Ambiental, SINA y se dictan otras disposiciones." www.secretariasenado.gov.co/senado/basedoc/ley_0099_1993.html. Also, Constitutional Court, Decision T-299 2008. www.corteconstitucional.gov.co/relatoria/2008/T-299-08.htm (Accessed 4 October 2020).

13 See Title 1, Art. 1 of Decision 391/1991. *Régimen Común sobre Acceso a los Recursos Genéticos*. www.sice.oas.org/trade/junac/Decisiones/Dec391s.asp (Accessed 2 November 2020).

14 Art. 7 of Decision 391/1991 "Régimen Común sobre Acceso a los Recursos Genéticos."

15 In Colombia, research projects involving biological diversity should have a Permiso de Estudio con Fines de Investigación Científica en Diversidad Biológica issued by the Autoridad Nacional Ambiental. Applicable norms: 1) Decreto 1076 de 2015: "Por medio del cual se expide el Decreto Único Reglamentario del Sector Ambiente y Desarrollo Sostenible," Capítulo 5 Investigación Científica. Sección 1 Investigación Científica Sobre Diversidad Biológica—which compiles Decreto 309 de 2000: "Por el cual se reglamenta la investigación científica sobre diversidad biológica." Resolución 068 de 2002: "Por la cual se establece el procedimiento para los permisos de estudio con fines de investigación científica en diversidad biológica y se adoptan otras determinaciones." Resolución 324 de 2015: "Por la cual se fijan las tarifas para el Cobro de los servicios de evaluación y seguimiento de licencias, permisos, concesiones, autorizaciones y demás instrumentos de control y manejo ambiental y se dictan otras disposiciones." Available at http://portal.anla.gov.co/permiso-estudio-fines-investigacion-cientifica-diversidad-biologica (Visited 10.04.2020). Academic studies on Permisos and Contratos de Acceso a Recursos Genéticos in Colombia: Rojas-Díaz, D.A., and Nemogá-Soto, G.R. 2007. "Evaluación de la normatividad vigente sobre permisos de investigación científica en diversidad biológica en Colombia. Primer caso: UAESPNN." In *Acta Biológica Colombiana*, 12: 128; Vargas-Roncancio, I.D., and Nemogá-Soto, G.R. 2010. "Contratos de Acceso a Recursos Genéticos: Un análisis comparado." *Revista Pensamiento Jurídico*, 27: 157–202; Nemogá-Soto, G.R., Ávila-Sánchez, L.A., Blanco-Martinez, J.T., Chaparro-Giraldo, A., Jimenez-Ariza, O.F., Lizarazo-Cortes, O.A., et al. 2010. *La investigación sobre biodiversidad en Colombia (Research on biodiversity in Colombia)*. Bogotá: Universidad Nacional de Colombia and Instituto de Genética. National regulations concerning the protection of traditional knowledge: Decreto 1080 de 2015, Artículo 2.5.1.2.8. and 3.; Ley 191 de 1995, "por medio de la cual se dictan disposiciones sobre zonas de frontera, se establecen dos mecanismos de protección para el CT desarrollado en las zonas de frontera: el consentimiento previo y la distribución equitativa de beneficio." On the subject see: Zerda, A. 2003. *Propiedad intelectual sobre el conocimiento vernáculo*. Bogotá: Universidad Nacional de Colombia.

16 Navarrete, D.M., and Buzinde, C.N. (2010). "Socio-Ecological Agency: From 'Human Exceptionalism' to Coping with 'Exceptional' Global Environmental Change." In *The International Handbook of Environmental Sociology* (2nd ed.). Cheltenham: Edward Elgar Publishing Ltd, pp. 136–149.

17 I first heard the word "conjuring" from a Cofán abuelo (elder) in Southern Colombia as he called upon the Yagé people in a ceremony by blowing into the Yagé concoction. Bajo Putumayo, Santa Rosa reservation, Amazonia, 2007. "Conjuring" also in the work of De la Cadena 2011.

18 For a comprehensive discussion of the place of ritual in the Western law, see the wonderful work by Allen Jessie: "A Theory of Adjudication: Law as Magic."

19 On the notion of excess see De la Cadena (2015).

20 In the Colombian legal systems, the expression "having the force of law" means that a legal act ("un acto normativo") which is not formally a 'law'—because it has not been issued by the Congress—nonetheless has the same hierarchical rank of a law. See Colombian Constitutional Court Decision C-893/1999. Moreover, the "force of law" raises a fundamental question: "what is the nature

of the force underlying legal authority? Frederick Schauer does an excellent job describing the history of two models of the nature of that force: coercion (i.e., sanction based) and sanction independent. Having identified these two distinct models, he then tries to make the case that the law is primarily about coercion and that the role of sanction-independent force has been overstated. His efforts to make this case rest upon an examination of the social science evidence in which he reaches different conclusions than those of many social scientists . . . social norms, moral values, and judgments about legitimacy all influence law-related behavior and, relying upon it, social scientists generally suggest that while sanctions matter sanction-independent forces are central to and often dominate the factors shaping people's law-related behaviors. Schauer argues that this considerable evidence is irrelevant to his analysis. He does so by creating a definition of sanction-independent motivation that he defines as "obey[ing] law because it is the law." He says that this category excludes the social science literature identifying the factors shaping compliance, and he suggests that moral values and legitimacy do not meet his definition of sanction-independent factors. . . . Schauer concludes that coercion is the central force underlying law." Tyler, T.R. 2015. "Understanding the Force of Law." *Tulsa Law Review*, 51(2), Art. 23: 507–519 (507).

21 I use the expression "nonstate" to highlight the participation of other-than-human agencies that the state considers as "natural resources" (See Brown 2004. "Are there natural resources?), or "cultural belief" (See De la Cadena 2010. "Indigenous cosmopolitics").

22 Fieldnotes, Don O, Nariño 2019.

23 See Chapter 7 "Conjuring" for a methodology to compare state and nonstate legal propositions.

24 Baptiste, B. 2011. *El Jaguar y la Telepatina del Yagé*. www.youtube.com/watch?v=gK3BWngw7oI (Accessed 30 July 2020). My translation.

25 A similar argument in Blaser (2016). As he argues, caring for atiku was, among others, about complying with local protocols to fully dispose of the animal remains. Caring for caribu, on the other hand, meant conducting a hunting ban to re-establish caribu populations. In my mind, this is a deeply legal question: atiku and caribu are two different reals rather than two different representations of a common external world or real. What if we probe this cosmopolitical argument in the legal field? What can we learn about ontology through the law—rather than the other way around?

26 The "law of the case" is a rule according to which the final judgment of the highest court is the final determination of the rights of the parties involved in a case: "If an appellate court has passed on a legal question and remanded the case to the court below for further proceedings, the legal question thus determined by the appellate court will not be differently determined on a subsequent appeal in the same case where the facts remain the same." *Allen v. Michigan Bell Tel. Co.*, 232 N.W.2d 302, 303.

27 The yajecero medics of the Colombian Amazon have written an ethical protocol for the responsible use of the plant. A protocol that all interested parties—including researchers—should follow. See Unión de Médicos Indígenas Yagéceros de la Amazonía Colombiana-UMIYAC. 2000. *El Pensamiento de los Mayores. Código de Ética de la Medicina Indígena del Piedemonte Amazónico Colombiano*. Mocoa: UMIYAC. https://umiyac.org/ (Accessed 3 October 2020).

28 Don O, Nariño, 2019. Interview.

29 I prefer this notion to underscore the situated and 'multi-being' origin of the agreement.

30 I am particularly referring to plants as people rather than objects of classificatory description and taxonomy.
31 See Tropical Plants Database, Ken Fern. tropical.theferns.info. 3 October 2020. tropical.theferns.info/viewtropical.php?id=Paullinia+Yoco (Accessed 5 October 2020). On Yagé, see Weiskopf 2002.
32 See Winter's Pioneering Work. 2001. *A Clearing in the Forest. Law, Life, and Mind.* Chicago: University of Chicago Press. Also, Chapter 3 ("Conjuring") of this dissertation.
33 See Andrade (1990, 1992). For the ritual aspects of this cultivation system see Echeverry and Kinerai (1993).
34 See Ken Fern. *Tropical Plants Database.* tropical.theferns.info/viewtropical.php?id=Paullinia+Yoco (Accessed 5 October 2020); Also see, Vickers, W.T., and Plowman, T. "Useful Plants of the Siona and Secoya Indians of Eastern Ecuador." *Fieldiana Botany New Series No. 15*, 1984. www.biodiversitylibrary.org, and Harvard Botanical Museum; Cambridge, MA. Botanical Museum Leaflets Vol. 10. 1942. www.biodiversitylibrary.org (Accessed 4 October 2020).
35 Ibid.
36 R.E. Shultes and Killip, *Paullinia Yoco.* https://pfaf.org/user/Plant.aspx?LatinName=Paullinia+Yoco (Accessed 22 December 2019).
37 Ibid.
38 On the concept of plants as teachers in Amazonia, Laura Dev (2018) suggests: "Shipibo healing practices, along with those of several other indigenous groups, have garnered global attention for their use of ayahuasca. I was under the impression that healers would learn their practices during an apprenticeship period, usually with older family members. However, when I began interviews, I was surprised that, though some of them had apprenticed with an elder, when asked who their teachers were and how they learned, most of them began by describing their plant teachers. Healers learn from plant teachers during quiet periods of deprivation and relative solitude called dietas (diets) (as described by, e.g., Jauregui, 2011). The dieta is a sensitive time in which the healer develops a relationship with a specific plant spirit that then assists them in learning and healing." (2018, 185)
39 The following text is based on ethnographic observations and the quotes do not represent the position of any Indigenous group. The quotes are translations from Spanish of selected excerpts of my field notes in the regions of Putumayo and Nariño, Southern Colombia (2019).
40 I will not refer to these plants in this section. On the use of tobacco among the Murui in Amazonia see the pioneering works of Colombian anthropologist Juan Alvaro Echeverry. Echeverry, J.A., and Kinerai, H.C. 1993. *Tabaco Frío. Coca Dulce. Palabras del Anciano Kinerai de la Tribu Cananguchal para sanar y alegrar el corazón de sus huérfanos.* Bogota: Concultura.
41 The Yoco intake seems to be decreasing in this region. Factors involve the accelerated deforestation of Amazonian forests for cattle, monoculture, and other forms of extraction. Chemical engineer Eduardo Bolivar explores the indigenous utilization of Yoco in the northwestern Amazonia, and its commercial extraction for the dietetic-supplements industry (w.d 153). See "Consejos para vivir bien: Una perspectiva histórica sobre los diferentes usos del bejuco Yoco, Amazonia noroccidental." In Digital Library National University of Colombia.
42 The Yagécero medics of the Colombian Amazon have written an ethical protocol for the resposible use of the plant. A protocol that all interested parties—including researchers—should follow. See Unión de Médicos Indígenas Yagéceros de la Amazonía Colombiana-UMIYAC. 2000. *El Pensamiento de los Mayores.*

Código de Ética de la Medicina Indígena del Piedemonte Amazónico Colombiano. Mocoa: UMIYAC. https://umiyac.org/ (Accessed 3 October 2020).

43 For the interaction between Yoco and Yagé in Amazonian shamanism see Belaunde and Echeverri (2008). Yagé is made from two plants: a vine (Banisteriopsis caapi), and a shrub, called chacruna (Psychotria viridis). See Caicedo (2015), Weiskopf (2002).

44 See Bolivar, E.E., Lopez, W., Gallego, L.M., and Huerfano, A. 2004. "Botando Pereza." In Echeverry, J.A. (ed.). *El Yoco entre los secoya del Putumayo*. Leticia: Universidad Nacional de Colombia-IMANI.

45 SeeBelaunde and Echeverri (2008, 103).

46 SeeBelaunde and Echeverri (2008, 102).

47 I will use the Spanish 'abuelo' throughout the text instead of the English term 'elder' to acknowledge the local dignity of this position of moral, political, and shamanic authority.

48 While theobromine is a diuretic, it mainly acts "as a smooth muscle relaxant and cardiac stimulant." See Coleman, W. 2004. "Chocolate: Theobromine and Caffeine." *Journal of Chemical Education*, 81(8): 1232.

49 Weiss and Kearns (2015).

50 On the notion of practitioners in the Southwestern region of Colombia see Lyons (2020).

51 My translation from the Spanish expression 'para [botar] la pereza y [purgar] la rabia' in Belaunde and Echeverri (2008, 107).

52 Abuelo O, Field notes, Mocoa, Putumayo, 2019.

53 Thanks to L4E colleague Shaun Sellers for a conversation about this issue (June 2020).

54 Here I draw inspiration from Kohn (2013, 2018).

55 Indigenous political leader H during a plenary meeting on the creation of an Indigenous university and intercultural knowledge. Mocoa, Putumayo, 2019.

56 For a recent conversation about this notion, see Luna, Luis Eduardo. 2019. "El Animismo Amerindio, las Plantas Sagradas y el Antropoceno." In *AYA Conference 2019*. www.youtube.com/watch?v=ZHiLl7NxP9w (Accessed 3 October 2020).

57 Rodriguez-Mora, David. Integrating ecomorphology and etnoecology to test Cofán etnovarietal classification of Banisteriopsiss caapi in southwestern Colombia. Description of Research project. Courtesy of author.

58 Varela et al. (1992), Varela (1999). See Gagliano (2018) for a similar argument.

59 Each of the stones that form the stove of the peasant and indigenos kitchens.

60 The minga took place in the city of Mocoa, Putumayo, 2019. The IPAU project is increasingly expanding its network of national and international friends and allies, for example, the Pedagogical University of Colombia, the National University of Colombia, the Javeriana University, among other, institutions and persons—most notably, Swiss artist and scholar Ursula Biemann.

61 On the notion of "conversation" between humans and plants, and between plants, see Urbina (2011, 201).

62 Anthropologist Eduardo Kohn discusses the sign-making capacities of nonhumans (2013).

63 For the notion of selva, see Lyons (2020).

64 The idea of learning to learn in the context of legal learning in the work of Anishinaabe legal scholar Aaron Mills (2019).

65 On the Amerindian notion of "cooling down" (enfriar) with the help of plants like the tobacco, see Echeverry and Kinerai (1993).

66 Fieldnotes, Abuelo O, Mocoa 2019.

67 Fieldnotes, Mama U, Mocoa 2019.
68 A discussion of the use of the coca leaf as a "corporeal discipline" in the next section. See also Echeverry and Echeverry and Pereira (2010), and Echeverry and Kinerai (1993).
69 It is a small plot for family agriculture based on successional rotation and regeneration of the forest, as well as a theater of socio-ecological relations of nourishment, medicine, spirituality, and political life for thousands of human communities across the region. See Andrade (1990, 1992), Correa (1990).
70 On the notion of perspectivism see Viveiros de Castro (1998).
71 On plants as selves in Gagliano (2018), and Kohn (2013). See Myers (2014).
72 Varela et al. (1992, 172).
73 On Yoco's ecology and pharmacology see: Guinard, M.L. 1927. "El yocco: nueva planta medicinal de la flora colombiana." *Boletín de la Sociedad Colombiana de Ciencias Naturales*, 89 February–March, pp. 3–5; Mitchiels and Denis (1926). "Sur la liane yocco, drogue a caféine, du genre Paullinia." *Bulletin de l'Academie Royal de Medecine de Belgique*, 6(VII): 424; Rouhier, A., y Perrot, E. 1926. "Le yocco, nouvelle drogue simple a caféine." *Bulletin of Pharmaceutical Sciences*, 33: 537–539; Schultes, R.E. 1943. "Plantae Colombianae IV. Una planta estimulante del Putumayo." *Revista de la Facultad Nacional de Agronomia*: 59–79; Schultes, R.E. 1986. "Recognition of Variability in Wild Plants by Indians of the Northwest Amazon: An Enigma." *Journal of Ethnobiology*, 6(2): 229–238; Schultes, R.E. 1943. "Plantae Colombianae IV. Una planta estimulante del Putumayo." *Revista de la Facultad Nacional de Agronomia*: 59–79; Schultes, R.E. 1942. "Plantae Colombianae II. Yoco: A Stimulant of Southern Colombia." *Botanical Museum Leaflets*, 10: 301–324; Vickers, William, y Plowman, Thimoty. 1984. "Useful Planls of the Siona Secoya Indians of Eastern Ecuador." *Fieldiana*, 15; Weckerle, C.S. 2003. "Purine alkaloids in Paullinia." *Phytochemistry*, 64(3): 735–742; Zuluaga, Germán. 2004. *El Yoco (Paullinia Yoco): La savia de la selva*. Bogotá: Universidad del Rosario; Zuluaga, Germán, y Amaya, Carolina (1991). "Uso de purgantes en la medicina tradicional colombiana." *Interciencia*, 16(6): 322–328.
74 On ethical training see Varela (1999), and Kohn (2018).
75 Belaunde and Echeverri (2008, 107).
76 On the "otherwise" in social theory see Restrepo and Escobar (2005).
77 Even beyond state granted personhood to non-human beings (see Part 2 of the dissertation: "Rights of Nature: Limits and Possibilities").
78 See Ianì, F. 2019. "Embodied Memories: Reviewing the Role of the Body in Memory Processes." *Psychonomic Bulletin and Review*, 26: 1747–1766. Iani explores the role of the body and its sensorimotor processes in memory. He claims: "The sensorimotor model of memory (SMM) claims that the body is the medium where (and through which) sensorimotor modalities actually simulate the somatosensory components of remembered events and predicts that memory processes can be manipulated through manipulation of the body" 2019, 1749.
79 Mills (2019) point "would be that it's not about law as norms at all, but about training and resources for making good decisions in the context of that web of relationships." Kirsten Anker, personal communication, January 2021.
80 In a recent conversation, McGill colleague Daniel Ruiz called attention to the semiotic character of these skills: identifying similarities as iconicity, and the ability to allow similar feelings to appear in a new situation as indexicality. Kohn (2013) suggests that icons and indexes are types of signs beyond human symbolic representation and therefore expressed by other beings. In the realm of ethics, this suggests that other-than-human beings are skillful (or skill-expressing) entities.
81 For a similar argument, see Ingold (2011) Ch. 9.

82 This argument is important for how we understand the notion of personhood in today's conversations concerning the rights of nature: it is becoming clear that the themes of the person and personhood are important not just for human rights theory but for the rights of nature theory as well. What we need is a theory of the person and personhood for the emergent rights of nature theory. However, there are ways to talk about the person based on non-modern ways. For example, the notion of self in Varela (1999) is very important for it emphasizes the idea of emergence rather than of bounded self: instead of thinking about persons from the vantage point of ontological separation, we can still think about persons from the vantage point of relational ontologies (See Chapter 5 "Conjuring" and 6 "Forest on Trial" of this book). For this second meaning of person, I prefer to use the language of "the self." The self is, then, an emergent property of living lines or what Ingold calls ways of life (Ingold 2011). The person is a meshwork in the context of a non-modern theory of rights of nature.
83 Koechlin, F. 2009. "The Dignity of Plants." *Plant Signaling & Behavior*, 4(1): 78–9. http://doi.org/10.4161/psb.4.1.7315.
84 Interview with A.A. 2019, referring to ritual plants, and particularly the *Yagé* vine. See next sub-chapter.
85 On this notion see Hall (2011), Gagliano (2018) and others.
86 For example, Study Permit for Scientific Research in Biological Diversity in Colombia and regulating laws, decrees, and resolutions.
87 See Table 1: Prevalence of the law of the place in the co-design of an ethnobotanical research agreement in Southern Colombia.

References

Allen, Jessie. 2008. "A Theory of Adjudication: Law as Magic." *Suffolk University Law Review*, 41(4): 773–831.

Andrade, Angela. 1990. "Sistemas Agrícolas Tradicionales en el Medio Caquetá." En Correa, F. (ed.). *La Selva Humanizada*. Bogotá: ICANH-FEN-CEREC.

Andrade, Angela. 1992. "Bases para el Estudio y diagnóstico preliminar de los Sistemas de producción en la Amazonía Colombiana." In *Amazonia Colombiana. Diversidad y Conflicto*. Bogotá: Colciencias, CONIA, CEGA.

Anker, Kirsten. 2017. "Law As . . . Forest: Eco-logic, Stories and Spirits in Indigenous Jurisprudence." *Law Text Culture*, 21: 191–213.

Anker, Kirsten, Burdon, Peter, Garver, Geoffrey, Maloney, Michele, and Sbert, Carla. (eds.). 2021. *From Environmental to Ecological Law*. London and New York: Routledge.

Baptiste, Briggitte. 2011. *El Jaguar y la Telepatina del Yagé*. https://www.youtube.com/watch?v=gK3BWngw7oI (Accessed September 2023).

Belaunde, Luis Elvira, and Echeverri, Juan Alvaro. 2008. "El Yoco del cielo es cultivado: perspectivas sobre Paullinia Yoco en el chamanismo airo-pai (secoya-tucano occidental)." *Anthropologica*, 26(26): 87–111.

Blaser, Mario. 2016. "Is Another Cosmopolitics Possible?" *Cultural Anthropology*, 31(4): 545–557.

Blaser, Mario. 2019. "On the Properly Political (Disposition for the) Anthropocene." *Anthropological Theory*, 19(1): 74–94.

Bolívar, Edgar. 2009. "Consejos para vivir bien: una perspectiva histórica sobre los diferentes usos del bejuco Yoco, Amazonía noroccidental." En Nieto, Juana

Valentina, y Palacio, Germán (eds.). *Amazonía desde dentro: Aportes a la investigación de la Amazonía colombiana*. Bogotá: Universidad Nacional de Colombia.
Bolivar, E.E., Lopez, W., Gallego, L.M., and Huerfano, A. 2004. "Botando Pereza." In Echeverry, J.A. (ed.). *El Yoco entre los secoya del Putumayo*. Leticia: Universidad Nacional de Colombia-IMANI.
Brown, Peter G. 2004. "Are There Any Natural Resources?" *Politics and the Life Sciences*, 23(1): 11–20.
Caicedo, Alhena. 2015. *La Alteridad Radical que Cura. Neo-chamanismos yageceros en Colombia*. Bogotá: Universidad de los Andes.
Capra, Frijoft, and Mattei, Ugo. 2015. *The Ecology of Law: Towards a Legal System in Tune with Nature and Community*. Oakland: Berrett-Koehler Publishers.
Coleman, William. 2004. "Chocolate: Theobromine and Caffeine." *Journal of Chemical Education*, 81(8): 1232.
Correa, Francois. 1990. "La Reciprocidad como modelo cultural de la reproducción del medio y la sociedad Taiwano." In Correa, F. (ed.), *La Selva Humanizada*. Bogotá: ICANH-FEN-CEREC.
De la Cadena, Marisol. 2010. "Indigenous Cosmopolitics in the Andes: Conceptual Reflections Beyond 'Politics'." *Cultural Anthropology*, 24(2): 334–370.
De la Cadena, Marisol. 2014. "Runa: Human But *Not Only*." Comment on Kohn, Eduardo. 2013. "How Forests Think: Toward an Anthropology Beyond the Human. Berkeley: University of California Press." *Journal of Ethnographic Theory*, 4(2): 253–259.
De la Cadena, Marisol. 2015. *Earth Beings. Ecologies of Practice Across Andean Worlds*. Durham: Duke University Press.
De la Cadena, Marisol, and Blaser, Mario. 2018. *A World of Many Worlds*. Durham: Duke University Press.
Descola, Philippe. 2013. *Beyond Nature and Culture*. Chicago: University of Chicago Press.
Despret, Vinciane. 2004. "The Body We Care for: Figures of Anthropo-Zoo-Genesis." *Body and Society*, 10(2–3): 111–134.
Dev, Laura. 2018. "Plant Knowledges: Indigenous Approaches and Interspecies Listening Toward Decolonizing Ayahuasca Research." In Labate, B.C., and Cavnar, C. (eds.). *Plant Medicines, Healing and Psychedelic Science. Cultural Perspectives*. London: Springer Nature.
Devenir Universidad. 2020. www.deveniruniversidad.org (Accessed 4 October 2023).
Echeverry, Juan Alvaro, and Kinerai, Hipólito Candre. 1993. *Tabaco Frío. Coca Dulce. Palabras del Anciano Kinerai de la Tribu Cananguchal para sanar y alegrar el corazón de sus huérfanos*. Bogotá: Concultura.
Echeverry, Juan Álvaro, and Pereira, Edmundo. 2010. "Mambear coca no es pintarse la boca de verde.' Notas sobre el uso ritual de la coca amazónica." In Chavez, Margarita, and Del Cairo, Carlos (comps.). *Perspectivas antropológicas sobre la Amazonía Contemporánea*. Bogotá: Instituto Colombiano de Antropología e História (ICANH) y Universidad Javeriana, pp. 565–594.
Escobar, Arturo. 2015. "Transiciones: A Space for Research and Design for Transitions to the Pluriverse." *Design Philosophy Papers*, 13(1): 13–23.
Escobar, Arturo. 2018. *Designs for the Pluriverse: Radical Interdependence, Autonomy and the Making of Worlds*. Durham: Duke University Press.

Escobar, Arturo. 2020. *Pluriversal Politics. The Real and the Possible*. Durham: Duke University Press.

European Parliament Think Tank. 2015. *The Precautionary Principle: Definitions, Applications and Governance*. www.europarl.europa.eu/thinktank/en/document.html?reference=EPRS_IDA(2015)573876.

Fern, Ken. 2014. *Tropical Plants Database*. tropical.theferns.info/viewtropical.php?id=Paullinia+Yoco.

Gagliano, Monica. 2018. *Thus Spoke the Plant. A Remarkable Journey of Groundbreaking Scientific Discoveries and Personal Encounters with Plants*. Berkeley: North Atlantic Books.

Gagliano, Monica, Grimonprez, Mayra, Depczynski, Martial, and Renton, Michael. 2017. "Turn in: Plant Roots Use Sound to Locate Water." *Oecologia*, 184(1): 151–160.

Gagliano, Monica, Renton, M., Depczynski, M., and Mancuso, S. 2014. "Experience Teaches Plants to Learn Faster and Forget Slower in Environments Where It Matters." *Oecologia*, 175: 63–72.

Garver, Geoffrey. 2013. "The Rule of Ecological Law: The Legal Complement to Degrowth Economics." *Sustainability*, 5: 316–337.

Garver, Geoffrey. 2019. "A Systems-based Tool for Transitioning to Law for a Mutually Enhancing Human-Earth Relationship." *Ecological Economics*, 157: 165–174.

Grear, Anna. 2017. "Anthropocene, Capitalocene, Chthulucene': Re-encountering Environmental Law and Its 'Subject' with Haraway and New Materialism." In Kotzé, Louis (ed.). *Environmental Law and Governance for the Anthropocene*. Oregon: Hart Publishing.

Grimes, Ronald. 2003. "Ritual and the Environment." In *The Editorial Board of the Sociological Review*. Oxford: Blackwell.

Gudynas, Eduardo. 2009. "La Ecología política del giro biocéntrico en la nueva Constitución del Ecuador." *Revista de Estudio Sociales*, 34: 34–47.

Guinard, M.L. 1927. "El yocco: nueva planta medicinal de la flora colombiana." *Boletín de la Sociedad Colombiana de Ciencias Naturales*, 89: 3–5.

Hall, Matthew. 2011. *Plants as Persons. A Philosophical Botany*. New York: State University of New York.

Haraway, Donna. 2007. *When Species Meet*. Minneapolis: University of Minnesota Press.

Haraway, Donna. 2016. *Staying with the Trouble. Making Kin in the Chthulucene*. Durham: Duke University Press.

Ianì, F. 2019. "Embodied Memories: Reviewing the Role of the Body in Memory Processes." *Psychonomic Bulletin and Review*, 26: 1747–1766.

Ingold, Tim. 2011. *Being Alive: Essays on Movement, Knowledge, and Description*. New York: Routledge.

Jamioy, Hugo, and Apushana, Vito. 2013. *Bonito debes pensar: luego bonito debes hablar*. Bogotá: Sudamericana.

Kimmerer, Robin Wall. 2013. *Braiding Sweetgrass. Indigenous Wisdom, Scientific Knowledge and the Teching of Plants*. Minneapolis: Milkweed Editors.

Kohn, Eduardo. 2013. *How Forests Think. Toward and Anthropology Beyond the Human*. Berkeley, CA: University of California Press.

Kohn, Eduardo. 2022. "Forest Forms and Ethical Life." *Environmental Humanities*, 14(2): 401–418.

Luna, Luis Eduardo. 1984. "The Concept of Plants as Teachers Among Four Mestizo Shamans in Iquitos, Northeaster Peru." *Journal of Ethnopharmacology*, 11(2): 135–156.

Lyons, Kristina. 2020. *Vital Decomposition. Soil Practitioners and Life Politics*. Durham: Duke University Press.

Mancuso, Stephano, and Viola, Stefano. 2015. *Brilliant Green. The Surprising History and Science of Plant Intelligence*. Washington, DC: Island Press.

Marder, Michel. 2013. *Plant-thinking. A Philosophy of Vegetal Life*. New York: Columbia University Press.

Martínez, Esperanza, and Acosta, Alberto. 2017. "Los Derechos de la Naturaleza como puerta de entrada a otro mundo posible." *Revista Dereito e Práxis*, 4(8).

Merleau-Ponty, Maurice. 1945 (1965). *The Phenomenology of Perception*. London: Routledge.

Mills, Aaron. 2016. "The Lifeworlds of Law: On Revitalizing Indigenous Legal Orders Today." *McGill Law Journal*, 61(4): 847–884.

Mills, Aaron. 2019. *Miinigowiziwin: All that Has Been Given For Living Well Together: One Vision of Anishinaabe Constitutionalism*. University of Victoria Dissertation, iii. https://dspace.library.uvic.ca/bitstream/handle/1828/10985/Mills_Aaron_PhD_2019.pdf?sequence=1&isAllowed=y.

Mitchiels, L., and Denis, P. 1926. "Sur la liane yocco, drogue a caféine, du genre Paullinia." *Bulletin de l'Academie Royal de Medecine de Belgique*, 6(VII): 424.

Myers, Natasha. 2014. "Conversations on Plant Sensing: Notes from the Field." *Nature Culture*, 3: 35–66.

Navarrete, David Manuel, and Buzinde, Christine. 2010. "Socio-Ecological Agency: From 'Human Exceptionalism' to Coping with 'Exceptional' Global Environmental Change." In *The International Handbook of Environmental Sociology* (2nd ed.). Cheltenham: Edward Elgar Publishing, pp. 136–149.

Nemogá-Soto, Gabriel Ricardo, Ávila-Sánchez, L.A., Blanco-Martinez, J.T., Chaparro-Giraldo, Alejandro, Jimenez-Ariza, O.F., Lizarazo-Cortes, Oscar, et al. 2010. *La investigación sobre biodiversidad en Colombia*. Bogotá: Universidad Nacional de Colombia and Instituto de Genética.

Perafàn, Carlos. 2000. *Sistemas jurídicos Tukano, Chami, Guambiano y Sikuani*. Bogotá: ICANH.

Pérez, D.H. 2002. *Plan de Vida del Pueblo Cofán y Cabildos Indígenas del Valle del Guamuez y San Miguel, Putumayo-Colombia*. Bogotá: Fundación ZIO-A' I.

Philippopoulos-Mihalopoulos, Andreas. 2017. "Critical Environmental Law in the Anthropocene." In Kotzé, Louis (ed.). *Environmental Law and Governance for the Anthropocene*. Oregon: Hart Publishing.

Piaget, Jean. 1935. *The Moral Judgment of the Child*. Glencoe: The Free Press.

Pike, Kenneth. 1967. *Language in Relation to a Unified Theory of Structure of Human Behavior*. The Hague, Netherlands: Mouton.

Restrepo, Eduardo, and Escobar, Arturo. 2005. "Other Anthropologies and Anthropology Otherwise: Steps to a World Anthropologies Framework." *Critique of Anthropology*, 25(2): 99–129.

Rojas-Díaz, Dali Alexandra, and Nemogá-Soto, Gabriel Ricardo. 2007. "Evaluación de la normatividad vigente sobre permisos de investigación científica en diversidad

biológica en Colombia. Primer caso: UAESPNN." *Acta Biológica Colombiana*, 12: 128.
Rouhier, A., and Perrot, E. 1926. "Le yocco, nouvelle drogue simple a caféine." *Bulletin of Pharmaceutical Sciences*, 33: 537–539.
Schultes, Richard E. 1942. "Plantae Colombianae II. Yoco: A Stimulant of Southern Colombia." *Botanical Museum Leaflets*, 10: 301–324.
Schultes, Richard E. 1943. "Plantae Colombianae IV. Una planta estimulante del Putumayo." *Revista de la Facultad Nacional de Agronomia*: 59–79.
Schultes, Richard E. 1986. "Recognition of Variability in Wild Plants by Indians of the Northwest Amazon: An Enigma." *Journal of Ethnobiology*, 6(2): 229–238.
Strathern, Marilyn. 2005. *Kinship, Law and the Unexpected. Relatives Are Always a Surprise*. Cambridge: Cambridge University Press.
Tsing, A.L. 2015. *The Mushroom at the End of the World*. Princeton: Princeton University Press.
Tuhiwai-Smith, Linda. 2012. *Decolonizing Methodologies* (2nd ed.). London and New York: Zed Books.
Tyler, Tom. 2015. "Understanding the Force of Law." *Tulsa Law Review*, 51(2): 507–519.
Unión de Médicos Indígenas Yagéceros de la Amazonía Colombiana-UMIYAC. 2000. *El Pensamiento de los Mayores. Código de Ética de la Medicina Indígena del Piedemonte Amazónico Colombiano*. Mocoa: UMIYAC. https://umiyac.org/
Unión de Médicos Indígenas Yagéceros de la Amazonía Colombiana-UMIYAC. 2019. *Declaration about Cultural Appropriation from the Spiritual Authorities, Representatives and Indigenous Organizations of the Amazon Region*. https://umiyac.org/2019/11/01/declaration-about-cultural-appropriation-from-the-spiritual-authorities-representatives-and-indigenous-organizations-of-the-amazon-region/?lang=en
Urbina Rangel, Fernando. 2011. "La coca. Palabras-hoja para cuidar el mundo." *Maguaré*, 25(2): 199–225.
Varela, Francisco. 1991. "Organism: A Meshwork of Selfless Selves." In Tauber, A.I. (ed.). *Organism and the Origins of Self. Boston Studies in the Philosophy of Science* (vol. 129). Dordrecht: Springer. https://doi.org/10.1007/978-94-011-3406-4_5
Varela, Francisco. 1999. *Ethical Know-How*. Stanford: Stanford University Press.
Varela, Francisco, Thompson, Evan, and Rosch, Eleanor. 1992. *The Embodied Mind: Cognitive Science and Human Experience*. Cambridge, MA: MIT Press.
Vargas-Roncancio, Ivan Dario. 2017. "Plants and the Law: A Perspective from Latin America." *Australian Feminist Law Journal*, 43(1): 76–81.
Vargas-Roncancio, Ivan Dario. 2021. "Yoco." In Ryan, John, Vieira, Patricia, and Gaglino, Monica (eds.). *The Mind of Plants: Narratives of Vegetal Intelligence*. Santa Fe: Synergetic Press.
Vargas-Roncancio, Ivan Dario, and Nemogá-Soto, Gabriel Ricardo. 2010. "Contratos de Acceso a Recursos Genéticos: Un análisis comparado." *Revista Pensamiento Jurídico*, 27: 157–202.
Vickers, William, and Plowman, Timothy. 1942. "Useful Plants of the Siona and Secoya Indians of Eastern Ecuador." *Botanical Museum Leaflets. Harvard Botanical Museum*, 10.
Viveiros de Castro, Eduardo. 1998. "Cosmological Diexis and Amerindian Perspectivism." *Journal of the Royal Anthropological Institute*, 4(3): 469–489.

Viveiros de Castro, Eduardo. 2013. *La Mirada del Jaguar: Introduccion al perspectivismo amerindio*. Buenos Aires: Tinta Limon.

Weckerle, C.S. 2003. "Purine alkaloids in Paullinia." *Phytochemistry*, 64(3): 735–742.

Weiskopf, Jimmy. 2002. *Yagé: El Nuevo Purgatorio*. Bogotá: Villegas Editores.

Weiss, Luke, and Kearns, James. 2015. "Caffeine and Theobromine Analysis of Paullinia Yoco, a Vine Harvested by Indigenous Peoples of the Upper Amazon." *Tropical Resources*, 34. https://tri.yale.edu/publications/tropical-resources-bulletin/tri-bulletin-archive/tropical-resources-vol-34/caffeine-and

Winter, Steven. 2001. *A Clearing in the Forest. Law, Life, and Mind*. Chicago: University of Chicago Press.

Wolhlleben, Peter. 2016. *The Hidden Life of Trees: What They Feel, How the Communicate—Discoveries from a Secret World*. Vancouver: Greystone Books.

Yearly, Lee. 1991. *Mencius and Aquinas: Theories of Virtue and Concepts of Courage*. Albany: SUNY Press.

Zerda, Alavaro. 2003. *Propiedad intelectual sobre el conocimiento vernáculo*. Bogotá: Universidad Nacional de Colombia.

Zuluaga, Germán. 2004. *El Yoco (Paullinia Yoco): La savia de la selva*. Bogotá: Universidad del Rosario.

Zuluaga, Germán, and Amaya, Carolina. 1991. "Uso de purgantes en la medicina tradicional colombiana." *Interciencia*, 16(6): 322–328.

Legal documents

Allen v. Michigan Bell Tel. Co., 232 N.W.2d 302, 303.

Autoridad Nacional de Licencias Ambientales, Resolución 324 de 2015: "Por la cual se fijan las tarifas para el Cobro de los servicios de evaluación y seguimiento de licencias, permisos, concesiones, autorizaciones y demás instrumentos de control y manejo ambiental y se dictan otras disposiciones." 17 de Marzo de 2015.

Comisión del Acuerdo de Cartagena, Decisión Andina 391/1991 "Régimen Común sobre Acceso a los Recursos Genéticos." 2 de Julio de 1996.

Congreso de la República de Colombia, Ley 57 de 1887, *Código Civil Colombiano*, 26 de Mayo de 1887.

Congreso de la República de Colombia, Ley 99 de 1993: "Por la cual se crea el Ministerio del Medio Ambiente, se reordena el Sector Público encargado de la gestión y conservación del medio ambiente y los recursos naturales renovables, se organiza el Sistema Nacional Ambiental, SINA y se dictan otras disposiciones." 22 de diciembre de 1993.

Congreso de la República de Colombia, Ley 191 de 1995, "por medio de la cual se dictan disposiciones sobre zonas de frontera, se establecen dos mecanismos de protección para el CT desarrollado en las zonas de frontera: el consentimiento previo y la distribución equitativa de beneficio." 23 de Junio.

Constitución de la Repúbica del Ecuador 2008, Decreto Legislativo No. 0, Registro Oficial 449 de 20 de Octubre de 2008, 2016.

Corte Constitutional de Colombia, Sentencia C-035 de 2016, 18 de Febrero.

Corte Constitucional de Colombia, Sentencia T-299 2008, 3 de Abril 2008.

Corte Constitucional de Colombia, Sentencia T-622 de 2016, 10 de Noviembre.

Corte Provincial de Loja [Ecuador], *Acción de Protección, Sentencia*, No. 11121 2011-0010 del 30 de marzo de 2011.

Corte Suprema de Justicia, STC 4390-2018 [Justice Supreme Tribunal STC 4390–2018], 5 de Junio.

Presidente de la República de Colombia, Decreto 309 de 2000: "Por el cual se reglamenta la investigación científica sobre diversidad biológica." Resolución 068 de 2002: "Por la cual se establece el procedimiento para los permisos de estudio con fines de investigación científica en diversidad biológica y se adoptan otras determinaciones." 1 de Marzo de 2000.

Presidente de la República de Colombia, Decreto 1076 de 2015: "Por medio del cual se expide el Decreto Único Reglamentario del Sector Ambiente y Desarrollo Sostenible." 26 de Mayo de 2015.

Presidente de la República de Colombia, Decreto 1080 de 2015, "Por medio del cual se expide el Decreto Único Reglamentario del Sector Cultura," 26 de Mayo.

República de Colombia, Constitucion Politica de Colombia, 1991.

Intertext 1

The elder and the seed

> **Note:** In the first part of the book, the reader will find two poetic references to plants, and one reflection on the continuities of matter and meaning in Amazonia. These intertexts are not meant as literary counterpoints to the theoretical aspirations of each chapter, but rather as conceptual forces that coud be woven into them. The intertexts therefore are meant to support the chapters in a way that feels less constrained by the formalities of scholarly writing.

It all started with a dream. I was at my grandmother's house in the Quindío neighborhood in the Southeast of Bogota. The two-story house was neat: rough painted walls and two large windows covered by bars. Let us say that the beautiful climbing vine that covered the front of the house was intact, and among the vertical bushes, white flowers peeked out as if they were the eyes of a forest suspended. An elder was in the house. He was sick with some cold of the Andean *cordillera*. We left the house on our way to the hospital and went up the steep and unpaved street that extended from the road to Villavicencio, as if it were an asphalt artery that gave consistency to the ethereal substance of the dream.

When we reached the intersection, we took a "*colectivo*" bus—in other places they call it a "guagua." The elder wore a striped shirt and gray pants, like those of an office worker, worn but infinitesimally comfortable, like cotton gloves. We boarded the bus and arrived a few minutes later at a house that looked like a health center. We found a beautiful garden inside. The garden had all kinds of plants: ferns, *bugambilias*, *cacao sabanero*, moriche palms, Yoco lianas and many others, in a sort of vegetal cacophony of forest, mountain and ornamental garden. The patio enjoyed a strange harmony, almost indecipherable. A few minutes later, the elder appeared, sitting quietly on a mat stretched over a stone bed, not extremely high off the ground of soil and granite. At that moment, a medical doctor appeared: a sort of hybrid between a Western physician in a clinic gown and a magician in a violet or dark blue tunic. The spotless gown and the tunic divided his body.

DOI: 10.4324/9781003349426-4

In the background, there was a projection of a bearded man on one of the white walls that enclosed the courtyard. The man was giving instructions while the physician, half Western doctor and half magician, was palpating the elder's chest on the mat with a "kaleidoscope" (instead of a phonendoscope). The elder had a *mochila* (a bag) woven with *chambira* fiber. The bag contained a fish wrapped in banana leaves. The voice of the image projected on the courtyard wall kept giving instructions to the half doctor/half magician. The elder lay down on the mat while I watched the scene. As I decided to sit down next to him, I witnessed how the elder shrank, little by little. Little by little, the elder was transforming; he was contracting as if it were a small implosion that had the cadence of a feather suspended in the air. It was shrinking, inwardly, until it became exceedingly small, until it became a seed: a humble seed.

Chapter 2

Yagé *(Banisteriopsis caapi)*

Moving words across worlds and entangled temporalities in Amazonia

Abstract

Chapter 2 invites another plant teacher in the Andean-Amazonian foothills of Colombia. This plant is central to the argument about learning law where the law is not named as such. Here the focus is on the disruption of linear time as a pre-analytical premise of Western legal epistemologies. *Yagé (Banisteriopsis caapi): Moving words across worlds* is based on ethnographic encounters with the Yagé vine in Upper Putumayo and the Guamuez Valley and investigates different modes of learning and practicing time in this region. The chapter focuses on the potential normative consequences of this disruption. A snapshot of personal experience with the Yagé concoction with the guidance of several practitioners from these regions, *Yagé* discusses how a non-modern approach to time—as a form of embodied practice—may contribute to a post-anthropocentric view of the law. How attending to entangled temporalities in Amazonia that involve visible and non-visible beings can transform legal imagination and practice. My larger goal here is to probe the limits and possibilities of what I have been calling the law of the place.

Ethical premises

Attending to entangled temporalities that involve visible and non-visible beings can transform legal imagination in Amazonia. Chapter 2 invites another plant teacher into the conversation. By disrupting linear time as a pre-analytical premise of Western legal epistemologies, this plant is key to the law where the law is not named as such. *Yagé (Banisteriopsis caapi): Moving words across worlds* is based on ethnographic encounters with the Yagé vine in Upper Putumayo and the Guamuez Valley and investigates different ways of practicing time in this region. The chapter focuses on the implications of this disruption for legal theory.

The *yagecero* medics of the Colombian Amazon have approved an ethical protocol to regulate the ritual use of medicinal plants such as the Ayawuasca also known as Ambiwuasca or Yagé (*Banisteriorpsis caapi*).[1] This protocol is known as "*El Pensamiento de los Mayores. Código de Ética de la Medicina Indígena del Piedemonte Amazónico Colombiano*" (Elders Thinking: Ethical

DOI: 10.4324/9781003349426-5

Code of the Indigenous Medicine of the Andean-Amazonian Piedmont).[2] The Code is based on accumulated experience with the plant over generations.[3] Before engaging with "time" as a form of practice, I will briefly summarize the main aspects of this form of Indigenous law, which shall guide the relationships between Indigenous practitioners, medicinal plants and other actors, including researchers, the state, companies and the general public.[4]

Elder's thinking: ethical code of the indigenous medicine of the Andean-Amazonian piedmont

The Code has numerous references to the notion that it is the plant *who* teaches or transmits knowledge to humans.[5] In 17 points, it summarizes the vegetal thinking of UMIYAC elders—*Association of Indigenous Yagecero Medics of the Colombian Amazon*—in relation to the following aspects: 1) the identity of traditional medics and their forms of legitimization; 2) the protocols to be followed by traditional medics and apprentices; 3) the relationship between traditional medics, communities and the outside world; 4) the behavior of medics when performing ceremonies; 5) the sale of healing services and advertising; 6) the relationship between traditional medics and Westerners; 7) Indigenous intellectual property rights; and 8) the trade in medicinal plants (UMIYAC 2000, 6–7). In addition, the Code 9) includes a proposal to certify traditional practitioners to ensure their authenticity, and provisions regarding the risks involved when charlatans administer traditional medicine (8).

10) The Code also addresses alcohol consumption and the risks associated with it, especially during healing ceremonies (25); 11) the refusal to consider the practice of traditional medicine as ambivalent, that is, as a practice to do good and evil at the same time (18) (it is always for the good of the patient); 12) the prohibition to advertise any therapeutic services without the permission of the traditional medics and their communities (25); 13) commitments to remain in Indigenous community with the purposes of healing (23); 14) the recovery of traditional garments (23); 15) the prohibition of any form of discrediting among traditional medics themselves (28); 16) the creation of an ethics tribunal (28); 17) the need for national and international legislation for the conservation of territories and cultural autonomy; 18) the prohibition of Yagé trafficking and of the sale of raw or prepared Yagé to be distributed to non-Indigenous persons (37); 18) the prohibition of other types of medicines and medics from taking on the name, practices, symbols and ceremonial garments of Yagé healers (31), among other important norms.[6]

Despite its written form, the Code is not reduced to this symbolic expression. It is an ongoing practice of accumulated experience between peoples and the territories they are part of. For Doña Y, a political leader of the Cofán community of Jardínes de Sucumbíos, "the mayores [elders] are the owners of this knowledge."[7] In fact, the knowledge of the yagecero healers concerning the practice of this form of medicine is protected by intellectual property laws on vernacular knowledge in Colombia and elsewhere (Zerda 2003).

Going beyond its symbolic expression—as enshrined in this Code—the law of the place can be formulated as follows: the practice of Yagé cannot take place if those concerned have not properly followed the provisions of the aforementioned Code. When a person enters the territory of the plant, so to speak, he or she must ask permission from its *sabedores*—the yagecero medics—who receive the knowledge and healing powers from the plant herself (Caicedo 2015; Weiskopf 2002). Moreover, while the law of place is situated and embodied in territories and practices, this type of law neither loses its generalizing properties nor its binding force: the law of place, or the law that arises from place, dictates the responsibilities that any concerned person must follow in their dealings with this powerful concoction.[8]

However, this kind of law goes well beyond the normative conventions of the multicultural state. It exceeds cultural belief tied to ethnicity as a modern category of difference (De la Cadena 2010). The law of the place is thus grounded on direct experience over generations of plants and humans in relentless entanglement and co-expression. It neither easily lends itself to modern taxonomies or multicultural accounts (Nieto 2000), nor to the constitutional reforms of a nation. The Yagé is ontologically elusive, and yet it is the root of the territory. The origin of law and well-being.[9]

Plan for the chapter: conceptual persons that aren't good to think with anymore

The idea that culture defines human-only modes of experience seems to travel well in social theory, material objects and everyday life. Ranging from people's conversations and academic journals to material objects, cities and natural parks, this conceptual personae (Deleuze and Guattari 2002) claims ownership over the territories of imagination, language, time and history. Specifying the human in relation to other living beings, the culture personae, so to speak, does not easily embrace the uncertain, the open-ended and the unexpected (Strathern 2005). Why do we insist in a particular mode of being—the modern human (Wynter 1992)—that separates us from the rest of life in times of planetary crisis?

The notion of nature, on the other hand, is often located at the periphery of human experience in words such as "environment" or "wilderness," when not at the very core of what some may push to the margins of scientific and social description: bodies, emotions, feelings and direct experiences.[10] Recourse to the nature *personae* when culture cancels out the possibility of other-than-human ways of being, doing, knowing and feeling does not necessarily solve the problem. The nature *personae* equally hinders imagination (see Chapter 7: "Conjuring"). How can we reimagine a shared experience of life and decay that involves beings and relations beyond the culture/nature divide? (Barad 2007; Bennett 2010; Descola 2013; Kohn 2013; Viveiros de Castro 2015).[11] The famous dualism tends to alternatively privilege one term over the other at the expense of the "radical interdependency" of our bodies, minds and experiences in the cosmos (Mills 2019; Escobar 2018; Berry and Swimme 1992; Dubashia 2018).

With this underlying critique, what follows is organized in three steps. First, I present the notions of common and altered temporalities (Part 1) to probe how a powerful other-than-human—the Yagé plant (*Banisteriopsis caapi*)—disrupts Western modernity's definitions of time as abstract, linear[12] and oriented towards the Euro-American *telos* of civilization, development and progress (Escobar 2008, 2016; Kothari et al. 2019; Mignolo 2011). In *Other-than-human Sources of Order* (Part 2), I delve into the potential normative properties of this disruption and re-center human and other-than-human bodies as the locus of environmental decision-making rather than the objects of environmental governance and critique (Law 2007). Finally, *A Biologist Becoming Bridge Between Worlds* (Part 3) briefly discusses Colombian biology professor Marcela Bravo's musings and experiences with the notions of space and time in Inga cosmologies, as she learns to become a "bridge" between worlds ("a *puente entre mundos*"),[13] thus "*trayendo y llevando palabra*,"[14] or moving words across worlds.

Part 1. Common and altered temporalities

How do you make place and history with plants? Historiographical accounts of the Amazonian region tend to conceal stratified temporalities that scape our modern-trained conceptualizations of time and history,[15] and define these layers as ritual or cultural belief (De la Cadena 2010). Yagé, the Andean-Amazonian concoction, could be a door into these other layers. With Yagé as people,[16] human people can learn that time also goes beyond human experience, that is, time is immanent to places rather than a transcendental norm of human abstraction imposed upon the movement of life.[17] Beyond abstract time, time is more than the relentless continuity of events and could also be conceived as a place-making practice shared by different kinds of beings.[18] And this idea challenges the way we organize history as a continuum of events with the dubious Eurocentric telos of civilization, development and progress (Mignolo 2011).

"When is this happening?" he asked, "It *is* happening yesterday, and *here*."[19] The future enters the past as the past enters the future in what Colombian anthropologist and Yagé practitioner William Torres calls an "aion-temporality" (2000). In aion-temporality, the actuality of the mundane and the virtuality of the sacred intertwine with each other, thus troubling the linear historical path that goes from a past of pre-modernity and stagnation into the future of modernity and progress of the Euro-American way of life (Quijano 2014).

I use the expression "common temporality" to refer to the human experience of continuity of everyday events, and "altered temporality" (Shanon 2001) to point out the disruption and discontinuity of this experience through encounters with the Amazon plant itself.[20] These encounters compel Yagé practitioners to reckon with the vanishing feeling of a human self while opening their bodies to the embedded continuities of other forms of life. Anthropologist Eduardo Kohn eloquently describes the ontological and ethical conundrums of this vanishing self:

> One of the most profound visionary experiences I had in my work last year in the Amazon was the complete dissolution of my 'self' as I became a conduit for the rush of forest life that today I can only call ongoingness

> itself. I allowed my bounded individual self to die—a bit—to a larger holobiome . . . a meshwork or assemblage of a host and other species living in or around it, which together form a discrete ecological unit[21] that engulfed the good in me, but I also felt the urgent need to hang on to a less than perfect kind of *me* as a historically committed site of difference that might make a difference. . . . In this process, I have become convinced that an ethics of ongoingness must involve some sort of orientation—which is not the same as belief—toward these powerful doubled and doubling kinds of beings whose reality is not at every moment palpably existent, and who, their generality notwithstanding, nonetheless risk becoming 'astralized' (p. 36) out of our worlds if too many of their tentacles become severed. For I am convinced that we need their orientation in these troubled times . . . how can we learn to inherit our connections to the powerful ones?
>
> (Kohn 2018)

The (human) self dissolves within broader continuities of human and nonhuman relations from the point of view of altered temporalities. Conversely, the (human) self can still appear as discontinuous, that is, as something separated from other selves from the point of view of the common temporalities of everyday life. In common temporalities, the self perceives the movement of the world (the change, decay and renewal of life) as taking place outside of her embodied experience.

What if, as Torres argues, the altered temporality of Yagé calls into question this sense of external, disembodied duration or the relentless unfolding of events—which is, supposedly, always susceptible to scientific description—by virtue of the dissolution of a self—any kind of self—within the broader "meshwork" of a forest that brings forth modes of participation beyond the human? (Kohn 2013. On meshwork, see Ingold 2011). How can we avoid "astralizing" (exoticizing) this altered temporality given the importance that this temporality seems to have for the care of territories and communities in the everyday?

Torres argues that the plant activates another time ("*un tiempo otro*") whose main property is to escape the immediate present, that is, the present of the "I think this and that," the present of "cogito," the present of "self-importance" and the present of "sedentary rationality." The brew activates an aion-temporality or **a time without duration**:

> In a single instant a foreseen event is activated. . . . The anaconda-ancestor emerges in the ritual space and embraces it, while the *selva's* spirits-ancestors appear with their feathers and crowns . . . quartz collars, jaguar tusks . . . and healing chants. The anaconda embraces the drinker's body [and] chants the conjurations close to their ear. . . . She devours the drinker's body, takes them away to the sub-aquatic world, then becoming a serpent-jaguar adorned with feathers, and finally catapulting the drinker into the celestial. . . . These past experiences narrated through myths are now lived in the future, in an instant with no thickness nor extension subdividing the Yagé practitioners into a past and a future life.
>
> (Torres 2000, 85–6. *Author's translation* from *Spanish*)

The temporality of Yagé, however, does not only refer to a ritualized moment during the Yagé ceremony, namely the return of the anaconda. The return of the anaconda is undoubtedly a mandate to take care of the communities and territories on a daily basis:

> After 500 years of Conquest, dispossession and death of our communities and our wisdom, this is the first time we have been able to gather the traditional Indigenous yagecero medics of Colombia to meet each other, exchange knowledge, befriend and unite for a single cause and in a single thought. . . . We consider that *Yagé*, the medicinal plant, and our wisdom to be a gift from God and a great benefit for the health of humanity. We are obliged to show the world, decisively and seriously, our values.
> (UMIYAC 2000, 6.*Author's translation from Spanish)*

For several Amazonian communities, everyday life is about dealing with neo-extractive economies, colonialism and physical violence as well as their impacts in their bodies, minds and territories.[22] The temporality activated by the plant—which is "the root of the territory"[23]—has a clear mandate: recovering community agricultural practices, systems of governance and strengthening communal hope as a transformative force in the present. While working with the Inga of the *Baja Bota Caucana* in Southern Colombia, biology professor Marcela Bravo calls this mandate *"saber vivir ahí"* ("learning how to live there"), which is a skill one learns with the plant.[24]

Indeed, the linear common temporality of the everyday becomes entangled with the spiral ceremonial time of the ritual: on the one hand, development projects, colonial occupations, political struggles and mobilizations, and on the other, the return of the anaconda to learn how to live well in the territory, or "to learn how to live there." This learning takes place with the plant as the root of the territory. In the words of Colombian attorney and Yagé practitioner A.A.,

> any decision of collective importance such as permitting a state's action or intervention in the territory (i.e., the provisioning of public services, any economic project, research activities etc.) requires the intake of the plant. The intake of the plant is a political act.[25]

That the plant activates an aion-like temporality seems crucial for the decision-making process in this region. However, due to colonialism, this methodology strays time and again away from any conventional decision-making model centered on the idea of rational deliberation between individual or collective human agents: "In the morning we already knew what we needed to do. We learned that with the *remedio* [the plant]. The *yagecito* told us"/*El yagecito nos dijo*."[26]

It is worth clarifying that the altered temporality of the plant does not cancel out rational deliberation. Quite the opposite, deliberation is further expanded to include other modes of participation, and, in that sense, the process of deliberation requires expanding the borders of the political community to include what Marcela calls other "*seres y existencias*"/beings and existents.[27] Moreover, as we learned earlier with Yoco, the relational protocol—getting attuned to the *law of the place* through a series of steps—involves cleansing the body of the human participant so that she can become a "conduit for the rush of forest life" (Kohn 2018, 101). Only in this way can the human participate in the layered temporalities beyond the present of "cogito" and "sedentary rationality" (Torres 2000), and the anaconda can take her "away to the sub-aquatic" and other worlds. Moving across worlds has an ecological function in times of planetary crisis.

The altered temporality of Yagé and the common temporality of everyday life co-intervene in the constitution of the real (Escobar 2018), namely ecological relations and systems; decision-making protocols and political struggles; local institutions of governance and sense of futurity. In the words of A.A., lawyer and Yagé practitioner, as she remembered the four constitutional pillars of the National Indigenous Organization of Colombia-ONIC ("unity, territory, culture and autonomy"):[28] "the Yagé is the root of the territory"/(*el Yagé es la raíz del territorio*).[29]

I am neither proposing an ontological discussion of time in this region (Fausto and Heckenberger 2007), nor reflecting on how altered temporalities interact with human cognitive processes of sorts (Shanon 2001). I am more interested in learning how an altered temporality that is woven into the tapestry of multispecies encounters may inform collective decisions about the forest beyond neo-extractivist projects and state-led conservation agendas.[30] By experiencing the whirl of past and future events, Yagé practitioners are able to disrupt this common-durational time as they weave back themselves after the Yagé experience. The plant conveys (teaches!) a mode of social and ethical participation that involves other-than-human peoples peopling the Amazon in a shared fabric of vitality, suffering, decay, renewal, hope and struggle "*por la defensa de la vida en el territorio*"/(in defense of life in the territory).[31]

Anthropologist Tim Ingold further suggests that human life involves the passage of time as an embodied experience (2011). However, when human relations become reassembled within the larger tapestry of other forms of life by virtue of these altered temporalities, the perception of time is a matter of partnership and composition in what Torres calls an "instant with no thickness nor extension" (2000, 86). In a way, the perception of time would be a shared practice (a work of art?) rather than a cognitive process whereby the human organize events that can be retrieved from an external world (Varela et al. 1992). There seems to be something fundamentally non-human (and even *un*-human) about time and all the things it organizes in life (the law!), for the human is already in partnership with other beings (plants, microbes, fungi, water, sunlight): the assemblage perceives time as a matter of an embodied composition of a world. In this sense, time cannot be reduced to chronology as a transcendental category of history, neither in biology nor in social thought.[32]

Based on similar accounts about the plant (Caicedo 2015; Weiskopf 2002; Luna 1984), time is about the making of a sentient ecology rather than a transcendental *a priori* to organize experience on a territory as a mindless stage for human action. My argument is thus about socio-ecological relations and human/other-than-human continuities by way of the analytics of entangled temporalities: the struggle between the time of development (pipelines, coca crops, soy monocrops) and the time of survival ("unity, territory, culture, and autonomy").[33] The next section will further explore the potential implication of this "temporal discussion" for normative systems such as the law.

Part 2. Other-than-human sources of order

I see temporality as a story about human and other-than-human alliances in the co-creation of a shared socio-normative whole. In my view, this powerful agent (the plant) intervenes in social life in a direct and often disruptive fashion. Reckoning with Yagé as a social agent or force troubles the assumption of separation, thus inviting us to embrace the radical interdependence of all that exists (Escobar 2018). However, this interdependence is not only about the shared physicality of all beings but also about cognition, ethics, and social life, or what Descola calls "interiority" (2013).

Yagé-as-person disrupts the modern separation between the materiality or "physicality" of human and other-than-human life and the "interiority" or meaning-making qualities of the human. In a sense, Yagé-as-person makes assemblages with the matter and energy flows of ecology, as well as the symbolic tissues of the social fabric where it is embedded. In the words of Viveiros de Castro, "[a]nimals impose the same categories and values on reality as humans do: their worlds, like ours, revolve around hunting and fishing, cooking and fermented drinks, cross-cousins and war, initiation rituals, shamans, chiefs, spirits" (1998, 477).

Plant personhood, however, is not an invitation to a modern "anthropomorphization" of other-than-human qualities and dispositions (see Chapter 8, "Forest on Trial," for a critique of the personhood of nature). This would imply that things like "action," "cognition," "morality" and the "experience of time" are defining features of a human being who, in an act of hospitality, grants human membership to prior objects such as plants, animals and rivers. Instead, these features co-emerge reciprocally. This has been confirmed by influential scientific insights committed to a mind-world monism, for example, the "embodied mind" of Francisco Varela et al. (1992), and the "endosymbiotic theory" of Lynn Margulis (1967). Yagé practices "echo the autopoietic dynamics and creativity of the Earth and the indubitable fact that no living being exists independently of the Earth" (Escobar 2015, 14; Varela 1991). Despite the flat distribution of this "condition of humanity" (Descola

2013) across different kinds of beings, how can we avoid the ontological divide in notions such as common and altered temporalities?

Among the Inga communities of the Colombian Amazon, the sources of political authority are not limited to the modern human being. Human interactions are regulated through the mandates, provisions and prohibitions set forth by the plant's master whose voice the *Iacha* or Yagé healer translates into rules for living a good life in the territory. In that sense, the common temporalities of history and the altered temporalities of plant-human encounters intertwine with each other, only revealing an analytical distinction between them. The Yagé weaves together a tapestry of cosmological, ecological (material) and historical continuities that brings into being a socio-ecological contract or form of local multispecies authority. In the words of Marcela Bravo as she describes Inga conceptions of territoriality and medicine:[34]

> People know how to live in the territory and the conception of the territory of the Inga indicates a lesson about living *with* the territory [my emphasis]: it is not about arriving and imposing one's form [point of view] because there, there is also a relationship, the agency of those who are in the territory: the macaw, the eagle, the river, the mountain, the moor and there are a lot of stories that I could tell you for hours and hours. I have drawn, I have thought about making books for children, stories, I have pictures of the stories . . . the real condition is the medicine [the "root of the territory" in terms of A.A.], and the force of survival for Indigenous peoples [in the territory] is the medicine [Yagé and other medicines including the territory itself] and it is something that is so scary [for modern thought] for that reason: the fact that there is a traditional doctor, a midwife, a *sobandero*, is politically irreverent. It is a [non-modern] re-existence amid modernity.[35]

If we, humans, share cognitive and moral capacities with other-than-human beings, how can we learn to perceive in partnership with these other beings in times of planetary crisis? In the context of the Yagé practice, I would argue that this learning and perception happens with the belly. In fact, bodily excess is part and parcel of the relational protocol, and it is via the ritual event of expulsion that we are compelled to question the bidimensional toolkit we use to organize our experience of the world: self and other, up and down, inside and outside, norms and ecologies, sacred and profane and reason and flesh, among other conceptual rifts. The plant teaches a political and legal theory of the flesh: "a glimpse into the non-temporal ongoingness of other-than-human forms of social authority" (Field notes, Mocoa 2019). Thus, the plant weaves together the "virtuality of a pre-cosmological" time (Viveiros de Castro 2014), or "the return of the anaconda" (Torres 2000), and the actuality of the historical and common temporality of life events in times of crisis and "re-existence amid modernity."

In this sense, the encounter between the plant and the human is an encounter for conversation (Grillo Fernández 1998). And this conversation is possible thanks to the meeting of bodies as minds as *abuelo* O said in Mocoa in Chapter 1. Again, the condition of possibility for this conversation is the *limpia*, the cleansing of the body and the expulsion of excess: "a deep cry begotten in the heart of his thinking esophagus, the only part of his body that the plant seemed to talk to. The only part that doesn't allow for second meanings." (Field notes, 2019) In this case, the conversation is conceived in a plane of asymmetry between the plant and the human: the drinker learns to loosen the self to encounter the law of the place.

In a process of plant-human conversation, the (vegetal) counterparty will dwell in the (human) drinker's body, or, in other words, the conversation takes the form of a mutual engagement between embodied selves. From the point of view of the human, for example, this form of interspecies conversation through ingestion depends upon the *limpia* (cleansing) of the body, namely the expulsion of excess as a way to achieve a *mente fresca* (clear mind) or readiness to radical listening (see Chapter 1, Yoco). The *limpia* allows for the emergence of a shared body that exceeds the conventions of dialogue between separated actors exchanging perspectives (symbols) in a space of rational deliberation.

However, this interspecies conversation is often not symmetrical: the human drinker must surrender to the will of Yagé and abandon any aspiration to control the outcome of the conversation.[36] As Inga *Iacha* V. would say, "the plant engages the human as a 'digestive tract'"—a part of the human body that the plants seems to talk to: "dialoguing" and "cleansing" are two sides of the same coin. The plant does not just appeal to the biography or ideas of the human drinker, but to the materials of their bare existence that allow for a dialogue between mind-*full* bodies. This brings us to the next and last part of the chapter: the ethical responsibility of translation across worlds. I've chosen to hold biology professor Marcela Bravo's authorial voice and therefore minimize my analytical intervention in this section.

Part 3. Becoming a bridge between worlds[37]

Carrying and bringing the word is a metaphor of weaving using a *guanga*,[38] says Marcela:

> The strings come and go and then they are tightened down below with a baton ("*la macana*") . . . the words, the threads, go back and forth, but they are never the same words. They are never the same threads. It is never the same bridge. And then, it is not always good to create bridges: sometimes we need to break them because there is no longer a need to go and return using the same path . . . the old path no longer serves us. In this back and forth something new emerges: the threads of time and space that

go back and forth are part of the same fabric. There are no words in Inga that treat time and space separately. It is always space-time: complementary pairs that arise together.[39]

Rooting oneself in the territory

"When you speak about spatialities and temporalities," she continues,

> I believe that there are different dimensions where one can experience space and time simultaneously. I have asked that a lot because, for example, to understand the case of midwifery, which is something that interests me a lot. . . . In relation to this *[she is referring to the question of space and time for the Inga]* the issue of seeding the womb *[the practice of sowing the placenta under the tulpa,*[40] *as a way to enraizar or rooting the newborn in her territory for ever]* I have approached them, the Inga, to see what they say about that, and it turns out that this [*placenta seeding*] can be done in many places as well, and not only the territory; these practices can be done regardless of the place where you are located [*earthing the placenta in the place where you were born creates a physical-spiritual connection to that place, and even when a person goes away, whatever happens in that place influences or dictates their life elsewhere. All because of the placenta seeding and the connection that it crates with the person whose placenta has been earthed]*.

"This is akin to Einstein's ideas of the curvature of the space and black holes [Einstein et al. 1935], don't you think?" she asked me. "So, don't you see that space and time can be curved and the Inga have known this for centuries so that life can exist?" Marcela continues,

> I have also asked [*this to the Inga*] and they [*always*] keep [*this material*] connection with their ancestral territory [*despite their mobility*]: they are merchants, as you know. [*The Inga are*] proud: they walk with all their necklaces all over the country; with all their garments; and they easily get money because they can sell a remedy [*she is here referring to plant-based medicines*]. We are all medicine [*and*] the medicine is sown [*like the placenta*] and if we need the medicine at some point, we can always activate that knowledge, and it comes out right away. It is not something like a predestination, or that there is a 'chosen one' because everyone has already been chosen when they're alive.

Marcela takes a deep breath, and then continues:

> So, time and space, as we understand them, are not like our time on the clock or this external reality that we touch: I can walk, I can go to different places, and I can know other cultures and others, but I always have *that*

> connection with the ancestral territory [*through the placenta*] and that is why they defend their territory, why they struggle. That is why even if they do not live there, it is their territory because there is medicine [*in each of us, because of our connection to the territory through the placenta even if we are far away*]. Let us say [*she continues*], for example, that the Yoco in the San Rafael reservation is almost gone, and why is that? Because the . . . guerrillas walk by and step on it; the peasants walk by and step on it; those who plant coca walk by and step on it . . . and then the Yoco is materially there, you see the lianas, but the spirit [of the plant] is already gone because this lack of respect,

Marcela cautions.

> There is a material basis, and in that sense, I am a materialist like Marx, because I do understand and conceive the Earth in a material sense, jut because it is the medium for the recreation of culture . . . but that territory must be there because that territory [makes] life. . . Now imagine the vine is planted, but it no longer has the spirit . . . to heal. What happens then with that plant? It is not a teacher anymore. We need to learn these rules of respect.

Marcela then asks:

> What happens with the medicine here in Bogotá? [*she is referring to Yagé practices in urban settings*] For example, here [*in the city*] there are also *iachas* [*medicine people*] and they do ceremonies. Where do they bring the plants from? Well, from Putumayo, from the territory, that is, they connect with their grandparents, cousins, and uncles, and there is a trade of plants and seeds, and all the time this medicine is moving, that is, all the time the territory walks because when an Inga walks . . . the territory also walks with her: they walk with the seeds, with the songs, with the *fluidos* [medicinal liquids], with the feathers, and the feathers come and go. . . . They move the word of the plant across all these different worlds. And the Inga go to Ecuador, to Peru, to Venezuela, and they all return on the date of the *Kalusturrinda* (Kusikuipuncha or Atun Puncha depending on the territory), the Carnival of Forgiveness and Reconciliation as we want to say it in Spanish. . . They come from wherever they are: Argentina, Germany . . . to be at the carnival in the territory. How do you explain this? There is a space and a time where people conceive that it is a time to be in the territory, which is a time to affirm the connection they have with the territory and to rekindle the ties of friendship and trust, to say sorry, to say . . . this happened to me, I have cried, I have eaten, I have been happy, I have learned, I worked and, again, I am in the territory. . . . They invite everyone to the carnival, but when they feel that you can already have a place in that world, it is no longer "I come because it is good," but it

is already [a responsibility]: "why didn't you come to the *Atun Puncha*? What happened to you?"

Conclusions

What we can learn with Yagé is quite clear from the point of view of the ecological ethos for our times: what we deem exclusively human is created with other-than-humans not as human praxis transforming nature to produce human history, but as the co-emergence of "all that exists" across time and space (Escobar 2018). History conceals layers of temporality that scape our perception. Yagé—the Amazonian brew—is a door to these other layers. In the words of biology professor Marcela Bravo:\

> On the way to the salt lake [salado], Mechas' companion tells him that "that sound . . . that's the sound of the clock bird [*pájaro reloj*] who sings every hour. That this is how they used to locate themselves in "time" when they went out to work, because there was not a clock in those times. When I told this story to Taita Pacho Tisoy, from Vichoy (a village in the Sibundoy Valley), he said that this bird is a liar; that the bird does not sing at the right time . . . I'm left wondering "who is the liar?", the bird or those who imposed the time system on us? Or better yet, what is it about time, about the hours?
> (Bravo 2015, 88)

In a recent conversation, she took this reflection even further:

> Those birds are no longer singing because their populations are shrinking due to mining projects in the area and the ensuing devastation of their ecosystems. But also, because climate change has confused them: the birds don't even know at what time they should sing anymore . . . It is not that the bird sings at the wrong time. What happens is that those who invented the clock to put time in it never consulted with the birds if it [the clock] had been well calibrated ["*los que se inventaron el reloj para meter el timepo en ese aparato nunca consultaron con los pajaros si les habia quedado bien calibrado.*"].
> (Interview, Oct. 2023)

With Ambiwaska, Ayawaska or Yagé we learn that time sits in places. Time is an embodied experience from beginning to end (Ingold 2011), and the placentas that kept us alive in the womb can be re-seeded in our territories so that we can maintain a viable and lasting connection with these territories, thus "bending time and space." Altering time and space in our life wanderings, while keeping alive in the present moment our past in our mother's womb, and enhancing our presence in the territories we have left (or never left), even if we live in new places where we can make a home.

Notes

1 My observations here are based on personal experience and interaction with some practitioners, and they do not represent a unified view of a particular community. Unless otherwise indicated, I use different names to protect the anonymity of my interlocutors.
2 See Unión de Médicos Indígenas Yagéceros de la Amazonía Colombiana-UMIYAC. 2000. *El Pensamiento de los Mayores. Código de Ética de la Medicina Indígena del Piedemonte Amazónico Colombiano*. Mocoa: UMIYAC. https://umiyac.org/ (Accessed 3 October 2020).
3 Ibid, preface.
4 This ethical protocol comprises 5 different Indigenous groups: Cofán, Inga, Siona, Kamentzá and Coreguaje.
5 See Caicedo 2005 for an outstanding ethnographic account of the Yagé circuits in Colombia, including a close reading of the Code.
6 See Caicedo (2015, 166) onwards, and Chapter 8 (*Forest on Trial*).
7 Doña Y, Nariño 2019 .*Interview*.
8 This form of law comes into being as a relational protocol, that is, the entangled lives of law and ecology in Amazonia.
9 AA, interview, Nariño 2019.
10 Varela (1999). See Gagliano (2018) for an argument about expanding the analytic horizon of science-making beyond human modes of representation.
11 See De la Cadena (2010, 2015), Kohn (2013), Descola (2013), Tsing (2015), Haraway (2016).
12 On linear time in the modernity-coloniality project, see Mignolo (2011, 158–164). A discussion of time in socio-ecological systems in Kolinjivadi et al. (2019).
13 A bridge between worlds. Interview with M. Bravo, June 2020.
14 Bravo, Marcela. 2015. *Ugpachisunchi i katichisunchi kilkaikunata—llevando y trayendola palabra-: territorio, "saber vivir ahí" y pensamiento Inga*. MA Thesis, Universidad Pedagógica Nacional. www.luguiva.net/admin/pdfs/Leidy-Saber%20vivir%20ah%C3%AD-marzo%202.pdf (Accessed 26 October 2020).
15 See Taussig (1980) for an argument against lineal historical narratives in Amazonia.
16 In Amazonia, animals, plants, and spirits are considered people. See Descola (2013), Kohn (2013), Viveiros de Castro (1998). According to Brazilian anthropologist Eduardo Viveiros de Castro, the corporeal form of each species "is a mere envelope which conceals an internal human form, usually only visible to the eyes of particular species or to certain trans-species beings such as shamans" (1998, 470–471).
17 See Luna (1984), Weiskopf (2002), Caicedo (2015), Taussig (1980).
18 See Ingold (2011) and Kolinjivadi et al. (2019) for a similar argument.
19 A dialogue between two practitioners during the ingestion of the brew. Field notes, Sibundoy Valley, Putumayo, 2019.
20 See Weiskopf's accounts of these kind of experiences (2002).
21 See the work of Margulis, Lynn and Fester, René. 1991. *Symbiosis as a Source of Evolutionary Innovation. Speciation and Morphogenesis*. Cambridge, MA: MIT Press.
22 See Mesa Permanente del Pueblo Cofán, *Histórica del Pueblo Cofán*. https://puebloCofán.org/nuestra-historia/ (Accessed 11 November 2020).
23 Interview with A.A., Nariño (Southern Colombia), 2019.
24 Interview with Marcela Bravo, June 2020. Also see her Master's thesis Bravo 2015.
25 Interview with A.A., Colombian attorney and Yagé practitioner, Nariño, 2019.
26 Cofán practitioner after a ceremony (field notes, 2019) referring to a prior consultation process with Ecopetrol (the Colombian national oil company).

27 Interview with Marcela Bravo, June 2020.
28 The First National Indigenous Congress adopted the principles of unity, territory, culture, and autonomy, which configure ONIC's lines of action and the mandate of the Organization concerning state's compliance of Indigenous legislation (particularly Ley 89 de 1890). ONIC thus recommends the adoption of these principles to all Indigenous people of the country to strengthen Indigenous autonomy and exercise their government protocols. See ONIC official webpage: www.onic.org.co/onic/143-nuestra-historia (Visited 10.26.2020).
29 Interview with A.A. Nariño 2019.
30 See Chindoy, Hernando. 2018. "A preservar el vestido de la tierra." In *La Silla Vacia*. https://lasillavacia.com/silla-llena/red-pacifico/historia/preservar-el-vestido-de-la-tierra-69172 (Accessed 26 October 2020).
31 Interview with M. Bravo, Zoom meeting, June, 2020.
32 Guerrero et al. (2013), Haraway (2016), Tsing (2015).
33 See ONIC official webpage: www.onic.org.co/onic/143-nuestra-historia (viewed on Oct. 26, 2020.)
34 Turner (2020) for a similar argument in the context of the First Nations on Turtle Island.
35 Interview with M. Bravo, June 2020.
36 See Riaño-Murcia, Diana. 2014. "Revisión crítica del derecho a la consulta previa de proyectos y sus procedimientos." Grupo Semillas. Available www.semillas.org.co/es/revisi (Nov. 11. 2020).
37 A bridge between worlds. This final section is a selection and translations of several excerpts of an interview conducted with M. Bravo in June, 2020.
38 A type of Andean loom. See Bravo (2015). For the guanga Weaving in the Andean world see also Chiran-Caipe and Hernandez-Burbano (2013).
39 My recollection of Marcela Bravo's explanation of "trayendo y llevando palabra," October, 2020. See also Bravo (2015).
40 The tulpa is a central cooking fire typical of Indigenous houses in the Andean-Amazonian region. It is made up of three stones that form a triangle.

References

Barad, Karen. 2007. *Meeting the Universe Halfway. Quantum Physics and the Entanglement of Matter and Meaning*. Duham: Duke University Press.

Bennett, Jane. 2010. *Vibrant Matter. A Political Ecology of Things*. Durham: Duke University Press.

Berry, Thomas, and Swimme, Brian. 1992. *The Universe Story. From the Primordial Flaring to the Ecozoic Era—A Celebration of the Unfolding of the Cosmos*. San Francisco: Harper.

Bravo, Marcela. 2015. *Ugpachisunchi i katichisunchi kilkaikunata—llevando y trayendo la palabra: Territorio, "Saber Vivir Ahí" y Pensamiento Inga*. Tesis de Maestria en Estudios Sociales. Universidad Pedagogica Nacional, Colombia.

Caicedo, Alhena. 2015. *La Alteridad Radical que Cura. Neo-chamanismos yageceros en Colombia*. Bogotá: Universidad de los Andes.

Chindoy, Hernando. 2018. "A preservar el vestido de la tierra." In *La Silla Vacia*. https://lasillavacia.com/silla-llena/red-pacifico/historia/preservar-el-vestido-de-la-tierra-69172 (Accessed 26 October 2020).

Congreso de la Republica de Colombia, Ley 89 de 1890.

De la Cadena, Marisol. 2010. "Indigenous Cosmopolitics in the Andes: Conceptual Reflections Beyond 'Politics'." *Cultural Anthropology*, 24(2): 334–370.
De la Cadena, Marisol. 2015. *Earth Beings. Ecologies of Practice Across Andean Worlds*. Durham: Duke University Press.
Deleuze, Gilles, and Guattari, Felix. 2002. *Mil Mesetas. Capitalismo y Ezquizofrenia*. Valencia: Pre-textos.
Descola, Philippe. 2013. *Beyond Nature and Culture*. Chicago: University of Chicago Press.
Dubashia, Nish. 2018. *The Unity of Everything. A Conversation with David Bohm*. Hamburg, Germany: Tredition.
Einstein, A., Podolsky, B., Rosen, N., and Podolsky, Rosen. 1935. "Can Quantum-Mechanical Description of Physical Reality Be Considered Complete?" *Physical Review*, 47(10): 777–780.
Escobar, Arturo. 2008. *Territories of Difference: Place, Movements, Life, Redes*. New Ecologies for the Twenty-First Century. Durham: Duke University Press.
Escobar, Arturo. 2015. "Transiciones: A Space for Research and Design for Transitions to the Pluriverse." *Design Philosophy Papers*, 13(1): 13–23.
Escobar, Arturo. 2016. "Sentipensar con la Tierra: Las Luchas Territoriales y la Dimensión Ontológica de las Epistemologías del Sur." *Revista de Antropologia Iberoamericana*, 11(1): 11–32.
Escobar, Arturo. 2018. *Designs for the Pluriverse: Radical Interdependence, Autonomy and the Making of Worlds*. Durham: Duke University Press.
Escobar, Arturo. 2020. *Pluriversal Politics. The Real and the Possible*. Durham: Duke University Press.
Fausto, Carlos, and Heckenberger, Michael. 2007. *Time and Memory in Indigenous Amazonia: Anthropological Perspectives*. Gainesville: University Press of Florida.
Gagliano, Monica. 2018. *Thus Spoke the Plant. A Remarkable Journey of Groundbreaking Scientific Discoveries and Personal Encounters with Plants*. Berkeley: North Atlantic Books.
Grillo Fernández, Eduardo. 1998. "Development or Cultural Affirmation in the Andes?" In Apffel-Marglin, Frédérique, and PRATEC (eds.). *The Spirit of Regeneration. Andean Culture Confronting Westerns Notions of Development*. New York: Zed Books.
Guerrero, Ricardo, Margulis, Lynn, and Berlanga, Mercedes. 2013. "Symbiogenesis: The Holobiont as a Unit of Evolution." *International Microbiology*, 16(3): 133–143.
Haraway, Donna. 2016. *Staying with the Trouble. Making Kin in the Chthulucene*. Durham: Duke University Press.
Hernandez-Burbano, J.P. 2013. "La dualidad andina del pueblo Pasto, principio filosófico ancestral inmerso en el tejido en guanga y la espiritualidad." *Plumilla Educativa*, 11(1): 136–156.
Ingold, Tim. 2011. *Being Alive. Essays on Movement, Knowledge, and Description*. New York: Routledge.
Kohn, Eduardo. 2013. *How Forests Think. Toward and Anthropology Beyond the Human*. Berkeley, CA: University of California Press.
Kohn, Eduardo. 2018. "What Kind of World an What Kind of We World? Staying with Donna Haraway's Staying with the Trouble." (Book review). *Dialogues in Human Geography*, 8(1): 99–101.

Kolinjivadi, Vijay, Vela Alemida, Diana, and Martineau, Jonathan. 2019. "Can the Planet be Saved in Time? On the Temporalities of Socionature, the Clock and the Limits Debate." *Environment and Planning E: Nature and Space*, 3(3): 904–926.

Kothari, Ashish, Salleh, Ariel, Escobar, Arturo, Demaria, Federico, and Acosta, Alberto. 2019. *Pluriverse. A Post-Development Dictionary*. New Delhi: Tulika Books.

Law, John. 2007. "Actor Network Theory and Material Semiotics." Version of 25 April 2007. hwww.heterogeneities.net/publications/Law2007ANTandMaterialSemiotics.pdf.

Luna, Luis Eduardo. 1984. "The Concept of Plants as Teachers Among Four Mestizo Shamans in Iquitos, Northeaster Peru." *Journal of Ethnopharmacology*, 11(2): 135–156.

Margulis (Sagan), Lynn. 1967. "On the Origin of Mitosing Cells." *Journal of Theoretical Biology*, 14(3): 225–274.

Margulis, Lynn, and Fester, René. 1991. *Symbiosis as a Source of Evolutionary Innovation. Speciation and Morphogenesis*. Cambridge, MA: MIT Press.

Mignolo, Walter. 2011. *The Darker Side of Western Modernity. Global Futures, Decolonial Options*. Durham: Duke University Press.

Mills, Aaron. 2019. *Miinigowiziwin: All That Has Been Given for Living Well Together. One Vision of Anishinaabe Constitutionalism*. Ph.D. Thesis. University of Victoria.

Nieto Olarte, Mauricio. 2000. *Remedios para el Imperio. Historia Natural y la Apropiación del Nuevo Mundo*. Bogotá. Universidad Externado de Colombia.

Quijano, Anibal. 2014. "Colonialidad del poder, eurocentrismo y America Latina." In *Cuestiones y horizontes: de la dependencia histórico-estructural a lacolonialidad/descolonialidad del poder*. Buenos Aires: CLACSO.

Riaño-Murcia, Diana. 2014. *Revisión crítica del derecho a la consulta previa de proyectos y sus procedimientos*. Bogota: Grupo Semillas. www.semillas.org.co/es/revisi

Shanon, B. 2001. "Altered Temporality." *Journal of Consciousness Studies*, 8(1): 35–58.

Strathern, Marilyn. 2005. *Kinship, Law and the Unexpected. Relatives Are Always a Surprise*. Cambridge: Cambridge University Press.

Taussig, Michael. 2010 (1980). *Devil and Commodity Fetishism in South America*. Chapel Hill: University of North Carolina.

Torres, William. 2000. "Liana del Ver, Cordón del Unvierso: El Yagé." *Boletin del Museo del Oro*, 46: 77–91.

Tsing, Anna. 2015. *The Mushroom at the End of the World*. Princeton: Princeton University Press.

Turner, Nancy (ed.). 2020. *Plants, People, and Places: The Roles of Ethnobotany and Ethnoecology in Indigenous Peoples' Land Rights in Canada and Beyond*. Montreal and Kingston: McGill-Queens's University Press.

Unión de Médicos Indígenas Yagéceros de la Amazonía Colombiana-UMIYAC. 2000. *El Pensamiento de los Mayores. Código de Ética de la Medicina Indígena del Piedemonte Amazónico Colombiano*. Mocoa: UMIYAC. https://umiyac.org/ (Accessed 10 March 2020).

Varela, Francisco. 1991. "Organism: A Meshwork of Selfless Selves." In Tauber, A.I. (ed.). *Organism and the Origins of Self. Boston Studies in the Philosophy of Science* (vol. 129). Dordrecht: Springer. https://doi.org/10.1007/978-94-011-3406-4_5

Varela, Francisco. 1999. *Ethical Know-How. Action, Wisdom and Cognition*. Stanford: Stanford University Press.
Varela, Francisco, Thompson, Evan, and Rosch, Eleanor. 1992. *The Embodied Mind: Cognitive Science and Human Experience*. Cambridge, MA: MIT Press.
Viveiros de Castro, Eduardo. 1998. "Cosmological *Diexis and* Amerindian Perspectivism." *Journal of the Royal Anthropological Institute*, 4(3): 469–489.
Viveiros de Castro, Eduardo. 2014. *Cannibal Metaphysics*. Minneapolis: Univocal.
Viveiros de Castro, Eduardo. 2015. *The Relative Native. Essays on Indigenous Conceptual Worlds*. Chicago: HAU Books.
Weiskopf, Jimmy. 2002. *Yagé: El Nuevo Purgatorio*. Bogotá: Villegas Editores.
Wynter, Sylvia. 1992. "No Humans Involved: An Open Letter to My Colleagues." *Voices of the African Diaspora: The CAAS Research Review*, VIII(2/Fall): 13–16.
Zerda, Alvaro. 2003. *Propiedad intelectual sobre el conocimiento vernáculo*. Bogotá: Universidad Nacional de Colombia.

Intertext 2

Tobacco as people

This story is about a Yagé vision. That of the elderly owners of healing plants such as tobacco and Yagé. I must first say that I am not an expert on the Cofán worlds. I do not speak the Aigae language, nor have I taken enough medicine—as they also call the Yagé brew—to say anything of much value. Some images, however, are tattooed in my memory with the clarity of an ink stroke on a blank sheet of paper. This piece is then about how tobacco creates people. The text comes from a longer narrative of an encounter with the Yagé brew in Lower Putumayo some 15 years ago.

At that time, D.V. was a professor of criminology at the National University of Colombia. We became good friends because of our humanistic quests outside the often-narrow frameworks of legal training. He had a remarkably close relationship with the Inga people—a *yagecero* community of Alto Putumayo. One of the traditional medics of that community, V.J., had studied law as well before becoming a traditional healer. This seemed particularly intriguing to me. A traditional healer who had studied Western law to find its root through the Yagé plant! The amazing thing, and what I want to narrate here, was how that encounter with D.V., and V.J. opened a world of worlds that continue to proliferate endlessly until today.

D.V. asked me if I wanted to come with him to Putumayo when I met him right at the entrance of my house in Bogota. He was wearing a traditional poncho called *sayo* and a rucksack by his side. I said "yes" to his invitation without suspecting what that simple monosyllable would open for me in the years to come.

We met at the bus terminal with V.J. and two of her daughters and left for Mocoa. It was a 14-hour trip. Arriving at the transport terminal of this Andean-Amazonian city, we had breakfast at the *Plaza de Mercado* followed by a six-hour trip to La Hormiga, Putumayo, and a ten-minute cab ride to the Cofán reservation of Santa Rosa del Guamuez where the worlds that I will narrate in these short pages are born.

The *Iacha* asked us to light a cigarette. With the words "here we are going to enter another world," V.J. also invited a different relationship with the tobacco plant—a protective being, a cleansing force. I felt that by entering

DOI: 10.4324/9781003349426-6

this new world with the lit tobacco I was crossing a new threshold. We walked for about 20 minutes through tobacco forests, plantains, *chontaduro* palms and other trees, and then arrived at the hamlet: about three small elevated wooden houses with palm roofs.

The next morning, we took a bath in the river and ate lightly during the day in preparation for the ingestion of the Yagé plant. The next morning—the other snippets of memory are not so important—we went to a nearby stream where a clear-eyed, jaguar-like presence of a wise man was waiting for us with a powerful vomitive: Yoco. Two gourds later I began to feel a kind of lightness in my body. The skin of the Yoco, scraped and dissolved in water, had a brownish-orange hue.

After cleansing my body, I felt even more ready to receive the strong medicine of the Yagé. The Yoco itself made me see the door to another world that was to be revealed during the night. We rested during the day between verses of Huidobro and the lullabies of palm trees. The night would bring its songs and premonitions. It was enough to wait. At the Casa de la Espiritualidad, we hung up our hammocks. The group was large: about 70 people, including elders, followers and Indigenous and non-Indigenous visitors. The hammocks were hung, and everyone was waiting. We waited. The Iacha called me to one of the corners of the "House of Spirituality" where he was.

There, in the Casita del Yagé, I tasted the famous concoction for the first time. I took it in slow sips, feeling the bitter potion slide down my throat like drops of volcanic rock in a millimetric slowness towards my stomach. Twenty or 30 minutes later, I began to feel its "reaction." Beyond the physical sensations, I would like to concentrate on the images. In the space-time of the concoction, everything, or almost everything, is beyond our control. The ingestion of the plant is already a surrender to another will. Thoughts have their own life and will, just like images. I felt my hammock widening and connecting to the images in my head: it is as if the reality we call "physical," and the "mental" reality were linked as part of the same fabric of the expanding and changing real. In the *chuma* or Yagé inebriation, the fabrics of the real were vegetable, and this integrating fabric of the material and the symbolic enveloped me with tenderness and without fear. I was entering the very womb of life at the hand of the vegetal threat that was coming out of the plant. A tissue that linked the bitter drink with my stomach, my head, my skin and the bodies of the world.

Already inside that womb of life, I imagined my body joining the skin of the soil. I was not on the Earth as if it were a secluded reality apart from me, but I was inside. I was part of her. I clearly saw the shapes, the threads that weave our ever-changing reality. From the widened hammock that joined my thoughts, I can say that even the hammock and myself were little parts of the same fabric of life. Once inside the Earth, being Earth, everything was more alive and elemental. The perception of reality and reality itself were one. Spirals, colorful resonance, loving meshworks that were the skin, flesh and spindles of all beings themselves. From the hammock I moved to the beams of the House of Spirituality that supported it: snakes, sinuous forms, slithered along those beams and entered the hammock to then enter inside of me. There were no boundaries between the self, the hammock and the House of Spirituality, or the boundaries were not fixed: this interdependence was the form of the real!

Already in the plant world, seeing through her eyes, an elder offered me a cigarette. The experience of smoking was of another *kind*: I felt the cigarette between my fingers as a continuity, again, of my own body. As if we were the same substance. I did not feel that the smoke was an external reality. Even if my mind managed to separate intellectually all these substances, I felt their continuity. If I wanted to be more precise, I would say that the tobacco was the person who smoked, and I was that tobacco and its smoke as well: tobacco created my body, my skin, my muscles and my bones with each inhalation. At times I was the smoke. As there was no fixed boundary between us, there were only expansive and changing continuities.

Of the feel of tobacco, I can only say that night I was formed by its own breath. It was not me smoking or the tobacco consuming itself, but it was me who was invented by the plant in every puff. In every exhalation. The tobacco and the human were alive as I was.

Time has made me forget a part of what I experienced that night. However, there are patterns in silent formation or, rather, snippets that are accentuated inside of me. One of those snippets is the beautiful episode of the circle of Amazonian elders—or at least this would be the imprecise denomination or verbal box to try to retain the image.

In a sort of semicircle, several elders dressed in feathers, fangs, necklaces and scarves, all symbols of power and status, beat the *wairas sachas* in unison. Each one was distinct: with their plants, stones and elements arranged in front of the thinking stool from which they ordered the world. I suddenly felt how each one of them fulfilled a function in the great chant of cosmic balance. Each one had his follower or apprentice who would have the responsibility to continue singing and teaching the songs to others and these to others until the sun sets and a new cycle began.

I wondered then what song I should learn to sing. The image of that council of elders ordering the world was tattooed in my memory. I did not know if they were the elders dressed in their ceremonial robes, or if they were the owners of the plants, those beings in the night between the smoke of tobacco and the rhythmic sounds of the *waira*.

Chapter 3

Coca leaf *(Erythroxylaceae coca)*

Territories in motion and learning law with the Amazonian "*mambe*"[1]

Abstract

As discussed in chapters 1 and 2, encountering the *legal* in Amazonia involves the active participation of other-than-human beings such as medicinal plants. Chapters 1 (Yoco: learning to learn) and 2 (Yagé: moving words across worlds) addressed the question of how we can learn law with the guidance of plants such as the Amazonian Yoco (*Paullinia Yoco*) and the Yagé (*Banisteriopsis caapi*), as well as the conceptual openings, ethical dilemmas and political possibilities of this vegetal approach. Following a similar line of work, chapter 3 discusses ritual and everyday encounters with a local preparation of the coca leaf (*Erythroxylon coca*) among the Indigenous Murui of Putumayo. The chapter further describes how humans and plants meet and make decisions together in this region. Don A, an elder and medicine man from the Murui community of Puerto Leguízamo, Putumayo, calls this process of co-decision "ordering the world" (*ordenar el mundo*). The chapter explores how bodily practices such as ingesting *plants-as-people* can be considered as a form of environmental co-governance that involves different kinds of beings. In doing so, it aims at expanding legal theory and practice beyond anthropocentrism, while probing the decolonial potentials of plant-human relations for legal theory and practice.

Introduction: vegetal co-making

A popular image describes the Amazon as a green wild vastness: home to millions of life forms that exchange matter and energy, proliferate and decompose to nurture new life (Slater 2002; Lyons 2020). A cycling system of massive dimensions where the mineral, the vegetal and the animal loop back into soils and waters relentlessly co-producing new forms of life and death. In contrast to the forest, the *chagra* has been imagined as the site of the measurable and human-like (Kawa 2016); yet, following a similar principle of metabolic exchange (Foster 2000; Saito 2022), the *chagra* system is based on successional crop rotation and the production of a secondary forest. This small agro-system has been considered a key source of anthropogenic forest

DOI: 10.4324/9781003349426-7

(Heckenberger and Fausto 2007) and, together with hunting practices, the most important transhistorical factor in the reproduction of social life in this region (Rodríguez 2010; Andrade 1990, 1992; Correa 1990). Far from clear-edged pieces of a complex vegetal puzzle, the "wild" forest and the "tamed" *chagra* remain in continuity co-forming each other: forest and *chagra* interact and overlap as they co-emerge in new relational fabrics.

Participants of this process of forest and *chagra's* mutual morphing, Don A, a local *sabedor* (knower) from the Murui community in the region of Puerto Leguízamo, Putumayo, and the plants he works with—particularly the coca leaf (Erythroxylum coca)—are integral to this meshwork of vital forces that embody the proliferating socio-ecological kinships of this region. As he tells the origin of the first *chagra* during a nightlong *sentada de mambia* (session of coca chewing until dawn), Don A is keen to affirm the primordial vegetal ontology of a world that he contributes to order every night *[ordenar el mundo]*, while ingesting the coca mix with other community members. The *sentada de mambia*, as Don A calls it, refers to the act of ingesting a coca-based preparation called *mambe* in ritual and everyday contexts. *Sentada* also refers to the act of discussing community matters while chewing the coca mix in the *mambeadero*, *coqueadero* (Urbina 2010) or spiritual community house:

> *Muinajeba*[2] was then sent with spirituality. *Guamo* confronted *Muinajeba* and soon after they both started to compete. *Muinajeba* found the *coca de monte* (this is the coca of the animals), as well as the human coca. Then, he found the tobacco, and a big tree where all the food comes from. There was about everything in that tree, and everybody ate from it. It grew tall and no one was able to climb up to the top. *Muinajeba* talked to some animals and then asked the frog to climb the tree, but he could only reach part of it. Then, he asked the fox to do it, but he climbed only to gather food for himself. Finally, *Muinajeba* asked one of the first chiefs that God created. He asked the hummingbird that brought the fire, and then sent a person with an ax. The tree was cut, and when it fell down the splinters became fish. The trunk formed the Putumayo River, and its branches the streams; the leaves were lakes. Now it was the time to sow the seeds, and thus the first *chagra* was created. *Muinajeba* created the first *chagra*.
>
> (Author's translation. See Vargas-Roncancio 2017, 257).[3]

Probing a non-anthropocentric approach to human-other-than-nonhuman interactions in this region of Putumayo, Chapter 3 begins by describing plant-human relations in the context of the ritual and everyday use of a specifically Amazonian preparation of the coca leaf (*Erythroxylon coca*). Combined with *yarumo* ashes (*Cecropia peltata)*, the coca leaves are thinly macerated to obtain a regionally distinct admixture known as *mambia*. Encounters between plants, humans and animals, as the *Muinajeba* story shows us, are crucial to local modes of knowing, living and shaping places such as the *chagra*

(Echeverry and Kinerai 1993). The second part describes how plant-human relations—via ritual and everyday use of the *mambia*—perform what I call a "nomadic ecology" or a "territory in motion." In light of recent fieldwork in Leticia (Amazon), I prefer this second notion because it highlights the metabolism of forest and *chagra*, as well as their situated stories of social relations.

Furthermore, I use the twin notions of nomadic ecology and territory in motion in two distinct but complementary ways. First, as a way to refer to the human act of traveling long distances with human and other-than-human beings, for example when Don A roams through the forest to hunt and collect wild seeds to sow in his *chagra*, as well as when this *chagra* co-shapes the forest as it successionally moves to another plot to allow the previous one to rest, regenerate and make the forest anew (Heckenberger and Fausto 2007). In the second sense, territory in motion refers to the act of planning community work in the *chagra*, as well as the traveling of thought *[el viaje del pensamiento]* through the forest with the aid of sacred plants, that is, without moving from one's physical position in the *coqueadero* or communal hut. The *coqueadero* is a representation of both the cosmos and the human body. Don A chews his *mambia* to order a world in continuity between the forest and the human (the vast and the small), as he performs this cosmological itinerancy. For him, *ordenar el mundo*—governing the forest—and *ordenar el* cuerpo—governing the body—are part and parcel of the same process of relational healing.

Ordering the world, in this manner, is a nonlinear action. The third part echoes Chapter 2 ("Moving words across worlds"), as it explores the notion of nonhuman temporalities to describe relations between being beyond teleological notions of time and history. The section also explores the decolonial potentials this time-with-the-plant can offer for legal theory and practice. An ethnographic conversation concerning what we may call the material speech of plants,[4] this chapter suggests that questions of corporality and ingestion are crucial for a legal theory beyond language, namely beyond the idea that the form of law is, or should be, primarily linguistic or propositional (Chapter 7: "Conjuring"). This legal vision has a direct bearing on current discussions around the nature/culture divide, and how undoing this modern division can push the "legal revolution" of the rights of nature beyond modern frameworks of analysis (Boyd 2017).

1. "La Mambia Dice": the vibrations of the coca leaf as knowledge[5]

The literature on the ritual and everyday use of the Andean coca is abundant (Chambi 2005; Manga 2003; Allen 2002). Comparatively, however, its Amazonian counterpart has received less scholarly attention, particularly when it comes to the ritual, political, aesthetic and pedagogical uses of this plant (Urbina 1992, 2010; Echeverry and Candre 1993; Echeverry and Pereira 2010). The *mambe* is a historical institution that "has been incorporated into myths, everyday life, and the ceremonial, and symbolic universe of many

Amazonian groups" (Echeverry and Pereira 2010, 590). However, the ritual and everyday use of this specific Amazonian preparation, the *mambe*, seems traditionally limited to the regions of the *Great Vaupés* (basins of the Vaupés, Apoporis and Mirití rivers, and towards the Caquetá River), and the Caquetá-Putumayo interfluve, "with some extensions to the South and East resulting from migrations of these groups" (2010, 590). W, a Murui man from Leticia, Colombian Amazon, describes the *mambe* in these terms:

> When they asked him "what is this?" he used to say: "that's coca, but learning what *mambe* is . . . well, that is something else. The *mambe* has to do with learning the sweet word and with learning the corporal and moral disciplines to live well." Once we arrived at his father's *maloca* we sat down on a trunk. The *abuelo* was sifting the coca with a blue cloth. A Ticuna from a nearby *resguardo* (reservation), his son-in-law piled the *coca* in a *pilón*, and there was a zinc tile with a pile of *yarumo* ashes right in front of him. The *abuelo* collected the ashes with his bare hands to mix them with the coca that was previously sifted. W speaks of the *mambe* as a tool. Like paper on which one writes words: "one wants that paper to be really clean!"—he says. "Just as white people write on these pieces of paper *(hojas de papel)*, we also write on the coca leaves *(hojas de coca)*. . . In fact, there is no separation between the Law of Origin and life for us, unlike the constitutions of the Colombian state, our Law of Origin does not change: it does not vary, it is not a 'transitory article'" (laughs).[6]

For the Murui, *mambear* coca is a practice associated with the education of the body and the spirit. It is a vehicle of sociopolitical and legal meaning that is best crystallized in the social institution of the *mambeadero*—"a place for the preparation and consumption of the coca dust, as well as a site of dialogue," and decision-making (Echeverry and Pereira 2010, 566). According to anthropologists Juan Álvaro Echeverry and Edmundo Pereira, the corporeal and social disciplines embedded in the institution of *mambe* have what they call "religious and spiritual meanings." The Murui people assert this dimension of *mambe* when they say that the coca "has a spirit." In fact, *mambear* coca "is not to paint one's mouth with green." The stimulant effects of *mambe* do matter, they argue, but also the social and bodily disciplines associated with each community's understanding and management of the coca plant itself (2010, 566), as a way to plan the work in the forest (i.e., the preparation of a terrain for a new *chagra*).

On the religious character of the *mambe*, Don A says:

> we pray at night, and then we work during the next day. We hope that the coca is sweet and to the service of our Lord. Otherwise, what is good could go away and what is bad could accumulate. We are in relation with God through the *mambeo*.

However, the "spirit of the coca" does not refer to an abstract entity since it is fully embedded in labor, practices of care, the education of children, and intertribal relations, among other aspects of community life.

> *Mambear* coca is about improving: when we *mambeamos* we remember the acts of the day and we correct ourselves to improve," says W, and one can derive crucial legal principles from this insight: "whomever do *mambe* does not get up, but this should not be interpreted literally. This means that whoever does *mambe* does not leave (does not get up) from their territory." Similarly, "whoever *mambea* does not sleep. Yet again, this does not mean that you cannot sleep at all. . . . Not sleeping means that you have to be attentive to everything that can cause harm to you, or to your community. Ultimately, *mambe* is about being awake, it is about living a good life. . . . There are three kinds of bodies in every human being: the physical body, the thinking body, and the spiritual body. There are diseases that can attack these three bodies and there is medicine (and food) for each of them: just as there is food to feed the body, there is food to feed our thought as well, and you feed thought with *mambe*.
>
> (Excerpts from conversation with W, Leticia, Colombian Amazon, field notes 2017)

The coca spirit expresses itself materially in different ways in the body of the *mambeador*, as was made clear during a nightlong *mambe* session with Don A and other men of his community: P, Don A's nephew, prepares the *mambia* by gently moving a bunch of coca leaves with his bare hands in a simmering copper pan, while a sheen of sweat bubbles sprouts on his forehead. Once toasted, the coca is poured into a wooden container, tenderized and then mixed with *yarumo* ashes. Seated next to him, Don A, the storyteller, goes on to explain the details of his roaming through the forest a couple of months back. As he pours a large spoon of the mix into his mouth, Don A tells us how the forest wanted him to survive: "it gave me food, it sheltered me, but it also scared me" (author's translation).

The most experienced *mambeadores* pour two to three full spoons into their mouths, while beginners like me unsuccessfully try to avoid the momentary lack of breath provoked by a modest teaspoon of the *mambia* mix. Quite an entertainment for the community men! With the *mambia* in the human body, her capacity to communicate is activated: "Let us see how everything goes with the word given by the plant."

The material spirituality of the *mambia*, so to speak, can best be described as a vibration or resonance that is enabled by the sensory acuity gained through the gradual ingestion and absorption of the plant in the bloodstream. The stimulation is mild as it sharpens concentration, facilitates communication with other people and helps recovering lost memories and stories. To be sure, the senses are open to the vivid perception of sounds, colors, smells and shapes of the forest. Such a resonance comes and goes, making the skin quiver in slow motion each time, almost like the wind shaking the top branches of a tall tree. These vibrations or *señales*, as Don A would describe them, take place in the skin as the canvas or "*hoja en blanco*" where the plant traces her particular mode of speech. To be sure, the skin is not rendered as the limit of bodies separating substances—that is, the human body and the body of the plant—but as an interface where the vibrational speech of the coca's vibrations and human perception meet co-shaping each another. Coca and human remain in continuity, connected through this vibrational tissue.[7]

Plant-human encounters, that is, the meeting of *mambia's* vibrational language and the human skin, can also be described as a "shared body" (Lyons 2016), that is, a material and semantic continuity between several beings and forces. The most experienced *mabeadores* can read these vibrations like an open book, like *hojas de papel (pieces of paper)* in W's words, to diagnose illnesses, or as signposts to mark different moments in the story that is being told. Vibrations might be a mode of plant communication, and the stories (knowledge) resulting from this form of embodied dialogue may well be a matter of collaboration between human and other-than-human modes of co-intentionality. The encounter between the *mambia* and the human through vibration is created, nourished, transmitted and sustained as a story: a fleshy story.

However, the plant wants to see us first while keeping us alert and open to the encounter (Gagliano 2018). Curious to learn about our intentions, stories and desires, the plant affords a new mode of inquiry into social life. In what sense is the plant curious? As any other human-like feature, curiosity may well be expressed materially. In the case of the *mambia*, this attribute suggests that the plant holds a form of interiority or agent-like capacity (Descola 2013): like a piece of clothing or envelope, the plant's body conceals underneath a form of intentionality.

However, this agential capacity comes into being by virtue of the relationship between the plant and the human via the act of ingestion as a material condition of plant/human co-emergence. How can we "know" if the plant can make decisions or choose between options?[8] Building on recent studies on plant bioacoustics (Gagliano 2013), I suspect that vegetal intentionality is revealed by virtue of her encounter with the human in the context of a nightlong *mambia* in the *mambeadero* or spiritual house. To encounter this mode of communication or intentionality, one needs to go beyond the mental anthropomorphizing of reality and, instead, embrace an anthropophagic approach, namely eating plants *as persons*. In fact, the encounter with the coca opens the issue of who counts as a subject of knowledge in human and other-than-human relations: Is the plant divesting the human from her epistemological command? Is the plant producing knowledge at all? And if so, what kind of knowledge?

Rendered a colonial subject after centuries-long negation and criminalization, the coca plant communicates with the human by means of its own mode of material language. On this point, Don A would agree with scholar Michael Marder when he affirms that vegetal beings express themselves otherwise "without resorting to vocalization" (Marder 2013, 74). For Marder,

> aside from communicating their distress when predators are detected in the vicinity by realizing airborne (or in some cases belowground) chemicals, plants, like all living beings, articulate themselves spatially. In a body language free from gestures, they can express themselves . . . in their postures.
> (Marder 2013, 75)

Similarly, anthropologist Eduardo Kohn studies this shifting focus towards nonhuman modes of communication while working with the Runa of Avila in the Ecuadorian Amazon (2013). For him, both humans and nonhumans use signs that are not necessarily symbolic, that is, language based. Kohn insists that "life-forms represent the world in some way or another, and these representations are intrinsic to their beings." In fact, what we, humans, share with other-than-human species is not only our embodiment "as certain strains of phenomenological approaches would hold, but the fact that we all live with and through signs . . . signs make what we are" (2013, 9).

The word "language" here describes plants' modes of communication as a form of spatialized materiality where intentions, desires and specific modes of agency are not *only* human but emergent in the context of interspecies interaction:

> Plants love each other. There are plants, however, that are more affectionate than others. This is why we cultivate diversified crops, so they can support each other. In the same way, there are plants that are more powerful than others, more jealous than others, more magical than others.
> (Interview with Muriu practitioner *Doña* C Puerto Leguizamo, Bajo Putumayo)

These plants can teach, but learning requires what W calls "an act of humility" on the part of the human learner:

> You cannot sit at the same level of the *abuelo* when you are learning with *mambe*. One must curl up . . . be on the ground. It is an act of humility. If you are sitting comfortably, you are either sleeping or not paying attention. The discipline of the *mambe* is corporal and learning those tools must be a corporeal discipline as well. . . . We have one foot in the West and we understand that teaching techniques must also change. People seek comfort to learn. To be well seated," W says as he pours a spoon full of *mambe* into his mouth: "whomever does *mambe* does not get up." They don't leave the territory." However, this metaphorical meaning does not cancel out the literal one. Around 3 p.m. we were hungry and got up from the *maloca*—which is also a form of territory—and we could not see how W prepared the *mambe*: "You got up earlier. When you start learning about these plants, you ought to control your craving to eat or doing other things. One does not get up to attend to other things. One focuses on what one is doing." W told us an anecdote about a young man who wanted to go to the bathroom after

> spending a few hours listening to the *abuelo* as he was doing *mambe*. But he remembered that "whomever *mambea* does not get up," and so he wanted to withhold his urge to go to the bathroom, and because he did not want to disobey the command, he did not get up (laughs). W also told the story of an *abuelo* who said the following in the *mambeadero*: "well, so as not to stay up late, let's leave it here" and it was already after 5:00 a.m. after sitting all around doing *mambe* the night before until dawn the next day (laughs).
>
> (Excerpts from a conversation with W, Leticia, Colombian Amazon. Author's translation)

This mode of communication between the human and the plant is made possible through a series of material transformations whereby the coca becomes *mambia* through human labor. Simultaneously, the human becomes a *mambeador* through the agency of the plant.[9] Colombian scholar Fernando Urbina, who is well-known for his work on the symbolism of coca use among Murui-Muinane communities, affirms that the coca leaf—itself a symbol of both tongue and speech—helps the human to remember what it was told in the *mambeadero*. There, the *hombre sentado*, the wise person seated on the ritual stool, "vertebrates reality with words" (Urbina 2010, 142). When the *mambeador* is just a boy, he listens to the words of power in the "germinal shadow of his mother's place" (Urbina 2010, 142).

When he grows up, like a plant, he is invited to the illuminated space of the *coqueadero* or *mambeadero* in the company of other men. These words will later become meaningful and real as they unfold in community rituals and the daily life of the adult. In this way, when a guiding word is needed, the coca, which is the tongue, will offer the right one. That is, the one that was heard next to the elder (Urbina 2010). More than the content of the learning (what), what matters is how something is learned, that is, next to the elder and *mambeando coca*.

The human learns the word of the coca ("*la palabra de la coca*") by incorporating it as *mambe*. In other words, social knowledge becomes a matter of eating. Eating the tongue, as it were, grants the human access to knowledge on community rituals and prepares them to plan and undertake the necessary labor to cultivate the *chagra*—where the coca and other foods grow. In other words, powdered coca embodies humanity through labor, while the human *mambeador* embodies planthood through the ingestion of *mambe*. A material feedback loop between living beings, this tissue of human and other-than-human agencies is itself a conversation on and of mutual nurturing, as well as legal principles embodied in practice and place (see Chapter 1's discussion on the "law of the place").

Legal cues of the coca leaf

As we have learned in Chapter 1 (Yoco) and Chapter 2 (Yagé), the law is not only a matter of state norms to govern socio-ecologies: it is also about following the relational protocol to learn how to live well with the territory, that is, learning how to live well with humans and other-than-human peoples. Encountering the law in this region is about participating in the entangled lives of norms and ecologies (i.e., plants, *chagras*, forests) and the human "corporeal disciplines" that teach people how to organize the world as a form of ecological governance (*ordenar el mundo*). It is about learning to work in the *chagra* and the forest according to ecological principles. To be sure, the *mambe* is a way to partake in this legal conversation between humans, plants and other beings of the forest. And this move implies pushing the normative boundaries of the law to consider its material entanglements and post-anthropocentric possibilities.

Andean intellectual Eduardo Grillo brilliantly puts it in the Andean context:

> here (in the Andean world), conversations cannot be reduced to dialogue, to the word, as in the modern Western's world but rather conversation engages us vitally: one converses with the whole body. To converse is to show oneself reciprocally, it is to commune, it is to dance to the rhythm which at every moment corresponds to the annual cycle of life. Conversation assumes all the complications characteristic of the living world. Nothing escapes conversation. Here there is no privacy. Conversation is inseparable from nurturance. For humans, to make *chakra* (or chagra), that is, to grow plants, animals, soils, waters, climates, is to converse with nature. But in the Andean-Amazonian world, all, not only humans, make and nurture the *chacra* (the chagra is the Amazonian counterpart). The human *chacra* is not only made (nurture) by humans; all, in one way or another, participate in the creation/nurturance of the human *chacra*: the sun, the moon, the starts, the mountain, the birds, the rain, the wind . . . even the frost and the hail.
>
> (Grillo Fernández 1998, 34)

Anthropologist and feminist science studies scholar Kristina Lyons goes a step further. Indeed, this conversation implies bodily contact between life entities as well as an emergent "shared body" (Lyons 2016) whose connecting tissue is what I call *skin*—so both tactility and ingestion are mutually implicated in Andean-Amazonian conversations with plants as a fertile site of social norms and institutions. A bundle of beings emerging as a single body, plant-human encounters—from sowing the land to the transformation of coca leaves into *mambia*; from ingesting the *mambia* to the planning of labor in the *chagra*—may well expand the scope of agency to include other beings and relations. When these entities emerge as a shared body, the word "agency" becomes a matter of material distribution of action across different life forms (vegetal or not). In other words, eating the plant, that is, eating the bundle of relations that make the plant emerge as such, is the condition of possibility of any collective mode of knowledge and action.

On this issue, Don A will insist on the notion of fostering a cyclical chain across human animals, animals and vegetal beings: "with the coca and tobacco plants (owners) we feed our spirit, and find the strength in order to work. In this way, we are able to hold the cyclical chain between the animal, the vegetal, and the human" (Author's translation).

How does the relational body of plants and humans look like? How would this relation appear to the plant as some*one* with a perspective? (Viveiros de Castro 2014). The *chagra*, where the coca grows, offers a unique image of this relational body or material continuum between life entities (forest and *chagra*). P says that

> in order to measure the complexity of the *chagra* one has to take into account several aspects, including the material, the dimension of health (human and not), the territory, the education, and the cosmogony, among others. The *chagra* is a heritage that is transmitted both orally and spiritually.
>
> (Author's translation)

To be sure, the *chagra* is the "shared body" of human and other-than-human entities, where the cyclical chain between the animal, the vegetal and the human is nourished.

Moreover, the *chagra* is not a stable being whatsoever. Much like Lyons describes in her work with *campesinos* in the region of Putumayo, Colombia:

> When farmers refer to what technicians call "soil" they are never referring to a stable object that can be managed by humans, but rather an entanglement of life-propagating relations that include microbes, insects, sunlight, *selva*, decaying leaves, animal feces and urine, human labor, and *mistica*.
>
> (Lyons 2014)

In fact, the *chagra* also becomes forest when the community (of human and other-than human) prepares another small area to cultivate, while the previous one is left to rest, gradually growing into a *berbecho* and then a secondary forest.[10] *Chagra* is forest, but forest is also *chagra*. Relations emerge from relations.

An expression of such embodied spirituality, material practices in the *chagra* are planned during the night in the *mambeadero* where *la palabra de decisión* (the word to decide) is co-produced along with the human. As Don A poetically expressed it: "*la coca es como un lago grande que da palabra en abundancia. El ambil es como un chorro que cae del cielo y orienta esa palabra y le da dirección (ordenar el mundo).*"/"The *coca* is like a big lake that gives words in abundance. The *ambil (liquid tobacco)* is like a cascade falling from the sky guiding those words towards a particular purpose (ordering the world)" (Author's translation). In a similar vein, Murui elder Don José García beautifully addresses this conversation of, and on, mutual nurturance between plants and humans, as follows:

> While you sow you sing and whistle, so the coca is happy. When you whistle the coca is happy because she senses that there is going to be a

> dance. And thus, she grows faster. These chants are prayers. As in the past, everything was done *coqueando* (using coca). When the crop is small and barely beautifying you take three or four small leaves from each plant. Then, you take a branch and put it on the top of a trunk in the middle of the *cocal*. This little branch calls the others saying: Come on! Come on! Come to my house! Don't stay behind! And thus, it makes them grow. And the branches underneath reply: Wait, don't let us behind! Wait for us! Thus, they try to climb. Some plants obey and others do not. That is why some plants grow faster.
>
> (*Abuelo José García*. From Urbina 2011, 201. Author's translation)

A counterpoint to Don A's teachings, Doña C, his wife, says that for plants to grow pretty ("*para que crezcan bonitas*"), one must converse with them—again the notion of conversation in its material sense comes to the fore:

> First one sows the manioc and the plantain. Then the *ñame*, the *daledale*, *caimarona* grape, *copoazú*, pineapple, *borojó*, *caimo*. You have to clean the terrain for the fruit to grow otherwise the *monte* will eat it. You need to talk with the plants, so they can grow. . . . I sow you here, plant, so that I can live off you, so that you offer good yields, a good tree, and they listen.
>
> (Author's translation)

The tropes of conversation and shared body are useful tools to engage with the ontology of the *mambia* in the Colombian Amazon. One night, *mambear* brought into being a woven object, almost like a soft piece of clothing gently pressing against the skin.[11] In fact, the coca speech is a material language of vibrations with the capacity to help us visualize the steps to give order to the world, for example, to take care of the *chagra* as a form of governance. But also, to visualize the forest and its events: the fabric of words and images Don A weaves together with his stories opens a window into the past of his wandering in the forest that almost cost him his life. A past almost cinematically made present with the aid of the *mambe*: *it was as if the story was alive*, I thought. "The *mambia* summons the past, and it is as if a window had been opened," *Don A* said as he poured another spoon full of *mambia* into his mouth.

A matter of sudden emergence, the *mambia* teaches us how the skin—rather than the brain only—can become a site of knowledge to *ordenar el mundo*—to give order to the world. In the relationship between the language of vibration of coca and the skin, the latter is neither the clean slate for the workings of perception, nor the exposed surface for the contingencies of sunrays, cold winds, scratches and the passing of time. The *mambia* becomes the site of active knowledge and embodied memory. When compared to the lettered legal archive, can vibrations and plants be considered sources of legal knowledge? During the *mambia* session, the skin becomes the canvas of a collective geometry of sensations and memories. The *mambia* holds a language on its own whose grammar is a bundle of vibrations rendered possible through the ingestion of the plant as *people.* As a someone with a perspective. These vibrations are a testimony of the itinerant and life-propagating character of the socio-ecological partnerships that I am calling a nomadic ecology: life partnerships that have moved, walked and shaped living beings, ecologies, territories, *chagras* and knowledge practices for centuries in Amazonia.[12] As an instance of this ecological nomadism where plants play an essential role, I will tell the story of Don A's roaming through the forest in the next section.

2. Making life in Amazonia: moving with the forest and its decolonial possibilities

More than 20 years ago, Don A wandered alone across the Amazon for several days. Eventually, he was able to recover the trail back home to tell the story of his roaming. He encountered vines, *ceiba* trees (Taíno: *ceiba.* Amaz. deno.: *Ceiba*; Lat. *Caiba pentadra*), *moriche* palms (Amaz. deno.: *Moriche; Lat. Mauritia flexuosa)* and hundreds of other members of a vegetal world in constant flux. Such plants, Don A said, led him back to his family and *chagra.* Negotiating his subsistence with any being willing to cooperate, Don A lived off of fruits, plants and small animals. The Amazon fed him, shared its hints and finally proposed a route for him to follow. As he would say, the forest *roamed* with him, thus showing a form of natural empathy whereby home and other-than-home, food and enemy, human and nonhuman, among other dualisms, were no precisely tenable distinctions to make sense of the event.

The forest partnered with the human by procuring his survival, while the human enhanced the boundaries of his family members. The distinction between dwelling in a single territory and the fabric of life beyond the human settlement became quite blurry for him: a new form of collaboration emerged in a place deemed as the other—the *forest*: a place turning into a nomadic ecology or territory in motion, that is, a place in continuous motion and transformation; a place becoming home as it moved with Don A as he moved with her.

Don A risked his life while becoming an integral part of a continuum of life forces morphing into socio-natural kin. To be able to reach his destination (the *chagra*), he had to establish agreements of survival and collaboration with the other-than-human others that he encountered along the way. "In the *chagra*," he said, "plants are together and closer to the house, but in the forest, one is alone, and it is not always easy to find the plant one needs." A family of life forms was in the making as Don A wandered alone. Yet this vital and changing relationality involved in his survival—plants and small animals, waters and soils, among others—*wandered* through him as well. This was an inner ecology on the move. Where can we locate, then, the precise limits between beings, family and place? The forest, also a product of human action, certainly had something about it that was entirely *chagra*-like.[13] In fact, Don A's intimate knowledge of forest ecology would later become the *chagra* for his family—a space made of the *stuff* of a different place: the roaming forest.

It is always surprising to encounter other beings. These encounters do not entice the universal moral choice of a community of settlers commanding action over their surroundings, but rather the embodied mode of skill, co-emergence and eventuality of the disperse community of foragers that make both place and people emerge from relations.[14] On the one hand, such interactions with this not-so-unfamiliar forest forced Don A to partake in sequences of collaboration, predation and survival with this emerging family of other-than-human relatives.[15] On the other hand, this dense yet ephemeral relationality made it difficult for him to dwell long in one single place: he had to move to live! Human and other-than-human mobility became the condition of possibility of survival, while *place*—also on the move—far from the backdrop of human action, became the resulting effect of human and other-than-human encounters. This is what Don A taught us: his return to the *chagra* was preceded by the formation of a nomadic community of life forms (plants and animals) that also inhabited him. *Chagra* and *forest* constitute a single continuum of Amazonian life. "*Selva* is home," Don A insisted, and *chagra* may be *selva* for other-than-human beings as well—plants included.

I heard this story in the *mambeadero* one night, and it occurred to me that the act of roaming through the forest was neither a single activity nor a prerogative of humans only. In fact, Don A was not alone as he moved through the forest. He was traveling with the *mambia*, while the *mambia* travelled with him (and within him). Moreover, what made him move also moved with him, for example, the small animals and plants that procured his survival. *What* travels, then? Or, better yet, *who* travels?

Humans and other-than-humans become a bundle of relations or, better yet, a shared body, namely life forms depending on the relations with other beings. Don A needed to connect with other entities by means of ingestion, tactility or even refusal to engage with several beings for his own sake. For that to happen, those entities moved underneath, like plant roots, or above ground, like leaves trying to catch sunlight. An emerging bundle of life relations on the move—of which Don A was already a part—as it were, this territory in motion transformed place with each new step. "*Mambia*-human," a "partially connected" entity (Strathern 2005), created its own dwelling as *they* moved.

Furthermore, *mambia*-human changed the surface of the Amazonian soil by leaving a material trace. Surely, this material imprint was made possible thanks to the *mambia* that inhabited Don A's body (i.e., ingesting the plant, eating the tongue to produce speech), which afforded him the necessary bodily capacities to orient himself through the forest. Similarly, the *chagra*, another nomadic ecology depending upon the *mambia* gathering where the work is planned and organized, leaves a material trace when it rotates through the forest. In fact, since many Amazonian soils are very acidic and have only a thin layer of organic matter (Lyons 2016), traditional agricultural systems of slash and burn (*chagra*) require the rotation of the area of cultivation from one place to the next. This *chagra* itinerancy through the forest is instrumental to the formation of a secondary forest: "*cuando quemamos los palos la ceniza se vuelve la comida del suelo*" . . . when we burn the trees the resulting ashes become soil's food], Don A said once. The human, therefore, moves to produce place, and, in return, the place, thus created, moves to co-shape other places, other humans and other-than-human beings. To put it bluntly, a nomadic ecology is another name for life relations.

Don A also travelled with seeds back and forth between sites:

> I brought some seeds from Ecuador, and I will research and experiment on them to see if they grow here. I have these peach seeds, for example, and I will put them in water for 15 minutes or so to make them softer. I will then sow them in seedbeds. Then, I will water them under the shadow to avoid insects.

I imagine the encounter between the human and the *mambia* as a learning moment about/with life amid a dense ecology of relations. They are ways to engage in knowledge practices that cut across the sedentary rationality of the Western legal archive. Such a learning moment may be able to tell us how *mambia* comes into being as a powerful non-modern teaching force where subjects and objects no longer precede their encounters in the social field. Moreover, such a learning moment with the *mambia* signals the option of a compositional relationality where eco-centric modes of knowing, feeling and acting in the social and legal worlds of the forest emerge amid entangled forms of violence and survival. Is the *mambe*, and the relations that it enables, a tool for the regeneration of human/nonhuman relationalities in this region? The next sub-section will tackle this issue.

"Mambear coca leaf": an Amazonian way with decoloniality?

In what way can the human use of coca leaves be considered as a legal decolonial practice in the Amazonian region? Decoloniality seeks to provincialize Western knowledge practices, including the law. It sheds light on colonial forms of direct and indirect violence across time and space—a violence that renders inferior and eliminates peoples, ways of being and epistemic practices that refuse to be accommodated within Euro-American reductionistic paradigms of knowledge and methodology. Moreover, decoloniality also emerges from the difference and multiplicity inscribed in race, gender, sexuality, class and ecological relations both in the present and in the past. In the case of human and other-than-human encounters, decoloniality highlights corporeal experiences of mobility over sedentary abstraction and universal reason. The term proposes a temporality and spatiality of co-existence attuned to Indigenous circular geometries of time and space. This is a temporality and spatiality that imagines ancestral and modern practices of life in a level of relative symmetry (Tuhiwai Smith 2012).

Affirming the existence of agents furnished with human-like attributes might expand legal decolonial agendas further to include other living beings as subjects of knowledge and sources of legality. Going back to the *mambia* night, the plant in relation with the human enacted a collective memory of co-existence, which colonial violence attempts to conceal time and again through civilizational fantasies, development agendas and extractivist ventures. To be sure, the methodology employed by the plant was to sensitize, awaken and empower the skin as a territory of knowledge. As a result of this capillary collaboration between the plant and the human, the *mambia* produced an effect of reality in everybody's *piel* [skin]; an ecology of vibrations translated into the language of skill, labor and emotions as collective forms of knowledge necessary for living and dwelling together as an ecology on the move: a nomadic ecology.

Again, I refer to a humble resonance that I was unable to translate into signs but also unable to represent or even to know at all. This very happening was telling stories of how the plant goes about telling stories, teaching and producing action beyond the horizontal transmission of lettered forms of (legal) knowledge, but also through the co-production of a form of ephemeral life [the vibration]. This ephemerality involved the active collaboration between the forest, the plant, the *mambia*, the chewer and the story as a decolonial collective of life enhancing forces (Escobar 2015).

It all started with the skin . . .

Is this a kind of knowledge and legal practice that the Western archive would be able to recognize, listen to or even foster? In what sense is this kind of knowledge decolonial? A methodology to account for the role of vibrations in decolonial knowledge practices should consider mechanisms to enhance plant-human encounters as well. In my view, lettered approaches about how this dense relationality comes into being are rather insufficient. Instead, vibrations telling stories emerge as a form of knowledge where the body becomes a potential decolonizing partner that troubles Western nonorganic approaches to theory and life.

More than a mode of critique, in this example, decoloniality is a conversational experience between different peoples (human and not). For instance, while foraging through the forest, Don A engaged in conversation with manifold beings that procured his survival and aided his return to the *chagra*. Moreover, he took part in bodily interactions with other-than-human peoples capable of cognition and memory. During the *mambia* session, for instance, the plant was keen to meet the visitors while upsetting the trajectory of Western epistemology (other-than-humans *knowing* humans) and affirming the relational ontology that made possible their encounter. In this sense, the plant was itself examining the very notion of human subjectivity.

In engaging with non-Western existential, epistemic and legal commitments, I also realized that the plant was pushing for another understanding of colonial relations in what Gunadule communities call Abya-Yala.[16] Thus, humans and other-than-humans could simultaneously be called upon as a decolonial praxis of delinking (Mignolo 2011). The *mambia* was a part of this praxis. Yet a change of epistemic direction also implies co-laboring a new body—a shared body: *mambia* was teaching a corporeal methodology necessary to weave unstable continuities between the world of the *forest*—the unfamiliar—and the world of the *chagra*—the humanized forest. In other words, delinking from the colonial matrix of power is to be achieved in partnership.

Moreover, the act of walking through the *chagra* is itself a way to retrieve the past from the standpoint of the present whereby all members of the natural family co-laborate. Don A was not the exclusive force in his own survival, for the forest was willing to offer him cues to recover the trail back to the *chagra*. Again, knowledge of survival through bodily skill was possible only in the context of such a dense relationality between the human walker and other beings (see Ingold 2000).

Finally, the *mambia*—and the vibrations it enabled that night with Don A—might inform a non-modern understanding of time in which the practice of the *mambia* could grant access to the past. However, the past is not deemed distant but co-existent with the present. The present of the *mambia* was, simultaneously, the possibility of a collective future experienced as memory in transformation. On the one hand, the co-existence of a plurality of times complicated the idea of temporal boundaries as a result of the agency of plants. The simultaneity of times also enabled the existence of a collective of beings in its convergent trajectories of becoming together (Despret 2004). On the other hand, liminal spaces proliferated everywhere: 1) between the slow-motionless of vibrations and the spins and accelerations of ecological cycles; 2) between knowledge embodied by words and knowledge embodied by experience (Maturana and Varela 1994) and skill; and 3) between the skin as a site of suffering and pleasure, and the skin as a site of meaning-making within a temporal register that superseded the linearity of modernity.

3. Embodied duration: on the temporalities of plant-human encounters

What can we learn about this temporality of co-existence and life relations between plants and humans beyond linear notions of time and history? As a possible contribution to this larger question, I suggest that several temporal registers inform relations between humans and plants in the Amazon.

Particularly, different understandings and practices *with* time co-shape the everyday of Amazonian human and other-than-human encounters (Ingold 2000). This meeting of times creates a space where different peoples as well as their stories and multiple experiences of duration foster what decolonial scholar Rolando Vasquez calls "relational temporalities" (2012).

Vasquez proposes a decolonial critique of time to liberate the past from the modern representations of history. He argues that "(t)he discourse of history, in its affirmation of modernity, the negation of its exteriority and the disavowal of the 'other' (including the other-than-human), has been a key mechanism of the modern/colonial control over representation. History as the monumentalization and inscription of the past in textuality," he argues, "produces a narrative of the past that functions as a teleology of the modern hegemony of the present." (2012, 7)

Thus far, his take on temporality works as a critique of history from a decolonial perspective. Yet, when exploring how the notion of relationality brings to the fore a different understanding of time beyond the past/present dichotomy, Vasquez pushes the decolonial critique of time beyond historiography: "When speaking of the *muntú*, the philosophy of Colombian afro-descendants, Manuel Zapata Olivella says:

> the muntú conceived the family as the sum of those dead (ancestors) and those alive, united by the word to the animal, to the trees, to the minerals (land, water, fire, star) and to the tools, in a world that is indissoluble.
> (2012, 8)

Relationality, then, is not only limited to present connections between different beings. For instance, this is true of the beings Don A encountered in his roaming through the forest. Rather, it also includes connections with the past populated by ancestors who are made present in the everyday. In the Aymara world, for example, the idea that the "future lays in the past" also speaks to the co-presence of all periodizations of time: past, present and future: ancestors, living people and people yet to be born are all part of the same community of life.

My take on temporality is slightly different when it comes to relations between plants—such as the coca leaf—and humans. I attempt to go beyond time organized as past, present and future, that is, as an experience of duration as perceived by a human mind. While Vasquez's relationality is premised on the co-presence of these three modes of duration, I consider temporality an embodied practice all the way through. More than recognizing the historical co-presence of beings from different times to overcome the dichotomy identified by Vasquez, I suggest exploring how different beings (humans and other-than-human, living or dead) enact temporalities together. In this way, I attempt to move beyond the ontology of the line implied in the notion of duration. In my view, time as duration insists in one real only (Escobar 2018).

Even though decolonial critiques of time—such as Vasquez's—plea for the co-presence of these three modes of temporal expressions in the now, in making the present and conjuring ancestors and nonliving people of the future, Vasquez confines the issue of presence to the plane of the present time from the point of view of the subject of enunciation. Again, the human is the one in command of the mechanism of representation. As I have suggested earlier, my interest is to reclaim plants as subjects of knowledge, but also to reclaim interspecies relations as sites of social (and legal) agency.

In this sense, I suggest switching the emphasis from duration to enaction. That is, from the idea of time as abstract duration to the idea of time as practice and embodied experience of multiple beings (Ingold 2000) to suggest that different temporalities create bodies and foster multiple historical trajectories of human and other-than-human encounters in the Amazon.[17] To be sure, the ancestral time of Indigenous sociality in the Amazon, the bio-social temporality of plants and the temporal registers of state agents become thickly entangled while compromising the messy materiality of multiple life forms in this region.[18] Let me try to exemplify this rather obscure couple of paragraphs by returning to the story of Don A as he *mambea* with the Murui community.

As suggested earlier, the plant meets the human in the space of colonial difference to form an alliance whereby the subaltern knowledge and political resistance of Indigenous peoples and their other-than-human partners become deeply entangled. However, such beings do not precede their encounters but become together through them. Here the past does not *exist*, since it is actualized in the moment of the relation. In the case of the *mambia* experience, I claim that neither the plant nor the human traverse individual durational trajectories leading to their actual forms, but instead become together as they practice the becoming together. The temporality of the coca leaf in the act of becoming with the temporality of the human feels like a humble resonance or vibration in the skin. I am unable to translate or represent such a resonance, and I do not claim *to know it* at all.[19] While the durational temporality of history is translatable into signs, this might not be the case with the enacted temporalities of coca vibrations which exceed human representation.

As the subject of enunciation of this experience, I have described such an encounter with the plant as a sensation of resonance in the skin. However, I will not claim that I was before a clear physical stimulus. That would be equivalent to saying that the plant behaves according to my own experience of duration and perception, thus granting me the capacity to represent such experience using words. As I resist the impulse of speculative elaboration on this matter, and since my goal is to exemplify what I mean by "enacted temporalities," I will stick to the premise of becoming together with the plant beyond the search of a stable ontology. However, the vibration was somehow telling of how the plant goes about telling stories, teaching and producing action: it was not through the horizontal transmission of lettered knowledge, but through the co-production of a form of an ephemeral life [the vibration] and resonance involving the active collaboration between forces activated by the plant. A methodology to recognize the role of vibrations in decolonial knowledge practices should also ask how plants, resonance, body and skin could all become the tissues of an archive of decolonial delinking from the modern matrix of power. Hence, the urgency to undo the temporal, spatial and subjective underpinnings of history-making to include other temporalities, locales, agents and relations.

I suggest that the *mambia*, along with the vibrations it enables, informs a non-modern understanding of time whereby the practice of the *mambia* grants access to a past already inscribed in the environment (rocks, rivers, forests, etc.). However, this past is not casted as a distant memory, but as a living memory co-existing with the present of the plant-human encounter. Appealing to duration seems less necessary when the embodied ecology of time collides it with place, perhaps cancelling the need for a predetermined *telos*. Again, the present of the *mambia* grants a collective future experienced as memory in transformation in the very present of the encounter with the plant. I certainly agree with Vasquez that going back to the past is bringing it to the present. Making presence cancels the need for duration while inviting us to think about ways of rendering the passing of time as an embodied experience all the way through.

In closing: decolonizing nature?

Over the last 20 years, Colombia has witnessed a state-led campaign that criminalizes and eradicates hundreds of hectares of coca crops in the country. '*La mata que mata*' (the plant that kills) was the motto behind the elimination of coca leaf yields around the country via the glyphosate aerial spraying (*fumigation*) (Lyons 2014). The campaign inadvertently acknowledged that a plant has itself the capacity to *end* life, thus holding a form of agency. However, coca crops, rather than the cocaine obtained by means of a complex global network of war, economy, politics and chemistry, is the one deemed capable of terminating a form of life rendered acceptable or rather legal by state law. However, the criminalization of plants and humans in the Amazon has been contested for decades in this region.[20] I suggest that plants have finally met humans in the space of colonial difference (Mignolo 2000, 2011),[21] and by this I refer to the space where the potentials for decolonization emerge not only from recognizing subalternized human knowledge but also from plant-human assemblages (or shared bodies) that official historiographies and legal narratives have rendered invisible or even harmful.

In this chapter, I have engaged with vibrations as active material events taking place in the skin and through the incorporation of certain plants. At the same time, I have argued that knowledge is a matter of partnership and co-intentionality between different sentient beings (plants and human): the skin is not only a membrane that separates interiorities from exteriorities but the locus of knowledge. This conceptualization of the skin may open up the evocative notion of *sentipensar* to other senses (Escobar 2015).

The event of vibration conflates with the event of thinking by making it almost impossible to distinguish between the two. The skin, as it were, is itself thinking. The relationship between thinking and feeling with the skin the plant enables has the potential to interrupt the division between knowledge practices and bodily perception through the senses. Perception as the act of engaging the world with the senses and thinking as the act of signifying it are both woven together. Engagement with the skin in decolonial practices poses the question of what it means to compromise modes of being in the world and not only the way in which one produces knowledge. Working with the *mambia* thus entails the task of confronting our own habits of thought and practice, but also how we are in (and as) place with other beings.

This might be a story of the decoloniality of nature, or about the ongoingness of decolonial life relations where other-than-humans and humans co-produce each other. In other words, humans and other nonhumans can engage in other forms of imagining, knowing and dwelling together. For instance, the plant communicates with us through vibrations and thus changes the direction of modern epistemologies (subject knowing objects) to experiment with the reverse logic whereby (former) objects get to "know" (former) subjects. This chapter was an attempt to bypass the binary division altogether. In my own academic work, I strive to participate in moments of evanescence and blissful vulnerability (Zakour and Gillespie 2013), but I attempt to engage with habits of thinking and doing whereby becoming with other forms of life is not always amenable to academic discourse.

The proposal of decolonizing research is somewhat closer to the experience of bodily exposure and co-creation with sentient ecologies (Smith 2012). This proposition requires further explanation. For now, it is sufficient to say that it aims at enhancing the scope of the decolonial conversation beyond the human by approaching the question of bodily exposure, tactility and suffering with other-than-human others and within the very practice of knowledge making. In that sense, this chapter is a story concerning the ongoingness of life relations and how humans and plants co-produce knowledge and place.

Notes

1 This section is a follow up of an earlier work in the region of Puerto Leguízamo, Lagartococha, Putumayo (Vargas-Roncancio 2017). Exploring the entangled lives of law and ecology in Amazonia via plant-human relations, several arguments of this section have been reworked and improved based on new ethnographic data (2019–2020). My observations here are based on personal experience and interaction with some practitioners, and they do not represent a unified view of a particular community. Unless otherwise indicated, I use different names to protect the anonymity of my interlocutors.

2 Besides Don A's account, I have not encountered the figure of *Muinajeba* in the ethnographic record about the region. I'm transcribing the word as I heard him pronouncing it. The word seems to refer to "moniya Amena"—the Tree of Abundance. Rather than a "person," it is a tree. "*Guamo*"—also my transcription—seems to refer to one of the four *buinaima* -creators: Moo, Jayo, jiko and Jitoma. See for different variations of the myth of the Tree of Abundance—connected to the origin of the *chagra:* https://nukanchipaeinushirafueup.files.wordpress.com/2019/09/versiones-del-c3a1rbol-de-la-abundancia.pdf (Accessed 7 March 2023).
3 Interview with Murui Elder *Don A* in the *mameadero,* Puerto Leguizamo, Bajo Putumayo.
4 For similar arguments about the agency of plants, see Gagliano (2018), Marder (2013).
5 This section brings new ethnographic insight into an earlier argument concerning the material language of the coca leaf as a vibration and "corporeal discipline" (see Echeverry and Pereira 2010; Vargas-Roncancio 2017).
6 Transliteration of a conversation with Murui leader W and some reflections. Field notes, 2017.
7 See Vargas-Roncancio (2017, 259–260) for details.
8 See Gagliano (2018) for an impressive scientific and experiential journey to plant agency.
9 I am referring here to the way the body of the coca plant is transformed by means of human, and nonhuman agencies. For a poetic and photographic description of the mambia process see Urbina (1992)
10 For a description of phases of the chagra, see Andrade (1992, 1990), Correa (1990) and Rodríguez (2010).
11 See Echeverry and Kinerai (1993). This text reminds us of the potentiality of vibrations as epistemic devices.
12 The term 'socioecological' has been discussed in a number of recent works in the fields of geography and anthropology. For a detailed review on this term see: Annals of the Association of American Geographers, Vol. 105, Number 2, March 2015. Special Issue: Futures: Imagining socio-ecological transformation. Other scholars prefer the use of 'cosmologies' or even 'natures' (where the human is already implicated in the concept) to refer to these arrangements between social relations and natural relations, while avoiding the Western heritage of the scholarly field of 'political ecology'.
13 See Kawa on *terras pretas* or dark soils of anthropogenic origin (2016).
14 On embodiment see Varela (1999).
15 On this point see the insightful text by Carlos Fausto (2007).
16 Abya-Yala is the Guna name for the expression 'land in its full maturity' or 'land of vital blood', and it is the name used by the Kuna people of today's Colombia and Panama to refer to the American continent. On the notion of coloniality and colonialism, see Mignolo (2000).
17 For instance, rain cycles, mythical time, and temporality of progress, among others.
18 On the notion of 'entanglement' in the Amazon see Slater (2002).
19 On the issue of vibration see Viveiros de Castro (2004).
20 See Maria Clemencia Ramírez (2011).
21 Colonial difference: 'The colonial difference is the space where coloniality of power is enacted. It is also the space where the restitution of subaltern knowledge is taking place and where border thinking is emerging. The colonial difference is the space where local histories inventing and implementing

global designs meet local histories, the space in which global designs have to be adapted, adopted, rejected, integrated, or ignored. The colonial difference is, finally, the physical as well as imaginary location where the coloniality of power is at work in the confrontation of two kinds of local histories displayed in different spaces and times across the planet. If Western cosmology is the historically unavoidable reference point, the multiple confrontations of two kinds of local histories defy dichotomies.' (Mignolo 2000, ix). Note: This definition does not pretend to be exhaustive. Colonial difference should be taken as a proposal always renewing itself contextually. It is an open space of decolonial imagination.

References

Allen, Catherine. 2002. *The Hold Life Has. Coca and Cultural Identity in an Andean Community*. Washington, DC: Smithsonian Institute Press.

Andrade, Angela. 1990. "Sistemas Agrícolas Tradicionales en el Medio Caquetá." En Correa, F. (ed.). *La Selva Humanizada*. Bogotá: ICANH-FEN-CEREC.

Andrade, Angela. 1992. "Bases para el Estudio y diagnóstico preliminar de los Sistemas de producción en la Amazonía Colombiana." In *Amazonia Colombiana. Diversidad y Conflicto*. Bogotá: Colciencias, CONIA, CEGA.

Boyd, David. 2017. *The Rights of Nature: A Legal Revolution That Could Save the World*. Toronto: ECW Press.

Chambi, Oscar. 2005. *Lenguaje de la Coca*. La Paz: MUSEF.

Correa, Francois. 1990. "La Reciprocidad como modelo cultural de la reproducción del medio y la sociedad Taiwano." In Correa, F. (ed.). *La Selva Humanizada*. Bogotá: ICANH-FEN-CEREC.

Descola, Philippe. 2013. *Beyond Nature and Culture*. Chicago: University of Chicago Press.

Despret, Vinciane. 2004. "The Body We Care for: Figures of Anthropo-Zoo-Genesis." *Body and Society*, 10(2–3): 111–134.

Echeverry, Juan Alvaro, and Kinerai, Hipolito Candre. 1993. *Tabaco Frío. Coca Dulce. Palabras del Anciano Kinerai de la Tribu Canangucbal para sanar y alegrar el corazón de sus huérfanos*. Bogotá: Concultura.

Echeverry, Juan Alvaro, and Pereira, Edmundo. 2010. "'Mambear coca no es pintarse la boca de verde.' Notas sobre el uso ritual de la coca amazónica." In Chavez, M., and Del Cairo, I. (eds.). *Perspectivas antropológicas sobre la Amazonía Contemporánea*. Bogotá: Instituto Colombiano de Antropología e História & Universidad Javeriana, pp. 565–594.

Escobar, Arturo. 2015. *Sentipensar con la Tierra. Nuevas lecturas sobre desarrollo, territorio y Diferencia*. Medellin, Colombia: Ediciones UNIAULA (Universidad Autonoma Latinoamericana).

Escobar, Arturo. 2018. *Designs for the Pluriverse: Radical Interdependence, Autonomy, and the Making of Worlds*. Durham: Duke University Press.

Fausto, Carlos. 2007. "Festing on People: Eating Animals and Humans in Native Amazonia." *Current Anthropology*, 48(4): 497–530.

Foster, John Bellamy. 2000. *Marx's Ecology*. New York: Monthly Review Press.

Gagliano, M. 2013. "Green Symphonies: A Call for Studies on Acoustic Communication in Plants." *Behavioral Ecology*, 24(4): 789–796. http://doi.org/10.1093/beheco/ars206.

Gagliano, Monica. 2018. *Thus Spoke the Plant. A Remarkable Journey of Groundbreaking Scientific Discoveries and Personal Encounters with Plants.* Berkeley: North Atlantic Books.

Grillo Fernández, Eduardo. 1998. "Development or Cultural Affirmation in the Andes?" In Apffel-Marglin, Frédérique and PRATEC (eds.). *The Spirit of Regeneration. Andean Culture Confronting Westerns Notions of Development.* New York: Zed Books.

Heckenberger, Michael, and Fausto, Carlos. 2007. *Time and Memory in Indigenous Amazonia: Anthropological Perspectives.* Gainesville: University Press of Florida.

Ingold, Tim. 2000. *The Perception of the Environment: Essays on Livelihood, Dwelling and Skill.* London: Routledge.

Kawa, Nicholas. 2016. *Amazonia in the Anthropocene. People, Soils, Plants, Forests.* Austin: University of Texas Press.

Kohn, Eduardo. 2013. *How Forests Think. Toward and Anthropology Beyond the Human.* Berkeley: University of California Press.

Lyons, Kristina. 2014. "Soil Science, Development, and the 'Elusive Nature' of Colombia's Amazonian Plains." *The Journal of Latin American and Caribbean Anthropology*, 19(2): 212—236.

Lyons, Kristina. 2016. "Decomposition as Life Politics: Soils, Selva, and Small Farmers Under the Gun of the US-Colombia War on Drugs.' *Cultural Anthropology*, 31(1): 56–81.

Lyons, Kristina. 2020. *Vital Decomposition: Soil Practitioners and Life Politics.* Durham: Duke University Press.

Manga, E. 2003. *Mito y realidad de la hoja de coca, en el tiempo de los Qhpaq Ingas del Tawantinsuyu.* www.andes.missouri.edu/andes/Especiales/EMQ_Coca.html.

Marder, Michael. 2013. *Plant-Thinking. A Philosophy of Vegetal Life.* New York: Columbia University Press.

Maturana, Humberto, and Varela, Francisco. 1994. *De máquinas y Seres Vivos. Autopoiesis: La Organización de lo Vivo.* Santiago de Chile: Editorial Universitaria.

Mignolo, Walter. 2000. *Local Histories/Global Designs. Coloniality, Subatern Knowledges, and Border Thinking.* Princeton, NJ: Princeton University Press.

Mignolo, Walter. 2011. *The Darker Side of Western Modernity.* Durham: Duke University Press.

Ramirez, Maria Clemencia. 2011. *Between the Guerrillas and the State: The Cocalero Movement, Citizenship, and Identity in the Colombian Amazon.* Durham: Duke University Press.

Rodríguez, Carlos Alberto. 2010. *Sistemas agrícolas—chagras y seguridad alimentaria.* Monitoreos comunitarios para el manejo de los recursos naturales en la Amazonía Colombiana (vol. 2). Bogotá: Tropenbos International.

Saito, Kohei. 2022. *Marx in the Anthropocene.* Cambridge: Cambridge University Press.

Slater, Candace. 2002. *Entangled Edens. Visions of the Amazon.* Berkeley: University of California Press.

Strathern, Marilyn. 2005. *Partial Connections.* Walnut Creek, CA: AltaMira Press.

Tuhiwai Smith, Linda. 2012. *Decolonizing Methodologies. Research and Indigenous Peoples.* New York: Zed Books.

Urbina Rangel, Fernando. 1992. *Hojas del Poder. Relatos sobre la Coca entre los Uitotos y Muinanes de la Amazonía Colombiana.* Bogotá: Centro Editorial Universidad Nacional de Colombia.

Urbina Rangel, Fernando. 2010. "El origen de la coca." En Urbina Rangel, Fernando (ed.). *Las palabras del origen. Breve compendio de la mitología de los Uitoto*. Biblioteca Básica de los Pueblo Indígenas de Colombia. Bogotá: Ministerio de Cultura.

Urbina Rangel, Fernando. 2011. "La coca. Palabras-hoja para cuidar el mundo." *Bogotá: Maguaré*, 25(2): 199–225.

Varela, Francisco. 1999. *Ethical Know-How: Action, Wisdom and Cognition*. Stanford: Stanford University Press.

Vargas-Roncancio, Iván Darío. 2017. "Nomadic Ecologies: Plants, Embodied Knowledge and Temporality in the Colombian Amazon." *Boletín de Antropología*, 32(53): 255–276.

Vasquez, Rolando. 2012. "Towards a Decolonial Critique of Modernity. Buen Vivir, Relationality and the Task of Listening." In Fornet-Betancourt, Raul (ed.). *Capital, Poverty, Denktraditionen im Dialog: Studien zur Befreing und Interkulturalitat* (vol. 33). Aachen: Wissenschaftsverlag Mainz.

Viveiros de Castro, Eduardo. 2004. "The Forest of Mirrors. A Few Notes on the Ontology of Amazonian Spirits." In *Symposium 'La nature des esprits: humains et non-humanis dans les cosmologies autochtones des Amériques'. Centre Interuniversitaire d'Études et de Recherches sur les Autochtones*. Québec: Universityé Laval.

Viveiros de Castro, Eduardo. 2014. *Cannibal Metaphysics*. Minneapolis: Univocal.

Zakour, Michael, and Gillespie, David. 2013. "Vulnerability Theory." *Community Disaster Vulnerability*: 17–35.

Intertext 3

On entanglements and encounters

An attempt at controlled speculation

This short speculative piece is about how empirical concepts probing physical phenomena such as the notion of "quantum entanglement" (QE), that is, the "nonlocal correlation" of two or more particles in nonphysical proximity or "spooky action at a distance" (Einstein et al. 1935), could illuminate an ethical-political dimension of matter and life that is not reduced to scientific description although it is deeply entangled with it (Barad 2007; Funtowicz and Ravetz 1994).[1] For analytical purposes, this dimension refers to the social conditions of emergence of scientific description of physical phenomena from sub-atomic particles to entire socio-ecosystems (Vargas Roncancio and Kosoy 2023).

The notion of continuity between meaning (ethics and politics) and matter (from sub-atomic particles to large objects in the universe) describe Amerindian worlds as well (Descola 2013). For example, Indigenous groups living on both sides of the frontier between Ecuador and Peru:

> differ little from the other tribes that make up the Jivaro group, to whom they are linked through both their language and their culture, when they declare that most plants and animals possess a soul (wakan) similar to that of humans. This constitutes a faculty that classifies these [as] "persons" in that it provides them with a reflexive awareness and intentionality that enable them to experience emotions and exchange messages with both their peers and also members of other species, including humans. This extralinguistic communication is made possible by the recognized ability of a wakan soundlessly to convey thoughts and desires to the soul of another being, thereby modifying the latter's state of mind and behavior, sometimes without it realizing this. For this purpose, humans have at their disposal a vast collection of magic incantations (anent) by means of which they are able, from a distance, to affect not only their fellows but also plants, animals, spirits, and even certain artifacts.
>
> (Descola 2013, 15 Digital Edition)

DOI: 10.4324/9781003349426-8

A central non-modernist premise of this continuity between humans and other-than-human worlds, between matter and meaning, is the notion that physical phenomena is intertwined with systems of value (Graeber 2001) which extend far beyond human language and representation.[2] A convergent Amerindian and Western insight around the continuity of meaning and matter, illustrated, for example, in the capacity to affect plants and artifact through incantations (words), implies the agential properties of matter and the kind of thinking and decision-making it capacitates (Bennett 2010).[3] I argue that these systems of value, or values, emerge when two or more agential forces distributed across human and other-than-human "selves" (Varela 1991; Kohn 2013) encounter one another to bring forth the real.[4] In other words, the relentless coming into being of life forms through processes of materialization and meaning—which are in tandem with each other—has a relational character (Escobar 2018).

Thus, values can be considered as the hinge between matter and meaning. Values emerge from matter and produce matter, but they emerge from meaning and produce meaning as well (Vargas Roncancio and Kosoy 2023). The idea of *encounter* accounts for these conditions of emergence of non-scientific and scientific description of socio-ecosystems in constant co-production. Knowledge traditions operate within the terrain of the ethical and the political so as to capacitate the coming into being of worlds—or "pluriverse" (Kothari et al. 2019)—beyond (and with) the human, symbolic representation and scientific description. *Encounters*, as it were, is another name for value systems that meet each other to bring forth a plural real.

These encounters between separated things (or things that not necessarily touch each other and yet affect each other) reveal an ethical/political/epistemological principle of sorts: the "radical interdependence of everything that exists" (Escobar 2016, 2018) depends on suspending any preconceived claim about the nature of the real. To illustrate the deep link between physical phenomena and what I am calling *encounters of systems of value*, we can draw from historical data and direct ethnographic experience. Historical data and direct experience in Amazonia teach two lessons: 1) the principle of relationality is a driver in evolutionary processes from sub-atomic particles to entire socio-ecosystems, and 2) decision-making concerning "nature" is amenable to this principle and thus involves the active participation of other-than-human beings as social agents rather than biological or physical forces only.

A central ontological claim here is that matter and meaning are deeply entangled properties of the *real* (Law 2007). And this is apparent in our case study about the invisible ones (Chapter 1: *Yoco*, and Chapter 4: *The Making of ERA*) where I attempt to describe how "the invisible people," as the Cofán community refers to these beings, intervene in the co-creation of an Ethnobotanical Research Agreement (ERA) in Southwestern Colombia. While this relational principle refers to how biophysical phenomena and social meaning are co-produced, the notion of *encounters* offers an important analytical nuance, namely different systems of value or plural values (Munda 2016) lie at the root of **any** ontological claim about what counts as *real.* It is in the encounter between values where socio-ecological assemblages emerge beyond the individual, the human and the market. Values, in other words, are prior to socio-ecological organization.

In this sense, "social institutions" (meaning) and "life" (matter) are always in dialectic co-construction through the *encounters of systems of value.* However, values are neither pre-given attributes of human behavior—for example, double dipping *is unethical*, or depositing a ballot in a box during election season *is a political action*—nor pertain to the domain of culture as opposed to the domain of nature. For the purposes of this book, values are the "emergent properties" (Varela 1999) of living systems at any scale, as they bring forth a world that creates them in turn. In other words, *world* and *self* specify each other (Varela 1991).

Encounters of values take place through often-intense negotiations between different kinds of agencies that might result in profound disagreements between the parties involved (Rancière 2004). In this book, I have concentrated on one such instance of potential disagreement, namely the co-production of ERA, which involved the contested participation of human and other-than-human agencies and institutions in a small region of the Colombian Amazon (see Chapter 4).

Final note on values: In the famous environmental conflict on bauxite mining in the sacred Niyamgiri Hills in India,[5] different agents understand and articulate the values around those hills in opposition to one to another. One group establishes that the hills are valuable due to the bauxite content in the mountain, hence only realizable through mineral extraction, while the local Indigenous group, the Dondria Ghong, renders the mountain as a deity to be revered and protected. For our purposes, (i) the values concerning the mountain do not exist in isolation; (ii) the value of the hills as mineral ore is reinforced by a value system that prioritizes mining extraction over any other value system (hence the notion of encounter—which is not always a conflict-free one; (iii) as the opposite is also true, the value of the hills as a God is reinforced through rituals and cultural practices that materialize the mountain as a deity; and (iv) different value systems give priority or respond to various configurations of power; (v) there is not an intrinsic value in "nature," for nature comes into being as the expression of a particular value system (coloniality/"Western modernity"/development. See Mignolo 2011; Quijano 2014). (vi) What we deem as "real" does not exist outside of the co-production between forces of the human and other-than-human kind.

Notes

1 Before we continue, a word about the word "entanglement." In quantum physics, "entanglement is the physical phenomenon that occurs when a pair or group of particles is generated, interact, or share spatial proximity in a way such that

the quantum state of each particle of the pair or group cannot be described independently of the state of the others, even when the particles are separated by a large distance." In Wikipedia (consulted 11.03.2020). Entry based on Einstein, A., Podolsky, B., and Rosen, N. 1935. "Can Quantum-Mechanical Description of Physical Reality Be Considered Complete?" *Physical Review*, 47(10): 777–780. http://doi.org/10.1103/PhysRev.47.777, among others.

2 For a similar argument, see Escobar (2018), Descola (2013) and Kohn (2013).

3 It is not clear whether QE can be experimentally modeled in living systems except for a recent study using bacteria and light (Marletto et al. 2018).

4 "Organism connotes a knotty dialectic: a living system makes itself into an entity distinct from its environment through a process that brings forth, through that very process, a world proper to the organism." (Varela 1991, 79)

5 See EJAtlas. *Niyamgiri-Vedanta Bauxite Mining, India*. https://ejatlas.org/conflict/niyamgiri-vedanta-bauxite-mining-india (Accessed 11 November 2020).

References

Barad, Karen. 2007. *Meeting the Universe Halfway. Quantum Physics and the Entanglement of Matter and Meaning*. Duham: Duke University Press.

Bennett, Jane. 2010. *Vibrant Matter. A Political Ecology of Things*. Durham: Duke University Press.

Descola, Philippe. 2013. *Beyond Nature and Culture*. Chicago: University of Chicago Press.

Graeber, David. 2001. *Towards an Anthropological Theory of Value. The False Coin of Our Own Dreams*. New York: Palgrave.

Einstein, A., Podolsky, B., and Rosen, N. 1935. "Can Quantum-Mechanical Description of Physical Reality Be Considered Complete?" *Physical Review*, 47(10): 777–780.

EJAtlas. *Niyamgiri-Vedanta Bauxite Mining, India*. https://ejatlas.org/conflict/niyamgiri-vedanta-bauxite-mining-india (Accessed 11 November 2020).

Escobar, Arturo. 2016. "Sentipensar con la Tierra: Las Luchas Territoriales y la Dimensión Ontológica de las Epistemologías del Sur." *Revista de Antropologia Iberoamericana*, 11(1): 11–32.

Escobar, Arturo. 2018. *Designs for the Pluriverse: Radical Interdependence, Autonomy and the Making of Worlds*. Durham: Duke University Press.

Funtowicz, Silvio, and Ravetz, Jerome. 1994. "The Worth of a Songbird: Ecological Economics as a Post-normal Science." *Ecological Economics*, 10(3): 197–207.

Kohn, Eduardo. 2013. *How Forests Think. Toward and Anthropology Beyond the Human*. Berkeley, CA: University of California Press.

Kothari, Ashish, Salleh, Ariel, Escobar, Arturo, Demaria, Federico, and Acosta, Alberto. 2019. *Pluriverse. A Post-Development Dictionary*. New Delhi: Tulika Books.

Law, John. 2007. *Actor Network Theory and Material Semiotics*. Version of 25 April 2007. hwww.heterogeneities.net/publications/Law2007ANTandMaterialSemiotics.pdf.

Marletto, C., Coles, D.M., Farrow, T., and Vedral, V. 2018. "Entanglement Between Living Bacterial and Quantized Light Withnessed by Rabi Splitting." *Journal of Physics Communications*, 2(10): 1010001.

Mignolo, Walter. 2011. *The Darker Side of Western Modernity. Global Futures, Decolonial Options*. Durham: Duke University Press.

Munda, Giuseppe. 2016. "Beyond Welfare Economics: Some Methodological Issues." *Journal of Economic Methodology*, 26(2): 185–202.

Quijano, Anibal. 2014. "Colonialidad del poder, eurocentrismo y America Latina." In *Cuestiones y horizontes: de la dependencia histórico-estructural a lacolonialidad/descolonialidad del poder*. Buenos Aires: CLACSO.

Rancière, Jacques. 2004. *Dis-agreement. Politics and Philosophy*. Minnesota: University of Minnesota Press.

Varela, Francisco. 1991. "Organism: A Meshwork of Selfless Selves." In Tauber, A.I. (ed.). *Organism and the Origins of Self. Boston Studies in the Philosophy of Science* (vol. 129). Dordrecht: Springer. https://doi.org/10.1007/978-94-011-3406-4_5

Varela, Francisco. 1999. *Ethical Know-How. Action, Wisdom and Cognition*. Stanford: Stanford University Press.

Vargas Roncancio, Iván Darío, and Kosoy, Nicolas. 2023. *The Agency Problem: From Individual to Relational Agencies in Ecological Economics*. SSRN. https://ssrn.com/abstract=4500678 or http://doi.org/10.2139/ssrn.4500678

Chapter 4

The making of an ethnobotanical research agreement in Southern Colombia

Yagé, invisible people and the law of the place*

Abstract

After analyzing several aspects of the entangled lives of law and ecology in Amazonia, Chapter 4 attempts a rather different format: it invites ethnobotanist David Rodríguez Mora to the conversation. The chapter discusses several aspects of year-long conversations about plants, law, the politics of naming nature, the invisible people and the ethical and conceptual dilemmas researchers faced as they engaged "law" and "ecology" with the guidance of humans and plants in Southern Colombia. The chapter tells a story of collaboration learning with Yagé (Banisteriopsis caapi (Spruce ex Griseb.) Morton, a.k.a. Ayahuasca) and members of the A'i (a.k.a. Cofán or Kofán) Indigenous people of Nariño in Southwestern Colombia, with whom David has been closely working since 2019. It centers on what the chapter provisionally interprets as "unseen conceptual and methodological challenges and ethical dilemmas" encountered during the co-creation of an ethnobotany research agreement seeking to integrate "Western" and Amazonian-Cofán epistemologies and ways of being concerning Yagé.

* Special thanks to Colombian ethnobiologist and anthropologist David Rodríguez-Mora for permission to publish this joint chapter based on our conversations and field collaborations in the Nariño region of Colombia. We both would like to acknowledge the Cofán of Colombia, the North Carolina State University and the National University of Colombia for their generous help and support enabling the fieldwork that rendered the present collaboration. A preliminary version was jointly presented at the Workshop: "From Ritual to Justice: towards a decolonial and feminist approach to ayahuasca" (Session 2). Paper: "Yagé as plant, teacher, and life practice: Weaving knowledge and worlds in Nariño, Andes-Amazon region of Colombia." SALSA XIII Biennial Conference, June 23rd, 2021. Workshop 2: From Ritual to Justice (Session 2). Our observations here are based on personal experience and interaction with some practitioners, and they do not represent a unified view of a particular community. Unless otherwise indicated, we use different names to protect the anonymity of our interlocutors. Special thanks to Michael Cepek for his critical and thoughtful comments and suggestions for improving this work.

DOI: 10.4324/9781003349426-9

As a mode of preface: documenting and interpreting key words pertaining to the *Yagé* practice

This joint chapter probes the limits and possibilities of contrasting yet complementary forms of knowledge and being in an ethnobotanical research project concerning the local variability of a ritual plant in Southern Colombia. On the one hand, the so-called "Western" ways of knowing comprised both a legal artifact (e.g., a research agreement) making each party accountable for specific responsibilities in the project, and the scientific design in the discipline of ethnobotany, providing measurable and replicable data about the Yagé liana (*Banisteriopsis caapi* (Spruce ex Griseb.) Morton) (a.k.a., Yajé). On the other hand, researchers' understanding of what they call "ways of knowing and being" of our Indigenous interlocutors that entailed Yagé ceremonies as a way to "consulting human and other-than-human persons" to deliver a verdict about the project's viability and research protocol. Finally, this account considers the importance and relegation of the role played by Indigenous "ways of knowing and being" for the co-production of knowledge and worlds in the Andean-Amazonian region of Colombia. These provisional approximations to the limitless world of Yagé derive from 12 weeks of ethnographic engagement and six months of ethnobotanical fieldwork in Spanish and not in A'ingae (Cofán language)—the mother tongue of four of our interlocutors, not spoken by the authors—conversing with and interviewing a total of 16 members of the Cofán (a.k.a., Kofán or A'i) community. Thus, we hope the initial shared hypotheses of this chapter to be tested in future ethnographic studies in A'ingae and with more A'i (Cofán) communities, to evaluate their scale of representation within the Cofán nation.

Throughout our research, there were important concepts in relation to the Yagé practice that we documented as we heard them used in multiple conversations and semi-structured interviews with 16 Cofán community members—self-identified as male or female and young or elder—during twelve weeks of ethnographic fieldwork and six months of ethnobotanical fieldwork. Furthermore, we have also incorporated into the discussion of this chapter some concepts related to the Yagé practice, which have been formerly treated in the relevant literature (Beyer 2010; Cepek 2012, 2018). As follows, we provide the list of such concepts with the provisional meaning we are adhering to for the present discussion. However, since most of these terms were taken from Spanish, we deem it important to disclose that their scrutiny in A'ingae language may likely provide very different translations.

Spirit: a noun colloquially used in the Cofán community regarding supernatural entities (i.e., *cocoya, tsampi'su, Yagé a'i* and *game owners/masters*), the agency, or capacity to act, of the *Yagé* liana (*B. Caapi*) and other plants. This term is also used by Cepek (2012, 2018) in association with Cofán life and worldviews and with gifts, objects and instruments (e.g., weapons), usually with power, provided by supernatural entities to people and, particularly, Cofán traditional medics. Following UMIYAC's ethical protocol, we prefer the use of this voice, rather than the common expression "shamans," which UMIYAC considers a colonial heritage. The protocol is known as "*El Pensamiento de los Mayores. Código de Ética de la Medicina Indígena del Piedemonte Amazónico Colombiano*" (Elders Thinking: Ethical Code of the Indigenous Medicine of the Andean-Amazonian Piedmont) (see Chapter 2).[1]

Supernatural: this adjective is used by Cepek (personal communication, 2021) as "beyond typical sensory experience." In the literature, it is employed regarding, on the one hand, three overlapping categories: malevolent agents or demons (e.g., *cocoya*), forest people (i.e., *tsampi'su*), invisible people (e.g., *Yagé a'i*) and game owners or masters—some of which may let themselves be seen at dawn or dusk, and all of which are contacted by traditional medics in their dreams and under the influence of Yagé (Cepek 2012, 2018). And, on the other hand, this adjective encompasses the traditional medic's action resulting from their interaction with such entities (2012, 2018). *Cocoya* is also a term used by many Cofán people in reference to Colombian paramilitaries and guerrilla members (2018). For further description on the *tsampi'su* and the traditional medic's relations with them, see Cepek (2012), and on the *cocoya*, game owners/masters and the *Yagé a'i*, see Cepek (2012, 2018).

Yagé science *(Ciencia del Yagé)*: many Cofán community members use this noun phrase as a parallel with the 'Western' science, seemingly to emphasize the legitimacy of the knowledge derivative from the Yagé practice, and the replicability—yet multiplicity—of the knower's actions through Yagé practices (see the entry "supernatural").

Esoteric languages: languages taught to the traditional medic and apprentice by *cocoya* and *Yagé a'i* (Cepek 2018).

Introduction

In January 2019, the Cofán authorities of a community in southwestern Colombia invited David Rodríguez-Mora to meet with them and to evaluate the possibility of conducting an ethnobotany project of their interest. They held three meetings in Spanish—which is spoken by all Cofán members in this community—during that visit, each followed by a *Yagé* ceremony.[2] During the first meeting, David suggested he could help to document their wild edible plants, but this was not a priority at the time. Instead, the Cofán authorities expressed that, since the spraying of glyphosate (e.g., Roundup) in the region had severely affected their main cash crop and most important sacred plant, *Yagé*, the Malpighiaceous liana *Banisteriopsis caapi* (Spruce ex Griseb.) Morton, it was helpful to them to assist their efforts to restore their *Yagé* populations and crops. In 2016, with the signing of the peace agreement between the Colombian government and the largest guerilla group, *Fuerzas Armadas Revolucionarias de Colombia* (FARC), glyphosate spraying ceased—although not for long. Thus, the opportunity to recover the Cofán Yagé crop seemed feasible at that time.

Although David was very grateful and excited with this potential research, he was wary that his ethnobotanical education had not prepared him to approach *Yagé* knowledge practices that involved ceremonies and plant "spirits" (see "spirit" in the preface to this chapter). He was taught that the "truth" of an external natural world is the pursuit of science and that such truth is objective, empirical, falsifiable and uncertain (Popper 2012)—an approach problematized and debated by several authors, such as Lakatos (1989), Lakatos and Feyerabend (2001) and Kuhn (2012). To be sure, his ethnobotanical training entailed recording replicable data of plant-human relationships to be put to the test through systematic observation and experimentation.

It seemed that "Cofán knowledge and ways of being" comprises both "natural" and "supernatural" worlds (see Preface), which the Cofán of Nariño seem to consider interconnected and pursue through *Yagé*. This constitutes, as some practitioners call it, "*la ciencia del Yagé*" (in English, "*the Yagé science*") (see Preface). Such knowledge, however, seems to derive from the interaction between two "agents," the *Yagé* drinker and the *Yagé* "spirit" or associated "entities" coined by Cepek (2012, 2018) as *cocoya, Yagé a'i*, and *game owners/masters*, amplified by the drink, and the *Yagé* drinker may learn this knowledge from their first-person point of view experience. In order to navigate these interactions, David relied both on his sensibility and intuition and on his ethnobotanical training. Interestingly, these skills seemed to work in tandem, after all, "mutually translating" each other (De la Cadena 2015).

During the *Yagé* ceremonies, three ideas surfaced in David's mind. The first idea was that the use of *Yagé* had many purposes. David was aware of its usefulness for healing and harming in Cofán traditional medicine (Cepek 2018). Still, in these ceremonies, he also considered that *Yagé* was being used as a trust assessment tool—and, in fact, protocol—to evaluate a potential collaboration with the Cofán community. It was *as if* he was being "tested" by the elder *Taita* Antonio (elder),[3] the community and the *Yagé* entities themselves in different ways. The second idea was that David needed to be determined to contribute to the Cofán eco-cultural revitalization. As he listened to the elder, sometimes chanting in esoteric languages (see Preface) and other times sharing some of his life stories, David felt the echo of his voice reverberating deeply inside of him. *Taita* Antonio's voice seemed to be the embodiment of a form of interspecies and inter-worlds communication under threat that longed to survive the test of time.

The third initial idea was that the medicinal benefits of *Yagé* needed to be more accessible to the people beyond the Cofán community. David felt that the global therapeutic potential of *Yagé* was mostly undermined by dominant "Western" mentalities (Mignolo 2011) and prohibitionist laws (CSA 1970; Lampe 2021). In the last ceremony of his visit, his wife had a tremendous healing session that significantly improved her well-being in the following weeks and months. Witnessing both the healing session and his wife's health improvement, David wanted others to experience this type of "benefit." By the end of this visit, the Cofán authorities confirmed their interest in establishing a collaboration with him to support their *Yagé* restoration, and he eagerly accepted this proposal.[4]

Whether he wanted it or not, it was clear that the unfolding of the research collaboration would entail the crucial learning process of weaving together different methodologies that, on the one hand, include the discipline of ethnobotany and, on the other, what we provisionally call "Cofán epistemologies and ways of being," regardless of the often-unnegotiable differences in their approaches and (de)colonial trajectories. In an attempt to articulate these methodologies, David let himself be guided by his experiences during the *Yagé* ceremonies and conversations with several Cofán community members, while rigorously documenting the ethnobotanical field data. A legal scholar working in the region—Iván—joined David as a field collaborator and interlocutor.

In this chapter, the collaboration between an ethnobotanist and a legal scholar concerns the entangled lives of law and ecology in Amazonia. Based on preliminary fieldwork material and ethnobotanical data, the chapter suggests that more than objects of research, territories and their invisible peoples are active shaping forces (Section 1). This affirmation requires a non-anthropocentric understanding of both biological knowledge and legal theory concerning the protection of rapidly declining populations of a highly regarded ritual plant, which, for the Cofán, we suggest, embodies "agential forces": forest people (i.e., *tsampi'su*) and/or invisible people (i.e., *Yagé a'i*). The second section (2) probes how ethnobotany and law co-emerge and seem to co-exist, "equivocally" nonetheless (Viveiros de Castro 2004), alongside what we tentatively call "Cofán epistemologies and ways of being" based on these agential capacities of the *Yagé* people (*Yagé a'i*). We suggest that these two complementary (and yet contested) onto-epistemic formations, "ethnobotany" and "law," are part and parcel of local strategies for the well-being of Cofán territories and peoples, and in the context of the research study's unfolding.

Part 3 and 4 probe the limits and possibilities of considering *Yagé*—the root of the territory—as a *someone*, that is, an other-than-human person (De la Cadena 2015) with the capacity to command behavior, and then discuss potential methodological and ethical implications of this "ontological opening" for "Western" science (De la Cadena and Blaser 2018). Based on preliminary ethnographic material concerning other-than-human commands or mandates (see Table 4.1) as articulated through the propositional language of the human actors involved in this collaboration, Part 5 suggests the working ethnographic notion of the legalities of the invisible: *los Invisibles* might come into being via non-symbolic ways such as "dreams" (Kohn 2013; Poirier 2003) that could nonetheless be translated into symbolic forms crystallizing a command or mandate. The translation, to be sure, exists as the "thing" and the "thing" lives through the "translation," ultimately mutually affecting each other.

These invisible legalities were recursively mediated by *Yagé* practices as a source of health, knowledge and decision-making in the community since the first day of research collaboration. Therefore, this provisionally suggests that *los Invisibles* co-participate in the making of an ethnobotany and law-otherwise (Restrepo and Escobar 2005), namely a shared field of practices, norms and procedures concerning the protection of a territory and the ongoingness of their people (human and not, visible and non-visible). To conclude, the chapter summarizes the two main aspects of the discussion and propose some questions for future research: first, how "the will of a plant" may become part of a larger conversation about knowledge and world-making in this region; and second, how may we come to learn the legal mandates of a place from encounters with different beings of a sentient and cognitive territory.

1. Law and science in the field: a legal scholar and a plant scientist meet

Soon after his first visit to the Cofán territory, David was introduced to Iván who was working on Indigenous legal traditions and Earth Law in the same region, particularly exploring whether the law, as a concept and life practice, could be thought from the plant's "perspective" (Viveiros de Castro 1998) in the context of growing jurisprudence on the rights of nature. They both realized that David's research collaboration with the Cofán also provided an ideal context for Iván to put his law work to the test of interspecies communication and methodologies outside of the legal field. With their prior experiences with *Yagé* and the Cofán community at hand, they engaged with the preliminary ideas of *Yagé* as a source of social norms and decision-making to fit well with the phenomenology of their shared *Yagé* encounters during the fieldwork.

They found themselves wondering, had the plant spirit and associated entities (see "spirit" and "supernatural" in the Preface) oriented them in the work that was unfolding? And if so, how can we "know" (or fail to know) this? As a scientist and a legal scholar, it was very troublesome for both to accept these ideas to be true solely based on personal experience with the plant and without extensive ethnographic and ethnobotanical research in A'ingae. They later learned, however, that the robust authoritative character of the *Yagé* encounters had been documented as a landmark of psychedelic experience (Pollan 2019; Gagliano 2018) and decision-making among Amazonian communities (Caicedo 2015; Weiskopf 2002).

Iván had the opportunity to join David's ethnobotanical research project as a field collaborator. The project's purpose was to study the diversity and classification of wild varieties of the *Yagé* vine (*Banisteriopsis caapi*) at a level above form or cultivar, among the Cofán traditional medics or "knowers" (UMIYAC 2000) and *Yagé* apprentices in the community:

> It was very exciting for me to contemplate the possibility to carry out a project that would contribute to the recovery of *Yagé*, the most sacred plant for the Cofán, purportedly the root of their knowledge, wisdom, cultural identity, and their ancestral territory. But at the same time, I knew this was a huge responsibility, not only with the community and the Cofán nation but also with the *Yagé* plant itself. Widely regarded as a sacred master plant (Luna 1984), the most important for the Amazonian people at large, I had heard numerous accounts that described the power of this plant's spirit. Additionally, I was aware that my training as an ethnobotanist had certainly not prepared me to know how to deal with plant spirits. Nevertheless, I felt reassured with the fact that this potential work was coming from the initiative of the Cofán authorities themselves and included the participation and endorsement of one of the most respected Taitas in the Amazon.

David framed this project to contribute to the "protection" of what we tentatively call the "root of the Cofán territory" and "traditional medicine," namely the *Yagé* vine itself. In his view, studying this plant's diversity was an important stepping stone in assessing the conservation status of *B.* caapi and designing sustainable harvesting methods and thus dealing with the purportedly rapidly declining wild populations of the plant, while contributing with the continuation of a world-known traditional medicine practice based on *Yagé*. While the purpose of the project was straightforward and seemingly aligned with the desires and expectations of the local community, the awaited co-creation of a scientific/legal protocol to guide the project was not without surprising and enriching "equivocations."

As mentioned earlier in the introduction, Brazilian anthropologist Eduardo Viveiros de Castro describes an "equivocation" as not only a failure to understand but "a failure to understand that understandings are necessarily not the same and that they are not related to imaginary ways of 'seeing' the world but to the real words that are being seen" (2004, 11). For example, during one of the numerous meetings with the community that year, Andrés, an Indigenous practitioner and *Yagé* trainee, considered that "since the territory protects itself, there was no need to do a project for that to happen."

Interestingly, David's understanding of "protecting the territory" via the (scientific) study of the variability and conservation status of individual ritual plant species was based upon a widely shared assumption that "protecting" the territory was a human endeavor and that the territory was simply the backdrop of this human decision. On the contrary, we suggest that for this local Indigenous trainee, any "protection of the territory" should count with the territory itself, which didn't seem to be the stage of human action, but rather an active shaping force. In a way, the territory and the human seemed to be in continuity (Descola 2013).

The initial reaction of the community to the ethnobotanical research proposal and David's diplomatic skills to respond to it stimulated a series of productive (dis)agreements (Rancière 2004) that eventually led to the contested co-creation of a research protocol, which conjured up what we provisionally call the "will of the plant" and the "will of the supernatural entities," including the "invisible peoples of the mountain" or *Yagé* A'i themselves (see "supernatural" in the Preface), and entailed a different understanding of the territory altogether. For us, it was apparent that establishing a research agreement with the community would require far more than the meeting of human minds via rational deliberation (Blaser 2013). More than objects of research, territory, plants and their invisible guardians appeared as their active shaping forces from the outset. We hypothesized that reckoning with this insight required different (and even equivocal) understandings and indeed enactions (Varela et al. 1991) of biological knowledge and decision-making theory concerning the protection of the rapidly declining populations of this ritual plant.

1.1. Finding the right pronoun

The ancestral Cofán territory is situated at the intersection of the Andean Cordillera and the Amazon basin encompassing the regions of Putumayo and Nariño. The territories of these interconnected regions express unique eco-cultural characteristics of both the Andes and the Amazon. The *Piedemonte*

Andino-Amazónico, for example, is considered one of the greatest sources of biophysical richness in the hemisphere with an enormous climatic and ecosystemic variability: the Amazon alone has been estimated to host about 50,000 plant species (Cardoso et al. 2017). Moreover, while the rich soils of the Andean slopes have favored an economy based on different cash crops, the Amazonian ecosystems are characterized by their fragility, as most of them are located on poor soils that are very vulnerable to rain and sun (Luizão et al. 2007).

This means that once the forest is cut down, the fertility of these acidic and thin soils quickly depletes. However, the great biological variability and resilience of this region is not due to its soils, but to the way in which its ecosystems function in a feeding cycle of aerial and subterranean interaction of Andean and Amazonian geographies, the prevailing environmental conditions of high humidity and heat (Clark et al. 2013; Clark et al. 2014; Torres et al. 2015), as well as the intimate ecological knowledge and effectiveness of Indigenous territorial governance systems (Thompson et al. 2020; Van et al. 2017). Local conceptions of territoriality are thus testimony of this great diversity of matter and meaning (see Intertext 3).

By the end of one of our first meetings with the Cofán authorities, it seemed plausible that conducting the project was not merely about (1) studying the classification of plants growing in territories with these unique eco-cultural characteristics, but about *learning with the plants as persons*; and (2) not only a matter of "protecting territories" and "shamanic legacies"—our initial shared assumptions—but about learning an entirely different way of engaging with a place and its sentient and even agential beings, and being even prepared to abandon the whole project altogether. And finally, (3) that any negotiation and eventual (dis)agreement with the community required calling respectful and humble attention both to the will of the community—with their internal deliberation procedures—as well as what we tentatively call the will of other-than-human beings (de la Cadena 2015).

If the territory could protect itself, we needed to learn whether it was feasible for us to "conduct research" with the set of epistemological, ontological and value assumption informing our thinking and action in the world daily. Responding to Andres' interpellation, David highlighted the "minimal needs of conservation of the vine" as a way to "protect the legacy of the Cofán medicine." Also, he insisted on how important it was to involve *all* the (human) community members in the design of this participatory endeavor. To be sure, studying the conservation status of ritual plants would, for him, contribute to the protection of the territory and culture of the community.

How can we even care for a territory that seems to protect herself, or a territory that governs herself? How does a plant *make* a place? How can we participate—or not—in the modes of decision-making that emerge from a willful place? One of the problems was, precisely, engaging with the territory as an "it." After the first meeting, words such as "community," "research," "territory," "agreement," "plant" and "research protocol" were subject to relentless negotiations and mutual ontological equivocations (see Blaser 2013; De la Cadena 2015 for a similar articulation of this idea). These and similar questions would linger all throughout our shared experience with the Cofán and their plant people from then on.

2. On a plane to Putumayo: two knowledges that co-emerged in conversation and disagreement

We were very excited about the whole thing. Iván wanted to learn about David's research as an ethnobotanist and how his encounters with different beings in the territory informed his scientific work. There was a sincere willingness to engage in mutual listening and co-learning. How did we "decide" to work with the *Yagé* vine from all different angles? As we travelled to Puerto Asís, Putumayo, pressing questions around the meaning of "research" and what the role of the "researcher" should be quickly emerged before us. While these issues were not initially explicit in our shared field experience, they were the elephant in the room from the onset.

It was clear that the research process would be as significant for us as its possible outcomes, and that the process would require deep reflection on our own positionalities. It was also clear that this process was one of opening up to a *world in place*—that is, colonial histories, extractivist economies, violence and stories of socio-ecological resilience—but also about opening to a *different world*: a set of values, practices and epistemological operations clashing against each other. Our attempts to remain open to other ways of thinking and doing things in the field would eventually defy well-established presuppositions about the nature of ethnobotanical knowledge as well as the nature of the law.

We set on to learn how to intertwine biology (the realm of life) and law (the realm of rules and decisions) to find out whether these two disciplines were kept in continuity, unraveled and reworked back again as we were learning to invite other humans and more-than-humans into the conversation. Two ways of being (biology and law) co-emerged in conversation and dis-agreement. Do territories make decisions? Are invisible people "real"? And to whom are they real? While these questions were not part of our initial repertoire in the making of ethnobotanical research with the Cofán community, they certainly were hovering in the background of our conversations like rapidly passing fireflies.

"Actually, it was the other way around," David insisted. "It was more like *something else* made that decision for me. I wanted to do a study on the ethnobotany of some fruit-bearing trees in the region. But, you see, in my subjective understanding this was more pressing for the community, and I suggest, for the mountain." David is a scientist, and he is also deeply invested in Indigenous practices with these plants. At first, he was serious about the possibility of a "willful" mountain and yet seemed less keen to allow the mountain to disturb the soundness of the scientific protocol: "It was the mountain, like, telling me that. It was not an invitation, but something like a *command*. Something I had to do regardless. But I want to be clear about a crucial point: one thing is science and quite another is what I believe about local spirit-life (see the entry "spirit" in the Preface) as important parts of the territory. We need to do the science right, with the method and all." We were both indeed very intrigued by the idea of a willful mountain or a mountain mandating someone to do something.

We needed to understand how to make things right by following the local protocol. To that extent, were we willing to acknowledge that the territory—and not only the community—could have been against the whole research project? This shared realization demanded what Cofán *cabildo*[5] leader Andrés had called "asking *permission* from the invisible ones" in various "*tomas de remedio*" (or *Yagé* ingestion ceremonies). What are the locally appropriate protocols to do anything related to obtaining—or not—agreement from the invisible ones?

"Now you made me think about that old law book, *The Spirit of the Laws*" (De Montesquieu 1989), Iván said. This memory made him realize that "spirits" are not quite the same across disciplinary boundaries and cultures. The spirit of the law that directed David to do his project was not quite the same *spirit of the law* as it exists in the 'Western' legal canon. Yet spirit life seemed quite pervasive across knowledge practices. Why not in science as well? If scientists like David could have received a mandate of sorts from the invisible people to perform what the "Western"-minded can only perceive as a stroke of imagination of a non-scientific sensibility, then what is really at stake is the status of *the real* (Escobar 2018). Yet we can also suggest that the territory is a force of law in the same way in which the constitution of a country is a force of law. After all, spirit masters (see "spirit" and "supernatural" in the Preface) from mountains to constitutional values guiding our "modern lives" are both invisible or absential phenomena, aren't they?

3. "*Tenía que hacer el proyecto*": the legal mandate of a mountain as narrated by a plant scientist

In the last ceremony during his first visit to the Cofán community, David witnessed what he felt was one of the most astounding insights of his personal and professional life. Given the importance of that ceremony as the stepping stone for the unfolding of the collaboration with the Cofán, he embraced the guidelines of the elder *Taita* Antonio, which were threefold: to drink *Yagé* fearlessly and abundantly, to bring a clear purpose to the ceremony and to let himself be guided by the *Yagé*—and the involved supernatural entities.[6] Naturally, that approach generated expectations that influenced David's experience. Before taking in a *Yagé* bowl, in his mind, he would 'ask' the *Yagé* spirit for guidance to conduct meaningful work for the Cofán and the *Yagé* liana populations. He was determined to follow the elder's advice, so he expected to undergo a very visual session. David was very observant throughout the night, paying close attention to the experience. Still, his expectations were not fulfilled in his eyes, as he could not *see* nor experience much.

He was amazed and confused by the ineffable nature of the experience. By the end of the ceremony, he felt that he lacked clear realizations from the *Yagé* experience regarding the research collaboration that was being established. Yet David was grateful to feel wide awake and energized, as he needed to move quickly to make it back in town before the first bus departed towards Puerto Asis. He and his wife had just the right amount of time to catch their flight, and a delay could have easily compromised their travel arrangements. So, David gathered his belongings, and it was time to say goodbye. He approached the elder *Taita* Antonio to say goodbye, and as he did, David broke into tears, weeping inconsolably as he had never wept before. Although it was the most honest farewell "words" to express his gratitude, admiration, respect and commitment with the Cofán, it was a very strange spontaneous expression of his being that, nonetheless, seem to have something to do with the research experience as well.

The governor accompanied him and his partner back in town, concerned that the effects of *Yagé* were only delayed, and that if they kicked in on the bus, he and his partner were going to miss their flight. David doubted that possibility, as he felt very sharp and strong—a very unusual sensation to feel right after a *Yagé* ceremony, deprived of sleep. It was a remarkably beautiful morning, with a gleam sunbathing the Andes-Amazon piedmont. The oropendolas were extremely active, singing and flying through the territory. And the mountains on the horizon radiated tremendous vitality.

He realized that he was experiencing what he could only frame as a déjà vu, as if at some point he had lived for a long time in that territory. David was invaded with a clear yet intimidating epiphany: the mountain was, perhaps, commanding him to do this work. That is, rather than the unfolding of an appealing research collaboration, that work was, he thought, more of a mandate of the mountain that David was *obligated* to carry out. Although he was certain that this message was presenting itself through *Yagé*, he did not know why he was certain about this. It was a crystal clear insight unbearably hard for him to defend as a scientist, for which the most objective explanation is that of a bizarre authoritative landmark of psychedelic experiences (Pollan 2019; Gagliano 2018).

He would wonder where such an unusual idea was coming from, seeming to be a factual belief yet corresponding to a secondary cognitive attitude derivative from the *Yagé* context (Van Leeuwen 2018). Was that idea a product of his mind, the *Yagé* spirit and/or the mountain? Regardless of the idea's provenance, and of David's acceptance of it as certainty rather than truth, the overall *Yagé* experience had transformed his perspective as a researcher and ethnobotanist in unseen ways, guiding the collaboration from what we provisionally call "a more culturally and territorially mindful framework."

4. Co-making a research agreement on the ethnobotanical classifications of a ritual plant

After the first visit to the Cofán community, with the guidance of his master's advisory committee, David developed an ethnobotany research study that enabled him to contribute to the *Yagé* restoration efforts of the Cofán. He sought to answer the question of whether the wild Cofán varieties of *B. caapi* could be recognized at the taxonomic level of subspecies. Dozens of varieties of *B. caapi* have been reported in the literature, including fifteen for the Cofán (Jütte 2016), which have been assumed to be solely chemical variants of that species (Gates 1982). However, no formal systematic revision has been conducted to assess their taxonomic diversity at a rank above form or cultivar (Oliveira et al. 2018). To conduct such a work, David proposed to document and analyze morphological, ethnobotanical and ecological data of the wild Cofán varieties of *Yagé*. That approach required for him to go into the Cofán territory with elders who knew how to recognize the wild *Yagé* plants and who would point them out to David for him to collect plant samples and bring them to the *Herbario Nacional Colombiano* (COL) (Colombian National Herbarium) in Bogotá, D.C. While doing these collections, he would also harvest stem cuttings of the lianas to hand over to the Cofán elders leading the field trips, for them and the rest of the community to utilize that material for their *Yagé* restoration efforts.

The botanical collections of the study were crucial to conduct the morphological analysis and to provide the physical scientific foundation supporting the work—that is, objective, empirical, replicable and falsifiable evidence. To serve as evidence, however, the samples needed to remain at the herbarium indefinitely. Yet a history of colonialism, extractivism and violence questions the research ethics in these kinds of works and their methodologies. In fact, during the first presentation of the research proposal that David carried out with the Cofán community and authorities, there was no shortage of opponents to the requirement to collect *Yagé* samples for this work. Some of the community members fiercely condemned the intentions behind the collections, and it seemed as if the collaboration was quickly coming apart.

After David thoroughly explained the rationale behind that requirement, everyone but one family approved. Instead, they invited him to partake in a *Yagé* ceremony at their place that night to discuss the matter further. Ironically, however, after the ceremony, this family became the most open and supportive of the project. What exactly triggered that shift in their perspective? That is hard to tell for a fact, but again, the *Yagé* ceremony seemed to have been the vehicle through which they assessed whether they could trust the collaboration. It appears to be common knowledge for the Cofán that *Yagé* is their guiding force, which may have also been helping everyone to navigate the unfolding of the ethnobotanical project.

4.1. Mutual learning: an ethnobotanical protocol and 'los Invisibles'

After the overall community had consented the proposed work, a research agreement was signed by the Cofán authorities, an Institutional Review Board was granted by the North Carolina State University and the collecting permits were issued through the Universidad Nacional de Colombia (the National University of Colombia), the home institution of COL as well as David and Iván during their undergraduate studies. The Cofán authorities facilitated the coordination of the specific Cofán participants accompanying the research collaboration (*Don Alvaro*, who was to lead it, and three community members who were to assist with the logistics in the field) as well as the gathering of the necessary supplies.

Two days before this collaboration, David and his field collaborators (Iván and two other colleagues) participated in a *Yagé* ceremony led by the maximum spiritual authority of the Cofán community in preparation for the fieldwork. That ceremony was further part of the protocol required by the Cofán authorities for the maximum spiritual authority to request permission from the supernatural entities of the territory known as "*los Invisibles*"—"the Invisible ones" (see the entry "supernatural" in the Preface)—to endorse the field trip to take place.

Just before embarking on the field, David and the field co-laborers were surprised to learn that the elder leading the research collaboration had not been present in the prior community meetings, yet he had been appointed to this role by the Cofán authorities, and he had eagerly accepted the invitation. Despite this surprise, the first field journey started very smoothly. Just as the field crew entered the protected territory of the Cofán, a troop of *bosilecho* monkeys approached them with curiosity in *what felt* like a greeting and a good omen. After several hours hiking in the woods, they reached the Cofán temporary settlement in the depths of the forest, and in the afternoon, they started the exploration of the area, seeking wild *Yagé* lianas. In a couple of hours, *Don Alvaro* found three wild *Yagé* lianas, and David, with his field collaborators, started to collect the liana's ecological data.

At night, David conducted an ethnobotanical semi-structured interview with the elder, documenting his life history with each wild *Yagé* variety that was found, in addition to the ethnoecological knowledge and the cultivation and/or harvesting practice. But the main emphasis centered on the characteristics that enabled the elder to tell each *Yagé* variety apart from each other and from the numerous other lianas in the forest. The following day, David set up tree climbing stations and climbed each liana's host trees to collect samples of the stems and of the leaves, flowers and fruits, which were located at the liana's apex, about 90 ft from the forest floor. Additionally, he harvested the lianas stem cuttings for *Don Alvaro* to use in the preparation of the *Yagé* drinks for the field ceremonies, but also for *Don Alvaro* to bring back and for the community to employ in their *Yagé* restoration efforts.

Although at first there seemed to be no misunderstandings in the field, the *Yagé* ceremonies and subsequent conversations with the accompanying Cofán members indicated that neither the elder leading the field collaboration nor "*los Invisibles*" were fully aware of the overall research that had been endorsed by the Cofán community and authorities. Thus, the ongoing work had not been yet "approved" by the supernatural entities of the territory, who, we hypothesize, are acknowledged by the Cofán as the legitimate owners (see the entry "supernatural" in the Preface) of the territory. In other words, despite the research agreement and protocols established up to that point with the human members of the community, the ultimate crucial permission, given by "*los Invisibles*," was pending.

At the last ceremony in the field, right before dawn, one of the Cofán collaborators called David outside of the ceremonial house, breaking the news "that *los Invisibles* had 'approved' the project." But he and his field collaborators "had to make sure to walk righteously, for *los Invisibles* were the owners (see the entry "supernatural" in the Preface) and masters of the territory and they could harm anyone who disobeyed their command." Never did they imagine during their research training that they needed to learn how to collaborate with supernatural entities to successfully complete a scientific work. The "unknowns" are too many to try to unravel. In short, the research protocol required trust in both directions and, more importantly, a humble acknowledgment of the limits of what we could know and the certainty that each other's knowledge was essential to carry out the project—even if the other's knowledge challenges our assumptions about what counts as knowledge.

In our all-too-human perspective, "knowing something well," that is, having complete or close to complete information, is essential to reaching "good" decisions, insofar as those decisions ensue the act of "knowing something well." However, information *is not always* essential for decision-making in cases where the *will* of a nonhuman party is essential for that decision to unfold: We, humans, may "make" decisions in contexts where our all-too-human knowledge can be put on hold, or even be yielded to the will of a more powerful being.

Decisions can sometimes be unexpected. Not knowing something, for example, ignoring who the agent is in a particular decisional field, can be crucial for decision-making. However, not knowing is not equivalent to ignoring, but rather to understanding the limits of what we can possibly *know*. After all, we cannot know the "invisible ones" by their forms, but rather by their effects: what they command is tangible in the everyday world. In fact, knowledge and/or information can be highly irrelevant in these contexts. Contrary to most agency theory, decisions sometimes precede information. However, this does not mean that these decisions are arbitrary or blind. This means that human language and decisions could find their limits in forms of decision-making that involve beings that *we can't fully know*—or that is better not to know at all, but rather to acknowledge and respect as a practice of an ecological ethics for our times.

5. "*Pedir permiso*": making decisions with "*los Invisibles*"

"We must ask permission from the invisibles ones for anything," said *Don Rogelio*, an Cofán *seguidor*,[7] after a four-hour trek from the community's municipality to their *Resguardo* up in the mountains where the whole community used to live before they migrated to the municipality several years ago to be closer to the health system and the school for their children.[8] We crossed the main river in a *tarabita*, a wire cable with a hanging basket (i.e., a cable car basket) to carry passengers and things across. Who are "*los Invisibles*"?

The following are some accounts by members of the Cofán people of Nariño with whom we interacted during the summer of 2019. They do not define who the invisible ones are, but rather express a mode of engagement with a place and the mandates and obligations concerning the care of the territory. This selection of local claims about the invisible ones expresses a normative language. To be sure, the invisible people seem to come into being as they allow or prohibit certain behaviors. These mandates, however, may not be reduced to their symbolic (human) expression: they may go beyond the propositional form of the law—in what we call a "law beyond the human" (Vargas-Roncancio et al. 2021)—and may therefore be woven into a territorial tapestry of living beings of which the invisible people seem to be a key constituent. Furthermore, the notion of the "invisible ones" is akin to what Varela calls "self-less selves" in the groundbreaking "Organism: A Meshwork of Selfless Selves" (1991). We might then ask, are "the invisible ones" emergent properties of the forest? Are they emergent properties of the interaction between Indigenous practices, plants, traditional medics, ethnobotanists, lawyers and the forest as a larger self? (Kohn 2013).

According to our interlocutors, "*los Invisibles*" are the owners of the territory and the plants that grow there (see the entry "supernatural" in the Preface), and we are all obliged to ask their permission before entering the territory. To ask permission, however, we need the mediation of the most respected and powerful medicine men (*abuelos mayores)* of the community. The *abuelos mayores* "communicate" this request for permission through the ingestion of the *Yagé* plant as part of what we call a relational protocol.[9] While asking for permission is the act of using symbolic language, it is also about a corporeal disposition (Echeverry and Kinerai 1993) or mode of engagement with other bodies through ingestion rather than representation (Vargas 2021): "How to ask permission?" we asked. "Well, just asking," the *abuela* replied.

However, the act of using symbolic language is not necessarily the best way to obtain permission from "*los Invisibles*." In our view, a crucial element of this relational protocol might be the cosmological translation of the

Table 4.1 A normative voice of "*los Invisibles*": a cosmological ventriloquism

Statement	*Normative function*
1. "The invisible ones **left me** necklaces and designs."—**Abuela Mariela**	1. Donation (invisible ones making gifts) (see the entry "spirit" in the Preface)
2. "When a person enters the territory, **they must ask permission** from its owners: the invisible ones. **Entering the territory without permission can bring unexpected consequences."** Associated with this are special care practices in handling plants. Here is a valuable normative source in regards to plants (mandates and prohibitions): "**do not go over** the plant; women **should not cook** Yagé; the **researcher should not harvest a wild plant without permission** from the invisible ones; the plant should not be removed from the territory." (Field notes, Southern Colombia, 2019)	2. Permission to do something/duty to consult prohibition of trespassing (the invisible people seem to prohibit access to their territory or to permit certain actions/*invisibles* as property owners
3. "It is not necessary to protect something that is **already being protected** by the invisible people."—Walter	3. Guardianship/mandate/ tutelage (the invisible ones seem to protect the interests of the territory as their owners) (see the entry "supernatural" in the Preface)
4. "Even the **invisible know**. They are present in our conversations. Perhaps they are also reading these lines that you are writing."—**Doña Yenni.** This does not mean that in the plane of daily life there is no permanent invocation of the spirits or the invisible, as **Doña Y** says: "The **invisible know** what we are talking about." (Field notes, Southern Colombia, 2019)	4. Witness/hearsay (the invisible ones seem to be witnesses)
5. "A research experience requires a strong agreement. **How can the invisible ones access the terms of this agreement**? How do you know if they agree to continue this work?" (Field notes, Southern Colombia, 2019)	5. Agreement/contract (the invisibles negotiate the terms of a relation or contract
6. "This breath (*soplo*) is to ask for protection and permission now that we enter the sacred territory of the Cofán whose spiritual owners are the invisible people who live in invisible citadels in the jungle." **Don Alvaro**	6. Prohibition of trespassing

(*Continued*)

Table 4.1 (Continued)

Statement	*Normative function*
7. "You have to **cover the food so that the invisible ones don't take it away**."—A **Doña Yenni**	7. Stealing (the invisible ones steal human property)
8. "The **invisible beings are ancestral grandparents of the Cofán** people who are living here and **did not allow themselves to be dominated by the Spaniards**. They are people like us [says the grandmother] . . . **they have their crops. They put feathers in their noses, they do their celebrations**. The grandmother was given a necklace at a Yagé ceremony and the invisible ones have a big maloca. There are bad invisible people and good invisible people. . . . Because of envy there are bad guys. They have their crops of cassava, chili . . . tobacco. [The grandmother] has been invited to celebrations with the invisible ones and they have painted faces . . . they also have a place to bathe. It seems that some invisible people steal children too." ***Don Alvaro***	8. Kinship relations/ inheritance/bequest (the invisible ones may be grandparents. Humans inherit their qualities and things)/gifting (see the entry "spirit" in the Preface)/kidnapping (invisible may steal human children)
9. "Grandma M told us about the invisible ones . . . they are ancestral people who live in big malocas and who allow us to be here today. "How to ask permission?" I ask. "Well, just asking," says the grandmother." (Field notes, Southern Colombia, 2019).	9. Kinship relations/duty to consult
10. "All morning it has rained. D wants to go out to climb the same tree as yesterday. *A* and the *abuelo* try to dissuade him by telling him stories of people to whom the invisible ones" untied the knots they made to climb up a tree and then they fell down." The grandfather also talks about a wild Yagé that is invisible. This plant cannot be found" (Field notes, Southern Colombia, 2019).	10. Injury/torts (invisible ones may injure humans)
11. "The grandfather talks about the many **spiritual wars** that he has waged to defeat his enemies. In one of those *rascas* (Yagé nigths), the Yagé showed the invisible beings who gave grandfather a *chonta* delivered in a precious box." (Field notes, Southern Colombia, 2019)	11. Self-defense/ proportionality/gifting (see the entry "spirit" in the Preface)
12. "If the invisible did not agree of your presence here it would be bad for us." **Abuela Mariela**	12. Consent (invisible people allow the presence of humans in their territory)

invisibles' will, which the elder performs during a *Yagé* ceremony as shown in Table 4.2:

Table 4.2 The *Yagé* as an interface between the human and the invisible people

"Invisible peoples" ↔ **Plant** (*Yagé*) ↔ humans (*abuelo mayor*)

"Making things right for the project," as David would put it, evokes a normative principle of sorts. According to this principle, the scientific method in ethnobotany and the relational protocol with the Cofán community and their more-than-human kin must work in tandem. To be sure, the ethnobotanical research protocol may well exceed the expectations of the plants' taxonomy or even a policy catalogue of best sustainability practices. Ultimately, we hypothesized that our field research was about different ways of encountering and interpreting (or even failing to interpret *correctly*) the will of human and other-than-human beings making this territorial tapestry of selves as they co-intervene in a decision-making process, aka granting permission to conduct ethnobotanical research.

In fact, we came to understand, provisionally, that David's ethnobotanical work would have been unthinkable without this "permission from the invisible ones": a piece of protocol that certainly exceeded language (scientific and otherwise) and the act of naming, and instead required the body and the act of ingesting another as a self: a bodily practice crucial to learning place and performing authority. Such permission refers to the limits and possibilities of what we conceptualize as "invisible legalities," that is, a series of mandates to do (or not) something in the territory that are neither reducible to the symbolic (Kohn 2013) nor to the mechanisms of human political deliberation (Blaser 2019; De la Cadena 2010). For the purposes of the ethnobotanical research agreement, these sources of authority to conduct a research project on the ethnovarieties of a ritual plant may have depended on a sentient and cognitive territory, although "*los Invisibles*" emerged through human symbolic language as well (see Table 4.1).

Perhaps here is where we both found our own limits to "knowing" radically different alterities (Caicedo 2015): "It is not necessary to protect something that is already being protected by the invisible people" and "even the invisible know," said an Cofán community member. These statements—which also are formal legal mandates—emerge via everyday encounters between humans and those "beings who may seem invisible to us, and yet have a word or two about how things should be done."[10]

While "*los Invisibles*" could grant permission to actively do things in their territory, they may have prohibited certain behaviors as well: "the *abuelo* tried to dissuade him by telling him stories of people to whom the invisible ones untied the knots they made to climb up a tree and then they fell down."

Table 4.3 Norms as relations between invisible people and traditional practitioners

"Invisible peoples" ↔ **norms** ↔ humans

For example, one **cannot** step or "go over the plant," or "women **should not** cook *Yagé*," or participate in a ceremony when they are menstruating (Cepek 2012, 2018; Caicedo 2015). Concerning David's interest to perform ethnobotanical research activities in the territory, "*los Invisibles*" seem to prohibit "harvesting a wild plant without their permission."

While these rules and prohibitions can be understood as binding cultural protocols at the local level, they must also be followed by anyone outside the community, and, in that sense, these rules are binding on everyone: they seem to be the law of the place (see Chapter 1). Moreover, these norms are not, simply put, a set of "cultural beliefs" of a particular community of humans, because they may also establish ecological functions of significant importance such as restricting the overexploitation of wild varieties of the sacred plant. In this sense, these norms may exemplify an ecological characteristic of the law beyond the exclusive attribution of human meaning (see Table 4.3).[11]

Again, who are "*los Invisibles*"? What is their ontological status? In what sense can they be considered as existent in the context of the ethnobotanical research protocol? Do "*los Invisibles*" matter for the law beyond the recognition of their official legal "status" as "local cultural beliefs" or "immaterial patrimony" within the conventional multicultural Constitution?[12] Viveiros de Castro explores the ontology of Amazonian spirits (2007) among the Yanomami:

> For the Yanomami "(w)e could say that the xapiripë [los invisibles, for the Cofán community members] is the name of the disjunctive synthesis that connects-separates the actual [the actual being and the normative expression of mandated behavior that emanates from her, for example, the obligation to ask permission to the invisibles to undergo any kind of "research"] and the virtual, the discrete and the continuous, the edible and the cannibal, the prey and the predator. . . . **A spirit in Amazonia is less a thing than an image . . . less an object than an event, less a transcendental figure than a sign of the immanent universal background**—the background comes to the surface in shamanism, in dreams and in hallucinations, human and the more-than-human, the visible and invisible trade places [it can be said that certain norms are given in a Yagé ceremony]. A 'spirit', in sum, is less a 'spirit' in opposition to an in-material body than a dynamic and intensive corporality . . . displaying sometimes terrifying appearance, superb body ornamentation, perfume, beauty. . . . In sum, a constitutive rather than a negation of corporality: **a spirit is something**

> **body insofar as it possesses too many bodies, capable of different corporal forms.** The interval between any two bodies rather than a non-body or no body.
>
> (Viveiros de Castro 2007, 20–21. Our highlights)

In the process of making the ethnobotanical protocol with the Cofán community, we came to believe that the invisibility of "*los Invisbles*" had less to do with our human sensory-motor capacities to perceive them as coherent external (to us) substances: "A spirit in Amazonia is less a thing than an image . . . less an object than an event, less a transcendental figure than a sign of the immanent universal background." Perhaps, the invisibility of "*los Invisbles*" had more to do with our (in)capacity to engage with what we can call the local coherence or socio-ecological efficaciousness of these in-between kind of *existents* as they participate in everyday situations by allowing or prohibiting certain behaviors, or even becoming involved in local decisions through human-plant assemblages.

This ability to "access," so to speak, the local coherence of the invisible people seems to be widely available in the Cofán community through dreams, images, symbolic language, material culture and, of course, ceremonial experiences with plants (on dreams see Poirier 2003, 2012). Insofar as "*los Invisibles*" come into being in all these different non-symbolic ways that nonetheless may also achieve a symbolic form (i.e., a mandate to do something in the forest), their social presence can be recognized as the law of the place, that is, a set of norms and procedures for making local decisions concerning the territory.

Therefore, "*los Invisibles*" may have more of a territorial existence anchored in concrete practices with other human and more-than-human selves than a metaphysical one separated from these practices; more of a socio-ecological immanence oriented toward cultural resilience and autonomy than a transcendental presence imposed by a constitutionally mandated "cultural value." In this sense, "*los Invisibles*" may be political beings performing a kind of politics of survival in multicultural contexts: "[t]he invisible beings are ancestral grandparents of the Cofán people who are living here and did not allow themselves to be dominated by the Spaniards," *Abuelo* Rogelio reminds us.

5.1. The legalities of the invisible

What has all this got to do with the law? Although representative democracy manifests itself the *spirit of democracy* through aggregate social behaviors (i.e., individual votes), the act of conjuring or calling upon in a *Yagé* ceremony may also enable the invisibles of the forest a to live through recursive territorial practice that is crucially contingent upon the material realities of the territory itself (i.e., the ecological availability of *Yagé* lianas). In these practices, invisibilities and materialities may be all essential to make decisions about/with the territory as a living, sentient and cognitive self (*Devenir Universidad*, 2021). However, here the "social" must not be equated with the (modern) social: this social (or rather socioecological) immanence of spirit life comprises all sorts of more-than-human agencies simply because all existents are or *can be* persons.

In this sense, Viveiros de Castro suggests that if all existents are not necessarily *de facto* persons, "the fundamental point is that there is *de jure* nothing to prevent any species or mode of being *[including invisible peoples]* from having that status" (Viveiros de Castro 2014, 58). A clear example of this is the rights of nature's clause where bundles of natural entities—from rivers to ecosystems—receive a personality of sorts to be considered existent before state law.

The problem, however, is not one of taxonomy and classification *only*. For example, in the case of the creation of the ethnobotanical protocol with the Cofán, the issue was not so much identifying *new* wild species of medicinal plants in their territory, but about determining whether the so-called "scientific expertise" was able to contribute with the protection of the territory by rendering visible these "unknown" (for western science) varieties of the "sacred plant" while at the same time purportedly integrating the local protocol or law of the place that required asking permission from "*los Invisibles*." (See Table 4.1.).

Perspectives, we suggest—including the point of view of "*los Invisibles*"—are not essences of a territory out there, but emergent attributes that are highly dependent on emplaced relationships (Blaser 2019). For example, we cannot claim that "*los Invisibles*" are always persons, that is, existents with the capacity to authorize and/or deny certain behaviors such as conducting a piece of research about *Yagé* (*B. caapi*) varieties in the wild. The *Invisibles*' capacity to act seem to emerge via the encounter with the human who "surrenders his or her will" to the *Invisibles* through the ingestion of the plant. To "access" spirit life and "negotiate" or even surrender our will to them, we must drink *Yagé* as a formal legal protocol to co-create the ethnobotanical agreement.

In this sense, learning or encountering this *other kind of law* and the principles it entails as one negotiates (or surrenders one's will to) with invisible peoples requires the act of carefully listening to these "others" with whom we share the territory. The ingestion of plants seems to be a vehicle for this kind of radical legal listening in this particular territory. As ***Abuela M*** narrates:

> They are people like us . . . **they have their crops. They put feathers in their noses, they do their celebrations.** I was given a necklace at a *Yagé* ceremony, and the invisible ones have a big maloca. There are bad invisible people and good invisible people. . . . Because of envy there are bad guys. They have their own crops of cassava, chili . . . tobacco. . . . I have

> been invited to celebrations with the invisible ones and they have painted faces . . . they also have a place to bathe. Some invisible people steal children too.

One may then assume that "*los Invisibles*" co-produce norms, or that all these "cultural features" are embodied forms of the social rules and conventions the territory-as-person lives by. What is the law from the vantage point or perspective of an *invisible* that might see us, "humans," as prey or (if we are lucky) persons? These legalities of "*los Invisibles*" complicate law and ecological knowledge in several ways in this region. Furthermore, they question our positionalities and roles as researchers attempting to translate complex cultural ways of life into a language distant from appropriation, and to give weight to an understanding of the world that may help us confront "Western" domination (Nadasdy 2003).

Concluding remarks

This chapter concerned the entangled lives of law and ecology in Amazonia, and we've focused on two main aspects of this assemblage: (1) how plants as persons may become part of a larger conversation about knowledge and world-making in this region, and (2) how may we come to learn the legal mandates that emerge from encounters with different beings of the forest. To probe this relationship between law and ecology, we have focused on the making of an ethnobotanical research agreement concerning wild varieties of the *Yagé* vine in the Cofán ancestral territory. This protocol or agreement seems to have involved the contested participation of human and more-than-human agencies including the plant as person.

There were, however, multiple epistemological, ethical and methodological challenges in the process of creating this legal artifact, for example, how may "*los Invisibles*" mediate norms for doing or not doing something in the forest? How can we know (or not) this? Rather than answering this difficult set of questions—which confronts us with the limits of our own knowledge "as long as we dare to ask the question"—this chapter has suggested, among other things, that the ingestion of plants as people may be a form of participation in the making of science and law (i.e., an ethnobotanical protocol) in one A´i community of Nariño. This participation is widely distributed and may involve more-than-human beings and thus may challenge the epistemic and ontological closure of symbolic forms of representation.

Furthermore, we suggest that the state may take these hypothetical broader forms of scientific and legal participation seriously when proposing viable models of intercultural environmental governance for this region (Nadasdy 2003). What we call the "legalities of the invisible," which state law has confined to the status of myth or cultural belief—that is, the purported mandates of the invisible people—are bound to place and yet may not lose their potential generalizing properties. A scientific and juridical theory and practice for this region must therefore probe the limits and possibilities of engagement with the cosmological, biological and "spiritual" (see the entry "spirit" in the Preface) life of a place. For example, beyond multicultural frameworks, state law may consider the serious implications of the law of place for emerging constitutional and legal articulations of the rights of nature.

Some questions emerged that intend to account for our experience of *Yagé* as a plant, protocol and life practice in the context of the making of an ethnobotanical research protocol with one Cofán community in Southern Colombia:

- Was partaking in *Yagé* ceremonies a legitimate and rather key approach to the study of this plant-human interaction? Was the first-person study with *Yagé* insufficient to the central questions of ethnobotany and the question outlined in this ethnobotanical collaboration? Is the standard ethnobotanical training missing to incorporate a crucial piece to further problematize and attempt to understand the human-plant relationship?
- Should the Cofán assessment about the researcher and the potential collaboration, hypothetically conducted during the *Yagé* ceremonies, be considered a protocol in its own right? Should the participation of the researcher in *Yagé* ceremonies be a requirement in studies with the Cofán in this community and in the Cofán nation at large? Are the research ethics of cultural studies missing to broaden their concepts of protocols, methods and agreements to articulate their own approach and work with local "cultures"? What happens with the words "research" and "researcher" after (*Yagé*) ingestion as method?
- Would the answers to these questions foster a decolonizing practice to conduct locally pertinent and methodologically open *Yagé* and other kinds of studies? How can we situate the word "research" in the context of a pervasive cognitive extractivism in Amazonia? Questions abound, and for us they will remain open to debate for years to come.

Notes

1 See *Unión de Médicos Indígenas Yajeceros de la Amazonía Colombiana*-UMIYAC (2000). *El Pensamiento de los Mayores. Código de Ética de la Medicina Indígena del Piedemonte Amazónico Colombiano*. Mocoa: UMIYAC. Available: https://umiyac.org/ (Visited 08.08.2021).

2 The traditional Amazonian Yagé or Ayahuasca ceremony has been practiced by several Indigenous peoples for several centuries and possibly since pre-Columbian times (Tupper 2006; Brabec de Mori 2011; Samorini 2014; Samorini 2015; Torres 2018; Samorini 2019a; Samorini 2019b; Brabec de Mori 2020). In this ceremony, a brew concocted from the stems of the Yagé liana (*Banisteriopsis caapi*) mixed with the leaves of the chakruna/pinta/chagropanga/oprito shrub (*Psychotria viridis* Ruiz & Pav.) is employed (Pinkley 1973; Schultes and Raffauf 1990; Schultes

et al. 2001). The term ayahuasca has been translated from the Quechua as the 'vine of the soul,' yet Highpine (2012) argues that 'vine *with* a soul' may be more adequate. Furthermore, ayahuasca is a term applied to signify the shamanic practice, the ceremony, the drink and the liana. The name chakruna comes from the verb 'chaqruy' and the verb root 'chakru' meaning 'to mix' (Highpine 2012), also from the Quechua language.

3 In the regions of Putumayo and Nariño, *Taita* is a term used by several Indigenous groups as a title of respect of political and spiritual leaders who have undergone the rigorous, demanding, and long training for mastering the Yagé practice. The equivalent word in A'ingae is atesu'cho, knowledge-able one (Cepek 2018). The word "shaman," commonly used as a synonym of Taita, has been rejected by multiple Taitas in the Colombian Amazon Piedmont given its colonial underpinnings (UMIYAC 2000). We use different names to protect the identity of our interlocutors.

4 After this visit, an additional meeting was conducted in June, 2019, to reiterate and document the consented decision to carry out the collaboration, and the terms under it was to be conducted. Furthermore, an Institutional Review Board from the North Carolina State University was granted.

5 An administrative/political council of a recognized Indigenous territory.

6 According to Cepek (Personal comm., 2021), in A'ingae language there is no clear reference to a Yagé spirit or spirits, but rather to "Yagé a'i" —i.e., Yagé people— present in the Yagé drunkness/inebriation (See the entry "supernatural" and "spirit" in the Preface).

7 *Seguirdor*: person who has the power to heal with plants but that is not yet considered a *Taita or atesu'cho* (Cepek 2018).

8 Conversation between David Rodriguez and Doña Y. Field notes, Nariño 2019.

9 The forest communicates agreement in other ways: rain, footprints of animals, the presence or absence of game, etc. The best way is by asking the plant and their related supernatural entities in a Yagé ceremony.

10 A.A, Nariño, 2019. For a discussion about the ontology of spirit life in Amazonia see Viveiros de Castro (2007).

11 On the ecological functions of ritual see Grimes, R. 2003. "Ritual and the Environment." In *The Editorial Board of the Sociological Review*. Oxford: Blackwell.

12 See Art. 7, Colombia's Constitution of 1991: "The State recognizes and protects the ethnic and cultural diversity of the Colombian Nation." Heller, Anna I. Vellve Torras, and Max Planck Institute). www.constituteproject.org/constitution/Colombia_2005.pdf (Accessed 9 November 2020).

References

Beyer, S.V. 2010. *Singing to the Plants: A Guide to Mestizo Shamanism in the Upper Amazon*. Albuquerque: UNM Press.

Blaser, M. 2013. "Ontological Conflicts and the Stories of Peoples In Spite of Europe: Towards a Conversation on Political Ontology." Accepted for publication in *Current Anthropology*, 54(5): 547–568.

Blaser, M. 2019. "On the Properly Political (Disposition for the) Anthropocene." *Anthropological Theory*, 19(1): 74–94.

Brabec de Mori, B. 2011. "Tracing Hallucinations. Contributing to a Critical Ethnohistory of Ayahuasca Usage in the Peruvian Amazon." In Labate, Beatriz C., and Jungaberle, Henrik (éds.). *The Internationalization of Ayahuasca*. Zürich: LIT-Verlag, pp. 23–47.

Brabec de Mori, B. 2020. *Is Ayahuasca Possibly Less than Five Hundred Years Old?* https://chacruna.net/is-ayahuasca-possibly-less-than-five-hundred-years-old/ (Accessed 5 February 2021).
Caicedo, Alhena. 2015. *La Alteridad Radical que Cura. Neo-chamanismos yageceros en Colombia*. Bogota: Universidad de los Andes.
Cardoso, D., Särkinen, T., Alexander, S., Amorim, A.M., Bittrich, V., Celis, M., . . . and Forzza, R.C. 2017. "Amazon Plant Diversity Revealed by a Taxonomically Verified Species List." *Proceedings of the National Academy of Sciences*, 114(40): 10695–10700.
Cepek, M.L. 2012. *A Future for Amazonia*. Austin: University of Texas Press.
Cepek, M.L. 2018. *Life in Oil: Cofán Survival in the Petroleum Fields of Amazonia*. Austin: University of Texas Press.
Clark, K.E., Hilton, R.G., West, A.J., Malhi, Y., Grocke, D.R., Bryant, C.L., Ascough, P.L., Robles, A.C., and New, M. 2013. "New Views on 'Old' Carbon in the Amazon River: Insight from the Source of Organic Carbon Eroded from the Peruvian Andes." *Geochemistry, Geophysics, Geosystems*, 14: 1644–1659.
Clark, K.E., Torres, M.A., West, A.J., Hilton, R.G., New, M., Horwath, A.B., Fisher, J.B., Rapp, J.R., Caceres, A.R., and Malhi, Y. 2014. "The Hydrological Regime of a Forested Tropical Andean Valley." *Hydrology and Earth System Sciences Discussions*, 11: 8603–8650.
Controlled Susbstance Act (CSA). Pub L. 91–513, 84 Stat. 1236, Enacted October 27, 1970, Codified at 21 U.S.C. 801 et. seq. Is the Statute Establishing Federal U.S. Drug Policy Underwhich the Manufacture, Importation, Posseon, Use and Distrubution of Certain Substances Is Regulated.
De la Cadena, M. 2010. "Indigenous Cosmopolitics in the Andes: Conceptual Reflections Beyond Politics Beyond Politics as Usual." *Cultural Anthropology*, 25(2).
De la Cadena, M. 2015. *Earth Beings: Ecologies of Practice Across Andean Worlds*. Durham: Duke University Press.
De la Cadena, M., and Blaser, M. 2018. *A World of Many Worlds*. Durham: Duke University Press.
De Montesquieu, C. 1989. *Montesquieu: The Spirit of the Laws*. Cambridge: Cambridge University Press.
Descola, P. 2013. *Beyond Nature and Culture*. Chicago: University of Chicago Press.
Echeverry, Juan Alvaro, and Kinerai, Hipolito Candre. 1993. *Tabaco Frío. Coca Dulce. Palabras del Anciano Kinerai de la Tribu Cananguchal para sanar y alegrar el corazón de sus huérfanos*. Bogota: Concultura.
Escobar, Arturo. 2018. *Designs for the Pluriverse: Radical Interdependence, Autonomy and the Making of Worlds*. Durham, NC: Duke University Press.
Gagliano, M. 2018. *Thus Spoke the Plants. A Remarkable Journey of Groundbreaking Scientific Discoveries and Personal Encounters with Plants*. Berkeley: North Atlantic Books.
Gates, B. 1982. "Banisteriopsis, Diplopterys (Malpighiaceae)." *Flora Neotropica*, 30: 1–237.
Grimes, R. 2003. "Ritual and the Environment." In *The Editorial Board of the Sociological Review*. Oxford: Blackwell.
Highpine, G. 2012. *Unraveling the Mystery of the Origin of Ayahuasca. Núcleo de Estudos Interdisciplinares Sobre Psicoativos* (NEIP). www.neip.info

Jütte, M. 2016. *Reisende im Strom der Zeit: zum Yagé (Ayahuasca)—Gebrauch der kolumbianischen Cofán* (vol. 64). Münster: LIT Verlag.

Kohn, E. 2013. *How Forest Think. Toward and Anthropology Beyond the Human.* Berkeley, CA: University of California Press.

Kuhn, T.S. 2012. *The Structure of Scientific Revolutions. 50th Anniversary.* Chicago: University of Chicago Press.

Lakatos, I. 1989. "La historia de la ciencia y sus reconstrucciones racionales." En *La metodología de los programas de investigación científica.* Madrid: Alianza Editorial, pp. 134–179.

Lakatos, I., and Feyerabend, P. 2001. *For and Against Method: Including Lakatos's Lectures on Scientific Method and the Lakatos-Feyerabend Correspondence.* Chicago: University of Chicago Press.

Lampe, J.R. 2021. *The Controlled Substances Act (CSA): A Legal Overview for the 117th Congress.* Washington: Congressional Research Service.

Luizão, Flávio J., et al. 2007. "Soil Acidity and Nutrient Deficiency in Central Amazonian Heath Forest Soils." *Plant Ecology*, 192(2), Springer: 209–224. www.jstor.org/stable/40212962.

Luna, L.E. 1984. "The Concept of Plants as Teachers Among Four Mestizo Shamans of Iquitos, Northeastern Peru." *Journal of Ethnopharmacology*, 11(2): 135–156.

Mignolo, W. 2011. *The Darker Side of Western Modernity. Global Futures, Decolonial Options.* Durham: Duke University Press.

Nadasdy, P. 2003. *Hunters and Bureaucrats: Power, Knowledge, and Aboriginal-State Relations in the Southwest Yukon.* Vancouver: UBC Press.

Oliveira, R.C., Fagg, C.W., Labate, B., and Sonsin, J.O. 2018. *The Urgent Need to Review the Botanical Classification of the Ayahuasca Vine.* https://chacruna.net/urgent-botanical-classification-ayahuasca/ (Accessed 22 July 2020).

Pinkley, H.V. 1973. *The Ethno-Ecology of the Cofán Indians.* Doctoral Dissertation. Harvard University Press, Cambridge, MA.

Poirier, S. 2003. "'This Is Good Country. We Are Good Dreamers'. Dreams and Dreaming in the Australian Western Desert." In Lohmann, R. (dir.). *Dream Travelers. Sleep Experiences and Culture in the Western Pacific.* New York: Palgrave Macmillan, pp. 107–125.

Poirier, S. 2012. "Dreams and Dreaming in the Australian Western Desert." In Barrett, D., and McNamara, P. (dirs.). *Encyclopedia of Sleep and Dreams.* Westport: Praeger Press.

Pollan, M. 2019. *How to Change Your Mind: What the New Science of Psychedelics Teaches Us About Consciousness, Dying, Addiction, Depression, and Transcendence.* London: Penguin Books.

Popper, K. 2012. *In Search of a Better World: Lectures and Essays from Thirty Years.* New York: Routledge.

Ranciere, J. 2004. *Dis-agreement. Politics and Philosophy.* Minneapolis: Minnesota University Press.

Restrepo, E., and Escobar, A. 2005. "Other Anthropologies and Anthropology Otherwise' Steps to a World Anthropologies Framework." *Critique of Anthropology*, 25(2): 99–129.

Samorini, G. 2014. "Aspectos y problemas de la arqueología de las drogas sudamericanas." *Cultura y Droga*, 19(21): 13–34.

Samorini, G. 2015. *Acerca de la presencia de beta-carbolinas en tejidos biológicos de los hallazgos arqueológicos sudamericanos.* www.samorini.it

Samorini, G. 2019a. "The Oldest Archeological Data Evidencing the Relationship of Homo Sapiens with Psychoactive Plants: A Worldwide Overview." *Journal of Psychedelic Studies*, 3(2): 63–80.

Samorini, G. 2019b. *Fake News About Ayahuasca's Archeological Antiquity*. https://chacruna.net/fake-news-about-ayahuascas-archeological-antiquity/ (Accessed 5 February 2021).

Schultes, R.E., Hofmann, A., and Ratsch, C. 2001. *Plants of the Gods: Their Sacred, Healing, and Hallucinogenic Powers* (revised ed.). Rochester, VT: Healing Arts Press.

Schultes, R.E., and Raffauf, R.F. 1990. *The Healing Forest: Medicinal and Toxic Plants of the Northwest Amazonia*. Portland: Dioscorides Press.

Thompson, K.-L., Lantz, T., and Ban, N.C. 2020. "A Review of Indigenous Knowledge and Participation in Environmental Monitoring." *Ecology and Society*, 25(2): 10.

Torres, C.M. 2018. "The Origins of the Ayahuasca/Yagé Concept. An Inquiry into the Synergy between Dimethyltryptamine and Beta-Carbolines." In *Ancient Psychoactive Substances*. Gainsville: University Press of Florida.

Torres, M.A., West, A.J., and Clark, K.E. 2015. "Geomorphic Regime Modulates Hydrologic Control of Chemical Weathering in the Andes-Amazon." *Geochimica et Cosmochimica Acta*, 166: 105–128.

Tupper, K.W. 2006. "The Globalization of Ayahuasca: Harm Reduction or Benefit Maximization?" *International Journal of Drug Policy*, 19(4): 297–303.

Unión de Médicos Indígenas Yageceros de la Amazonía Colombiana-UMIYAC. 2000. *El Pensamiento de los Mayores. Código de Ética de la Medicina Indígena del Piedemonte Amazónico Colombiano*. https://umiyac.org/

Van Leeuwen, N. 2018. "The Factual Belief Fallacy." *Contemporary Pragmatism*, 15(3): 319–343.

Van Vliet, N., L'haridon, L., Gomez, J., Vanegas, L., Sandrin, F., and Nasi, R. 2017. "The Use of Traditional Ecological Knowledge in the Context of Participatory Wildlife Management: Examples From Indigenous Communities in Puerto Nariño, Amazonas-Colombia." In Nóbrega Alves, Rômulo Romeu, and Albuquerque, Ulysses Paulino (eds.). *Ethnozoology: Animals in Our Lives*. Cambridge, MA: Academic Press.

Varela, Francisco. 1991. "Organism: A Meshwork of Selfless Selves." In Tauber, A.I. (ed.). *Organism and the Origins of Self*. Boston Studies in the Philosophy of Science (vol. 129). Dordrecht: Springer.

Varela, Franciso, Thompson, Evan, and Rosch, Eleanor. 1991. *The Embodied Mind: Cognitive Science and Human Experience*. Cambridge, MA: MIT Press.

Vargas Roncancio, Iván D. 2021. *The Legal Lives of Forests: Law and the Other-Than-Human in the Andes-Amazon, Colombia. An Anthropological and Legal Theory Approach*. Doctoral Dissertation. McGill University, Montreal.

Vargas Roncancio, Iván D., Grear, Anna, Boulot, Emille, and Sterlin, Joshua (eds.). 2021. *Posthuman Legalities: New Materialism and Law Beyond the Human*. Cheltenham and Northampton: Edward Elgar Press.

Viveiros de Castro, Eduardo. 1998. "Cosmological Diexis and Amerindian Perspectivism." *Journal of the Royal Anthropological Institute*, 4(3): 469–489.

Viveiros de Castro, Eduardo. 2004. "Perspectival Anthropology and the Method of Controlled Equivocation." *Tipití: Journal of the Society for the Anthropology of Lowland South America*, 2(1).

Viveiros de Castro, Eduardo. 2007. "The Crystal Forest." *Inner Asia*, 9: 13–33.
Viveiros de Castro, Eduardo. 2014. *Cannibal Metaphysics*. Minneapolis: Univocal.
Weiskopf, Jimmy. 2002. *Yagé: El Nuevo Purgatorio*. Bogota: Villegas Editores.

Part II

On the rights of nature

Limits, possibilities and challenges in neo-extractivist worlds

After a detailed review of literature on what we may call a post-humanist approach in social theory, Part II contributes a theory on the conceptual limits and possibilities of the rights of nature in Latin America in the context of an emerging global Earth Law movement. By attending to the social and legal worlds of human and other-than-human beings studied in Part I, ***Rights of Nature*** reimagines core ontological, epistemological and methodological premises of social and legal sciences at present. For example, it critically reassesses key concepts of Western law such as "legal personhood," "standing" and "rights," thus joining activists and scholarly efforts to reorient the law as an instrument of socio-ecological transformation in contexts of neo-extractivism and colonial violence.

DOI: 10.4324/9781003349426-10

Chapter 5

Sowing concepts

Towards a post-humanist understanding of the encounter of beings

Abstract

The relentless multiplicity of Indigenous knowledge around "natural systems" can hardly be confined to concepts whose fundamental ontological premise is the modern separation between knowledge and life, culture and nature and body and mind. This chapter reviews post-humanist and relational approaches in social theory to discuss legal questions beyond anthropocentric principles. A detailed conceptual framework for the second part of the book, the chapter is divided into four parts, namely: 1) post-humanist theory and material agency; 2) plant studies and plant-human relations; 3) Earth Law and the rights of nature; and 4) Indigenous legal traditions and decoloniality.

1. Post-humanist theory and material agencies

The notions of traditional knowledge (Vallejo 2007; Torres et al. 2004), traditional ecological knowledge (Lauer and Shakar 2009; Langton and Zane 2005; Pierotti and Wildcat 2000), Indigenous know-how (Yavo 2013) and Indigenous science (Snively and Corsiglia 2000) populate scholarly and institutional discussions around local ways of dealing with plants, animals, soils, mountains and other beings and relations. In one way or another, the heuristic potentials and political capaciousness of these concepts have been the object of critique in the anthropology of knowledge (Green 2008), political ecology (Rocheleau 2008; Escobar 2015), post-humanist anthropology (Kohn 2013; Descola 2013; Viveiros de Castro 1998, 2014, 2015), political ontology (Blaser 2013; De la Cadena 2015; Escobar 2018) and cultural studies (Castro-Gomez and Grosfoguel 2007), to mention just a few fields.

The place-based and relational character of local "knowledge practices" in the Andean-Amazonian region concerning the "natural world" require novel languages as to convey the highly asymmetrical character of environmental knowledge practices in colonial contexts (Walsh 2009; Taussig 2010 [1980]), as well as the limits of human representation of forest life (Kohn 2013; Descola 2013). Notions such as cultural translation (Buden et al. 2009), transposition of knowledge (Lundberg and Kilhamn 2016),

DOI: 10.4324/9781003349426-11

re-appropriation and re-signification (Rappaport and Cummins 2011), cultural hybridity (MaClean 2015), other-than-human agencies (De la Cadena 2015) and perspectivism and multi-naturalism (Viveiros de Castro 1998) are paramount to an epistemology and ontology of Amerindian forest practices and territorial governance models in the Andean-Amazonian region today.

What follows reviews some streams of relational theory that inform and inspire a post-anthropocentric legal theory.

1.1. Beyond Marx's "metabolic rift" and the possibility of "other" materialism

An earlier approach to the relationship between the "social" and the "natural" world can be found in Marx—deemed by some scholars as one of the first modern ecologists (Bellamy Foster 2000).[1] Marx employed the concept of metabolism to describe the material exchange between nature and society, that is, a physical process prescribed by nature's own laws of sustainability mediated by the force of human labor.[2] Marx's materialist approach is grounded upon a notion of practical materialism that asserts the constitutive role of human agency in the reproduction and transformation of social relations.[3] Such relations of "man" to "nature" were "practical from the outset, that is, . . . established by action," he argues.[4] The notion of metabolism thus entails the "essential" role of human action in transforming the material conditions of their own existence by mediating, regulating and controlling "nature." For instance, soil nutrients absorbed by plants later become part of the human diet vis-à-vis the production of food.[5] Marx cautions, however, that the metabolic relations between humans and nature remain possible when premised on a principle of (metabolic) restitution, a process by which some of the nutrients that have been extracted from the soil are resituated under the form of manure. Yet, for Marx, nutrients, soils and plants are all material conditions of production devoid of agentive properties. In fact, the notion of agency is out of the picture in Marx's work.[6] These "natural elements" are mere forces of causality, while human praxis remains the eminent shaping force of nature and social life. The ontological premise of this kind of materialism is dualistic as opposed to relational, since "nature" and "culture" are considered separate spheres of life governed by different principles. An epistemological rift, as it were, this principle of separation lays at the root of our modern anthropocentrism with its widely known ecological, economic and political impacts (Escobar 2015).

1.2. The possibility of other-than-human agencies

Notwithstanding Marx's contributions to understand the relationship between nature and society, a call for a "nonhuman turn," on the other hand, attempts to bypass the dualistic foundation of his metabolic theses. A recent history of nonhuman agency could be traced back to mid-1990. This date saw the emergence of manifold theoretical approaches considering natural beings and material things as social agents themselves. Instead of privileging culture and human praxis—as Marxism would have it—these scholars have focused on what Donna Haraway calls "nature cultures," and Bruno Latour referred to as "collectives." (Haraway 1991; Latour 1993).

On this novel relation between "nature" and "culture," Haraway suggests that historically specific human relations with 'nature' must somehow

> linguistically, ethically, scientifically, politically, technologically, and epistemologically—be imagined as genuinely social and actively relational. . . . 'Our' relations with 'nature' might be imagined as a social engagement with a being who is neither 'it', 'you', 'thou', 'he', 'she' nor 'they' in relation to 'us'. The pronouns embedded in sentences about contestations for what may count as nature are themselves political tools, expressing hopes, fears, and contradictory histories. . . . Curiously . . . efforts to come to linguistic terms with the non-representability, historical contingency, artefactuality, and yet spontaneity, necessity, fragility, and stunning profusions of 'nature' can help us refigure the kind of persons we might be.
>
> (Haraway 1991, 3)

Similarly, on the notion of "collectives" or assemblies between former natures and cultures, Bruno Latour argues that

> science studies are talking not about the social contexts and the interests of power, but about their involvement with collectives and objects. The Navy's organization is profoundly modified by the way its offices are allied with its bombs;. . . . I will use the word 'collective' to describe the association of humans and nonhumans and 'society' to designate one part only of our collectives, the divide invented by the social sciences.
>
> (Latour 2004)

Thus, these concepts propose a radical rethinking of modern dualisms while describing how they are produced in discourse and action. Their focus is on "the morphology of change giving special attention to matter (materiality, processes of materialization) as it has been so much neglected by dualist thought."[7] Here, attention to the cultural capacities of matter and the "nonhuman" that, contra Grusin (2015) and others, I am calling an "other-than-human" turn[8] has influenced fields such as anthropology (Ingold 2011; Kohn 2013; Viveiros de Castro 1998), political theory (Bennett 2010), cultural studies and legal theory (Braverman 2018), among other fields (Escobar 2018). Moreover, several emergent approaches and fields of practice foreground the agency of things (Hodder 2012), materials (De Landa 1997) and other-than-humans beings such as plants (Pollan 2002), soils (Lyons 2016) and animals (Few and Tortorici 2013) in contemporary Latin American social theory. As indicated, these approaches range from political ecology to political ontology (Escobar 2015; Blaser 2013; De la Cadena 2010), and from Amerindian perspectivism (Viveiros de Castro 1998) to post-humanist anthropology (2007, 2013), to only name a few.

Many of these works have very actively deconstructed the institutional and academic production of nature as an object of knowledge, exploitation, management and conservation.[9] They have shown how what Western modern epistemologies (Mignolo 2011) call "natural beings" are produced as material forces of life, however devoid of agentive properties, a feature deemed exclusively cultural or human-like. For instance, in the case of political economy, to which political ecologists target their critique, nature is designated as the point of departure of economic processes having nothing to do with either the production of meaning or political action. The co-emergent articulation between other-than-humans and humans, instead, suggests a new framework that is centered on the relation rather than the entity (Varela et al. 1991). A shift with major repercussions for the understanding of political and legal subjectivity and agency, this new framework suggests, among others, that life entities such as plants and humans do not precede the relationships from which they emerge (Haraway 1991; Escobar 2015):

> The law does not recognize a relationship as a legal subject. Only individuals (individual persons) can be legal subjects. It would not be too far off to say that . . . relationships [can be] the equivalent of legal subjects, insofar as they are embodied in persons ("including plants and animals") subject to political-ritual protocols and public attention.[10]

This *encounter* between other-than-humans and human beings in social theory and practice therefore points to the limits of human representation as the only source of any social form (i.e., practices, institutions, norms, decisions). Here, "representation" stands for the language-mediated outcome of cognition, for example, the names given to the stuff of reality, as well as the act of standing for another person by contract or legal right, for example, when certain humans speak on behalf of other beings, including animals, rivers and ecosystems, among others. Therefore, "other-than-human" attention to social form can offer crucial analytical tools around the limits of human representation as the privileged site of meaning and action in a context of acute planetary crises. Following French anthropologist Philippe Descola, the project of post-humanism is

> repopulating the social sciences ("including the law") with nonhuman beings, and thus of shifting the focus away from the internal analysis of social conventions and institutions and toward the interactions of humans with (and between) animals, plants, physical processes, [and] other forms of beings.
>
> (Descola 2014, 268)

Similarly, anthropologist Eduardo Kohn's work with the Runa of the Ecuadorian Amazon suggests a shifting focus towards other-than-human–human relations and other-than-human modes of meaning (Kohn 2013, 9). He argues that both humans and other-than-humans use signs that are not necessarily symbolic, that is, all species are capable of producing forms of meaning which are not limited to the creation of conventional, referential and linguistic symbols.[11] Following Peirce's semiotics, Kohn considers other semiotic modalities: iconic signs (that share likenesses with what they stand for) and indexical signs (that are in a relation of spatial or temporal contiguity with what they represent). These representational modalities, to be sure, "have to be brought into the anthropological agenda . . . because icons and indexes are the signs that nonhuman organisms use to represent the world and communicate between life forms" (Descola 2014, 269).

Following a similar line of inquiry for the case of plants, philosopher Michael Marder argues that vegetal life expresses itself otherwise and "without resorting to vocalization." For him,

> aside from communicating their distress when predators are detected in the vicinity by realizing airborne (or in some cases belowground) chemicals, plants, like all living beings, articulate themselves spatially; in a body language free from gestures, they can express themselves only in their postures.
>
> (Marder 2013, 75)[12]

The word "language" here describes plants' modes of expression as a form of spatialized materiality. Thus, when it comes to plants, representation stands for "any network of (material) traces, of which consciousness is a highly circumscribed instance" (156). By a similar token, Kohn insists that "life-forms represent the world in some way or another, and these representations are intrinsic to their beings." What we, humans, share with other-than-human species is not only our embodiment "but the fact that we all live with and through signs . . . signs make what we are" (Kohn 2013, 9).

According to these post-humanist approaches, cognition, memory and communication are material-semiotic attributes distributed among different types of beings, rather than the exclusive domain of humans endowed with brains, centralized nervous systems, consciousness and language. In this sense, all living beings have the capacity to perceive, establish modes of communication and create dwellings by means of different modes of non-symbolic representation that are expressed through indexes and icons, or as forms of "spatial materiality." With Kohn, non-symbolic representation is "intrinsic" to all forms of life.

Cognitive and social "attributes" such as the capacity to signify, make choices and create norms are materially and semiotically expressed in concrete places. This approach has the potential to expand concepts of society (Viveiros de Castro 1998), politics (De la Cadena 2010) and law (Anker 2017) beyond the human and the symbolic (Kohn 2013) since such attributes speak to the continuity rather than the separation between humans and other beings. In the opening story of my introduction (*Law and the pluriverse*), the *frailejones* of *Sumapaz* were *active* social actors in the production of a place that exceeded the material as something external to the human "observer." Both the Spanish invaders and the local *frailejones* (moor plants) co-emerged as "humans" insofar as these "humans" were considered events rather than substances. The idea of the "human as an event of co-emergence" presupposes a form of continuity across all life forms.

Up to his point, the basic premise is the co-participation of *all* agencies in the cosmos, or relationality (Escobar 2018) in the production of multiple domains of theory and practice.[13] Let us further expand on this relational principle.

1.3. Sentience and interdependence: a relational principle

Recent studies in the field of animal cognition have discussed the moral basis of welfare beyond vertebrate animals, showing how human cognitive and affective biases towards beings such as arthropods shape our notions of what counts as moral standing (Mikhalevich and Powell 2020).[14] Mikhalevich and Powell (2020) suggest that once science has sufficiently demonstrated cognitive capacities in other-than-human species, its members should be granted moral consideration. This assumes that cognition is a potential attribute of *all* organisms. For example, a beetle should be considered capable of cognitive function if research confirms their capacity to perform tasks that humans recognize as cognitive or cognitive-like. This is an anthropocentric bias: cognition might not be a *property within* individual organisms, but an emergent effect of the relationships between organisms and the world they continuously co-create (Varela et al. 1991; Varela 1999; Ingold 2011).

The implications of this anthropocentric bias for the understanding of other-than-humans and morality are, therefore, multiple. For example, in relation to the human attribution of morality to other-than-human others, the anthropocentric bias considers moral values as matters of political concern if science is able to certify the cognitive *in* nature. There is certainly nothing wrong with establishing cognition beyond the human. The issue arises when science is considered as something preceding and separated from the very conditions of its emergence (Gagliano 2018; Haraway 2016; Tsing 2015), for instance, the cultural values, ethical orientations, political stances, epistemological preferences and socio-economic determinants of research practice.

Confronting this often-inescapable anthropocentric "bias"—or, rather, presupposition—demands to pay attention to the ontological, epistemological and axiological conditions of emergence of any scientific inquiry (Castro-Gomez 2005; Quijano Valencia 2016). From this, it follows that moral consideration of non-vertebrates, such as our beetle, emanates from scientific claims about cognition, in general, and other-than-human cognition.

Scientific claims, as a set of practices from an externally positioned human, cast meaning over our speechless beetle, and in doing so, science without the other-than-human perspective reinforces the ontology that separates ecologies, knowledge practices and socio-cultural values. This, of course, is not about science negationism, but a call to expand scientific practice beyond the confines of modern epistemologies that separate humans from the rest of life (Berry 1999) in times of acute socio-ecological crises.

While this anthropocentric bias suggests that human experience shall delimit the cognitive and the moral *in* the other-than-human, an ontological bias neatly separates our beetle from the human "observer" in a material and semiotic sense. This ontological "discontinuity" (Descola 2013) suggests the existence of an objective nature out there (i.e., the beetle is *in* nature), which the human shall describe with some level of standardized accuracy. This ontology of separation, namely the idea that "nature" is the domain of life while "science" and "culture," more generally, are the domains of *human* life, underpins both cognition research and moral philosophy.

Thus, more than expanding the scope of moral attribution to wider aspects of an external nature, we could examine how a theory of relational cognition and ethics may transform the underlying ontology that separates humans from the rest of life (Akhtar-Khavari 2020). Conceptualizing nature as an objective reality composed of a collection of discrete elements (Escobar 2018) therefore mobilizes moral philosophy to expand the circle of concern towards non-vertebrates at the expense of the relationships from which they emerge (Haraway 2016). This means that those new beings *exist* as discrete moral agents to the extent that science produces them as such (as discrete entities).

The strategy of "uncovering" what we may call a "dualist premise of scientific inquiry" challenges what we mean by human and other-than-human cognition and ethical standing in society. How can we reorient normative systems in light of these assumptions? More than a property of beings assigned from external sources, could normative systems be considered as a sort of emergent property of inter-being relations? Describing cognition as something *intrinsic* to beings rather than an emergent property of the ongoing and often unpredictable relations between them (Varela et al. 1991; Varela 1999) removes the beetle further away from the ecologies that make her emerge as such (Haraway 2007; Strathern 2016). We grant moral consideration to the beetle to separate her from her systemic relations (living and not), without paying much attention to the fact that the beetle's cognitive dispositions do not exist outside of these relations. Unless science can prove that these relations are cognitive in the same way in which substances or selves such as beetles, plants and humans are, these relations are not given moral consideration at all. In other words, these relations are considered part of neither law nor ethics as subjects of protection and standing (see Chapter 7, "Conjuring"). If we give rights to one being—the beetle—only to ignore the relations from which she emerges, what we tentatively call epistemological bias further separates ecologies, values and knowledge practices.

As we pay attention to relations, the moral consideration of non-vertebrate beings challenges cognition as a property *of* beings. This also means that cognitive science is not the only source of knowledge about what is cognitive and what is not, nor that cognition is the only adequate description of the mind-like properties of living and nonliving relations (Ingold 2011). For some people, nonliving beings like rocks have thoughts and feelings, and science cannot disprove this. This does not mean that the alternative is a matter to be discarded as mere cultural belief (De la Cadena 2015).

However, a question remains, if science cannot prove or disprove the sentience of the nonorganic (perhaps the next moral frontier), can we then assume that rocks should not be considered as subjects of moral and legal attribution? Indigenous people from Australia to the Amazon and from the Andes to the boreal forests of Canada would certainly say otherwise. Having a "mind" is not an attribute of beings, nor a property that you can find *in* an external nature (i.e., plants, beetles, glaciers, rivers). Mind "is" *minding*, that is, process and emergence. What kind of law is then a law that is attentive to "emergence" and "social relations" between humans and other beings? Let us keep this question in mind as this review progresses.

In addition to plants and other living beings in relentless co-emergence, things, objects and "matter" participate in agency assemblies and express a type of social life of sorts (Bennett 2010; Ingold 2011). This idea is important to push contemporary social and legal theory beyond the symbolic and multicultural frameworks in which they seemed to be trapped (De la Cadena 2010). In the next section, I will examine in detail one of those cases where "things" not only have a social life but also a form of agency in the Andean context (for a similar argument in Amazonia, see Santos-Granero 2011). The fact that "things" do things is crucial for relational approaches to the law as well (see Chapter 8, "Forest on trial").

1.4. Writing history with clay and stone: indigenous material literacies in the Andean region

In 2012, a major archaeological exploration took place in the Colombian municipality of Soacha, Cundinamarca, located only a few miles south of Bogotá. A group of 170 archeologists unearthed what is considered the largest archaeological site in Colombia dated from the *Herrera* period.[15] It covers an area of approximately 8 hectares and has been described as a unique case in Colombian history given its potential to account for a human group that inhabited this part of the country almost 3,000 years ago.[16] Thus far, archeologists have found evidence of a village-like settlement with some vestiges of family dwellings, ceremonial constructions and funerary deposits:[17] over 30 well-preserved ceramic objects and hundreds of stone-carved tools to spin wool, 30,000 fragments of pottery and more than a 100 tombs, remains of ceremonial houses and several other constructions all pointing to a major human settlement in the area.

Given the lack of symbolic inscriptions on the surfaces of these materials, for example hieroglyphics, it may be inferred that *Herrera* peoples were not concerned with the practice of recording memory, and much less that objects hold a form of memory in and of themselves. In fact, the materials found at this site offer cues on how the *Herrera* peoples lived and the tools they used, but not so much on how they inscribed their own way of living. This connection between materials and history by means other than the inscription of symbolic signs hold space for socialities beyond the human. I use the notion of material inscription of memory to refer to practices that both express daily life activities, as well as the recording of events in the vein of the largely studied *khipu*, namely the Andean cord notation system.[18] Practices within the domain of material culture such as weaving, stone carving and pottery making can be considered forms of inscription of memory. However, the criteria to determine which practices count as *material literacy*[19] is beyond the scope of this review. Suffice it to say that materials are not only inserted into human affairs but actively create what counts as society as well.

In what follows, I will discuss the notion of intercultural literacy in the work of anthropologist Joan Rappaport and art historian Tom Cummins (Rappaport and Cummins 2011). *Beyond the Lettered City: Indigenous Literacies in the Andes* studies the Spanish imposition of alphabetic and visual regimes on Indigenous modes of inscribing memory and the Indigenous re-appropriation of colonial techniques in Colonial Andes (Colombia). Probing how humans and materials make history together, a working notion of material writing and literacy illustrates how both non-lettered practices such as weaving, pottery and stone carving as well as the materials they are made of co-produce history. To be sure, the notion of material literacy rethinks pre-colonial modes of memory making and historical consciousness. By stressing the role of materials, this line of work bears a special interest for the law as well (Pottage 2012): material literacies go beyond the symbolic and re-establish historical continuities before and after the Colonial encounter, while expanding the sources of legal meaning based solely on the symbolic. In a sense, this line of work is part of a larger argument on how "peoples" and "things" make history and law together (Salomon and Niño-Murcia 2011).

1.4.1. Matter, meaning, history

A central tenet of the material turn in social theory[20] is that the "understanding of things that are written must . . . go beyond (the) study of textual meanings and take account of the *material worlds* in which writing is inextricably embedded" (Piquette and Whitehouse 2013, 1. My highlight). For instance, in the absence of symbolic inscriptions or traces on the surfaces of the objects found in *Soacha*, the very materials of which they are made off hold some form of meaning to their finders. As British scholars Piquette and Whitehouse argue, the notion of material writing implies that "analytical and interpretative priority (is) given, not (only) to the linguistic and semantic meanings of graphical marks, but to their physicality and the ways in which this relates to creators, . . . users," and interpreters (2013, 1).

Expanding the notion of writing to include material objects, post-humanist approaches bring forth the theme of historical continuity between pre-colonial and colonial ways of writing events by means of material artifacts. What if we open the notion of the archive to consider non-lettered forms of inscribing events? This is a crucial methodological premise of a law-otherwise insofar as it expands legal sources beyond symbolic inscription or propositional language (Anker 2014, 2017). What might happen to the notion of intercultural literacy expressed, for instance, in legal documents such as Indigenous testaments, when we consider material practices as active sources of history? (Rappaport and Cummins 2011, 9, 66, 157). In other words, do weaving, stone carving and pottery contribute to a colonial culture predominantly based on symbolic expressions of memory? (Rappaport and Cummins 2011, 126, 162). These questions, again, are far beyond the scope of this review, but they are good to think about as we consider how legal theory and practice is embedded in larger assemblages of meaning and matter. Attention to the material worlds in which the social is inscribed help us to trace out the social action arising from "humans" and "other-than-humans" encounters. "What happens when this approach to materiality takes on the question of law?" (Pottage 2012, 167).

1.4.2. Literacy beyond the letter: an archive of stones?

For Rapapport and Cummins, the expression *colonial culture* stems from the difficulty of separating into discrete entities with manifold cultural trajectories that contribute to the formation of a common colonial world. The expression "colonial culture" describes "the voices of numerous cultural actors from different historical periods" (Rappaport and Cummins 2011, 29) and how they become "inextricably intertwined" over the years. The cultural contestation of this period is not visualized "as the confrontation of two opposite poles," but as a series of modulations that unfold over time. Such modulations took place "as much among Europeans as among Andeans, both of whom belonged to heterogeneous social constellations marked by a multitude of cultural, racial, occupations, and gender identities that could be altered by administrative petitions" (Rappaport and Cummins 2011, 29).

Discussing the colonial archive as mainly formed by the letter, the visual and the interpretation of the spoken word (Rappaport and Cummins 2011,

21, 24), the notion of the text is still central to Rappaport-Cummins' larger claims about the formation of a "colonial culture" and history making more broadly. The problematization of the archive beyond the symbolic, then, is relevant to the possibility of writing history with "things" or considering things as historical agents themselves. The Argentinian critic Cesar Paternosto (1996) writes the following on the connections between text, textile and stone of special interest to the social agency of things in history and law:

> Tectonic derives from the late Latin *tectonicus*, which derive from the Greek *tektonikos*, from *tekton*, carpenter or constructor. Inspired by Cecilia Vicuna's poetic work with metaphors that are hidden in the intimate heart of a word, I discovered that the Indo-European root *teks*—the etymon, the true meaning of the tectonic—means "to weave," and also to make a wicker or wattle framework for mud walls; in Latin, *texere* (to weave) is the word from which "text," "texture" and context are derived. And one of the root's suffix forms, *teks*-la, is in Latin tela (net, warp, spiderweb), while another of its suffix forms, *teks-na*, means "artisanry" (weaving or fabricating), which in Greek is *tekhne* (art, artisanry, skill). Thus, in its hidden meanings, the word "tectonic" illuminates the primordial meaning of art ('and the creative work of memory inscription'), in which weaving and constructing are identified with the same semantic resonance—a resonance that, from my point of view, becomes the subtext, the weft that interweaves with the expositive warp of the history of Andean art.
>
> (1996, 165)

Can "things" be considered agents of history rather than passive objects of historical claims? The connection between the "text" and the "stone" offers potentials for grounded speculation on what expanding the archive to material practices might entail.[21] Whereas practices such as weaving, pottery and stone carving are expressive acts in and of themselves, a post-humanist reading suggests that these things are *not only* pieces of external matter from which humans derive meaning but part and parcel of relational constellations of history where meaning and matter are deeply entangled.

Rappaport and Cummins' focus on the lettered archive does not consider practices of Indigenous colonial subjects who neither engaged with the letter nor with intercultural forms of literacy (2011, 11). To be comprehensive, the notion of colonial culture should expand the focus on Indigenous *ladino* practices such as issuing testaments as a form of intercultural literacy to material practices of Indigenous artisans such as weaving. Stemming from Paternosto's etymological account of the "text" (*tek*, *textere*, *tek*-tonic), an archive is also an archive of stones.

1.5. Intercultural literacy, colonial culture and historical continuity

Beyond the Lettered City is a study on Indigenous literacies in Northern Andes (present-day Colombia). It examines the colonial imposition of alphabetic and visual regimes of the Spanish culture, while describing how Andean peoples received, maintained and subverted these dominant literacies by adding their own local traditions. Rappaport and Cummins' focus was on the formation of a colonial culture by way of the reception, appropriation and reinterpretation of lettered practices, particularly legal documents, notarial manuals, dictionaries, religious images, catechisms and sermons, as well as a vast amount of administrative records produced by colonial authorities and their Indigenous scribes. While the book focuses on textual literacy, it "goes beyond the obvious point that alphabetically written archival documents provide the major source of . . . information on the colonial period" (2011, 11), and it leaves open the question of how different modalities of memory inscription beyond the symbolic played a role in the formation of a colonial culture. The lack of reference to the historical continuity of vernacular modes of engagement with memory can be explained by the book's primary focus on the lettered or alphabetic archive.[22]

However, Rappaport and Cummins suggest that colonial Andean studies have just recently paid attention to the intricate connections and interfaces between different social actors (2011, 28). The focus has shifted from the study of discrete social agents to the study of an emergent colonial culture that integrated different sectors of society in often-surprising ways (2011, 29): they were not so much closed worlds "as they were critical scenarios within which representations and, ultimately power, were wielded by colonial administrators and indigenous agents alike" (2011, 28). Citing Carolyn Dean's study on a seventeenth-century series of paintings of Corpus Christi processions in Cuzco (Dean 2010), "colonial culture is best comprehended as a complex process of 'relexification,'[23] in which Andean (Indigenous) syntax was used to frame European utterances" (Rappaport and Cummins 2011, 28). In other words, European worldviews were transmitted using the grammar of the colonized. The authors explain this process in detail:

> This is a striking example of the internalization of a new visual culture in the psyche of a native woman [the authors are referring to a Christian vision that a *muisca* woman had]. Her dream experience was shaped by a painting before which she may very well have prayed but whose iconography she probably did not fully comprehend. Nevertheless, in her vision the canvas becomes a vehicle mediating between her pagan past and her Christian future; the former is literally represented by the *jeque* (shaman), and the latter by the Dominicans . . . in this instance, the structures of the new civil and religious order are manifest in the woman's accessing of a

> particular form of colonial literacy over which her command was only partial. . . . The exemplary nature of her tale is what caused it to be cast in writing, to enter into an epistolary genre and to be forwarded to the Jesuit General in Rome, where the letter is now stored. As a result, the traces of visual literacy that impacted the vision are recast in alphabetic form.
>
> (Rappaport and Cummins 2011, 253)

As this passage suggests, the alphabetical form is the dominant form of historical record. An Indigenous woman's exposure to a painting whose iconography she did not "fully comprehend" and the ensuing alphabetic recording of this experience cast the letter a source of truth. Indeed, the cultural relexification hypothesis 1) signals a complex process of cultural *mestizaje* in the colonial period (Rappaport and Cummins 2011, 30), and the profound power asymmetries between different colonial actors;[24] 2) the emergence of a colonial culture that was heavily influenced by the Spanish lettered city[25] and 3) the re-appropriation of the "Spanish letter" to secure the continuity of the colonial rule. However, the relexification does not fully account for the other kind of continuity, namely the transmission of practical knowledge through material artifacts that refused a process of *mestizaje* and, nonetheless, surely influenced what the authors call "colonial culture."[26] A "material semiotics"[27] approach to the archive thus affirms the historical continuity between pre-colonial Andean modes of engaging with memory (such as the cited *Herrera* period) and material practices that survived the colonial rule.

As indicated, the notion of "intercultural literacy" describes how Indigenous populations have engaged with alphabetic writing during the colonial period. However, when the letter and the visual are the main streams running towards the archive's well, they might become the privileged source of historical evidence at the expense of materials that carry historical meaning. The notion of intercultural literacy embodied in practices such as *ladino* testaments have obscured local forms of material memorialization that were not dependent on the alphabetic and the visual. Nonetheless, Rappaport and Cummins (2011) do refer to "native literacies" (5, 9) as something other than "learning to read alphabetically inscribed texts and producing Western forms of pictorical representation" (9). In fact, they were richer than "mere adaptations of European practices of reading and viewing; they also transformed them, spawning intertextual reading that interacted with indigenous forms of recording and representation, including knot records (khipus), textiles, and sacred geography" (10). The affirmation that "Andean (Indigenous) syntax was used to frame European utterance" does not seem to extinguish possible sources and practices of literacy based on material cultural expressions such as stone carving, weaving and pottery making.[28]

Thus, the relexification hypothesis describes Indigenous nobility's lettered forms of memorialization and inheritance such as testaments. These testaments show how *ladino* Indigenous property owners progressively adopted the Catholic, and, therefore, the hypothesis do not sufficiently account for lay Indigenous folk and their modes of inscribing memory through materials. I am referring to people, however incorporated into the "Spanish juridical arrangement" (2011, 29), who might have not been totally deprived of their forms of memory, nor necessarily influenced by the alphabetic mentality.

On this issue, the Austrian scholar Ivan Illich argues that any fundamental concept exists in relation to the alphabet in the Western world. Thus, the alphabetic mentality is a sort of relapse to the realm of the letter at the expense of other modes of representation. The alphabetic mentality differs from *literacy*—the capacity to read and write—in that it has become a mode of perception where the alphabet is the main metaphor through which the "I" is conceived and situated (Illich 2006, 555). I am using this expression in a slightly different way to include both the alphabetic "function" (to read and write) and a sort of reductionism of memorialization and social agency to the alphabetic mentality,[29] that is, Indigenous syntax to European utterances (lettered-alphabetic). Despite this overreliance on the "text," *Beyond* makes an explicit reference to the inscription of memory through weaving:

> Within colonial culture, the performative efficacy of multiple literacies that crosscut indigenous and European genres of inscription and narration was played out in administrative and ritual space. For example, royal decrees read at the investiture of northern Andean caciques shared ritual space with native weavings, which were conferred upon new caciques in a culture in which textiles were a prime vehicle for inscription of memory and power.
>
> (Rappaport and Cummins 2011, 149)

In the next section I will suggest a notion of material writing to underline how crucially entangled matter and meaning are in the construction of history. Matter as a social agent is central to the formation of a colonial culture and its historical continuities up until today.

1.6. Writing and material writing

Writing can be broadly defined as a human practice of inscribing meaning. This practice alters an object, for example, a piece of paper, a headstone, a piece of cloth, among other materials, to retain the alphabetic trace or any other symbol (Ingold 2007).[30] Conventionally, things can't convey meaning unless human practitioners assign meaning to them, that is, things are surfaces or mere carriers of meaning. This definition implies a separation between sign and matter, or human agency and bare objects. Does this cultural definition of writing foreclose meaning beyond the symbolic?

According to British archaeologist John Bennet, the term writing embodies two different meanings: 1) "a *process* involving the interactions of human bodies with materials normally mediated through various tools (pen, keyboard, etc.), and 2) a *substance* or the material residues of those bodily actions on, or in, the surface of media of many kinds" (Bennet 2013: 335). This double sense of writing as the material process of inscription, and its ensuing substance, requires another step, namely the act of reading from which the effect of meaning emerges. For Bennet, the practice of reading is also deemed a bodily process of engagement with the substance of writing through the senses, for example, the tactility involved in the Braille system. However, reading can potentially refer to a "broader set of engagements than merely making sense of and absorbing a representation of language" (336). Such is the case of the Andean cord notation system—khipu—considered a nonlanguage-based form of writing (Salomon and Niño-Murcia 2011).

The material process of writing is just one possible form of representation, and, like other forms, "its appreciation is not limited to the visual dimension" (Bennet 2013: 337). In other words, it is not limited to writing in the sense of a material process of inscription of meaning on a surface (the production of traces). Since representational practices are not limited to the lettered inscription of memory, the archive can be expanded to other forms of representation that might open space for other ways of the human inscription of memory, as well as the co-participation of *things* as co-agents of history rather than mere recipients of meaning (Ingold 2011). Yet not all things make history. The scope of this review is limited to expand on this issue.

As Bennet suggests, "writing is a *particular* form of representation" (337), or a form producing meaning among many other forms. Certain definitions of writing emphasize the content of writing systems, for example, as symbolic systems rather than the material embodiment of the writing process itself (Bennet 2013, 338). Similarly, Berry Powel defines writing as "a system of markings with a conventional reference that communicates information" (2009, 313). Here writing moves between the inscription of signs and the communication of meaning rather than the relationship between inscription and production of meaning. Other authors point to the relation between writing and speech (Robertson 2010), while others challenge definitions that limit writing to the representation of speech (Salomon and Niño-Murcia 2011). Bennet (2013) goes a step further to affirm that "not all writing is for reading by human eyes (i.e., certain inscriptions in Egyptian tombs or Greco-Roman curse tablets), or strictly representative of human language (i.e., magic spells)" (Bennet 2013, 337).

Textile-making, pottery, stone carving, among other practices, can be considered expressions of the material inscription of memory. These expressions act as bearers of memory and knowledge and testify to the historical continuities of Indigenous struggles in the Andes.[31] Rappaport and Cummins' notion of literacy includes practices of urban planners, painters, *escribas* and members of the Indigenous nobility. The fact that certain forms of literacy are not explicitly taken into account in the colonial archive opens up new considerations of special interest in understanding the place of the other-than-human in the constitution of the social field: 1) the colonial archive is lettered both in the sense of the "lettered city" (the alphabet) as well as the local Indigenous re-appropriation of Spanish modes of engaging with memory, or intercultural "literacy." From this, it follows that historical claims depend upon symbolic evidence at the expense of other forms of representation; 2) the symbolic *is* memory, and since memory is what exists in the archive, the symbolic *is* history. Therefore, making history beyond the symbolic holds space for things as social agents rather than bearers of human memory; 3) a "colonial culture" based on the letter creates a history without materials, and these materials are left out of social inquiry to enter the realm of naturalistic description.

Rappaport and Cummins (2011) further argue that Indigenous Andean communities

> did not know narrative pictorial representation or alphabetic or hieroglyphic literacy before the arrival of the Spaniards, and that to enter into such literate conventions they needed to learn a new set of technologies, but also had to understand that what was represented was not embodied in the image or symbol, but referred to something outside of it.
>
> (Rappaport and Cummins 2011, 254)

This suggests that local peoples were forced into a series of cognitive transformations to engage with European symbolic systems at the expense of their own ways of producing memory.

Indeed, adopting a form of literacy by means of alphabetic and visual inscription was part of a colonial symbolic system of occupation of local historical continuities, institutions, values and territories. This occupation presupposed the separation between human representation and de-animated material world that was rendered as the external referent of symbolic description. In *Beyond*'s words, local peoples need to understand that "what was represented was not embodied in the image or symbol but referred to something outside of it" (254). Conversely, objects such as pottery, textiles and stones can become a material grammar where the 'thing' and its linguistic representation become a unit. Thus, 'things' can form a *tek archive* or an archive of stones insofar as the representation of the world cannot be separated from their material entanglements.

For instance, it appears that in the pre-colonial Mayan world, the act of reading was already associated with three rather fleshy actions, "one of which has to do with speaking (usually calling out or shouting), a second with counting and a third with looking (or looking specifically at paper)" (Tedlock 1992, 216). By analyzing Mayan forms of writing, the ethnographer and linguist Dennis Tedlock finds that the use of writing among the pre-colonial Maya "argues against . . . suggestions that literacy was not widely diffused among Mayan peoples until the alphabet was introduced" (Tedlock 1992, 218). Further, "there is certainly no lack of Mayan terms and phrases that deal with the process by which speech is made into visible texts and texts are interpreted" (Tedlock 1992, 218). Well before the introduction of the Roman alphabet in the so-called New World, this linguistic evidence suggests that reading and writing were both forms of material practice.

This seems to speak to our current interest in opening the question of 'material literacy' as a set of operations to record memory beyond the conventional notion of literacy, but also as a way to collide literacy and material culture. What is 'inscription' in the face of memory forms that some consider to be 'alive' and in permanent flux? The double risk of reducing past events to different expressions of material culture or material reductionism, while reducing the narration of events to alphabetic inscriptions or formal reductionism, should be considered as we try to expand the notion of literacy beyond the symbolic and the human. Illich offers an interesting approach to this 'double risk' by weaving together the notion of dwelling and the idea of inscribing memory:

> To inhabit was to remain in his own footsteps, to let daily life write the networks and articulations of his biography on the landscape. This writing could be inscribed on the stone by successive generations or reconstructed in each rainy season with some gray hairs and leaves.
>
> (My translation)[32]

The acts of writing and inhabiting are similar insofar as both try to trace paths and boundaries of meaning and matter in specific places. The landscape becomes a text or an archive of stones: "the dwelling was never finished before it was occupied, contrary to contemporary accommodation which deteriorates from the very day it is ready to be occupied" (Illich 2006, 464).

The notion of "material literacy" expands the archive beyond symbolic representation, while affirming the factuality and continuity of historical events that cannot be explained by the symbolic form only. Thus, material literacy in the pre-colonial and colonial Andes refers to the material inscription of memory that, despite colonial domination, continues until now through practices with clay, stone and wool, among other materials (Ingold 2011 for the notion of lively materials). Different peoples create stone archives that represent historical continuities of sign and matter despite ongoing colonial rule in the Andean region. The fact that these artifacts cannot be "translated" into written text speaks to a non-literary form of literacy in which things themselves are texts embedded in the materials from which they are made. Again, the agency of things is a matter of relationship or association with human creators. In a sense, humans and things co-make history and each other. This entangled reality of sign and matter can "speak."

Building upon the study of materiality, I suggest that attention to situated "inter-being" collaborations (Harris 2014) and their role in the production of legal concepts at different scales poses important ontological challenges to modern understandings of law, politics and knowledge production in the Andean region and beyond.[33] In short, this book develops a proposal in which the relations between human beings and nonhuman beings become a place for the transformations of legal systems. These legal transformations are part of the post-extractivist transitions that are emerging in Latin America. (Gudynas 2009; Escobar 2015). The role other-than-human/human entanglements play in social theory lays at the heart of fundamental questions of modern social institutions. In the following section, I will review several studies on the encounters between humans and plants, as they help us think about society and law differently.

2. Plant studies and plant-human relation

2.1. The (vegetal) other-than-human and the law

Questions about the role of other-than-humans in legal theory and practice "shed light on some of the most fundamental assumptions and constructions of contemporary modern law" (Braverman 2016, 2018, 127). A groundbreaking work in this direction, *Forest Law|Selva Jurídica* (Biemann and Tavares 2014), addresses Indigenous engagements with legal forms of activism in the face of 'neo-extractive' industries in Amazonia (Svampa 2019). Turned into a quarry for the world's economy since the seventeenth century, this region has been the source of rich epistemic diversity that is already transforming legal institutions: while granting rights to nature, the 2008 Constitution of Ecuador holds space for a non-anthropocentric view of law that is slowly but surely spreading to other areas of the legal discipline (Zelle et al. 2021; Harris 2014; Papadopoulos 2012).

In fact, this review is attentive to what De la Cadena rightly calls "politics beyond politics," that is, a form of power that conjures "sentient entities (mountains, water, and soil—what we call 'nature') into the public political arena" (2010, 334). My approach to normative systems such as law and ethics foregrounds the limits of human representation as the privileged site of social, political and legal meaning. In the words of Kohn, other-than-human 'selves' create forms of meaning beyond conventional, referential and language-based symbols (2013). As "skilled practitioners," mountains, rivers, plants and animals can co-create legal institutions as well (Ingold 2011, 11).

The question of other-than-human agency has been widely addressed in contemporary social theory. However, it has received much less attention in the legal field (Vermeylen 2017). In the Latin American context, contemporary legal scholarship generally approaches the rights of nature either as state-granted norms or as political achievements of Indigenous social movements (Acosta and Martínez 2011; Gudynas 2009). While these approaches are central to the theory and practice of the rights of nature, they have not paid sufficient ethnographic attention to the modes of participation of other-than-humans in the legal field. By probing how the law emerges from life relations themselves (Anker 2017), my book engages legal questions beyond normative and multicultural frameworks, that is, beyond a form of law recognized by a state. Other-than-human beings are then contested sources of legal concepts and practices, and I will provisionally call this space of legal creativity Indigenous-forest relational jurisprudence.

Along with the living entities that make up Indigenous collective worlds, Indigenous epistemologies and world-making practices in Amazonia suggest an altogether different approach to the law. What if other-than-human beings are the site of legal meaning rather than the passive receiver of natural rights? What if what we call 'law' in contemporary eco-centric approaches to legal concepts such as the rights of nature is already enmeshed in human/other-than-human alliances? Thinking with Indigenous Kamentzá Hugo Jamioy from the Upper Putumayo region in Colombia, plants and other beings may have a saying in what he refers to as the *law of nature*, which is not the same as the Western natural law.

Similarly, anthropologist Philippe Descola argues that in Amazonia animals, plants and other beings see themselves as people whose bodies conceal an internal human form (2014). Moreover, Eduardo Viveiros de Castro distinguishes between Western multicultural ontology—as the diversity of cultural representations of a common nature—from Amerindian multi-naturalism—as the multiplicity of natures (i.e., life entities) sharing a common culture or interiority (1998).[34] Here, this review proposes a relational rather than an entity-oriented view of 'organisms' (Ingold 2011) as they partake in the making of socio-legal worlds in Amazonia and the Andes. Paraphrasing ecologist and theologian Thomas Berry considered one of the founding figures of the Earth Jurisprudence movement, the historical treatment of the Andean-Amazonian region of Colombia is a prime example of the 'radical discontinuity' between human and other-than-human beings and the ensuing "bestowal of all rights on the humans" alone (Berry 1999, 4). This radical discontinuity is at the root of the ecological and cultural devastation of this region. Conversely, the new approaches I have just briefly summarized provide elements for the task of reinventing the human (Berry 1999) and the other-than-human by re-embedding socials institutions such as the law within the broader community of entangled forms of life and meaning (Berry 1999; Brown 2015).[35] In this sense, plants are good persons to think with about the law (Gagliano 2018; Hall 2011).

Plants are not only the vegetal stuff of the world's economy and scholarly imagination. Instead, they are sentient, political and legal entities that do not precede the relationships from which they emerge (Haraway 2007). This insight poses a major shift for a theory of legal subjectivity in this region. For example, political philosopher Roberto Esposito (2010) asks whether the concept of rights can survive without the notion of personhood. Traditionally, only persons [natural or juridical (Stone 1972)] have been considered legal subjects. Insofar as relationships are embodied in persons, the first can also be subject "to political-ritual protocols and public attention" (Strathern 2010, 95).

Assessing the limits of epistemology in legal scholarship, these scholars address the debate through relational lenses as well. Adding to this discussion, I suggest that plants embody and exceed Amerindian concepts of relationality and interdependency between living and nonliving entities. In other words, plants emerge as a sort of cognitive prototype of a relational (and contested) legal agency I believe central to Indigenous legal systems in contemporary Andes-Amazon. Section 5 thus focuses on the modes of socio-legal participation of plants.

2.2. *Plants: a prototype of other-than-human (legal) agency?*

As we have seen, other-than-human beings have been casted as agents of knowledge, shaping forces in social life, as well as subjects of rights in today's legal theory and practice.[36] Thinking with plants can provide a good entry point to reimagine what (else) counts as 'society', 'politics' and 'law' (Marder 2013; Gagliano 2018). Plants and humans, however, do not precede their encounters (Myers 2015): subterraneous and aquatic, aerial and aural, literal and metaphoric, plants are constituted through vital relations with other beings and forces. They are embedded within life assemblages or 'meshworks' (Ingold 2011) that extend far beyond plants' perceived forms above ground, as well as their modes of movement.

As discrete entities, plants can accomplish tasks considered exclusive to humans according to anthropocentric concepts of agency (Calvo et al. 2020; Franks et al. 2020; Mancuso and Viola 2015). Plants are sentient beings capable of perception, cognition and communication (Gagliano et al. 2018; Gagliano et al. 2016; Gagliano and Grimonprez 2015). For instance, they can sense their immediate environments and transform light into food; they can interact with other plants through their roots; they can also alert their vegetal kin about the presence of predators, and even hunt, among other qualities. This is not to say that plants' 'attributes' are valuable because they resemble human 'attributes.' Again, that would be an anthropocentric stance to plant-human encounters. The case might be that plants are far more resourceful beings than their human counterparts, and the cited studies tend to approach plants' abilities in their own terms (Myers 2015). Moreover, plants have been brought into contemporary legal debates: to what extent can plants be subjects of rights? When does the human right to obtain food from plants collide with the plants' rights to the regeneration of the soil where they grow? (Pelizzon and Gagliano 2015; Federal Ethics Committee on Non-Human Biotechnology 2008).

Some studies have focused on the relationship between plants and territories—"we think with plants about the nature of territory" (Betsky and Padwe 2016, 10), while others explore local-based alternatives to extractivist practices such as the free exchange of seeds and traditional banks of germplasm (Grupo Semillas 2016).[37] Furthermore, while vegetal beings are incapable of 'speech' in the linguistic sense, convergent examples of Amerindian cosmologies and Western sciences consider them capable of communication, meaning-creation and a form of social action in accord with their own perspectives (Turner 2020; Wall Kimmerer 2013). Indeed, plants are windows into larger conversations over representations of nature across time and space, legal personhood beyond the human and alternatives to profit-oriented economies (see Chapter 8: "Forest on trial"). A short step towards an other-than-human theory of legal agency, the next sub-section will review some works in the field of plant sensing and intelligence, and how "plant-thinking" may help us *think* through notions of socio-ecological justice and the natural contract.[38]

2.2.1. "They are sentient beings." A Western convergence

In the field of plant studies, scholars use different analytic frameworks to probe plants' modes of agency and intentionality. Botanical philosophers invite us to "consider the moral standing of plants arguing that they are other-than-human persons," (Hall 2011) while science and technology scholars offer a more nuanced take on vegetal intentionality in particular techno-scientific settings (Myers 2015). For example, they explore how different practitioners, for example, scientists, assign meaning to the plants they work with and how "plants sense and make sense of their (own) worlds" as well (Myers 2015, 36. See Wohlleben 2015; Mancuso and Viola 2015). This is the case of anthropologist Natasha Myers who explores how plants perceive and respond to their own environments suggesting that plants are perspectival entities whose meaning-making capacities are not reducible to the conceptual toolkit of their human counterparts—including notions of intentionality or even intelligence. To be sure, the locus of plant 'intelligence' is not a centralized brain, but a decentralized body, which might ask for different conceptual frameworks (see Chapter 1, "Yoco").

These studies attempt to overcome anthropomorphic categorizations of plant behavior as they discuss the possibility of a plant point of view. Philosopher Michael Marder proposes the notion of *plant-thinking* to refer to what plants can do—and what *we* can achieve learning with plants—as well as to their "unique perspective, expressed at the cellular, organismic and environmental levels." The challenge, he argues, "is to look at the world from a plant 'point of view,' for if biology is to be a science of living beings, it must investigate the particular perspective correlated with each distinct form of life." (Marder 2013, 136) Marder implies, however, that life is a collection of discrete entities connected through vectors of predation and symbiosis. What if a focus on relations redefines attributes such as 'intelligence', 'memory' and 'intentionality' as emergent effects of inter-being encounters, rather than specific capacities of the modern human or the plant? Our current discursive and practical overreliance on self-contained entities (i.e., humans, plants, animals, among others) may overlook the importance of interspecies relations in social theory (Escobar 2018). This point is crucial as we explore a non-dualist approach to legal agency in sync with Amerindian relational views of life and justice.

Plant scientist Monica Gagliano investigates plants' ability to detect vibrations from distant sound sources for orientation towards water (2018). Similarly, an increasing number of studies ranging from plant communication and intelligence (Trewavas 2016) to vegetal neuro-physiology (Mancuso and Viola 2015) and plant bio-acoustics (Gagliano 2018) reveal a vegetal sensorium functionally similar to organisms with centralized nervous systems. Yet, again, plants' perspectival capacities (Viveiros de Castro 1998), as it were, are neither a mere analogue of human cognition nor an enclosed set of vital attributes. In fact, plants are part and parcel of a shifting assemblage of distributed agencies and material politics (Harvey et al. 2014) that weave together soil, water, humus, deforestation, technologies, spirits and legal codes reconfiguring political relations and environmental governance models.

Intelligence and sentience, therefore, are not *in* plants but *with* plants, and this relational focus opens theoretical questions with potential legal interest. The case of plants invites us to rethink society and the law as exclusive cultural attributes of organisms endowed with brains and nervous systems: as plant scientists Viola and Mancuso have argued, plants can "breathe without having lungs, nourish themselves without having a mouth or stomach, stand erect without having a skeleton, and . . . *make decisions without having a brain*" (Mancuso and Viola 2015, 34. My emphasis). Yet this framework is not without limitations: How "anthropocentric" is this brain-centered rendition of plant life? How can we study the social lives of plants *in their own terms*?

Indeed, the idea that plants and other organisms are capable of intelligent behavior may expand notions of representation beyond the human and the person as bonded selves. Plants modes of representation, this research is set off to demonstrate, are not reducible to those specific to the human, that is, symbolic and language-based signs (Kohn 2013; Marder 2013). Broadly speaking, this research builds upon a well-established scholarship that expands the notion of representation usually defined in two complementary ways (de la Cadena 2015; Escobar 2018). First, as the language-mediated outcomes of human perception, that is, the names human assign to exterior objects and the relations between them (Westermann and Mareschal 2014). And second, as the act of standing for another party by contract or legal right, for example, when humans speak on behalf of others in a congress or a court of law. This suggests that neither the language-mediated perception of a single reality nor the act of speaking on behalf of others forecloses the possibility of other-than-human (legal) representation beyond symbolic signs (Kohn 2013).

2.3. Plants: relationality and indigenous botany in colonial contexts

From earlier histories of colonization and development to current scientific and economic uses of plant life, relations between humans and plants have been largely overlooked by social theory in colonial contexts. How do Indigenous peoples in Southwestern Colombia interact with plants for food, medicine, ritual and decision-making purposes? What concepts people use to describe vegetal beings in relation to other aspects of culture? Theoretically situated at the intersection between Indigenous studies (Santos-Granero 2011) and ethnobotany (Balée 2000, 1994; Berlin 1992; Rätsch 2005; Schultes et al. 2001), this review further adopts a relational point of view to study local engagements with plants in the Andean-Amazonian foothills. Perhaps overstated, this perspective considers 'plants' as entities already enmeshed in constitutive relations with other beings. Joining this conversation, some ethnographic works have discussed how human and plants co-produce each other and the kind of knowledge practices that emerge from this interface, while others focus on how local practices with plants are central to understand how territories come into being (Betsky and Padwe 2016).

Indigenous classifications of plants and plant uses, on the other hand, are deeply rooted in local representations of plants as sentient beings, former humans and even family members in Amazonia (Santos-Granero 2011; Echeverry and Kinerai 1993; Urbina 2010). Cultural representations of *certain* plant species as bearers of 'interiority' and even agency determine local taxonomies in this region (Descola 2013; UMIYAC 2000. See Pinkley 1973 for Cofán taxonomies). While this research tracks a series of discourses and material practices with plants, it is particularly attentive to certain Andean-Amazonian vegetal beings whose capacities for action and histories of colonization have determined Indigenous' political struggles for centuries (see Chapters 1 and 2). This is the case of the tobacco plant *(Nicotiana tabacum)*, the coca *(Erythroxylon coca)* and the *caapi* vine, all thinking companions and decision-making partners for many Andean-Amazonian communities today (Echeverry and Kinerai 1993). Plant-human relations have been at the root of territorial and political practices for centuries in this region (ZIO—A'I Foundation and Humboldt Institute 2004; Allen 2002; Caicedo 2015),[39] and today they are part of growing post-development responses to extractivist economies worldwide (Turner 2020).[40] New eco-centric articulations of the law are part and parcel of these responses.

3. Earth Law and the rights of nature

3.1. *Ecological law: a new ontological framework*

National constitutions, court decisions and governance models across the world are increasingly recognizing the role of other-than-human entities in law-making processes, while scholars study how this new legal framework interact with (post-) development agendas in Latin America (Acosta and Martínez 2011; Gudynas 2011). The contested rights of nature clause is a growing response to (neo-) extractivist practices (Svampa 2019) underpinning the global "inter-related crises of climate, food, energy, poverty, and meaning" (Escobar 2016). While this response recognizes the inherent value and integrity of natural systems, beings and relations (Berry 1999; Brown 2015), the increase of intensive extractive practices in this region is not matched by this growing development of jurisprudence on nature rights.[41] This telling discrepancy is the point of departure for this section.

A central tenet of my research is that the 'social' and the 'legal' are expressions of a continuum between human and other-than-human beings (including the supernatural and the 'inert') (Descola 2013). Moreover, the 'social' is an expression of the world-making possibilities of the law as exemplified by the notion of the natural contract (Serres 1992). In conversation with non-dualist approaches in cognitive science (Varela 1999), plant science and plant studies (Gagliano 2014, 2015) and Amerindian ethnography in Amazonia (Viveiros de Castro 1998), this review and research asserts that living entities besides the human are endowed with cognitive and agent-like capacities and therefore have integral roles to play within the social and the legal field.

A second tenet is that the law is embedded in larger onto-epistemic, material and ecological contexts (Vermeylen 2017; Philippopoulos-Mihalopoulos 2017). This attention to the material and post-humanist dimensions of the law is closely related to eco-centric proposals in the Northern hemisphere, for example, the work of historian of ideas and theologian Thomas Berry. Berry proposes a deep transformation of social institutions and practices based on ecological principles in what he calls the Ecozoic era, or the transition toward a "mutually enhancing human-Earth relationship" (Berry 1999). While these works conceptualize the limits of a legal paradigm based on the separation between humans and the larger community of life (Berry 1999), legal norms and ecological relations (Capra and Mattei 2015), social and ecological justice (Harris 2014), among other dualisms, there hasn't been sufficient attention to the relational, systems-based (Garver 2019) and experience-grounded ontologies in which an emergent legal paradigm shall be based. This emergent paradigm seeks to de-center the human and the 'person' (see Chapter 4: "Forest on trial") in legal norms, practices and scholarship (Grear 2017).

De-centering the human, an emergent legal paradigm adopts a relational approach that signals the recursive co-emergence between all beings. This paradigm privileges the integrity of the whole Earth community in the long term over the interests of humans or any other species (Cullinan 2011). What *is* law under this new paradigm? (Davies 2017 for a critique of essentialist questions concerning nature of the law). Broadly speaking, the law is concerned with relations between individuals, communities (human and not), collectives, states and "elementary groupings themselves" (Graham 2011, 15 cited in Burdon 2012, 28. See Burdon 2010). It can therefore be defined as a system of norms about relations.

Paradoxically, explained in terms of norms and procedures separated from the ecological processes it is set off to regulate, legal theory often overlooks the relational and material dimensions of law-making and takes for granted notions of objectivity and subjectivity (personhood) profoundly tied to mechanistic worldviews (Capra and Mattei 2015).

An ontological or relational approach to the law considers the world-making capaciousness of legal institutions, and not only their prescriptive or normative attributes. In this vein, legal norms are already grounded in the concrete experience of humans and other beings as they relate to one another in concrete places, beyond the state formalism of top-down legal codification (Winter 2001). This perspective suggests a systemic and emergentist legal ontology, as opposed to a mechanistic and deterministic approach (Capra and Mattei 2015). The rules we live by emerge in recursive engagement with a world we (humans) co-create along with other species (Winter 2001).

In fact, these rules are not circumscribed to a set of abstract norms separated from the concrete sensory-motor handling of living organisms (Varela 1999). According to this perspective, the law or any other normative system does not precede the mind (Winter 2001) but is something that all organisms engage in "by moving, touching, breathing and eating" (Varela 1999, 7) insofar as all organisms are mind-bearing selves in relentless co-emergence. This relational framework offers an important point of departure toward a new legal paradigm for the post-extractivist Andean-Amazonian region.

Furthermore, while the law is conceptualized as a system (Van de Kerchove and Ost 1994), it is rarely approached from the vantage point of the systems it regulates at ever-increasing pace, for example, geological, biological and social systems (Garver 2019). Within this predominant mechanistic paradigm, the law is conceptualized as an autonomous human institution severed from larger socio-material processes, while these processes are considered external to other-than-human 'nature' (Burdon 2012; Braverman 2018). At its root, this ontology of separation is responsible for the reinforcing relations between top-down environmental governance models, socio-economic disparities and the overall degradation of socio-ecological systems in the Global South.

The field of ecological law (Garver 2013, 2019) reacts against these top-down and command and control approaches of environmental law, thus posing an important challenge to the anthropocentric legal narratives of Western modernity (Mignolo 2013). While ecological law scholars critically integrate the law within larger ethical and scientific concerns (Brown 2015; Garver 2013; Brown and Garver 2009), the relationship between ecological law, neo-extractivism and colonial violence remains largely overlooked (Gudynas 2009). In this sense, this book studies how three non-anthropocentric legal approaches take up the challenge of other-than-human normativities in the context of rampant extractivism and ongoing colonial violence, namely Indigenous legal theories and systems and the emergent ontological turn in legal studies.

This non-anthropocentric approach borrows from Kohn and others to contribute to a new legal paradigm that entails a form of "ecologized" law.[42] Here, I distinguish between "ecological law" and "ecologized law." The latter foregrounds the *active* role other-than-humans play in making the law that emerges through various sets of practices. Ecological law, on the other hand, refers to the normative principles that can be applied to different legal subjects as they attend to relational principles and planetary limits (Garver 2019). While the former is grounded in legal theory and ecological economics, the latter is ethnographically based. Both are inspired by Indigenous conceptual practices and need to work in tandem.

Moreover, this review builds upon a well-established body of literature that seeks to understand and reverse the predominant colonial relation between Western modernity (Mignolo 2013; Escobar 2015) and "Indigenous conceptual worlds" (Viveiros de Castro 2014, 2015). Rather than focusing on how anthropocentric conceptions of the law might impact Indigenous life and cosmologies, I study how Amerindian ways of knowing and being challenge anthropocentric conceptions of the law. Brazilian anthropologist Eduardo Viveiros de Castro has termed this inversion a "remarkable reversal" (2014, 39).

In brief, the law stages the tension between anthropocentric and ecocentric claims about socio-ecological change. Thus far, ecologically oriented legal scholarship sometimes reinforces the separation between humans and other-than-humans because it takes for granted terms such as 'personhood', 'standing' and 'rights' (see Chapter 7: "Conjuring"). In a way, this review and the following chapters remain attentive to the limits and possibilities of an ontological/relational turn in the social sciences and the humanities, and its potential itineraries within the legal field in Latin America.

3.2. *Ecologizing the law: a question of method?*

As indicated, anthropologist Eduardo Kohn's work with the Runa of the Ecuadorian Amazon offers rich ethnographic evidence and methodological guidance on the intrinsic meaning-making and sign-producing capacities of other-than-humans such as plants and animals. In Amazonia, living beings create modes of meaning that are not limited to conventional and language-based symbols. As outlined earlier in this review, Kohn identifies two representational modalities beyond symbolic signs, namely icons, and indexes. Signs are iconic when they share likeness with what they stand for. For example, a picture of my grandmother is an icon of my grandmother. Words like *splash* and *hiccup* are also iconic. Words such as *ta* stand for

> [a]n image of chopping: *tap*. *Pu oh* captures the process by which a tree falls. The snap that initiates its toppling, the swish of the crown free-falling through layers of forest canopy, and the crash and its echoes as it hits the ground are all enfolded in this sonic image.
>
> (2013, 30)

Indexical signs, on the other hand, express a relation of spatial or temporal continuity with what they stand for. Or, in other words, an index stands for some physical feature that points to something other than itself, for instance,

> the sound of the palm tree crashing frightened the monkey from her perch. . . . The crash, as sign (of danger for the monkey), is not a likeness of the object it represents (*like an icon*). Instead, it points to something else. Peirce calls this sort of sign an index.
>
> (2013, 31)

Life represents the world in myriad ways, and this sign-making capacity is also intrinsic to nonhuman beings, Kohn argues. Thus, what we humans share with nonhuman species is not (only or even most crucially) our embodiment, "but the fact that we all live with and through signs . . . signs make what we are." (2013, 9) Non-symbolic representation, then, is common to all life, so life *is not* without signs. Consequently, signs are not the monopoly of (human) language and let alone legal language. Kohn's ontological and methodological argument concerning the mind-manifesting capacities of forests is of special interest for *Law, Humans and Plants* and has been explored in detail in Chapters 1–4.

4. Indigenous legal traditions and decoloniality

Conventionally described in terms of norms and procedures, the law remains separated from larger social and natural systems. As a result, legal orders have become instrumental to the ongoing socio-ecological crisis of our time. How do Indigenous Legal Traditions (ILT) in the Americas conceptualize the relationship between law and life? Can ILT contribute to knowledge-grounded and life-enhancing legal paradigms? For the purposes of this review,

I conceptualize ILT as situated and cross-generational indigenous governance protocols rooted in the principle of interdependence between humans and other than humans. ILT are already in relation to their underlying cosmological and historical contexts and could offer important guidance to probe the limits and possibilities of transforming conventional legal systems in times of planetary crisis. This section is a mouth-opener on the relationship between law and life in Indigenous legal scholarship.

4.1. Decolonizing legal imagination

Scholarship and regulatory proposals around Indigenous Traditional Knowledge (TK) and Traditional Ecological Knowledge (TEK) abound in the Andean-Amazonian context (Caldas 2004). Comparatively, however, there is less explicit attention to Indigenous legal traditions in this region, as well as how they challenge dominant environmental legal models in extractivist contexts. By creating partnerships with a range of national and international NGOs, academics and state actors, indigenous legal systems and decision-making protocols are "partially connected" (Strathern 2005) to state and "colonial" norms in often complicated and surprising ways.

Several scholars explore the interface between decoloniality and legal theory. For example, Barreto's (2012) work on human rights and emotions and Upendra Baxis's work on postcolonial legality (2005) are attempts to bring legal theory into conversation with critics of modernity. In addition, these works explore possible intersections between decolonial theory and legal philosophy in the Latin American context, for example 1) Barreto's recovery of the decolonial theories of Dussel and Mignolo to address human rights issues in a global perspective (Barreto 2012), 2) Baxis' (2005) critique of Western law from the point of view of the subaltern and 3) Acosta (2017) and Gudyna's work on the rights of nature, political ecology and environmental constitutionalism in Ecuador and Bolivia.

On the basis of this scholarship, I analyze issues of legal philosophy such as the sources of legal norms (Law of Origin), the relationship between law and ecological processes, but also urgent debates on territoriality and the collective rights of Indigenous people. I am also interested in Indigenous legal scholarship, as it probes decolonial critiques of modernity to go beyond rationalist theories of law, while refocusing life on the legal systems themselves. More than the critique of rationalism itself, I am interested in exploring how legal scholarship might benefit from relational ontological frameworks and decolonial theories. Some works point in that direction. Once again, Baxi (2005) and Barreto (2012) explore the role of emotions and suffering in human rights discourses (HHRR) as a way of placing the voice and experience of subalternized victims at the center of the debate. They consider not only their experiences as victims but also the role of emotions in the construction of political subjectivities. The 'decolonial gesture' (Mignolo 2014) could not be more explicit in these proposals.

Table 5.1 Comparison of ontological and epistemological features of Anthropocene and Earth-centered paradigms in selected legal concepts

What is emerging in current transitions to an earth-centered paradigm	*Law*	*What some describe as the 'anthropocene'*
Humans and nonhumans, relations	**Legal agent**	Humans (i.e., individuals, groups, collectives, states)
Territories, land, mother earth, plants, ancestry, the non-visible	**Sources of the law**	God, reason, law, power
For ecological relations and between different life forms Socio-ecological justice	**Justice**	For humans and between humans Social justice
Natural contract	**Legal institutions (property, contracts, etc.)**	Social contract

In the Global North, Harris (2014) discusses a notion of socio-ecological justice that integrates what she calls 'trans-species relations'. Thus, she clearly advocates a notion of justice that considers not only human beings but also other beings (organic and nonorganic), while appealing to a relational framework to challenge other categories such as legal capacity, compensation for damages, constitutional justice, among others. Furthermore, Indigenous legal scholarship explores the relationship between Indigenous cosmologies and collective land claims (Consejo Regional Indígena de Huila 2012), thus providing fertile ground for a legal theory that re-centers life in legal thought and practice. Finally, Pottage (2012) contributes to a "material ontology of legal studies" beyond the notion of a "system of rules," while Monateri traces the multicultural origins of the Western legal tradition (2006). These approaches go beyond the ubiquitous logocentric, rationalist and extremely formalistic approach to law and modernity by drawing attention to what Mignolo calls "shifting the geopolitics of knowledge, feeling and belief" (2011). See Table 5.1.

Notes

1 This idea has been challenged in Martinez-Alier (1995).
2 Carl Marx (Grundrisse) 1973, 489 and 527; Carl Marx, (Capital (I)) 1976, 283–290.
3 A materialist approach to reality considers that the origin and development of all that exists depends upon nature as a physical reality. Thus, a philosophical materialism as a complex worldview comprises, among others, a practical materialism that asserts the constitutive role of human agency in the reproduction and transformation of social relations. See Bellamy Foster 21.

4 Marx, (Texts on Method) 1975, 190).
5 Marx, (Capital (I)) 1976, 637; Bellamy Foster 200, 141.
6 Nicolas Kosoy, personal conversation. Nov. 21, 2020.
7 The NonHuman Turn and the New Materialist Turn are tightly related. For a comprehensive account of the latter, see Rick Dolphijn and Iris van der Tuin (2012).
8 On nonhumans: "nature is not a domain defined by animality in contrast with culture as the domain of humanity. The real problem with the use of the category of 'nature' . . . lies . . . with the assumption of a unified non-human domain." Viveiros de Castro (1998, 470).
9 Eduardo Gudynas, Derechos de la Naturaleza y Políticas Ambientales (Jardín Botánico Bogotá 2014); Eduardo Gudynas, 'Alcances y Contenidos de las Transiciones al Post-extractivismo' (2011a) 82 Ecuador Debate 61; Eduardo Gudynas, 'Buen Vivir: Germinando Alternativas al Desarrollo' (2011b) América Latina en Movimiento.
10 Strathern (2005, 13). Roberto Esposito's philosophy of the impersonal, however, offers some analytic keys to the idea of 'the rights of nature' beyond the notion of the person. (2010). Can the idea of 'rights' survive without the notion of personhood? Esposito argues that in order 'to be able to assert legitimately what we call subjective rights (at least in the modern juridical conception of rights), one needs beforehand to have penetrated the enclosed space of the person. Thus, to be a person means enjoying these rights in and of themselves.' (Esposito 2010, 121). See Chapter 4 of this book "Forest on Trial."
11 Here Kohn uses Peirce's definition of a sign "as something that stands to somebody for something in some respect" (cited in Descola 2014, 271).
12 Taking cues from Marder's philosophical project, Vanessa Lemm discusess various characteristics of vegetal life in Nietzsche's work—i.e., the plant as a living entitiy that is capable of measuring; the plant as a living being that is able to incorporate other beings and create value—in order to address the philosofical issue of the origin of value. Nietszche, according to Lemm, concludes that in terms of our (human) capacity to perceive the world, we are not that different from neither plants nor animals. In other words, the way in which humans feel and percieve the world does not differ from the way plants relate to the world as well. See Lemm (2016, 152).
13 A new-materialist theory of law in Alain Pottage, The Materiality of What? (2012) 39(1) Journal of Law and Society 167. An etnnographic account on soy agency as it pertains to the law in Hetherington, Kregg. 2013. "Beans Before the Law: Knowledge Practices, Responsability, and the Paraguayan Soy Boom." *Cultural Anthropology*, 28(1): 65.
14 Comments of an earlier version of this short piece by M. Gagliano, A. Khavari, and S. Whalan.
15 The name herrera comes from the first place where ceramics from this period were found: the Herrera lagoon in the department of Boyaca. See Oquendo, Catalina. 2013. "Viaje a traves de la excavacion arqueologica mas grande del pais." *El Tiempo Magazine*. See www.eltiempo.com/archivo/documento/CMS-13242355 (Accessed 23 November 2019). The Herrera Period or Pre-muisca (900 b.c.—900 a.d) is the first period of archaeological occupation from which there are a good number of records. The presence of agro-potter groups from this period—prior to Muisca settlement—has been registered in all these sites during the last few decades. The influx of agro-potter cultures, perhaps coming from the Northern plains of the country, explains why agrarian practices achieved significant 'progress'. Also, the domestication of useful species such as corn favored the occupation of diverse terrains alongside the rivers of the mountain chain (cordillera).

See www.banrepcultural.org/blaavirtual/faunayflora/paramo/para213.htm (Accessed 23 November 2019).
16 EFE and Semana. 2013. "El Descubrimiento arquelogico mas grande de Colombia." *Semana Magazine*. See www.semana.com/nacion/articulo/descubrimiento-arqueologico-mas-grande-de-colombia/367219-3 (Accessed 23 November 2019).
17 Ibid, Semana, p. 1
18 See Salomon, Frank. 2013. "The Twisting Paths of Recall: Khipu (Andean Cord Notation) as Artifact." In Piquette, K.E., and Whitehouse, R.D. (eds.). *Writing as Material Practice: Substance, Surface and Medium*. London: Ubiquity Press, pp. 15–43.
19 The Enyclopedia Britannica defines literacy as the "capacity to communicate using inscribed, printed, or electronic signs or symbols for representing language. Literacy is customarily contrasted with orality (oral tradition), which encompasses a broad set of strategies for communicating through oral and aural media. In real world situations, however, literate and oral modes of communication coexist and interact, not only within the same culture but also within the very same individual." Available at www.britannica.com/EBchecked/topic/343440/literacy.
20 On this particular issue, see Hicks, Dan. 2010. "The Material-Cultural Turn: Event and Effect." In Beaudry, Mary, and Dan, Hicks (eds.). *The Oxford Handbook of Material Culture Studies*. New York: Oxford University Press. Hicks: "The terms 'material culture' and 'material culture studies' emerged, one after another, during the twentieth century in the disciplines of archaeology and sociocultural anthropology, and especially in the place of intersection between the two: anthropological archaeology. The purpose of this article, however, is to excavate the idea of 'material culture studies', rather than to bury it. Excavation examines the remains of the past in the present and for the present. It proceeds down from the surface, but the archaeological convention is to reverse this sequence in writing: from the past to the present. In the discussion of the history of ideas and theories, a major risk of such a chronological framework is that new ideas are narrated progressively, as paradigm shifts. The main argument of the article relates to the distinctive form taken by the 'cultural turn' in British archaeology and anthropology during the 1980s and 1990s." (2010)
21 The historian Achille Mbembe affirms that 'the term 'archives' first refers to a building, a symbol of a public institution, which is one of the organs of a constituted state. However, by 'archives' is also understood a collection of documents—normally written documents kept in this building. There cannot, therefore, be a definition of 'archives' that does not encompass both the building itself and the documents stored there.' (2002, 19)
22 On the notion of the vernacular see Illich, I., Obras Reunidas, Mexico: Fondo de Cultura Economica, Tomo II, 2006 (in particular the collection of essays "En el Espejo del Pasado").
23 This notion comes from linguistics, and refers to the 'the mechanism of language change by which one language replaces much or all of its lexicon, including basic vocabulary, with that of another language, without drastic change to its grammar. It is principally used to describe pidgins, creoles, and mixed languages. Relexification is not synonymous with lexical borrowing, which describes the situation where a language merely supplements its basic vocabulary with words from another language.' (Wikipedia, consulted on 11–23–2014). On the relationship between relexification, and culture see Brightman, Robert. 1995. "Forget Culture: Replacement, Transcendence, Relexification." *Cultural Anthropology*, 10(4): 509–546. www.jstor.org/stable/656256

24 I am well aware of the anachronistic use of the term 'actor' to refer to groups of peoples in the colonial period. I am using it to assert their active role in this process of hybridization.
25 Rama, Angel, The Lettered City (trans. Chasteen, John). Durham: Duke University Press, 1996.
26 I am not suggesting that instead of cultural mestizaje there was 'cultural purity'. On the contrary, I am suggesting that even holding onto this binary, both processes might have taken place simultaneously.
27 Bluntly put, this expression refers to the semantic value of materials, but also to their capacity to 'convey' meaning on their own. Refer to the following works on this particular issue (the agency of materials). Bennett, Jane. 2010. *Vibrant Matter. A Political Ecology of Things*. Durham: Duke University Press; Law, John. 2007. "Actor Network Theory and Material Semiotics." Version of 25 April 2007. hwww.heterogeneities.net/publications/Law2007ANTandMaterialSemiotics.pdf. See also Keane, Webb. 2003. "Semiotics and the Social Analysis of Material Things." *Language and Communication*, 23: 409–425. townsendgroups.berkeley.edu/sites/default/files/webb_keane_semiotics_and_things.pdf. See Bolt, Barbara. 2007. "Material Thinking and the Agency of Matter." *Studies in Material Thinking*, 1(1). www.materialthinking.org/sites/default/files/papers/Barbara.pdf.
28 Examples of this 'colonial culture' as well as the 'cognitive and philosophical transformations' (R & C 2012, 254) that it implied are cited in their work: "It is precisely in the learning of a perspective by walking the streets of a reduccion, the observation of a corregidor kissing a royal decree, the recounting of a dream sequence that mirrors a painting, the introduction of Spanish tilework in a wattle-end-daub Andean village, that we can begin to perceive the process through which such cognitive transformation occurred." (R & C 2012, 254)
29 Illich, Ivan. 2006. "Por un estudio de la mentalidad alfabetica." In *Obras Reunidas II*. Mexico: Fondo de Cultura Economica, pp. 555–570.
30 Ingold, Tim. 2007. *Lines. A Brief History*. New York: Routledge.
31 For instance, ladino testament is an expression of intercultural literacy with legal purchase, but also guane textiles are expressions of pre-colonial literacies that might be treated as legal evidence of possession of a particular territory.
32 Iván Illich in H20 The Waters of Forgetfulness refers to the change from Mnemosina (el pozo de los recuerdos) into the alphabetic text—where memory is monopolized by the 'letter'. gets inscribed: "el poeta clásico de Grecia ya no necesita de recuerdos de un mas allá. Sus fuentes están congeladas en textos. Sigue las *líneas de un texto escrito; el rio épico que alimenta su propia fuente ya no se recuerda. Ni una sola ciudad griega ha conservado un altar dedicado a Mnemosina ["Las Corrientes llevan los recuerdos que Leteo lavo de los pies de los muertos hacia ese pozo, transformando de esa manera a los seres desaparecidos en meras sombras, a este pozo del recuerdo que los griegos lo llamaron Mnemosina" (Illich, "Las Aguas de Leteo," 370)]. Su nombre se convirtió en un termino técnico para designar la "memoria," ahora imaginada como una pagina; el material de la memoria pasa del agua a la vasija; el leguaje escrito, que ha fijado las palabras en tabletas de arcilla, adquiere mas autoridad que la re-evocación del fluido, habla viviente. Antes se conocían muchos tipos de "escritura," pero todos eran como carriles, mojones o flechas que guiaban el flujo del habla en la dirección correcta. Los pictogramas o los ideogramas no tenían la exclusiva función técnica de fijar los sonidos tal como se pronunciaban, para que pudieran proferirse posteriormente y por algún otro en la misma forma. Antes de que la tradición épica se registrara; antes de que la costumbre pudiese fijarse en ley escrita, el pensamiento y la memoria estaban entrelazados en cada enunciación; el que hablaba*

no tenia modo de imaginar la distinción entre el pensamiento y el lenguaje. La voz no podía almacenarse, no dejaba sedimentos. La composición solmene tenia que adecuarse para seguir el ritmo del hexámetro, enfatizado por la pulsación de las cuerdas de la lira. La conciencia, a falta de la metáfora del alfabeto, tenia que imaginarse como una corriente llena de tesoros. Cada expresión era como un madero que el hablante pescaba en un rio, algo arrojado del mas allá que en ese momento había sido traído a las playas de su mente." (Illich, El Estanque de Reflexión de Mnemosina, 372–3, FCE)

33 Constitución de Ecuador de (2008), and Ley Marco de la Madre Tierra y Desarrollo Integral para el Buen Vivir. See www.harmonywithnatureun.org/content/documents/157Bolivia%20Ley%20300.pdf.

34 I use the notion of 'multi-naturalism' to analyze the rights of nature. See the postscriptum in Chapter 3 "Conjuring."

35 The expression "Ecozoic era" was coined by Thomas Berry and Brian Swimme in their groundbreaking The Universe Story. The term broadly describes "the geologic era that Earth is entering—when humans live in a mutually enhancing relationship with Earth and the Earth community." See https://ecozoictimes.com/what-is-the-ecozoic/what-does-ecozoic-mean/ (Accessed 22 February 2019).

36 See this review: "Post-humanist theory."

37 See Semillas, Grupo. 2016. *La Lucha por las Semillas Libres de los Pueblos Latinoamericanos: Experiencias de Brasil, Ecuador, Colombia, Honduras y Guatemala.* www.semillas.org.co/es/la-lucha-por-las-semillas-libres-de-los-pueblos-latinoamericanos-experiencias-de-brasil-ecuador-colombia-honduras-y#_ftn23 (Accessed 11 November 2020).

38 On plant-thinking, Marder (2013, 152); on 'socio-ecological justice', Lyons (2016); on the 'natural contract', Serres 1995.

39 ZIO—A'I Foundation and Humboldt Institute. 2004. Manual Botánico para el reconocimiento ambiental y cultural de Ukumari Kankhe (Resguardo del Oso.) Also see Cofàn People (with the support of various organizations), Plan de Salvaguarda del Pueblo Cofán. See www.mininterior.gov.co/sites/default/files/p.s_Cofán.pdf (Accessed 11 November 2020).

40 A reconstruction of this genealogy in Escobar, Beyond the Third World. In www3.nd.edu/~druccio/Escobar.pdf (Accessed 11 November 2020).

41 Extractivism in the Latin American context can be better described as 'capitalocene' (Moore 2015). This term accounts for human geological impacts on the planet across humans depending on differential levels of consumption, ownership of the means of production, and ecological footprint. Therefore, this notion accounts for concrete modes of production, division of labor, and power asymmetries, rather than abstract and generic human impacts on the planet. Therefore, a theory of accountability for global ecological damage should reflect these differentials.

42 Kohn (2014). Also see Capra and Mattei (2015).

References

Acosta, Alberto. 2017. "Post-Extractivism: From Discourse to Practice—Reflections for Action." In *Alternative Pathways to Sustainable Development: Lessons from Latin America.* International Development Policy Series No. 9. Geneva, Boston: Graduate Institute Publications, Brill-Nijhoff, pp. 77–101.

Acosta, Alberto, and Martínez, Esperanza. 2011. *Naturaleza Con Derechos : De La Filosofía a La Política* (1st ed.). Quito, Ecuador: Ediciones Abya-Yala.

Akhtar-Khavari, A. 2020. "Restoration and Cooperation for Flourishing Socio-Ecological Landscapes." *Transnational Legal Theory*, 11(1–2): 62–74.

Allen, Catherine. 2002. *The Hold Life Has. Coca and Cultural Identity in an Andean Community*. Washington, DC: Smithsonian Books.
Anker, Kirsten. 2014. *Declarations of Interdependence: A Legal Pluralist Approach to Indigenous Rights*. New York: Routledge.
Anker, Kirsten. 2017. "Law as . . . Forest: Eco-logic, Stories and Spirits in Indigenous Jurisprudence." *Law Text Culture*, 21: 191–213.
Balée, William. 1994. *Footprints of the Forest: Ka'Apor Ethnobotany. The Historical Ecology of Plant Utilization by an Amazonian People*. New York: Columbia University Press.
Balée, William. 2000. "Antiquity of Traditional Ethnobiological Knowledge in Amazonia: The Tupi-Guarani Family and Time." *Ethnohistory*, 47(2): 399–422.
Barreto, Jose Manuel. 2012. "Decolonial Strategies and Dialogue in the Human Rights Field. A Manifesto." *Transnational Legal Theory*, 3(1): 1–29.
Baxi, Upendra. 2005. "Postcolonial Legality." In Schawarz, S., and Ray, S. (eds.). *A Companion to Postcolonial Studies*. Oxford: Blackwell.
Bellamy Foster, John. 2000. *Marx's Ecology*. New York: Monthly Review Press.
Bennet, John. 2013. "Epilogue." In Piquette, K., and Whitehouse, R. (eds.). *Writing as Material Practice: Substance, Surface and Medium*. London: Ubiquity Press.
Bennett, Jane. 2010. *Vibrant Matter. A Political Ecology of Things*. Durham: Duke University Press.
Berlin, B. 1992. *Ethnobiological Classification: Principles of Categorization of Plants and Animals in Traditional Societies*. Princeton: Princeton Unviersity Press.
Berry, Thomas. 1999. *The Great Work. Our Way into the Future*. New York: Bell Tower.
Betsky, Sarah, and Padwe, Jonathan. 2016. "Placing Plants in Territory." *Environment and Society*, 7(1).
Biemann, Ursula, and Tavares, Pablo. 2014. *Forest Law—Selva Jurídica*. East Lansing: Eli and Edythe Broad Art Museum, Michigan State University.
Blaser, Mario. 2013. "Ontological Conflicts and the Stories of Peoples in Spite of Europe: Towards a Conversation on Political Ontology." Accepted for publication in *Current Anthropology*, 54(5): 547–568.
Braverman, Irus. 2016. "Introduction. Lively Legalities." In Braverman, Irus (ed.). *Animals, Biopolitics, Law. Lively Legalities*. New York: Routledge.
Braverman, Irus. 2018. "Law's Underdog: A Call for More-Than-Human Legalities." *Annual Review of Law and Social Science*, 14: 127–144.
Brown, Peter. 2015. "Ethics for Economics in the Anthropocene." In Brown, P., and Timmerman, P. (eds.). *Ecological Economics for the Anthropocene*. New York: Columbia University Press.
Brown, Peter, and Garver, Geoffrey. 2009. *Right Relationship. Building a Whole Earth Economy*. San Francisco: Berreth-Koehler Publishers.
Buden, Boris, Nawotny, Stefan, Simon, Sherry, Bery, Ashok, and Cronin, Michael. 2009. "Cultural Translation: An Introduction to the Problem, and Responses." *Journal of Tranlation Studies*, 2(2): 196–219.
Burdon, Peter. 2010. "The Rights of Nature: Reconsidered." *Australian Humanities Review*, 49: 69.
Burdon, Peter. 2012. *Exploring Wild Law: The Philosophy of Earth Jurisprudence*. Cambridge: Wakefield Press.

Caicedo, Alhena. 2015. *La Alteridad Radical que Cura. Neo-chamanismos yageceros en Colombia*. Bogotá: Universidad de los Andes.
Caldas, Adressa. 2004. *La regulación jurídica del conocimiento tradicional*. Bogotá: ILSA.
Calvo, P., Gagliano, M., Souza, G.M., and Trewavas, A. 2020. "Plants Are Intelligent, and Here Is How." *Annals of Botany*, 125: 11–28.
Capra, Fritjof, and Mattei, Ugo. 2015. *The Ecology of Law: Toward a Legal System in Tune with Nature and Community*. Oakland: Berrett-Koehler Publishers, Incorporated.
Castro-Gómez, Santiago. 2005. *La Hybris del Punto Cero: Ciencia, Raza e Ilustración en la Nueva Granada (1750–1816)*. Bogotá: Editorial Pontificia Universidad Javeriana.
Castro-Gómez, Santiago, y Grosfoguel, Ramón. 2007. *El Giro Decolonial: Reflexiones para una Diversidad Epistémica más allá del capitalismo global*. Bogotá: Siglo del Hombre Editores.
Consejo Regional Indígena de Huila. 2012. *La Ley de Origen de los Pueblos Indígenas*. www.crihu.org/2012/09/la-ley-origen.html
Constitución de la Repúbica del Ecuador 2008, Decreto Legislativo No. 0, Registro Oficial 449 de 20 de Octubre de 2008 2016 [Constitution of the Republic of Ecuador 2008, Legislative Decree No. 0, Official Registration 449, 20 October 2008].
Cullinan, Cullinan. 2011. *Wild Law: A Manifesto for Earth Justice* (2nd ed.). White River Junction, VT: Chelsea Green.
Davies, Margaret. 2017. *Law Unlimited. Materialism, Pluralism, and Legal Theory*. London: Routledge.
De la Cadena, Marisol. 2010. "Indigenous Cosmopolitics in the Andes: Conceptual Reflections Beyond 'politics'." *Cultural Anthropology*, 24(2): 334–370.
De la Cadena, Marisol. 2015. *Earth Beings. Ecologies of Practice. Ecologies of Practice Across Andean Worlds*. Durham: Duke University Press.
De Landa, Manuel. 1997. *A Thousand Years of Nonlinear History*. Zone Books.
Dean, Carolyn. 2010. *A Culture of Stone. Inka Perspectives of Rock*. Durham: Duke University Press.
Descola, Philippe. 2013. *Beyond Nature and Culture*. Chicago: University of Chicago Press.
Descola, Philippe. 2014. "All to Human (Still). A Comment on Eduardo Kohn' How Forest Think." *HAU: Journal of Ethnographic Theory*, 4(2): 268.
Dolphijn, Rick, and van der Tuin, Iris. 2012. *New Materialism: Interviews & Cartographies*. Ann Arbor: University of Michigan.
Echeverry, Juan Alvaro, and Kinerai, Hipólito Candre. 1993. *Tabaco Frío. Coca Dulce. Palabras del Anciano Kinerai de la Tribu Canangucbal para sanar y alegrar el corazón de sus huérfanos*. Bogotá: Concultura.
Escobar, Arturo. 2015. *Sentipensar con la Tierra. Nuevas lecturas sobre desarrollo, territorio y Diferencia*. Medellin, Colombia: Ediciones UNIAULA.
Escobar, Arturo. 2016. "Sentipensar con la Tierra: Las Luchas Territoriales y la Dimensión Ontológica de las Epistemologías del Sur." *Revista de Antropologia Iberoamericana*, 11(1): 11–32.
Escobar, Arturo. 2018. *Designs for the Pluriverse: Radical Interdependence, Autonomy, and the Making of Worlds*. Durham: Duke University Press.

Esposito, Roberto. 2010. "For a Philosophy of the Impersonal." *CR: The New Centennial Review*, 10(2): 121–134.

Federal Ethics Committee on Non-Human Biotechnology (ECNH). 2008. *The Dignity of Living Beings with Regard to Plants. Moral Consideration of Plants for Their Own Sake*. www.ekah.admin.ch/inhalte/ekah-dateien/dokumentation/publikationen/e-Broschure-Wurde-Pflanze-2008.pdf

Few, Martha, and Tortorici, Zeb. 2013. *Centering Animals in Latin American History*. Durham: Duke University Press.

Franks, B., Webb, C., Gagliano, M., and Smuts, B. 2020. "Conventional Science Will Not Do Justice to Nonhuman Interests: A Fresh Approach Is Required. Commentary on Treves et al. on 'Just Preservation'." *Animal Sentience*, 27(17): 1–5.

Gagliano, Monica. 2015. "In a Green Frame of Mind: Perspectives on the Behavioural Ecology and Cognitive Nature of Plants." *AoB Plants*, 7: plu075.

Gagliano, Monica. 2018. *Thus Spoke the Plant: A Remarkable Journey of Groundbreaking Scientific Discoveries and Personal Encounters with Plants*. Berkeley: North Atlantic Books.

Gagliano, Monica, Abramson, C.I., and Depczynski, M. 2018. "Plants Learn and Remember: Lets Get Used to It." *Oecologia*, 186: 29–31.

Gagliano, Monica, and Grimonprez, M. 2015, "Breaking the Silence—Language and the Making of Meaning in Plants." *Ecopsychology*, 7: 143–152.

Gagliano, Monica, Vyazovskiy, V.V., Borbély, A.A., Grimonprez, M., and Depczynski, M. 2016. "Learning by Association in Plants." *Scientific Reports*, 6: 38427.

Garver, Geoffrey. 2013. "The Rule of Ecological Law: The Legal Complement to Degrowth Economics." *Sustainability*, 5: 316–337.

Garver, Geoffrey. 2019. "A Systems-based Tool for Transitioning to Law for a Mutually Enhancing Human-Earth Relationship." *Ecological Economics*, 157: 165–174.

Glenn, Patrick. 2014. *Legal Traditions of the World*. Oxford: Oxford University Press.

Graham, Laura. 2011. *Lawscape: Property, Environment, Law*. New York: Routledge.

Grear, Anna. 2017. "Anthropocene, Capitalocene, Chthulucene': Re-encountering Environmental Law and Its 'Subject' with Haraway and New Materialism." In Kotzé, Louis (ed.). *Environmental Law and Governance for the Anthropocene*. Oregon: Hart Publishing.

Green, Lesley. 2008. "Anthropology of Knowledge and South Africa's Indigenous Knowledge Systems Policy." *Anthropology Southern Africa*, 31(1&2).

Grupo Semillas. 2016. *La Lucha por las Semillas Libres de los Pueblos Latinoamericanos: Experiencias de Brasil, Ecuador, Colombia, Honduras y Guatemala*. www.semillas.org.co/es/la-lucha-por-las-semillas-libres-de-los-pueblos-latinoamericanos-experiencias-de-brasil-ecuador-colombia-honduras-y#_ftn23

Grusin, Richard. 2015. *The Nonhuman Turn*. Minneapolis: University of Minnesota Press.

Gudynas, Eduardo. 2009. "La Ecología política del giro biocéntrico en la nueva Constitución del Ecuador." *Revista de Estudio Sociales*, 34: 34–47.

Gudynas, Eduardo. 2011. "Más allá del nuevo extractivismo: transiciones sostenibles y alternativas al desarrollo." En Wanderley, Fernanda (coord.). *El Desarrollo en Cuestión. Reflexiones desde América Latina*, La Paz: Oxfam y CIDES, pp. 379–410.

Hall, Mattew. 2011. *Plants as Persons. A Philosophical Botany*. New York: State University of New York.

Haraway, Donna. 1991. *Simians, Cyborgs, and Women. The Reinvention of Nature.* New York: Routledge.
Haraway, Donna. 2007. *When Species Meet.* Minneapolis: University of Minnesota Press.
Haraway, Donna. 2016. *Staying with the Trouble. Making kin in the Chthulucene.* Durham: Duke University Press.
Harris, Angela. 2014. "Vulnerability and Power in the Age of the Anthropocene." *Washington and Lee Journal of Energy, Climate, and the Environment*, 6: 98–160.
Harvey, Penny, Casella, Eleanor, Evan, Gillian, Knox, Hannah, McLean, Christine, Silva, Elizabeth, Thoburn, Nicholas, and Woodward, Kath. 2014. *Objects and Materials. A Routledge Companion.* London: Routledge. Taylor and Francis Group.
Hodder, Ian. 2012. *Entangled. An Archeology of the Relationships between Humans and Things.* London: Wiley-Blackwell.
Illich, Ivan. 2006. *Obras Reunidas. II.* Mexico: Fondo de Cultura Economica.
Ingold, Tim. 2007. *Lines. A Brief History.* New York: Routledge.
Ingold, Tim. 2011. *Being Alive: Essays on Movement, Knowledge, and Description.* New York: Routledge.
Kimmerer, Robin Wall. 2013. *Braiding Sweetgrass. Indigenous Wisdom, Scientific Knowledge and the Teching of Plants.* Minneapolis: Milkweed Editors.
Kohn, Eduardo. 2013. *How Forests Think. Towards and Anthropology Beyond the Human.* Berkeley: University of California Press.
Langton, Marcia, y Ma Rhea, Zane. 2005. "Traditional Indigenous Biodiversity-related Knowledge." *Australian Academic and Research Libraries*, 36(2): 47–72.
Latour, Bruno. 1993. *We Have Never Been Modern.* Cambridge, MA: Harvard University Press.
Latour, Bruno. 2004. "Why Has Critique Run Out of Steam? From Matters of Fact to Matters of Concern." *Critical Inquiry*, 30(2): 225–248.
Lauer, Matthew, and Aswani, Shakar. 2009. "Indigenous Ecological Knowledge as Situated Practices: Understanding Fishers' Knowledge in the Western Salomon Islands." *American Antropologist*, 111(3): 317–329.
Lemm, Vanessa. 2016. "Filosofía en los Bordes de lo Humano. La Filosofía Vegetal de Friedrich Nietzsche." In Iván Darío, Ávila Gaitan (ed.). *La Cuestión Animal(ista).* Bogotá: Ediciones Desde Abajo.
Lundberg, Anna, and Kilhamn, Cecilia. 2016. "Transposition of Knowledge: Encountering Proportionality in an Algebra Task." *International Journal of Science and Mathematics Education*, 16: 559–579.
Lyons, Kristina. 2016. "Decomposition as Life Politics: Soils, Selva, and Small Farmers Under the Gun of the US-Colombia War on Drugs." *Cultural Anthropology*, 31(1).
Maffie, James. 2012. "Ethnoepistemology." *Internet Encyclopedia of Philosophy.* www.philpapers.org/rec/MAFE
Mancuso, Stefano, and Viola, Alessandra. 2015. *Brilliant Green. The Surprising History and Science of Plant Intelligence.* Washington, DC: Island Press.
Marder, Michel. 2013. *Plant-thinking. A Philosophy of Vegetal Life.* New York: Columbia University Press.
Martinez-Alier, Joan. 1995. "Political Ecology, Distributional Conflicts, and Economic Incom-Mensurability." *New Left Review*, 211: 70–88.

Marx, Carl. 1973. *Grundrisse*. New York: Vintage.
Marx, Carl. 1975. *Texts on Method*. Oxford: Basil Blackwell Oxford.
Marx, Carl. 1976. *Capital (I)*. New York: Vintage.
MaClean, Kristen. 2015. *Cultural Hybridity and the Environment: Strategies to Celebrate Indigenous Knowledge*. New York: Springer.
Mignolo, Walter. 2011. *The Darker Side of Western Modernity. Global Futures, Decolonial Options*. Durham: Duke University Press.
Mignolo, Walter. 2013. "Geopolitics of Sensing and Knowing: On (De)Coloniality, Border Thinking, and Epistemic Disobedience." *Confero*, 1(1): 129–150.
Mikhalevich, I., and Powell, R. 2020. "Minds Without Spines: Evolutionarily Inclusive Animal Ethics." *Animal Sentience*, 29(1): 1–25.
Monateri, P.G. 2006. *Gayo, el negro: una búsqueda de los orígenes multiculturales de la tradición jurídica occidental*. Bogotá: Siglo del hombre editores.
Moore, Jason. 2015. *Capitalism in the Web of Life. Ecology and the Accumulation of Capital*. Lodon: Verso.
Myers, Natasha. 2015. "Conversations on Plant Sensing: Notes from the Field." *Nature Culture*, 3: 35–66.
Papadopoulos, Dimitris. 2012. "Worlding Justice/Commoning Matter." *Occasion: Interdisciplinary Studies in the Humanities*, 25: 3.
Paternosto, Cesar. 1996. *The Stone and the Thread*. Austin: University of Texas.
Pelizzon, Alessandro, and Gagliano, Monica. 2015. "The Sentience of Plants: Toward a New Regime of Plant Rights, or the Intersection of Animal Rights and Rights of Nature?" *AAPLJ*, 11: 5–13.
Philippopoulos-Mihalopoulos, Andreas. 2017. "Critical Environmental Law in the Anthropocene." In Kotzé, Louis (ed.). *Environmental Law and Governance for the Anthropocene*. Oregon: Hart Publishing.
Pierotti, Raymond, and Wildcat, Raimond. 2000. "Traditional Ecological Knowledge: The Third Alternative (Commentary)." *Ecological Applications*, 10(5): 1333–1340.
Pinkley, Homer Virgil. 1973. *The Ethnoecology of the Cofán Indians*. Doctoral Dissertation, Harvard University Press, Cambridge, MA.
Piquette, K., and Whitehouse, R. 2013. *Writing as Material Practice: Substance, Surface and Medium*. London: Ubiquity Press.
Pollan, Michael. 2002. *The Botany of Deisre. A Plant's Eye View of the World*. New York: Random House.
Pottage, Alain. 2012. *The Materiality of What?* Rochester, NY: Social Science Research.
Powell, B.B. 2009. *Writing: Theory and History of the Technology of Civilization*. Oxford: Wiley-Blackwell.
Quijano Valencia, Olver. 2016. *Ecosimias. Visiones y practicas de diferencia economico/cultural en contextos de multiplicidad*. Popayan: Editorial Unviersidad del Cauca.
Rama, Angel. 1996. *The Lettered City* (J. Chasteen, trans.). Durham: Duke University Press.
Rappaport, J., and Cummins, T. 2011. *Beyond the Lettered City. Indigenous Literacies in the Andes*. Durham: Duke University Press.
Rätsch, C. 2005. *The Encyclopedia of Psychoactive Plants: Ethnopharmacology and Its Applications*. New York: Simon and Schuster.

Robertson, J.S. 2010. "The Possibility and Actuality of Writing." In Houston, S.D. (ed.). *The First Writing: Script Invention as History and Process*. Cambridge: Cambridge University Press, pp. 16–38.
Rocheleau, Dianne. 2008. "Political Ecology in the Key of Policy: From Chains of Explanation to Webs of Relation." *Geoforum*, 39: 716–727.
Salomon, F. and Nino, M.M. 2011. *The Lettered Mountain*. Durham: Duke University Press.
Santos-Granero, Fernando. 2011. "The Virtuous Manioc and the Barbasco: Sublime and Grotesque Modes of Transformation in the Origino of Yanesha Plant Life." *Journal of Ethnobiology*, 31(1): 44–71.
Schultes, R.E., Hofmann, A., and Rätsch, C. 2001. *Plants of the Gods: Their Sacred, Healing, and Hallucinogenic Powers*. Rochester, VT: Healing Arts Press, pp. 124–135.
Serres, Michel. 1992. *The Natural Contract*. Ann Arbor: University of Michigan Press.
Snively, Gloria, and Corsiglia, John. 2000. "Discovering Indigenous Science: Implications for Science Education." *Science Education*, 85(1): 6–34.
Stone, Christopher. 1972. "Should Trees Have Standing? Toward Legal Rights for Natural Object." *Southern California Law Review*, 45: 450–501.
Strathern, Marilyn. 2005. *Partial Connections*. Waltnut, CA: AltaMira Press.
Strathern, Marilyn. 2010. *Kinship, Law and the Unexpected. Relatives Are Always a Surprise*. Cambridge: Cambridge University Press.
Strathern, Marilyn. 2016. "Revolvendo as raízes da antropologia: algumas reflexões sobre 'relações'." *Revista de Antropologia*, 59(1): 224–257.
Svampa, Maristella. 2019. *Las Fronteras del Neoextractivismo en America Latina*. CALAS-Maria Sibylla Merian Center. Ciudad de Mexico.
Taussig, Michael. 2010 (1980). *Devil and Commodity Fetishism in South America*. Chapel Hill: University of North Carolina.
Tedlock, D. 1992. "On Subsistence Transitions: Response to Hawkes and O'Connell." *Current Anthropology*, 33(2): 216–218.
Torres, R., Rincón, M., y Ceballos, N. 2004. "Elementos para la definición de una política de recuperación, protección y fomento del Conocimiento Tradicional." In *Proyecto Política de Acceso y Aprovechamiento de los Recursos Genéticos en Colombia*. Bogotá: Instituto de Investigación de Recursos Biológicos Alexander von Humboldt.
Trewavas, Anthony. 2016. "Plant Intelligence: An Overview." *BioScience*, 66(7): 542–551.
Tsing, A.L. 2015. *The Mushroom at the End of the World*. Princeton: Princeton University Press.
Turner, Nancy (ed.). 2020. *Plants, People, and Places: The Roles of Ethnobotany and Ethnoecology in Indigenous Peoples' Land Rights in Canada and Beyond*. Montreal and Kingston: McGill-Queens's University Press.
Unión de Médicos Indígenas Yagéceros de la Amazonía Colombiana-UMIYAC. 2000. *El Pensamiento de los Mayores. Código de Ética de la Medicina Indígena del Piedemonte Amazónico Colombiano*. Mocoa: UMIYAC. https://umiyac.org/
Urbina Rangel, Fernando. 2010. "El origen de la coca." In Urbina Rangel, Fernando (ed.). *Las palabras del origen. Breve compendio de la mitología de los Uitoto*. Biblioteca Básica de los Pueblo Indígenas de Colombia. Bogotá: Ministerio de Cultura.

Vallejo, Trujillo Florelia. 2007. "Fundamentos constitucionales para la protección del conocimiento tradicional." *Pensamiento Jurídico*, 18: 147–178.

Van de Kerchove, Michael, and Ost, Francois. 1994. *The Legal System between Order and Disorder*. Clarendon Press.

Varela, Francisco. 1999. *Ethical Know-How. Action, Wisdom and Cognition*. Stanford: Stanford University Press.

Varela, Francisco, Thompson, Evan, and Eleanor, Rosh. 1991. *The Embodied Mind. Cognitive Science and Human Experience*. Cambridge, MA: MIT Press.

Vermeylen, Saskia. 2017. "Materiality and the Ontological Turn in the Anthropocene: Establishing a Dialogue between Law, Anthropology, and Eco-philosphy." In Kotzé, Louis (ed.). *Environmental Law and Governance for the Anthropocene*. Oregon: Hart Publishing.

Viveiros de Castro, Eduardo. 1998. "Cosmological Diexis and Amerindian Perspectivism." *Journal of the Royal Anthropological Institute*, 4(3): 469–489.

Viveiros de Castro, Eduardo. 2014. *Cannibal Metaphysics*. Minneapolis: Univocal.

Viveiros de Castro, Eduardo. 2015. *The Relative Native. Essays on Indigenous Conceptual Worlds*. Chicago: HAU Books.

Walsh, Catherine. 2009. *Interculturalidad, Estado, Sociedad: Luchas (de)coloniales de nuestra época*. Quito: Universidad Andina Simón Bolívar/Abya-Yala.

Westermann, Gert, and Mareschal, Denis. 2014. "From Perceptual to Language-Mediated Categorization." *Philosophical Transactions of the Royal Society of London. Series B, Biological Sciences*, 369: 1634.

Winter, Steven. 2001. *A Clearing in the Forest. Law, Life, and Mind*. Chicago: The University of Chicago Press.

Wohlleben, Peter. 2015. *The Hidden Life of Trees: What They Feel, How the Communicate—Discoveries from a Secret World*. Vancouver: Greystone Books.

Yavo, Philippe. 2013. *Technical Know-how in the Indigenous Knowledge System Underlying Batammariba Traditiona Architecture in Togo and Benin*. Doctoral Dissertation. University of Kwazulu-Natal, Kwazulu-Natal, South Africa.

Zelle, Anthony, Wilson, Graham, Adam, Rachel, and Greene, Hermann (eds.). 2021. *Earth Law: Emerging Ecocentric Law. A Practitioner's Guide. Aspen Coursebook Series*. New York: Wolters Kluwer.

ZIO—A'I Foundation and Humboldt Institute. 2004. *Manual Botánico para el reconocimiento ambiental y cultural de Ukumari Kankhe*. Narino, Putumayo, Colombia: Resguardo del Oso.

Chapter 6

Plants and the law

Vegetal ontologies and the rights of nature

Abstract

The chapter proposes two anthropological and legal readings and textual methodologies concerning the rights of nature clause in Latin American constitutionalism. Taking cues from the science of plant sensing and intelligence, the chapter probes how plants can serve as a prototype of constitutional analysis that fully asserts Amazonian principles of relationality and interdependency between all entities. It concludes with an invitation to take seriously interspecies encounters and forms of agency as well as how they unfold in Indigenous law and constitutional analysis and practice in neo-extractivist contexts.

1. Nonhumans and the law: eco-centric analysis and multinaturalist jurisprudence

Over the last three decades, Latin American constitutional history has focused on the social, political and economic effects of institutional reforms that incorporate the nation's cultural diversity within the state law. However, during the last few years, the emergence of environmental constitutions in countries such as Colombia, Ecuador and Bolivia has opened questions about the limits of multiculturalism, as nature is made an important political player within the state's legal and political narratives (Hale 2002, 485). Is Latin America creating room for the point of view of the nonhuman world in legal theory and practice? How is standing before a court of law transformed when using the lens of situated nonhuman (vegetal) agencies? In recognizing the rights of nature and *pachamama*, the Article 71 of the CRE 2008 suggests, on the one hand, that multicultural frameworks are incapable of including forms of cultural difference profoundly tied to ecological realities:

Art. 70. Persons, communities, peoples, nations and communities are bearers of rights and shall enjoy the rights guaranteed to them in the Constitution and in international instruments. Nature shall be subject of those rights that the Constitution recognizes for it.

DOI: 10.4324/9781003349426-12

> **Art. 71.** Nature, or Pachamama, where life is reproduced and occurs, has the right to integral respect for its existence and for the maintenance and regeneration of its life cycles, structure, functions and evolutionary processes. All persons, communities, peoples and nations can call upon public authorities to enforce the rights of nature.

On the other hand, several instances of the application of Article 71 that favors the protection of the environment against the implementation of development projects assert natural beings as social agents in their own right:

> On 30 March 2011 the Provincial Court of Loja granted an injunction against the Provincial Government of Loja to stop violating the Constitutional Rights of the Vilcabama River to exist and maintain its vital cycles, structure, function, and evolutionary processes. This is the first successful Rights of Nature case under Article 71 of the Ecuadorian Constitution. The government's project to build a road without required environmental impact studies detrimentally affected the river's flow causing flooding, and disrupted wildlife and local communities' livelihoods. . . . The Court upheld the precautionary principle that until the Government can prove that the widening of the road would not affected Nature the presumption is for the protection of the rights of Nature.[1]

This constitutional innovation has successfully challenged long-standing principles of Western law and some of the main tenets of modernity itself. In particular, the radical separation between nature and culture and the exclusive social agency of humans. Paradoxically, however, this constitution emerges in a context of intensive extraction of natural "resources" or neo-extractivism (G Gudynas 2009). To be sure, "nature," the emergent subject of rights, still remains the perennial object of knowledge and economic value for the state and capital alike. As Eduardo Gudynas has argued, Latin America's long history of colonization has always been marked by an extractivist ethos.[2]

In this context, indigenous movements and social scholars alike discuss the possibility of a post-extractivist era in the face of global environmental problems and its ensuing socio-economic inequalities. In fact, the juridicization of Amerindian principles of relationality and interdependency casts natural beings as repositories (and producers) of value-in-itself (i.e., the "bio-centric" turn), as it is represented in folk stories, knowledge systems, material culture and local ecologies.[3] In other words, the intrinsic value of nature is an opportunity to "slow down capitalism" and legal fetishism (Stengers 2010). How should we understand the limits of this constitutional clause in the midst of neo-extractivist activities? Are multiculturalism and extractivism related? Is nature falling within a multicultural narrative? The next section (2) offers two legal anthropological readings of the rights of nature clause. It suggests that non-anthropocentric thinking in Latin American legal theory could help us to redefine concepts such as justice and legal standing, among others, to better face the socio-ecological challenges of the present. We, humans, represent and relate to other beings in the context of legal production and circulation does matter when it comes to living together in a world deeply troubled by the interrelated crises of social and ecological systems. Taking cues from the science of plant sensing and intelligence, section 3 suggests (3) that plants can serve as a sort of prototype of (vegetal) nonhuman agency that fully asserts Amerindian principles of relationality, and interdependency between all living and nonliving beings—as suggested in Article 71 of the CRE 2008. For this purpose, (4) the chapter closes with a reference to the use of an Amazonian ritual plant in the context of Indigenous politics and legalities.

2. Two anthropological readings of the rights of nature

The clause on the rights of nature is becoming a well-established reference in contemporary Latin American legal culture, as well as a powerful instance of political transformation (Acosta and Martinez 2011). For several reasons, this clause represents a discontinuity in our regional constitutionalism.[4] First of all, it asserts the material and semantic continuity between "nature" and "culture," while proposing a new socio-ecological contract in the subcontinent (Serres 1995). As the French anthropologist Philippe Descola puts it when highlighting the continuity of the human and the nonhuman world, "this is not a matter of a metaphorical correspondence of a quite classic nature between human development and plant (nonhuman) development. Instead, what we find is a material ('and semantic') continuity between two orders of life" (Descola 2013). However, the juridicization of the nature in national constitutions[5] raises concerns about how this novel set of rights will affect local ecologies, upset dominant representations of nature as the backdrop of human action so central to "sustainable" development projects and how these rights will impact the rule of law across the region.[6] It could be argued, for instance, that extending the circle of rights to nonhuman beings does violence to non-Western systems of justice grounded upon relations of reciprocity with local territories, ancestors and future generations,[7] as well as the non-separation between (legal) knowledge and life. In part, the issues raised by the nonhuman clause are related to a strong multicultural heritage in the region. Thus, what are the limits of a multicultural reading of this clause?

2.1. *From "Western multiculturalism" to "Amerindian multi-naturalism"*

The word "nature" can be enacted in several ways, for example, a multiplicity of animals, plants and minerals, among others, inhabiting the planet; nature as the material and biological aspect of a given culture or society, or as an all-encompassing ecology of relations that includes the human; and nature as a "society" of humans and other-than-human beings dwelling, collaborating and suffering together. A list of possible associations can go on and on. However, I will engage in the following provisional classification on the relationship between "nature" and "culture" as one of the founding binaries of modern ontologies: first, multiculturalism, which states the existence of one nature and multiple cultural representations of it; and, second, multi-naturalism, which asserts the existence of many natures and one single culture (or interiority) shared among different beings (human and not).

These two conceptual schemes populate today's conversations in environmental anthropology and discussions on environmental policy in South America. On the one hand, we have Descola's retrieval of the ubiquitous animism, which he defines as a plurality of natural beings "endowed with (one) identical soul and culture." (Descola 2013, 173). This model resonates with what Viveiros de Castro calls multi-naturalism, "to designate one of the contrastive features of Amerindian thought in relation to Western multiculturalist cosmologies." Viveiros de Castro argues that where multiculturalism is "founded on the mutual implication of the unity of nature and the plurality of cultures—the first guaranteed by the objective universality of body and substance, the second generated by the subjective particularity of spirit and meaning," the Amerindian multinaturalist conception of this relation, "would suppose a spiritual unity and a corporeal diversity" (Vivieros de Castro 1998, 471). On the other hand, the model of naturalism or multiculturalism in Viveiros de Castro's definition conveys one single nature and multiple cultural representations of it. In other words, this model refers to a singular world endowed with as many interpretations and social engagements as there are human cultures. The fundamental difference between these models rests on the continuity or discontinuity on the axis of corporeal differences, and the multiplicity or unity of cultural expressions or perspectives on the axis of interiority. Thus, we are within a multinaturalist framework whenever we affirm the "corporeal heterogeneity of classes of existing beings" (Descola 2013, 173) but the cultural unity or non-fragmentation of culture (interiority). Conversely, if we propose the oneness of nature and the multiplicity of cultural perspectives and expressions in relation to it, we step into a multicultural framework.

This distinction becomes useful to comprehend the terms in which the CRE 2008 conceptualizes nature, as well as the political significance of using one ontological framework over the other. Overall, whenever we say nature—in the singular—we enact the plural *cultures*, thus confirming the singularity of the world from where there can be as many cultural expressions or interpretations as possible. In fact, Article 71 refers to the "rights of nature" seemingly backing a multicultural perspective since it enacts one single nature as a material continuum of nonhumans to which distinct cultural expressions (communities, persons, organizations, tribes, social movements, among others) relate in different ways. However, this interpretation seems to reinstate the ontological difference between nature and culture, rather than its material and semantic continuity—more attuned to a conception of nature as a value-in-itself (biocentrism). In fact, a material continuity between humans and nonhumans only accounts for a shared materiality, but not for a shared experience of collaboration in the making of multiple worlds, which requires common moral and cognitive capacities distributed across multiple species. As Descola argues:

> If the sociability of humans . . . and plants are so intimately connected in Amazonia, that is because their respective forms of collective organization stem from a common model that is quite flexible and that makes it possible to describe interactions between nonhumans by using the named categories that structure relations between humans.
>
> (2013, 9–10)

Within a multicultural framework, however, nature is not casted as a partner in ethical symmetry with the human, but the marginalized *other* to which humans relate differently (Descola 1986, 120). The multicultural interpretation of the rights of nature resonates with what legal hermeneutics calls exegesis or literal interpretation. To be sure, nature is defined as a singular entity that embraces all living beings in a continuum of shared materiality (or physicality), but at the same time affirming the semantic (or internal) discontinuity—ontological difference—between them (see Table 6.1):

Table 6.1 Multicultural interpretation of Art. 71, Constitution of the Republic of Ecuador, 2008

Multicultural Interpretation: ontological discontinuity of humans and nature
Art. 71. Nature (SINGULAR: *a singular materiality, or a singular material world*), or *Pachamama*, where life is reproduced and occurs, has the right to integral respect for its existence and for the maintenance and regeneration of its life cycles, structure, functions and evolutionary processes. All persons, communities, peoples and nations (PLURAL: *a multiplicity of cultural expressions and interpretations*) can call upon public authorities to enforce the rights of nature.

A multinaturalist (Viveiros de Castro) or animist (Descola) interpretation, on the other hand, restores the ethical symmetry between humans and nonhumans, which the naturalist interpretation seems to cancel out when reducing the latter to their bare materiality. By the same token, this new interpretation affirms the subjectivity of nature by recognizing the agent-like capacities of nonhumans and pluralizing its material expressions (different worlds) as well. A multinaturalist approach, therefore, requires an organic interpretation of the Constitution—as opposed to a literal one—whereby, despite the singularizing language used to evoke nature in Articles 70 and 71, expressions such as "life cycles" and "elements comprising an ecosystem" (Art. 71) open up room for natural multiplicities. When pluralized in this way, nature turns into nature(s) (a plurality of worlds), and the notion of rights can be attributed to different "elements comprising the ecosystem." For instance, the rights of waters, the rights of animals, the rights of forests, the rights of plants and, following British anthropologist Marilyn Strathern, "the rights of relations" (2004, 13) (see Table 6.2).

Indeed, if we say nature(s), we are saying one culture—in singular—indicating that to each natural world there corresponds a common cultural

Table 6.2 Multi-natural interpretation of Art. 71, Constitution of the Republic of Ecuador, 2008

Multi-natural Interpretation: ontological continuity between humans and "nature"

Art. 71. Nature (PLURAL: *An internal plurality of beings sharing the same culture or interiority: that is, cognitive and moral capacities*), or *Pachamama*, where life is reproduced and occurs, has the right to integral respect for its existence and for the maintenance and regeneration of its life cycles, structure, functions, and evolutionary processes. All persons, communities, peoples and nations (SINGULAR: *a singularity of cultural expressions, or a shared interiority.*)

continuity (a human condition in Descola's expression), whereby humans and nonhumans alike share common cognitive attributes:

> Animals (and plants) are people or see themselves as persons . . . the manifest form of each species is a mere envelope (a 'clothing') which conceals an internal human form, usually only visible to the eyes of the particular species or to certain trans-species beings such as shamans.[8] This internal form is the 'soul' or 'spirit' of the animal; an intentionality or subjectivity formally identical human consciousness, materializable in a human bodily schema concealed behind an animal mask.
>
> (Vivieros de Castro 1998, 470–471)

In other words, humans, animals and plants—for that matter—all share a common condition which Descola calls humanity: "the site of intentionality, subjectivity, and ultimately, culture" (472). Furthermore, the multi-natural approach attempts to challenge this anthropocentric bias in the legal field, and plants' modes of engagement with the world offer a unique image to undertake this kind of constitutional interpretation. In my view, the multi-natural approach achieves a double task. First, it opens room for a multiplicity of natures (vegetal and otherwise), instead of an all-encompassing natural world endowed with abstract rights. Second, it precludes the impulse of interpreting natural realities through a multicultural lens, thus translating the issue of nature from the field of epistemology into the field of multiple ontologies populating the law. When it comes to the multicultural approach, instead, the possibility of one single nature subjected to multiple representations could take away modes of agency with a role to play in today's ecological crises. Yet what do plants have to do with this multi-natural interpretation of Article 71 of the CRE 2008? What legal lessons can we learn from plants' modes of engagement with other beings?

3. Plants: a prototype of nonhuman (legal) agency?

While nature emerges as an agent of knowledge, a shaping force in social life and a subject of rights in the CRE 2008, thinking with plants can provide a good entry point to collectively reimagine what (else) counts as law in the Latin American region. First, as I tried to point out in the opening introduction, plants and humans do not precede their encounters: subterraneous and aquatic, aerial and aural, literal and metaphoric, plants are constituted through vital relations with other beings and forces. They are embedded within life meshworks that extend far beyond plants' perceived forms above ground, as well as their modes of movement. In the introductory vignette, for example, the withdrawal of the Spanish troops was enabled by the limits of (human) representation, which made it possible for the *páramo* and its plant inhabitants to survive for centuries to come. Yet *plants* and *humans* did not precede this encounter, but emerged from it. Second, plants can accomplish tasks considered exclusive to humans according to anthropocentric concepts of agency. Indeed, plants are sentient beings capable of perception, cognition and communication. For instance, they sense their immediate environments and transform light into food; they interact with other plants through their roots; they also alert their vegetal kin about the presence of predators; and they even hunt, among other qualities (Mancuso and Viola 2015). This is not to say that plants' attributes are valuable because they resemble human ones.

Again, that would be to endorse an anthropocentric stance. The case might be that plants are far more resourceful beings than their human counterparts. Third, plants can also be brought into contemporary debates over, first, the rights of nature: To what extent can plants be subjects of rights? When does the human right to obtain food from plants collide with the plants' rights to the regeneration of the soil where they grow? Second, the creation of territory and place: Can "we think with plants about the nature of territory"? (Betsky and Padwe 2016, 10).[9] And, third, local-based alternatives to neo-extractivism in the region such as the free exchange of seeds and traditional banks of germplasm. Indeed, plants are windows into larger conversations over representations of nature across time and space, legal personhood beyond the human and alternatives to profit-oriented economies.

Moreover, vegetal others are considered incapable of "speech" in the linguistic sense. Yet several instances of Amerindian cosmologies and Western sciences alike consider them capable of communication, meaning-creation and a form of social action in accord with their own perspective. A short step towards a nonhuman theory of legal agency, the next few lines will briefly review some works in the field of plant sensing and intelligence and how "plant-thinking" may help us to think through notions of socio-ecological justice and the natural contract.

3.1. Plants: intelligent and sentient beings

In the ample field of plant studies, several scholars use a phenomenological framework to study plants' modes of intentionality. Others invite us to "consider the moral standing of plants arguing that they are other-than-human persons" (Hall 2011, 5). Science and technology studies/ethnographic approaches with a wide range of actors, however, may offer a more nuanced take on plants intentionality. First, they explore how different practitioners, for instance, peasants and scientists, assign meaning to the plants they work with, but also how "plants sense and make sense of their (own) worlds" (Myers 2015, 36). Anthropologist Natasha Myers explores how plants perceive and respond to their own environments. She suggests that plants are perspectival entities whose meaning-making capacities are not reducible to the conceptual toolkit of their human counterparts—including notions of intentionality or even intelligence. In other words, the locus of their intelligence is not a centralized brain, but a decentralized body, which might ask for different concepts (13).

All these studies attempt to overcome anthropomorphic categorizations of plant behavior as they discuss the possibility of a plant point of view. Marder, for example, proposes the notion of plant-thinking to refer to what plants can do—and what *we* can achieve learning with plants—as well as to their "unique perspective, expressed at the cellular, organismic and environmental levels." The challenge, he argues, "is to look at the world from a plant 'point of view,' for if biology is to be a science of living beings, it must investigate the particular perspective correlated with each distinct form of life" (Marder 2013, 136). Marder implies, however, that life is a collection of discrete entities connected through vectors of predation and symbiosis. What if a focus on relations redefines attributes such as "intelligence," "memory" and "intentionality" as emergent effects of inter-being encounters, rather than specific capacities of the modern human? Our current discursive and practical over-reliance on self-contained entities (i.e., humans, plants, animals, among others) may overlook the importance of interspecies relations in the plane of social theory. This point is crucial as we explore a non-dualist approach to legal agency in sync with Amerindian relational views of life and justice.

3.2. *Socio-ecological justice as seen through the vegetal grid*

As mentioned earlier, some studies have looked at how nonhuman entities partake in legal theory, challenging divisions such as norm/fact, law/life, among others (Pottage 2012; Papadopoulos 2012). There, attention to situated inter-being relations poses several challenges to modern understandings of justice. The notion of socio-ecological justice, for instance, is rooted in indigenous *Ley de Origen* (Law of Origin) and *Derecho Mayor* (Earth Law) across the Andean-Amazonian region (Muelas 2000). First, Law of Origin and Earth Law are neither abstract notions actualized in positive law as principles, rules and procedures, nor expressed through customary law. Law of Origin and Earth Law practices of situated justice and responsibility are embedded in material labor, family care, communal nurturing, plant sowing and practices of commensality, among others. Second, they are embodied as a "common material world," whereby matter stands for shared conditions of existence between living and nonliving entities (Papadopoulos 2012, 1). As Dimitris Papadopoulos suggests, creating alternative material conditions of existence requires local associations of co-responsibility between different species, that is, a natural contract as a form of embedded relationality. Here law seems to stand for life, and life forms—indexically—seem to stand for legal principles of living together.

At the same time, such practices of justice are non-future-oriented in that they strive for a common and situated material world beyond (or before) a normative command that guides action. Hence, Law of Origin and Earth Law propose embodied justice, rather than justice to come; justice through material practices of living together, rather than abstract principles of conviviality that only a few people can read, translate and control.

Moreover, feminist African-American legal scholar Angela Harris discusses a notion of socio-ecological justice that integrates what she calls "trans-species relations." For Harris, a theory of socio-ecological justice underscores nonhuman vulnerability as part and parcel of a concept of justice for the Anthropocene. The fact that human life is "inextricably intertwined with life and non-life, human and not" suggests that the notion of justice should include nonhumans as entities that can potentially be subjected to various forms of injustice. In her words, "just sustainability embraces just social relations among persons, and sustainable relations between humans and the nonhuman world . . . care of the earth and for social justice simultaneously" (Harris 2014, 53). In brief, she suggests integrating social justice and environmental justice, and forms of social inequality to environmental injustice. Again, can plant life inspire law-otherwise? At the beginning of the introduction to this book, I asked: What did Federmann's soldiers see through the fog? This question pointed to the problem of the production of humanity in the context of interspecies encounters. As suggested earlier, plants' modes of engagement with other beings might be a sort of prototype of social (distributed) agency. A sort of interface between worlds, plants connect and foster new relations among living beings. Additionally, in the context of a multinaturalist approach to the CRE 2008, plants, rather than animals, offer a unique image of the plurality of natures that emerge from the constitutional clause. Plants' movements above and below ground, moreover, exemplify Amerindian principles of relationality and interdependency between all living and nonliving entities (i.e., sun, dirt, bees, microorganisms and water, among others). Providing an ethnographic vignette on the experience of *Yagé* among some Amazonian practitioners, the following section attempts to clarify what I mean by vegetal (distributed) agency, and why it pertains to the law (constitutional law).

4. Final remarks: "*De Aquí Viene el Derecho*." The jurisprudence of the plant

D and *E* slowly drank the brew in three long sips, feeling an irresistible nausea. A brief spasm crowned their heads. They sat down, shivering, while waiting for ten, 15 or perhaps 20 minutes. The plant sent them back to the hammock. *D* and *E* travelled far, inwardly, while crossing the lakes of lucid moments and the feverish fields of dreaming. They felt the vibrations of the candlelight in their eyes, feeling a profound isolation. "I can feel my blood moving fast through my veins," one of them said. The plant branched out through their limbs, heads and organs as well. They asked for help.

Almost stumbling up to the *taita's* [elder] corner, *D* and *E* pleaded for a cure. "This is too much," somebody said. The *taita* asked them to sit down: "*Calma! Mejor salga y saque lo que tiene adentro*" [Calm down! Or better go out and expulse all that you have inside], he said with a soft yet firm voice. "*Carajo*! The plant got us!" The drinkers imagined a time before time, or something very special that was preceding and sustaining "all of this."[10] Plants such as those combined in the *Yagé* brew play a central role in Amazonian communities' political and legal dealings within and outside their territories. In fact, Indigenous peoples often invite plants to the negotiation table with other (human) actors, as I have learned with them on several occasions in the regions of Putumayo and Leticia, Colombian Amazon. From the point of view of these communities, for instance, the use of ritual plants is a necessary condition to the *consulta previa* (prior consent) with states or companies attempting to develop economic projects in their territories.[11] From the point of view of the state or the company, however, this consultation rightfully excludes potentially affected nonhuman inhabitants and allies—forests, lagoons, plots, grass and animals, among others—whom, from their point of view, are not asked about their "opinion." However, the consultation with the plant always requires a form of embodied dialogue—that is, ingestion, tact, etc.—as its condition of possibility and emergence. Thus, the "counterparty" arguably inhabits the drinker's body itself: on the one hand, this encounter between the plant and the human is set for a bodily conversation between entities. In our example, it was apparent that the plant was materially questioning the dichotomies that sustained human lives. However, the conditions of possibility for any conversation between the human and the plant depended upon the *limpia* (cleansing) of the human body, that is, the expulsion of excess. The *limpia* allows the emergence of bodily forces that exceed the conventions of dialogue between rational actors and yet provide both meaning to the encounter, as well as full political efficacy. On the other hand, the conversation happened asymmetrically because the drinker was totally surrendered to the world of *Yagé* in the same way in which the prey offers itself to the hunter. In fact, the plant considered the human as a "digestive tract"—the only part of their body that the vegetal *other* seemed to talk to, for "dialoguing" and "cleansing" were both casted as the same action. The plant did not appeal so much to the biography or ideas of the human drinker, but to the materials of their bare existence that would allow for a (corporeal) dialogue between living beings.

The *Yagé* was initially more interested in the stomach than in any other organ because a trans-species dialogue involved a process of bodily cleansing [*limpia*]. Some drinkers may represent this dialogue as an inner conversation with themselves as opposed to a conversation with a plant that was acting at the level of a powerful purge. Indeed, once the plant meets the human in the belly, however, there emerges a condition of shared materiality that makes the dialogue a possible event. In fact, the effective incorporation of the body of the plant into the body of the drinker propitiated this shared materiality in a very intimate sense: a radical embodiment that cancelled the need for divisions. From then on, the collaboration was possible as an effect of an intimate encounter, whereby both the human and the plant engaged in a process of thinking and doing together, for instance, negotiating a contract with a state actor. Some indigenous practitioners I have encountered in the cities of Bogotá and Puerto Leguízamo (Colombian Amazon), for instance, say that the plant teaches them how to organize labor, the production of food and medicinal practices. In fact, following the guidance of the plant makes it possible to have future encounters with her. Yet the plant itself needs the human to persist as a learning partner, that is, to persist as the co-responsible party of their mutual survival.

Yagé is a combination of various elements put together through human action, and "human action" here stands for the emergent effect of plant-human encounters through food, medicine and ritual-political practices. Thus, interactions between species might call our attention to other ideas of what counts as social. This being said, both the CRE 2008 as well as *Yagé* encounters seem to exemplify what Amazonian communities have lived and experienced for centuries in the Andean- Amazonian region, that is, the material intimacy, conviviality and plane of social (yet often antisocial) symmetry between species. From this place of partnership emerges a set of ecological values linked to everyday practices. Also, as Descola, Viveiros de Castro and Kohn, among others, have pointed out, the capacities for interiority are not the exclusive resort of humans. In fact, an ontological difference is not enough to claim ethical superiority since social norms might well be already socio-ecological as well as the by-product of collaborations between living and nonliving entities.

What we learn with *Yagé* is rather obvious from the point of view of an ecological *ethos*, namely that what we deem exclusively human (societies included) is produced in relation with other- than-human beings. In fact, I am not referring to human labor intentionally transforming nature to reproduce human history (i.e., Marx). Again, this seems to be a self-reproduction of the human-through-human praxis. I am suggesting that there are multiple modes of nonhuman production of the social through labor, nonhuman speech and, certainly, nonhuman instances of law-making such as the CRE 2008, which incorporates Ecuadorian indigenous principles of thick life relationality. The case may well be that nonhuman beings force the recognition of their own rights in collaboration with their human Indigenous allies. These allies might have considered vegetal modes of conversation—such as the one just described—in their dealings with lawmakers. Yet if plants and humans co-create one another, first, neither politics nor law are (exclusive) anthropocentric attributes; second, the only subject of rights might be the relation itself (aka M. Strathern), and, finally, bodily conversations are, perhaps, a good mechanism to come to an ecologically sound understanding between species—humans and not. Plants might be a good entry point to imagine this (vegetal) nonhuman rootedness of legal institutions and practices in the Andean-Amazonian region.

Notes

1 Acción de Protección de la Corte Provincial de Loja, Sentencia No. 11121–2011–0010 del 30 de marzo de 2011 [Protective Action issued by the Provincial Court of Loja, Sentence No. 1121–2011–001, 30 March 2011]. See also Gaia Foundation 'Recognition of the Rights of River Vilcabama' *Earth Law Precedents* (online) 27 January 2012 <gaiafoundation.org/earth-law-precedents> (last accessed 6 November 2016).
2 For example, 17th—19th centuries silver mining economy in Potosi to contemporary and ubiquitous forms of coal, oil, timber, and gold extraction.
3 On the bio-centric turn in Latin America, Gudynas (2009). On Indigenous Legal Theory, Lorenzo Muelas (2000).
4 I am referring to a discontinuity within the anthropocentric legal narrative whereby the human is considered the subject of the law, while nature is casted as its object.
5 On green constitutionalism, see Skagen (2007).
6 On law and the environment, see Palacio (2009).
7 On state's self-proclaim 'universal validity' of legal principles, and local indigenous knowledge systems see Iván Vargas, *Sistemas de Conocimiento Ecológico Tradicional. El Caso de una Chagra Amazónica* (online) 22 August 2011 <www.bdigital.unal.edu.co/4097/1/ivandariovargasroncancio.2011.pdf>.
8 The example of *ayahuasca,* the ritual brew used by many Amazonian communities, might be helpful to understand the politics of nonhumas such as plants.
9 On plants and place-making see Betsky and Padwe (2016).
10 Taken from my field notes in Putumayo, Colombian Amazon.
11 See Gobierno Colombiano, *Decreto 1320 de 1998 que 'Reglamenta la Consulta Previa con las comunidades indígenas y negras para la explotación de recursos naturales dentro de su territorio.'* [Colombian Government decree on prior consultation with indigenous and black communities in the context of the exploitation of natural resources in their territories] 13 July 1998. www.urosario.edu.co/jurisprudencia/catedra-viva-intercultural/Documentos/Decreto_1320_de_1998.pdf (Accessed 6 November 2016).

Bibliography

Acción de Protección de la Corte Provincial de Loja, Sentencia No. 11121-2011-0010 del 30 de marzo de 2011 [Protective Action issued by the Provincial Court of Loja, Sentence No. 1121-2011-001, 30 March 2011].

Acosta, Alberto, and Martínez, Esperanza (eds.). 2011. *Naturaleza con Derechos: De La Filosofía a La Política*. Quito: Ediciones Abya-Yala.
Betsky, Sarah, and Padwe, Jonathan. 2016. "Placing Plants in Territory." *Environment and Society*, 7(1).
Descola, Philippe. 1986. *La Nature Domestique: Symbolisme et Praxis dans l'écologie des Achuar*. Paris: Les Editions de la MSH.
Descola, Philippe. 2013. *Beyond Nature and Culture*. Chicago: University of Chicago Press.
Gaia Foundation. 2012. "Recognition of the Rights of River Vilcabama." *Earth Law Precedents* (online), 27 January. gaiafoundation.org/earth-law-precedents (Accessed 6 November 2016).
Gobierno Colombiano. 1998. *Decreto 1320 de 1998 que 'Reglamenta la Consulta Previa con las comunidades indígenas y negras para la explotación de recursos naturales dentro de su territorio* [Colombian Government Decree on Prior Consultation with Indigenous and Black Communities in the Context of the Exploitation of Natural Resources in Their Territories], 13 July. www.urosario.edu.co/jurisprudencia/catedra-viva-intercultural/Documentos/Decreto_1320_de_1998.pdf (Accessed 6 November 2016).
Gudynas, Eduardo. 2009. "La Ecología política del giro biocéntrico en la nueva Constitución del Ecuador." *Revista de Estudio Sociales*, 34: 34–47.
Gudynas, Eduardo. 2011. "Más allá del nuevo extractivismo: transiciones sostenibles y alternativas al desarrollo." En Wanderley, Fernanda (coord.). *El Desarrollo en Cuestión. Reflexiones desde América Latina*. La Paz: Oxfam y CIDES, pp. 379–410.
Hale, Charles. 2002. "Does Multiculturalism Menace? Governance, Cultural Rights, and the Politics of Identity in Guatemala." *Journal of Latin American Studies*, 34(3).
Hall, Mattew. 2011. *Plants as Persons. A Philosophical Botany*. New York: State University of New York.
Haraway, Donna. 2016 *Staying with the Trouble. Making Kin in the Chthulucene*. Durham: Duke University Press.
Harris, Angela. 2014. "Vulnerability and Power in the Age of the Anthropocene." *Washington and Lee Journal of Energy, Climate, and the Environment*, 6: 98–160.
Mancuso, Stephano, and Viola, Stefano. 2015. *Brilliant Green. The Surprising History and Science of Plant Intelligence*. Washington: Island Press.
Marder, Michel. 2013. *Plant-Thinking. A Philosophy of Vegetal Life*. New York: Columbia University Press.
Muelas, Lorenzo. 2000. "El Derecho Mayor no Prescribe." *Ecología Política*, 19.
Myers, Natasha. 2015. "Conversations on Plant Sensing: Notes from the Field." *Nature Culture*, 3: 35–66.
Palacio Castañeda, German. 2009. 'El Papel del Derecho en el Cambio Material y Simbólico del Paisaje Colombiano, 1850–1930." *Pensamiento Jurídico*, 25.
Papadopoulos, Dimitris. 2012. "Worlding Justice/Commoning Matter." *Occasion: Interdisciplinary Studies in the Humanities*, 3.
Pottage, Alain. 2012. "The Materiality of What?" *Journal of Law and Society*, 39(1).
Serres, Michel. 1995. *The Natural Contract*. Ann Arbor: University of Michigan Press.
Skagen, Ekeli Kristian. 2007. "Green Constitutionalism: The Constitutional Protection of Future Generations." *Ratio Juris*, 20(3): 378–401.

Stengers, Isabelle. 2010. "Including Nonhumans in Political Theory: Opening the Pandora's Box?" In Braun, Bruce, and Whatmore, Sarah J. (eds.). *Political Matter: Technoscience, Democracy, and Public Life*. Minneapolis: University of Minnesota Press.

Strathern, Marilyn. 2004. *Partial Connections*. Waltnut-California: AltaMira Press.

Vargas Roncancio, Iván Dario. 2011. *Sistemas de Conocimiento Ecológico Tradicional. El Caso de una Chagra Amazónica*. Master's Thesis. www.bdigital.unal.edu.co/4097/1/ivandariovargasroncancio.2011.pdf> (Accessed 4 March 2017).

Vivieros de Castro, Eduardo. 1998. "Cosmological Diexis and Amerindian Perspectivism." *Journal of the Royal Anthropological Institute*, 4(3): 469–489.

Chapter 7

Conjuring sentient beings and relations in the law

Rights of nature and a comparative praxis of legal cosmologies

Abstract

Conjuring contributes to rethinking fundamental premises of legal sciences in times of planetary crises, namely the idea that the law is primarily linguistic or propositional and the notion that rights and responsibilities are commensurable across different legal cultures and cosmologies. Drawing from legal theory, post-humanist anthropology and Amazonian ethnography, *Conjuring* proposes a new comparative methodology for legal analysis. It compares two overarching pre-analytical assumptions of a constitutional text and their diverging consequences for constitutional adjudication: on the one hand, *right of nature as text*, that is, a set of textual propositions based upon the ontological premise that the 'real' is divided into nature and culture. And second, *rights of nature* as *teks*, based on what I have called the *Principle of Radical Interdependence* (PRI). Discerning this new ontological premise and its consequences for legal analysis implies a tectonic reading that goes beyond the human, language and the state.

Introduction

Recent norms and judicial decisions on the rights of nature (RON) place life at the center of legal discourse in Latin America (Martínez and Acosta 2017). This "legal revolution" (Boyd 2017) thus purports to upend the paradigm of solely human legal subjectivity in recognizing the personhood of nature. Nevertheless, the RON approach seems to depend on an assumption that the form of law is primarily linguistic and propositional. In this way, it reveals another critical assumption: that law is a system of norms made by humans to regulate human conduct in relation to an externally existing natural world, thereby insisting on a separation between law and life processes. This chapter argues that recognizing nature as a legal person and subject of rights falls short if law is understood as a matter of human language only and nature is understood as an adequate conception of cosmological interdependencies between "all that exists" (Escobar 2018). The thesis of law as language seems to reinforce a much-contested rift between mind and body, culture and nature, among other boundary-making notions at the root of modern thought and practice

DOI: 10.4324/9781003349426-13

(Descola 2013). In what sense, then, could conjuring other-than-human beings as agents of legal meaning, rather than mere recipients of state-sanctioned rights, transform what we mean by law and RON in Latin America?[1]

This chapter probes this question in three steps. First, it discusses a relational ontology of law based on the principle of radical interdependence of all that exists (Escobar 2018; Mills 2019), then explores how this approach may challenge understandings of RON premised on an ontology of separation or fragmentation of the living.[2] As a way to encounter radical interdependencies in law, the third part discusses a methodology to harness RON's potentials to heal socio-ecological relations[3] concealed by a theory of "law as language" (Anker 2017, 208). The chapter concludes that repairing[4] these relations through the law involves the crucial speculative step of rethinking our ontological commitments to an all-too-human law to hold space open for another legal imagination and practice (Stone 1972. See Cullinan 2011; Pelizzon and Gagliano 2015).

1. Relational ontologies in legal thought

The principle of "radical interdependence" suggests that entities do not precede the relationships that comprise them (Escobar 2018). In fact, all existents, whether minerals, animals, plants, human or rivers, co-emerge relationally. From discrete entities to interdependencies, the implications of this "remarkable reversal" (Viveiros de Castro 2014, 39) for legal theory and practice are profound. This section argues that the law can be imagined as a *way of life* and thus embraces Anker's radical proposal to consider "what it is to take forests, mountains, and rivers as law" (2017, 194) or as more-than human language (Kohn 2013). A theory and practice of law based upon this principle, namely a relational legal ontology, could leverage much-needed socio-ecological transformations in Latin America.[5]

1.1. Law as meshwork

Anthropologist Tim Ingold defines a way of life as the trajectory of movement and growth of all beings. Every being is instantiated in the world "as a path of movement along a way of life" (2011, 4), and these paths or lines form a tapestry of co-emergent lifeways that he calls a "meshwork" (2011, 63). To further clarify this notion, Ingold contrasts the meshwork with the idea of "network," which represents the interconnection between preexistent entities in space. He notes that what is commonly known as the web of life, that is, the material relationships between organisms in an ecological community, is not a "network of connected points but a meshwork of interwoven lines" in a particular place (2011, 63). For example, winding rivers, growing plants, moving animals and humans, and even legal propositions, are all ways of life or trajectories of growth and movement relentlessly emerging together. The notion of a way of life then blurs the dividing lines between life as the domain of biological phenomena and law as the domain of social meaning in Western metaphysics.[6]

Depicting ways of life and movement rather than substances, indigenous concepts of the self in Amazonia further illustrate this relational ontology.

In Amazonia, animals, plants, mountains and rivers, among other beings, are endowed with a form of interiority or soul with attributes "identical to those of humans, such as reflexive consciousness, intentionality, affective life, and respect for ethical principles" (Descola 2013, 14).[7] In this region, the world is not intrinsically organized through the stable categories of nature and culture since all beings (human and not) share a common interiority concealed underneath the mask of their own bodies (Descola 2013). This theory of the self as multiple "natures" or bodies sharing a common interiority or "culture" across different kinds of beings affords quite a different understanding of the law as something beyond cultural or human meaning. For indigenous communities in Southwestern Colombia, legal protocols come into being through ritual and everyday relations between animals, plants, spirits and humans mediated by the *taita* (often a traditional political authority), or the shaman (medicine and spiritual person).[8] Applied in instances ranging from ritual procedures to research contracts and from prior consultation between the state and local authorities to the allocation of justice in the community itself, legal meaning in these protocols is the emergent effect of inter-being engagements rather than the will of the human expressed through the vehicle of language.[9]

This legal cosmology imagines the law as a meshwork and challenges "Western" legal theory on at least two fronts. First, it expands the arc of legal subjectivity to include humans and more-than-human beings as ways of life or movement rather than settled bodies with predesigned limits. Strathern claims that, although the modern conception of the (natural or corporate) individual as the archetypal legal person prevents the recognition of relationships as legal subjects, both relationships and legal subjects "are embodied in persons (human and not) subject to political-ritual protocols and public attention" and so can be equivalent (2005, 13). An ontological commitment to relations rather than substances has a special bearing in concrete scenarios of adjudication where legal redress requires politically contentious demarcations of socio-ecosystems (see *Corte Constitucional de Colombia*, Decision T-622/2016; *Corte Suprema de Justicia de Colombia*, Decision STC 4360–2018; *Ley de Derechos de la Madre Tierra*, No. 071, 21, 2010).

Secondly, this relational principle exceeds or destabilizes the dualistic categories that structure legal thinking from the ground up in modern law. For example, in its Decision SU-510/1998, the Colombian Constitutional Court grasped that the non-separation between the plane of spirituality and the plane of the mundane practiced by the Ika (an indigenous group in Northern Colombia) was part of the general integration of systems (religious, social, legal) in Ika life. Non-separation is expressed by Ika through *pagamentos* (payments) to Mother Earth—such as through offerings of food, archaeological objects, human hair, semen, blood, cotton-threads, seashells and communal work—and precedes almost any human act from the most ordinary to the most arcane. The Ika were seeking to prevent the proselytizing activities in their communities of an evangelical church, which prohibits *pagamentos* as superstitious beliefs. The Court upheld an Action of Protection on the basis that proselytism was a threat to local forms of embodied spirituality as an expression of the Ley de Origen (the Original Law of Universal Balance) and therefore to indigenous rights to cultural diversity. The Court writes that "each thought, act, fact or object, regardless of the field in which it occurs or is found, has a religious meaning that is essential to individual and collective existence" (Decision SU-510/1998, p. 64). To explain the relational principle, the Court highlights the Ika metaphor of weaving, noting that weaving fabric literally means "weaving the fabric of one's life," that is, participating in a way of life that both create material forms (a piece of fabric) while exceeding these forms to *do* persons with thoughts and social roles. A relational practice with material and social/semiotic orientations, weaving "organizes and intertwines the web of social relations where the weaver is also inserted." (44) Thus, it is through weaving that "thoughts are organized and embedded in the universal order that fulfills . . . the Mother's (Earth) Law" (44). Powerfully, in drawing on Ika cosmologies and material practices of interdependence to uphold the Ika Ley de Origen, the Court itself engaged in a relational practice of weaving between the dualistic categories of law "proper" and Indigenous "custom."

So how does a relational ontology transform our understanding and practice of the RON beyond the recognition of state-granted rights to natural entities? What does it mean to grant rights to relationships instead of substances and/or persons? In the next section, I claim, first, that although it promises to draw on these relational ontologies, RON does so in a limited way. Taken as legal language to shift the idea of actors, namely as a human-*only* issue, the RON approach transposes the notion of the individual as a legal subject onto nonhuman fluid agencies without integrating their constitutive interdependencies. Secondly, and perhaps more crucially, RON's *realpolitik* is far removed from the ontological commitment to the nonhuman as a value in itself (Gudynas 2011). Although several Latin American nations recognize nature as a subject of rights via their constitutions,[10] legislation[11] and case law,[12] the RON approach has had the effect of concealing extractivist economies (Weitzner 2017) and the rights that enable these economic practices (i.e., property, entrepreneurial freedom, patents), to the detriment of the rights advanced, for example, the rights "to exist, persist, maintain . . . vital cycles, structure, functions and . . . evolutionary processes" of nature (Constitution of Ecuador 2008, Art. 71). Taken as a set of normative propositions to expand the arc of legal subjectivity to rivers, forests and animals, RON actually conceals the lifeways where these rights are embedded, namely a tapestry of territories, indigenous struggles, forms of legal meaning and economic systems,[13] among others. Partly thanks to a deep-seated conception of the law as a human domain separated from and on top of the living relations it aims to regulate, RON forms a seemingly autonomous set of normative propositions in a meshwork of lifeways turned into resources, commodities and environmental services through the circuits of capital (Kosoy and Corbera 2010). As autonomous propositions, these rights can be played off—balanced, cost-benefited—against other abstract rights to resources that ignore the lifeways that sustain them both.

2. Rights of nature and ontologies of separation

A game-changing leap in legal theory, the rights of nature approach is still grounded in the ontology of separation between law and life that endorses a conception of law as human language only (Anker 2017). However, RON has the potential to heal socio-ecological relationships. This section summarizes important challenges this pervasive ontology of separation poses for the implementation of RON and the final section, *Reweaving the legal fabric: a tectonic methodology*, probes how enacting RON as meshwork can become a tool for what Escobar calls the "political activation of relationality" (Escobar 2018. See Blaser 2013). This activation of relational ontologies

> can be gleaned from developments in fields as varied as local food and environmental activism, opposition to extractivism, alternative economies . . . and some varieties of urban environmentalism, as well as from emerging transition frameworks such as degrowth in the Global North and 'alternatives to development' and *Buen Vivir* in the Global South.
>
> (Escobar 2018, 101)

Yet this activation will need to go hand in hand with ensuing legal transformations not only at the level of positive law but also at the level of legal imagination. A tectonic methodology can be a step forward in this direction.

2.1. The challenges: diffuse nature, collision of cosmologies, discreteness and human mediation

Generally speaking, Western legal theory is based upon the primacy of separation between social facts and ecological interdependencies; norms and values; positive law and local customs, among others. And it is precisely because of this separation that it is possible to speak of rights for *external* natural beings. It is challenging, however, if one takes a rights approach, to say that nature should be *in* law without radically transforming what we mean both by nature and law. The difficulty of a legal embeddedness of "nature" speaks to the limits of using categories of a legal ontology based on "nature," and of the concept of rights as trump-style claims conferred by the state on nonhumans, giving them legal meaning which they would otherwise lack. There are a number of conceptual, but also deeply political, challenges in understanding rights of nature:

- *Diffuse nature*: The notion of nature is diffuse because this word may refer to humans and nonhumans, or to nonhuman beings only (Greene, *unpublished*, 1). Since nature is pervasive in human life and human impacts are pervasive in nature, they cannot be separated. Whereas this argument is common parlance in social theory today (Ulloa 2005), it highlights the need for a new language of interdependence to overcome the primacy of separation and its cascading effects on socio-ecosystems. This diffuse character of nature speaks to the encounters between divergent ways of seeing and worlding, or different cosmologies.

- *Collision of cosmologies*: The second challenge refers to what we can call the collision of legal cosmologies (Western and non-Western). The Constitution of Ecuador, for example, recognizes an ample set of rights for natural beings in the following terms: "Art. 71. Nature, or Pachamama, where life is reproduced and occurs, has the right to integral respect for its existence."[14] The clause undoubtedly expands the circle of rights to a generic nature as an index of a legal paradigm shift in contexts of socio-ecological collapse. Do we need to seek the consistency between this clause and the principle of radical interdependence outside of the legal text (the proposition)? At the propositional level, the clause extends personhood to a *generic* nature that is immediately equated to the Andean Pachamama. For Quechua-speaking people, however, Pachamama encompasses the Earth/time; the Sun and the Moon; the Goddess of Fertility; and the prime origin of all that exists.[15] Does this generic nature 2.0, that is, as legal person,[16] encapsulate the inter-existences of Pachamama? Does granting rights to the Andean Condor or the Amazonian manatee secure the ongoingness of the relations that make these nonhuman selves thrive? And what about the rights of the Andean mountains and the Amazonian rivers where these (non)human people co-emerge? This challenge brings us closer to the problem of rendering all existents either as discrete substances or as fluid lifeways or "paths of movement and growth" (Ingold 2011).
- *Discreteness*: This nature is composed of millions of species and "each aspect of nature involves a different (socio-legal) interest" (Greene, 2). As a result, it is impossible to articulate legal claims for each component of nature (see Burdon 2010), which means that a democracy of rights based on discrete beings is impracticable and may lead to an identity politics for nature with challenges similar to those already faced by humans groups, such as the state recognition of peasant communities as collective actors beyond markers of ethnicity or race. Here is a telling example to illustrate this point:

> one may say an ant has a right to live, to eat, and to protect itself by stinging, but does it have such rights at all times and in all places? If not, what are the ant's rights relative to other components of nature, especially humans?
> (Greene, 2)

Therefore, the state recognition of rights refers to the problem of representation and mediation of (human and nonhuman) interests.

- *Human mediation*: The nonhuman will always require the mediation of a human guardian because nonhuman beings cannot articulate legal claims before a court of law using a symbolic system of communication (Kohn

2013). The self-standing of nonhumans, as it were, is impossible within a legal system based on an idea of law as language only, or a conception of law as a human-only system of meaning.[17] However, this difference in modes of communication between human and nonhuman selves should not foreclose *other forms of speaking and listening in the legal field.* The understanding of rights as a human language only performs a particular kind of difference between the human and other lifeways, for example, a mountain. And this kind of difference is specific to the so-called naturalist ontology of modernity that pro-claims the existence of a single common nature shared between different human cultures that have different representations of it (Descola 2013), or different cultural systems.

These challenges raise at least three crucial questions for legal theory. What should be considered as existent for concrete scenarios of adjudication? What kind of people should act on whose behalf? And what is the procedure for adjudicating rights in contexts of pervasive extractivism and war? The preceding assessment calls for a radical transformation of RON's legal imagination. As RON highlight substantial territorial and cultural claims by indigenous and peasant communities in Latin America, established critique has underlined the dangers of reducing those rights to a mere icon of "environmental statehood" (Rossotto 2014) in contexts of extractivism. The gap between aspirational legal propositions, on the one hand, and increasing neo-extractivist practices, on the other (Svampa 2019; Gudynas 2011), is but a symptom of a deeper rift between the co-emergent logic of life and the mechanistic logic of the law in modern societies (Capra and Mattei 2015).

3. Reweaving the legal fabric: a tectonic methodology to encounter RON in life

By following RON to their underlying life-worlds and bringing the latter back to the surface of adjudication, in this section, I propose a tectonic reading methodology as an invitation to harness RON's potential to "heal the web of life," following Colombian anthropologist Arturo Escobar (2018, 2019). Escobar suggests a relational concept of health as the interaction between elements stemming from an entire range of systems (biophysical, economic, political, cultural, environmental, spiritual). According to this holistic perspective, we can also define healing as "an emergent property of the dynamic interaction of the self-organizing networks entailed in these systems, not the result of a few factors" (Escobar 2019, 3). Adopting this perspective, Escobar suggests, "one reaches the conclusion that what needs to be healed is the entire system of relations, not just bodies or ecosystems" (3). With this in mind, the next section fleshes out a methodology to harness these healing possibilities in the law.

The methodology should be considered as a mode of asking questions and following legal propositions to their underlying life-worlds and compares two contrasting RON imaginaries. The first one will be referred to as the state proposition, which describes RON as (state) language to grant legal subjectivity to nature. The second one, the cosmological proposition, imagines RON as a meshwork of lifeways, namely an opportunity for the legal activation of relationality. This section claims that RON as simply *language* makes nature as network (ontology of separation), whereas RON as *lifeway* makes cosmos as meshwork (relational ontology).

3.1. Reading RON as text and as teks

A tectonic reading of the law refers to the act of comparing two different albeit partially connected enactments of the law. In this context, "proposition" designates a unit of comparison. For the purposes of my argument, the phrases "X has a right to Y" or "X has a responsibility to Y" are examples of such a propositional language. In addition, I use the term "tectonic" in two ways:

(1) As the underlying plates of the earth's crust shifting us inexorably around the globe, crashing into each other. Following RON's relations all the way to their underlying life-worlds is, first and foremost, to encounter the collision of two different modes of worlding through the law, namely separation and interdependence.
(2) The act of weaving, for example, a fabric like that woven by the Ika community in Northern Colombia. The Indo-European root of tectonic (teks) means to weave and "to make a wicker or wattle framework for mud walls" (Paternosto 1996, 165). In fact, the words "text," "texture" and "context" all derive from the word textere, which comes from the same root as teks. "One of the root's suffix forms, teks-la, is in Latin tela (net, warp, spiderweb), while another of its suffix forms, teks-na, means 'artisanry' (weaving or fabricating), which in Greek is tekhne (art, artisanry, skill)" (Paternosto 1996). I use these two meanings analogically.

Once we notice the collision of ontologies represented in these two propositions (state and cosmological), we can now begin to analyze how they are enacted through the law vis-à-vis the rights of nature. For our purposes, the tectonic analysis refers to the legal proposition both as a text, that is, the words written in a document, as well as teks, that is, the action of weaving a meshwork (spiderweb, *tela* or fabric) in the Ingoldian sense. This tectonic strategy reveals different modes of worlding through the law. A corollary of the radical ontological difference between separation and interdependence, RON-as-text would be akin to a state proposition that enacts rights for nature as a delocalized abstract person. At the same time, RON-as-*teks* would be akin to a cosmological proposition that enacts rights for a radically situated bundle of socio-ecological relations in particular places vis-à-vis fluid legal meshworks. RON as *teks* recursively emerges from local ecologies and places with histories that cannot be transplanted into other places without some form of colonial damage. In brief, RON-as-text makes nature as network, whereas RON-as-teks makes cosmos as meshwork (see Table 7.1).

In Table 7.1, I bring these two RON ontologies together and engage in a comparative analysis between them. In a way, the table attempts to call attention to the mutual incommensurability between these two ontologies (and the different worlds they *world*) as it follows RON to their constitutive meshworks. The comparative methodology includes the following steps: (1) the selection of propositions *a* and *b* (*state* and *cosmological* propositions respectively); (2) defining criteria of comparison between them while acknowledging the limits of cross-ontological translation—or the impossibility of ontological equivalence or incommensurability (Munda 2016); (3) determining the fluid "outcomes" of comparison; as well as (4) possible questions for practical scenarios of adjudication (see Table 7.2).

This comparative analysis attempts to encounter legal language differently, that is, as one thread in a living tapestry of human and more than human lifeways. This analysis is then an invitation to read the state proposition (e.g., "Nature has rights to") in the broader context of extralegal and extra-human

Table 7.1 Collision of cosmologies

State proposition	*Cosmological proposition*
RON as language	RON as lifeways
RON as text	RON as teks
Network	Meshwork
Nature	Cosmos

Table 7.2 Tectonic reading of the rights of nature

(a) State proposition	*(b) Cosmological proposition*
Pre-analytical assumption: The rights of nature are transparently listed in the law (i.e., a Constitution). They "exist" as language.	**Pre-analytical assumption:** The rights of nature may not *exist* as legal language and the general notion of "rights" may not have a local equivalent. Strictly speaking, the comparison may not be possible and this itself can be considered an outcome of the act of comparison. "Rights" to something might be locally articulated as "responsibilities" towards something or oneself.
(3) Selecting the proposition **Chapter 7: Rights of nature**	***(1) Selecting the proposition*** **Conception and Application of the Law of the Origin of the Inga People (Colombia)**

(Continued)

Table 7.2 (Continued)

(a) State proposition	*(b) Cosmological proposition*
Art. 71: Nature or Pachamama, where life is reproduced and exists, has the right to exist, persist, maintain and regenerate its vital cycles, structure, functions and its processes in evolution. Every person, people, community or nationality will be able to demand the recognition of rights for nature before the public organisms (Constitution of Ecuador 2008).	Wasikamas law (the law of the guardianship of the Earth) is recognized in daily life as the existence of an infinite web of relationships between humans, animals, plants, spirits and minerals. Wasikamas is found in the Inga language as one of the most important sources where the Ancestral Knowledge of our community is revitalized; this knowledge holds the key to the Andean and Amazonian worlds. Wasikamas is *samai* (joyful resting) or encounter between beings in time and space.[18]
(2) Criteria of comparison a. What is considered as existent (e.g.): • Nature or Pachamama (partition of beings) • Humans • . . . b. Who has (or has not) rights • Nature and all its partitions • . . . c. What kind of rights does this "who" has? • Right to exist • Right to evolutionary processes • . . . d. Who speaks at the court of law • Humans (person, people, community or nationality . . .) on behalf of nature. e. Reading strategy and aim of the proposition • Exegesis under conditions of law as a system of norms • Aim: allocating rights and responsibilities among existents	***(2) Criteria of comparison*** a. What is considered as existent (e.g.): • Web of relationships • Plants, animals, humans, minerals (continuity of beings) • . . . b. Who has (or has not) rights • It is hard to determine based on this propositional form only. • More than rights, the law is about the guardianship of the Earth. • Existents are inter-dependent, and this interdependence can be subject to rights. Ensuing need to "compose" this local interdependence before adjudicating rights. c. What kind of rights does this "who" have? • Those emerging from encountering what is considered as existent • Guardianship of the Earth • Responsibilities rather than rights • Rights (to exist, etc.) d. Who speaks at the court of law • Web of relations where humans are embedded. • Humans as bundles of relations speak on "behalf" of those socio-ecological relations e. Reading strategy and aim of the proposition: • Tectonic: following relations through propositions and experience • Aim: harnessing RON as a tool to re-compose "the infinite web of relationships" or healing life in a place (see later)

(a) State proposition	*(b) Cosmological proposition*
(3) Determining fluid "outcomes" of comparison • Legal ontology of separation • RON as text • Providing a normative horizon for protection for nature (i.e., environmental law)	***(3) Determining fluid "outcomes" of comparison*** • Legal relational ontology • RON as *teks* can heal socio-ecological relations • Offering a normative horizon of regeneration of life relations in contexts of extractivism (i.e., Earth Law, ecological law)
(4) Determining possible questions for practical scenarios of adjudication • *Pachamama* is the Fertility Goddess who presides over planting and harvesting, embodies mountains, rivers and forests and causes natural disasters as well. Are nature and *Pachamama* the same? Are we granting rights to the same kind of *person*? • Are these persons (nature and *Pachamama*) partially connected? • Does granting rights to nature, with all its partitions, harm *Pachamama* in any way?	***(4) Determining possible questions for practical scenarios of adjudication*** • What are the challenges and possibilities of considering this story as a source of law? • "How much" ontological uncertainty about the subject of rights is acceptable before engaging in the act of adjudication? • Does the idea of the sacred impose yet another dualism between a transcendental entity and the inherent powers of a creative Earth itself?

"evidence." In this sense, it aims to probe the possibilities and limits of translation between different legal systems and the worlds they capacitate, and, perhaps more importantly, it is an invitation to consider the nonhuman seriously in legal theory and practice. Although schematic, the analysis suggests that healing relations through the law—or, paraphrasing Escobar (2018), the legal activation of relationality—is also a task of comparison between propositions (and between relations). But it is also a task of following RON's lifeways as far as they can take us in a particular legal case. Next, I unpack the elements of this comparison.

3.2. Comparing propositions: what do we make of this analysis?

Pre-analytical assumptions: The state proposition—RON as a set of normative claims—suggests that the rights of nature exist first and foremost as state language. This premise brings into being a particular kind of legal entity: nature. The cosmological proposition—RON as meshwork—suggests exactly the opposite, that is, RON might not *exist* as such and even the notion of "rights" might not have a local equivalent where the web of life has been broken and yet the activation of legal redress is still needed. This radical difference could cancel out the "resolution" of a case vis-à-vis the mere recognition of rights. In fact, the comparison between these two propositions reveals the possibility of their mutual incommensurability given the absence of a common ground of comparison. In other words, what the state proposition sees as rights, the cosmological proposition might see as responsibilities (a sort of legal "perspectivism," Viveiros de Castro 1998). The underlying tectonic effect—the collision of cosmologies—presents us with an interesting realization, namely there are different ways of conceptualizing what the law *is* as well as different ways of worlding through the law, and they might not be mutually commensurable.

Selecting the proposition: In the state proposition, RON is ontologically prior to acts of comparison and adjudication. Hence, these rights *exist* primarily as language vis-à-vis positive law. Conversely, in the cosmological proposition, RON *becomes* both (a) an emergent property of cross-ontological comparison or its impossibility (that is, RON is what comes after (dis) agreements between agents of the human and nonhuman type) as well as (b) what is already recognized as "an infinite web of relationships" in the everyday of a particular collective, for example, the Law of the Guardianship of the Earth of the Inga People. While selecting the state proposition is somewhat straightforward, this is not the case when it comes to deciding about the cosmological proposition. The sources of cosmological propositions can be multiple (storytelling as law, locally codified law, deliberative law, material culture, etc.), and the selection mechanism is not extinguished simply by selecting isomorphic equivalences across cultures (i.e., what is the definition of "nature" in modern and non-modern societies?). Is the act of comparison even possible? Is there something akin to "rights" in a local community that allows comparison? Is comparing actually translating? What are the risks of translating across ontologies when it comes to local law, culture and territory?

Criteria of comparison: Five themes come to mind once we've established the limits and possibilities of cross-ontological comparison (Descola 2013) in contexts of adjudication. First, we have to determine what is considered as *existent*, for example, "nature," "human and more-than-human persons," "inter-being relations," and "meshworks," among other *existents*. Depending on what is rendered as existent, we've to establish who has (or hasn't) rights to *what* and what kind of rights does this "who" have. Once we have established what is deemed as existent and the kinds of rights predicated upon them, for example, the regeneration and respect for reproductive cycles, we'll then need to establish who will be considered as a legitimate spokesperson for the rights-holder. And this question is not only about legal representation in the context of adjudication but also about learning the local protocols of representation outside of the court. These protocols could involve careful and respectful engagement with locally appropriate decision-making protocols with different kinds of beings. The fourth step would be then to determine the proposition's reading strategy and aims.

In general, we imagine two general kinds of reading strategies, namely *exegesis* under conditions of law as a system of positive norms, and *tectonics*—in the double sense of encountering the collision of ontologies and following the socio-material relations of rights—under conditions of law as meshwork. The first strategy (exegesis) leads to the allocation of rights among predetermined existents, while the second (tectonics) harnesses RON's capacities to heal relations in flux and becoming (ways of life). Exegesis and tectonics are both important and complementary strategies, which means that comparing between them is not a zero-sum game. How can the law heal relations? Following the cosmological proposition, the law can heal relations by cultivating and stimulating their conditions of emergence in a particular place. In this context, the word "healing" refers to the holistic regeneration—to the extent possible—of the fabric of dynamic and self-organizing interactions between ways of life (i.e., minerals, plants, humans, animals, spirits, legal propositions) that make up the meshwork of a particular place. More than allocating rights between existents, the cosmological proposition aims at articulating a kind of law that can become a tool to regenerate (re-weave) socio-ecological relationships that make up a place (spiritual payments, ecological corridors, seed diversity). And this requires a kind of legal imagination and language where beings are not only considered subjects with rights but also law-producing selves. This is what we've called the legal activation (or healing) of relationality.

Determining fluid outcomes of comparison and possible questions for practical scenarios of adjudication: Both the state proposition and the cosmological proposition open up a shared horizon of environmental protection. Where RON as text provides a normative horizon for the protection of "nature," RON as *teks* offers a normative horizon for the regeneration and "ongoingness" (Haraway 2016) of life relations in contexts of extractivism (i.e., the principal source of harm). Again, they are partially connected. Although the state proposition weaves *Pachamama* and nature together, this begs the question of whether nature and *Pachamama* are the same kind of entities. Are we granting rights to the same kind of *subjects*? On the other hand, the cosmological proposition opens the critical question of how far we can go with ontological uncertainty when it comes to deciding who is a "subject" of rights and what is an "object" of protection. Is this sort of ontological undecidability acceptable in practical contexts of adjudication? These questions will remain open for the time being. Suffice it to say that this methodology is as much about learning to ask questions as it is about learning to weave RON's relational field for a particular case involving unsettled existents such as nature and *Pachamama*.

4. Conclusion: healing socio-ecological relations through the law

This chapter has explored two different projects. The first, RON as text, is based upon the ontological assumption that the real is divided into nature and culture and other cascading divisions. This ontology leads to seeing what positive law calls "nature" as a legal person, often at the expense of the relations behind the mask of legal subjectivity. The second, RON as *teks*, is based upon another pre-analytical assumption, which, following Escobar, I have termed the Principle of Radical Interdependence. Translated into a legal principle, this cosmological premise suggests that the project of the law is also about discerning (legal) meaning in relationships beyond the human, language and the state (Davies 2017), and I have proposed a methodology to encounter such relations in the law: tectonic reading.

The current coupling of textual RON with the persistence of the development/extractivist project in Latin America demands yet another braiding move, namely to imagine economic relations from the vantage point of indigenous cosmologies of interdependence (see Atleo 2011). A potential future step for this line of inquiry would be to explore an animist framework for economic practice as part of a post-extractivist agenda for this region. Understanding law as meshwork and economics as reciprocity is an integral part of a relational imagination and practice to heal the web of life and nurture its radical ongoingness.

Notes

1 Similar argument in Cullinan (2003); law and language in Anker (2014); language and other sign modalities beyond the human in Kohn (2013).
2 Drawing from Escobar (2018), as used here, the word "ontology" refers to how people, human and not, enact different worlds or "reals" rather than different cultural representations of a singular and common reality. Ontology also refers to the normative attributes of these world-making practices and the limits and possibilities of comparing and translating between them.
3 Law as a healing practice in Swaim (2006).
4 Escobar (2018) suggests the notion of "design" as a political-ontological praxis of repair.
5 For the ontological dimensions of law see Vermeylen (2017), Davies (2017); Boulot and Sterlin (unpublished).
6 Drawing from Ingold (2011), I am making an analytical distinction between life—a cell, for example—and living as the capacity to move or act, which life shares with nonlife such as rocks, mountains, and rivers, among others.
7 Also see De la Cadena (2015), Kohn (2013); Viveiros de Castro (1998).
8 Conversation with A.A. former education advisor in Colombia, and Yagé practitioner. Southern Colombia. Field notes, 2019.
9 Conversation with David Rodríguez, biologist and plant scientist working on the preservation of wild populations of medicinal-ritual plants in Southern Colombia. Field notes, 2019.
10 Constitution of the Republic of Ecuador (2008), Legislative Decree No. 0, Official Registration 449 October 20, 2008.
11 Statute of the Rights of Modern Earth No. 071, 21, Dec. 2010, Bolivia.

12 Colombian Constitutional Court, Sentence C-035 2016; Colombian Constitutional Court, Sentence T-622 2016; Justice Supreme Justice Court, Colombia, STC 4360–2018.
13 On the relationship between ecological law and degrowth economica see Garver (2013).
14 See Political Databases of the Americas, 2012.
15 Diccionario Quechua-español-Quechua Edición de la Municipalidad del Cusco, 1995.
16 Critique of personhood in Vargas (2020).
17 On decision-making in plants, Gagliano (2015). On more-than-human legalities, Braverman (2018).
18 Taita Hernando Chindoy, Personal communication, Feb. 2020.

References

Anker, Kirsten. 2014. *Declarations of Interdependence: A Legal Pluralist Approach to Indigenous Rights*. New York: Routledge.

Anker, Kirsten. 2017. "Law as . . . Forest: Eco-logic, Stories and Spirits in Indigenous Jurisprudence." *Law Text Culture*, 21: 191–213.

Atleo, Richard. 2011. *Principles of Tsawalk: An Indigenous Approach to Global Crisis*. Vancouver: University of British Columbia Press.

Blaser, Mario. 2013. "Ontological Conflicts and the Stories of Peoples in Spite of Europe: Towards a Conversation on Political Ontology." *Current Anthropology*, 54(5): 547–568.

Boyd, David. 2017. *The Rights of Nature: A Legal Revolution That Could Save the World*. Toronto: ECW Press.

Braverman, I. 2018. "Law's Underdog: A Call for More-Than-Human Legalities." *The Annual Review of Law and Social Science*, 14: 127–144.

Burdon, Peter. 2010. "The Rights of Nature: Reconsidered." *Australian Humanities Review*, 49: 69.

Capra, Frijoft, and Mattei, Ugo. 2015. *The Ecology of Law: Toward a Legal System in Tune with Nature and Community*. San Francisco: Berrett-Koehler Publishers.

Cullinan, Cormac. 2003. *Wild Law: A Manifesto for Earth Justice* (2nd ed.). White River Junction, VT: Chelsea Green.

Davies, Margaret. 2017. *Law Unlimited: Materialism, Pluralism, and Legal Theory*. New York: Routledge.

De la Cadena, Marisol. 2015. *Earth Beings: Ecologies of Practice Across Andean Worlds*. Durham: Duke University Press.

Descola, Philippe. 2013. *Beyond Nature and Culture*. Chicago: University of Chicago Press.

Escobar, Arturo. 2018. *Designs for the Pluriverse: Radical Interdependence, Autonomy and the Making of Worlds*. Durham: Duke University Press.

Escobar, Arturo. 2019. "Healing the Web of Life: On the Meaning of Environmental and Health Equity." *International Journal of Public Health*, 64: 3–4.

Gagliano, Monica. 2015. "In a Green Frame of Mind: Perspectives on the Behavioural Ecology and Cognitive Nature of Plants." *AoB Plants*, 7: plu075.

Garver, Geoffrey. 2013. "The Rule of Ecological Law: The Legal Complement to Degrowth Economics." *Sustainability*, 5: 316–337.

Gudynas, Eduardo. 2011. "Más allá del nuevo extractivismo: transiciones sostenibles y alternativas al desarrollo." In Wanderley, F. (ed.). *El Desarrollo en Cuestión. Reflexiones desde América Latina*. La Paz: Oxfam y CIDES.

Haraway, Donna. 2016. *Staying with the Trouble: Making Kin in the Chthulucene*. Durham: Duke University Press.

Ingold, Tim. 2011. *Being Alive: Essays on Movement, Knowledge, and Description*. New York: Routledge.

Kohn, Eduardo. 2013. *How Forests Think. Toward and Anthropology Beyond the Human*. Berkeley, CA: University of California Press.

Kosoy, Nicolas, and Corbera, Esteve. 2010. "Payment for Ecosystem Services as Commodity Fetishism." *Ecological Economics*, 69(6): 1228–1236.

Martínez, Esperanza, and Acosta, Alberto. 2017. "Los Derechos de la Naturaleza como puerta de entrada a otro mundo posible." *Revista Dereito e Práxis*, 4(8).

Mills, Aaron. 2019. *Miinigowiziwin: All That Has Been Given for Living Well Together. One Vision of Anishinaabe Constitutionalism*. Ph.D. Thesis. University of Victoria, Victoria.

Munda, Giuseppe. 2016. "Beyond Welfare Economics: Some Methodological Issues." *Journal of Economic Methodology*, 26(2): 185–202.

Paternosto, Cesar. 1996. *The Stone and the Thread: Andean Roots of Abstract Art*. Austin, TX: University of Texas Press.

Pelizzon, Alessandro, and Gagliano, Monica. 2015. "The Sentience of Plants: Animal Rights and Rights of Nature Intersecting?" *Australian Animal Protection Law Journal*, 11: 5–13.

Rossotto, Ioris Antonio A. 2014. *The Political Ecology of the State: The Basis and the Evolution of Environmental Statehood*. London: Routledge.

Stone, Christopher. 1972. "Should Trees Have Standing? Toward Legal Rights for the Natural Objects." *Southern California Law Review*, 45: 450–501.

Strathern, Marilyn. 2005. *Kinship, Law and the Unexpected. Relavites Are Always a Surprise*. Cambridge: Cambridge University Press.

Svampa, Maristella. 2019. *Las Fronteras del Neoextractivismo en America Latina*. Guadalajara, MX: CALAS-Maria Sibylla Merian Center for Advanced Latin American Studies.

Swaim, Susan. 2006. "Law as a Healing Profession: The Comprehensive Law Movement." In *Research Paper Series 05/06 # 12*. New York: New York Law School Clinical Research Institute.

Ulloa, Astrid. 2005. *The Ecological Native: Indigenous People's Movements and Eco-Governmentality in Colombia*. New York: Routledge.

Vargas Roncancio, Ivan Dario. 2020. "Forest on Trial: Towards a Relational Theory of Legal Agency for Transitions into the Ecozoic." In Orr, C., Kish, K., and Jennings, B. (eds.). *Liberty and the Ecological Crisis: Freedom on a Finite Planet*. New York: Routledge.

Vargas Roncancio, I.D. 2021. "Conjuring Sentient Beings and Relations in the Law: Rights of Nature and a Comparative Praxis of Legal Cosmologies." In Anker, K., Burdon, P., Garver, G., Maloney M., and Sbert, C. (eds.). *From Environmental to Ecological Law*. London—NY: Routledge.

Vermeylen, Saskia. 2017. "Materiality and the Ontological Turn in the Anthropocene: Establishing a Dialogue Between Law, Anthropology and Eco-philosophy."

In Kótze, L. (ed.). *Environmental Law and Governance for the Anthropocene*. Oxford: Oxford University Press, pp. 137–162.
Viveiros de Castro, Eduardo. 1998. "Cosmological Diexis and Amerindian Perspectivism." *Journal of the Royal Anthropological Institute*, 4(3): 469–489.
Viveiros de Castro, Eduardo. 2014. *Cannibal Metaphysics*. Minneapolis: Univocal.
Weitzner, V. 2017. "Nosotros Somos Estado: Contested Legalities in Decision-making about Extractives Affecting Ancestral Territories in Colombia." *Third World Quarterly*, 38(5): 1198–1214.

Legal documents

Constitución Política de la República del Ecuador [Ecuador], 20 October 2008.
Corte Constitucional de Colombia, Decision C-035 2016 [Colombia], 8 February 2016.
Corte Constitucional de Colombia, Decision SU-510 1998 [Colombia], 18 Septiembre 1998.
Corte Constitucional de Colombia, Decision T-622 2016 [Colombia], 10 November 2016.
Corte Suprema de Justicia de Colombia, Decision STC 4360–2018 [Colombia], 5 April 2018.
Ley de Derechos de la Madre Tierra, No. 071, 21 [Bolivia], 21 December 2010.

Chapter 8

Forest on trial

Towards a relational theory of legal personhood[1]

Abstract

Forest on trial explores the notion of *personhood* through an ethnographic and *ius*-philosophical prism. Persons such as humans and corporations can seek redress before a court of law. This chapter claims that the notion of legal personhood seems to actualize the contested modern tension between nature and culture in most of the social and legal theory at present. More than discontinuous and self-contained beings, Amazonian forests embody sentient and mind-bearing relations involving humans and other-than-human beings such as plants, animals and spirits. Can the forest speak law? Do forests endlessly require the mediation of human modes of legal representation? Overflowing the person's ontological stability, forests teach a notion of legal personhood beyond the human, the state and the norm. An attempt to overcome anthropocentric concepts of personhood and agency, this chapter furthers the empirical argument advanced in Part I of the book concerning Amazonian legal cosmologies. The chapter approaches law both as a particular kind of symbolic representation, that is, a text, as well as a non-symbolic form of representation that conjures up other-than-humans in legal theory and practice.

1. Introduction: vegetal agencies in the law

National legislations and governance models across the world increasingly recognize the legal subjectivity of other-than-human beings (Acosta and Martínez 2011; Harris 2014; Youatt 2017). The contested clause of the rights of nature (RN),[2] for instance, is a growing response to economic practices underpinning the "inter-related global crises of climate, food, energy, poverty, and meaning" (Escobar 2016, 13). Are human engagements with other beings limited to the dubious epiphany that we all depend on the mineral, vegetal and animal life of the world? What do other-than-human beings have to do with the law in contexts of territorial dispossession?

While the RN express the radical interdependence between natural and social systems, dominant environmental governance models in Amazonia seem deeply entangled with what Colombian legal scholar Gregorio Mesa

DOI: 10.4324/9781003349426-14

calls an "ethics of consumption." With this notion, he highlights the social mindsets and institutions casting nature an endless quarry of material goods and ecosystems services to meet ever-expanding human needs (2008, 333).

Increasing eco-centric legal proposals such as the RN emerge amid neo-extractivist/colonial practices with often disastrous impacts on socio-ecological systems and ways of being (Gudynas 2009). As discussed in earlier chapters, this tension is an expression of the pervasive ontology of separation between nature and culture in much of environmental law and governance models today (Atleo 2011; Vargas et al. 2019). How can a new legal ontology contribute to a shifting paradigm: from a highly regulatory environmental approach to a relational and knowledge-grounded Earth jurisprudence? (Burdon 2012; Cullinan 2011; Pelizzon 2014).

By drawing connections between the law and larger socio-ecological systems (Garver 2013, 2019), the first section of this chapter challenges a standard definition of the law as a "system of norms," while rendering visible the ontological and cognitive dimensions of legal theory and practice (Vermeylen 2017; Philippopoulos-Mihalopoulos 2017; Winter 2001).

In particular, it analyses how the notion of personhood (see Anker 2017)—central to Western theories of rights and justice [López 2018 (2004)]—conceals understandings of the law as a potential emancipatory and world-making tool for transitions into the Ecozoic, an era of mutually enhancing human-Earth relationships (Berry 1999; Berry and Swimme 1992).

Are human engagements with other beings limited to the dubious epiphany that we all depend on the mineral, vegetal and animal life of the world? Based on ethnographic encounters in the Colombian Amazon, as well as a short review in the field of plant communication and intelligence (Gagliano 2018; Mancuso and Viola 2015; Marder 2013, 2016; Myers 2015), the second section illustrates how nonhuman collectives, which I tentatively call nonpersons, overflow the ontological stability of objects and subjects. This working notion offers analytical keys for a concept of legal agency beyond the modern divide actualized by the idea of personhood.

While much of current debates about the RN are framed in terms of granting legal personhood to nonhumans (Youatt 2017), I suggest calling attention to the relational framework of Indigenous epistemologies and ontologies foregrounding the earthly co-emergence of humans and other-than-humans in legal systems (Borrows 2016; Kimmerer 2013). Inspired by the principle of interdependence (Atleo 2011), the chapter concludes by asserting how other-than-human legalities might become compelling sources of a legal ontology beyond human-only, hyper-regulatory and interculturality-blind environmental legal frameworks today, as well as the questions this effort raises for legal theory and practice.

2. Why plants?

I am considering the case of plants, among others, for two main reasons. First, much attention has been given to the figure of the animal in social theory (Few and Tortorici 2013), while studies on the relationship between plants and social theory have received much less attention (Marder 2013; Gagliano 2013; Gagliano et al. 2014). Moreover, the sessile character of plants foregrounds a compelling critique of an idea of agency solely based on human perceived movement as an index of change.

An increasing number of studies, ranging from plant communication and intelligence (Trewavas 2016) to vegetal neurophysiology (Mancuso and Viola 2015) and plant bio-acoustics, reveal a vegetal sensorium functionally similar to organisms with centralized nervous systems (Gagliano 2018). For example, as sign-making selves, some plants can locate water sources through their roots by sensing the sounding vibrations of water moving inside pipelines. Plants' ability to detect vibrations "may represent a very efficient way of capturing information from distant sound sources for orientation towards water" (Gagliano et al. 2017, 152).

A suggestive proposition, the idea that plants can "listen" and orient themselves towards water sources might well sound a mere humanization of biological phenomena. Yet, as anthropologist E. Viveiros de Castro would argue, "when everything is human, the human is an entirely different thing" (Viveiros de Castro 2014). Moreover, Myers develops an ethnographic argument on the limits of anthropogenic classification of plant life, namely the tendency to define plant attributes in terms of human attributes. She uses expressions such as the "plant turn" (2015, 40) or "vegetal epistemology" (42) to account for a non-anthropocentric stance to plant modes of knowledge and being.

However, a focus on relations, encounters and "mutual differences" (de la Cadena 2015) may redefine much-praised human attributes such as intelligence and memory as emergent properties of inter-being encounters (Haraway 2007). They are not specific capacities of neither humans (i.e., the human point of view) nor plants (i.e., the plant point of view) defined as discrete entities themselves (Escobar 2016, 2018). Plants and humans co-emerge in symbiosis in worlds of social and legal meaning entangled with life and matter (Barad 2007; Margulis and Sagan 2003).

3. Personhood reinforces the ontological dualism between humans and nature. Can we think of legal agency beyond this divide?

In the foreword to *Lively Legalities*, Wolfe asks his readers the following compelling question:

> What sense does it make that a highly developed animal such as a tiger or an orca is regarded as 'the same' as a toaster or a pile of bricks, while in US law at least, corporations and ships of state are legally designated as persons?
>
> (Wolf 2016, xiv)

Indeed, natural and juridical persons such as humans and corporations equally hold legal standing, such as the ability to seek redress before a court of law (Stone 1972). While the distinction between the natural (i.e., laws of "nature") and the juridical (i.e., positive norms sanctioned by a state) is not a settled discussion, the fact that legal entities such as corporations can be considered persons intriguingly expands the notion of personhood beyond the human.

For Dewey the "'person' signifies what the law makes it signify," and it is therefore an empty and positional signifier in the legal arena. Similarly, Marder elaborates on the neighbouring notion of subjectivity as the capacity to act with intent to "actively shape the world" (2016, 56). For example, organisms such as plants can actively shape their own milieus, thus expressing a subjective or person-like property akin to the notion of rights.[3]

Does reckoning the legal personhood to nonhumans such as plants and forests reinstate the ontology of separation between humans and the rest of life at the root of dominant legal systems? An almost-commonsensical perspective would say that to be a person entails "enjoying . . . rights in and of themselves" (Esposito 2010, 121). In the field of legal theory, however, it remains rather unclear whether the idea of rights—including the right to obtain legal remedy—can exist without the modern concept of the person. For Esposito, "the enclosed space of the person" in not a necessary condition of legal rights (2010, 122); in fact, "no one is born a person. . . . Some might become a person, but precisely by pushing those that surround him into the dimension of the thing" (2010, 126).

Pushed into the dimension of "thing-like phenomena," entities and processes such as water systems, forests and nitrogen cycles are devoid of agency (and rights) unless they are made into persons through the law. In other words, nonpersons (things or assemblages of things) would be, at best, objects of environmental protection with no rights "in and of themselves."

Thus, the ability to have rights and duties expresses the inherent legal capacity of persons as opposed to the inherent natural behavior of things. Dewey furthers this ontology of separation when affirming that "molecules or trees" behave "exactly as they do" by force of nature—rather than by the rule of law (1926, 661). As he allocates agency on the side of the person at the expense of the passive materiality of nonpersons ("molecules and trees"), Dewey actualizes the pervasive distinction between subjects and objects via a theory of personhood. Similarly, Stephens suggests a compelling tripartite spectrum to define nature: from "*relatively* untransformed nature at one pole, borderline places such as traditional farms and country paths . . . and the world of completed artifacts and radically instrumentally transformed goods . . . the other pole" (Stephens 2019). While this notion differentiates the intensity and scale of human intervention over an *external* nature, it seems to locate agency on the human end exclusively, thus re-inscribing the modern tension between subjects and objects just described. To state it in terms of geologian Thomas Berry, the radical discontinuity between human and other-than-human beings, and the ensuing "bestowal of all rights on the humans" alone, underpins the ecological and cultural devastation of the planet (1999, 4). The task ahead is then "reinventing the human" by re-embedding social institutions such as the law within the broader community of life. I see this project connected to the reevaluation of deeply entrenched notions such as the pair subjectivity/personhood.

3.1. *Situating non-personhood within legal ontologies*

While some scholars contest the idea of rights given the little evidence of their real effectiveness (Posner 2014), legal theory might benefit from a conception of agency beyond the legal twins of personality/subjectivity, thus expanding the notion of rights. This endeavor re-conceptualizes the limits of a legal ontology based on the separation between persons and things; the disentanglement of legal norms and vital relations; and the decoupling of social and ecological justice, to only name a few cascading implications of this ontological critique.

A relational and experience-grounded approach to the law, on the other hand, seeks to de-center the human in legal systems (Grear 2017) to acknowledge the recursive interactions between humans and other-than-human selves (Kohn 2013). This relational idiom privileges the integrity of the whole Earth community in the long term over the interests of humans alone (Cullinan 2011). Yet what does the expression legal ontology refer to in this context?

Broadly speaking, the law deals with a universe of relations between individuals, communities (human and not), states and "elementary groupings themselves" (Graham 2011, 15 in Burdon 2010, 28). However, usually depicted in terms of norms and procedures separated from the larger socio-ecological processes they regulate, Western legal theory tends to overlook the relational and material dimensions of law-making. It takes for granted notions of personhood and subjectivity profoundly tied to mechanistic/Cartesian worldviews (Capra and Mattei 2015. See Anker 2017).

Under this predominant mechanistic paradigm, the law is conceptualized as an autonomous human institution separated from its socio-material processes (Burdon 2012; Braverman 2016). Rather than something circumscribed to a set of abstract norms separated from the concrete sensorimotor handling of living organisms (Varela 1999), the rules we live by arise in recursive engagement with the world humans co-create with other selves. The law does not denote something pre-given to the mind, but "something we (humans and not) engage in by moving, touching, breathing and eating" (Varela 1999, 7).

In contrast, an ontological approach to the law considers the world-making potentials of legal systems, and not only its prescriptive attributes. Beyond the universalistic formalism of top-down legal codes (Winter 2001), legal norms are grounded or embedded in the concrete experience of humans and, I will later argue, other-than-humans. A systems-based legal ontology thus brings to trial mechanistic and deterministic approaches to the law.

3.2. *On how ontological choices may determine legal frameworks*

As early as 1972, US Justice William O. Douglas argued that trees should have legal standing. For him,

> [i]nanimate objects are sometimes parties in litigation. A ship has a legal personality, a fiction found useful for maritime purposes. . . . So it should be as respects valleys, alpine meadows, rivers, lakes, estuaries, beaches, ridges, groves of trees, swampland, or even air that feels the destructive pressures of modern technology and modern life.[4]

To the extent that the entities in this list should be granted rights, can we say that they should be considered persons as well? What ontological commitments do we make when personifying "nature" and "natural relations"?

More than enclosed entities, forests, meadows, swamplands and the like are often defined as bundles of ever-renewing relations eluding the stability of the bounded self (Haraway 2007). In order to have standing, however, these entities require the legal quality of personhood regardless of their living and human-like attributes. To be sure, the entity in question ought to be a person first (it needs to occupy the "enclosed space" of the bounded self) to be able to hold rights. Personhood precedes standing, and standing precedes rights.

To be a person, however, one does not necessarily need to be alive. For example, a corporation can become a person to hold legal standing and rights. Personhood, then, is a productive legal fiction. It creates effects in the world. This decoupling between "personhood" and "life" creates fictional persons (corporations) with rights regardless of ecological considerations. This ontology of separation, again, divorces the law from larger socio-ecological processes by affording legal standing to the person and thus re-inscribing the rift between humans and other-than-humans. A "'person' signifies what the law makes it signify" (Dewey 1926, 655), or, in other words, the law is made into an autonomous sphere of action fictionally—but quite productively—separated from the life systems it depends upon.

Fluid relations with elusive embodiments, nonpersons such as water cycles, soils and forests best describe what Amazonian Indigenous Nonuya elder and artist Abel Rodríguez calls the "figure of life"—or how life emerges and takes hold (Rodríguez 2014). Extending this argument to the legal realm, nonpersons could claim a strong presence within the law that includes the language of rights but is not reducible to it. Rather than bearers of rights afforded by humans, these relations are sources of the law (Borrows 2016), as well as law-making agents in their own right (Strathern 2005).

In this context, to *create the law* stands for a quality of what I provisionally call semiotic relations, namely the relational and meaning-producing character of life (Kohn 2013).

3.3. *Standing on the legal stage, the actor conceals the human and its constitutive relations underneath the mask of the person*

As the idea of corporate legal personality illustrates (Dewey 1926), the realm of person-like phenomena is rather stable, predictable and limited. The realm of relational-like phenomena, on the other hand, appears rather vast, unpredictable and politically contentious. What happens with obliterated life relations unaccounted for by the law as persons? In the multiple and relentlessly productive field of Andean and Amazonian cosmologies, humans, animals, plants and spirits—the invisible peoples of Chapter 4—conceal an internal human form (Descola 2013; Viveiros de Castro 1998, 2014). The person stands for a mask or clothing (Rodriguez's "figure of life") concealing underneath human-like properties of nonhuman selves such as rivers, plants and forests (Kohn 2013). While living beings can only become juridical persons through an act of legal recognition reinstating the separation between the "person" and the "thing" (Esposito 2010), non-personality re-organizes the relational and distributed web of legal agencies. Here is an example: An 80,000-year-old organism, the *pando (Populus tremuloides)*, looks like a grove of separated trees with a densely intertwined complex root system underneath the topsoil.[5] As legal theory increasingly grounds its conceptual toolkit within the life sciences, nonpersons such as the *pando* pose uncanny challenges to a theory of legal agency based on the twin notions of subjectivity and personhood. Especially when we learn that more than half of the biomass of this life system reverberates under our feet and beyond the human purview (Wohlleben 2015, 85). The notion of personhood here reveals itself inadequate, for it manages the elusive stability of life relations through the counting of persons-for-the-law.

The legal person-making machine seems to eclipse that which stands behind the legal mask of personhood: a messy and often unpredictable "meshwork" of relations escaping the logic of the enclosing law (Ingold 2011). In other words, while the notion of personhood is a legally produced quality of humans and other-than-human beings, this notion renders invisible the relations that make life entities emerge from underneath the field of human regimes of perception. I am suggesting that life relations often shape the legal purview of personhood and thus require concepts attuned to its material unfolding. Deemed a necessary legal fiction, the notion of personhood can certainly be extended to highly heterogeneous kinds of entities from corporations and states to forests and rivers. The list is endless. My argument advocates for a legal ontology that considers how life works and what kind of legal theory emerges from this realization. I will further explain this point later.

In a context of increasing recognition of the rights of nature (Gudynas 2009; Burdon 2010), one may wonder whether legal categories used to adjudicate human affairs can easily be transferred over to nonhuman beings, particularly in the case of interconnected entities seen as discrete selves above ground (the *pando*), while concealing underneath a complex organization beyond the reach of direct human perception (the law).

Legal adjudication of personhood not only meets the constraints of human perception—and their specific modes of symbolic representation—but also the unexpected materiality of inter-being encounters reverberating under our feet. Before any juridical personalization, Esposito insists, living beings constitute a plane of indivisibility whereby life (human and not) *is* to itself; "in which the form, precisely of life, is the form of its own content (2010, 132)." The mask (the person) and the actor (life relations) become one and the same thing.

I suggest that life entities such as plants and forests can either be persons epistemologically separated from their vital relations or fully emplaced within them. Shifting our dominant Western theories of rights necessitates an opening up of the enclosed space of the person as to consider the relations behind the legal fiction (or mask) of personhood. It is the law that needs to be integrated into the logic of life, and not the other way around. Partially guided by the threads of plant science, the next section offers empirical grounding for the larger argument on the relational (or non-personal) ontologies of the law I have discussed. I ask how the legal adjudication of rights may look from the vantage point of plants and forests as relations rather than (bounded) substances.

4. Legal plants: how vegetal others invite us to think about environmental law and governance otherwise

Several studies in the fields of Amazonian anthropology and plant science render vegetal beings capable of performing tasks considered exclusive to the human per anthropocentric definitions of language and agency.[6] For instance, plants are deemed intelligent and sentient entities, thus opening up a cascade of theoretical considerations with potential legal interest.[7]

The case of plants invites us to rethink culture (and the law) as an exclusive attribute of organisms endowed with brains and nervous systems (Varela 1999). As plant scientists Viola and Mancuso argue, plants can "breathe without having lungs, nourish themselves without having a mouth or stomach, stand erect without having a skeleton, and . . . make decisions without having a brain" (Mancuso and Viola 2015, 34).

The idea that plants and other organisms are capable of intelligent behavior expands notions of representation beyond the human and the person as a bounded self. Yet plants' modes of representation are not reducible to those specific to the human, that is, symbolic and language-based symbols (Kohn 2013). Broadly speaking, I expand the notion of representation usually defined in two complementary ways. First, as the language-mediated outcomes of human perception, that is, the names assigned to exterior objects and the relations between them (Westermann and Mareschal 2014). And second, as the act of standing for another party by contract or legal right, for example, when humans speak on behalf of others in a congress or a court of law (Vieira and Runciman 2008). Yet neither the language-mediated perception of a single and stable reality nor the act of speaking on behalf of others forecloses the possibility of other-than-human (legal) representation and practice beyond symbolic signs.

Anthropologist Eduado Kohn's work with the Runa of the Ecuadorian Amazon offers rich ethnographic evidence on the intrinsic meaning-making and sign-producing capacities of other-than-humans such as plants and animals of interest to my argument. In Amazonia, he argues, life forms create modes of meaning not limited to conventional and language-based signs. Utilizing Pierce's semiotic framework, Kohn identifies two other representational modalities beyond symbolic signs, namely icons and indexes. Signs are iconic when they share likeness with what they stand for. For example, a picture of your family is an *icon* of your family. Terms like *splash*, *hiccup* and *meow* are also iconic.

Indexical signs, on the other hand, express a relation of spatial or temporal continuity with what they stand for. Or, in other words, an index stands for some physical feature that points to something other than itself, for instance,

> the sound of the palm tree crashing frightened the monkey from her perch. . . . The crash, as sign (of danger for the monkey), is not a likeness of the object it represents. Instead, it points to something else . . . this sort of sign (is) an index.
>
> (Kohn 2013, 31)

Therefore, what we humans share with nonhuman species is not only (or even most crucially) our embodiment, Kohn argues, "but the fact that we all live with and through signs . . . signs make what we are" (2013, 9). Non-symbolic representation, then, is common to all life, so life *is not* without signs. Consequently, signs are not the monopoly of (human) language—let alone legal language—thus living selves represent the world in myriad ways, and this sign-making capacity is intrinsic in all life forms.

Living organisms such as humans, animals and plants are not only persons, for life recursively exceeds what the law deems as such for the purposes of granting legal rights. Paraphrasing Dewey, *life* "does not signify what the law makes it signify." Quite the opposite, the *law* does signify what life makes it signify. Sign-making life, then, overflows the norm, namely the classic *ought-to-be* of the law putting "life in order" (Foucault 1978, 138). The norm, however, cannot exist outside the material and the living where it is embedded (Braverman 2016, 2018; Davies 2017; Graham 2011), for life constantly exceeds the purview of the law as well as its person-making machine.

Additionally, if representation is not a property of human persons alone (as "legal fictions"), then representation is not only the human attribution of meaning upon semiotic-devoid matter. Representation, then, becomes a strong property of nonpersons; simply put, nonpersons-as-relations exist outside the purview of the law-as-a-system-of-norms. A system that governs what kind of life shall be granted with rights. Paradoxically, however, nonpersons are the *rule*, while persons, or what the law defines as such, are the exception (Teubner 1987). In the example, *pando* represents the world through other-than-symbolic modalities (indexes and icons), and these representations are essential to its life experience. Marder furthers this argument when arguing that vegetal life expresses itself otherwise and without resorting to vocalization or language. For him,

> aside from communicating their distress when predators are detected in the vicinity by realizing airborne (or in some cases belowground) chemicals, plants, like all living beings, articulate themselves spatially; in a body language free from gestures, they can express themselves only in their postures.
>
> (Marder 2013, 75)

To summarize, as sign-producing entities, nonhuman selves such as the *pando* operate in a double register. On the one hand, they can be *persons* and thus "signify what the law makes it signify" (Dewey 1926, 655) through environmental governance models and the rights of nature clause. In this sense, *pando*, as a subject of rights, shall claim legal remedy via the figure of legal guardianship (Stone 1972).

However, as Roberto Esposito has made clear, it needs to "penetrate the enclosed space of the person" first (2010, 121). That is, the *pando* (and *pando's* guardian) needs juridical personality through the codifying legal apparatus, so that it can claim legal standing to be recognized and protected. On the other hand, the *pando* can be a nonperson, or the excess of the law. Such non-personality amounts to what escapes the purview of the legal eye (of human regimes of perception), namely the rhizome that makes up more than half of *pando*'s biomass beneath the soil (Wohlleben 2015) making it more than a collection of surface trees. Insofar as *pando* is more than trees, it occupies a non-personal body. Yet, in order to live, this body does not need to be purified as a person by the legal machine. As a person, however, *pando* is within the purview of an endangered species act, a biological resources protection treaty or a constitutional clause granting them rights as well.

As a nonperson, I wonder if the *pando* would prefer to go unnoticed so that it can occupy the generative excess of the law, that is, the material-semiotic processes that make the law possible through the *pando*'s relational self. The elusive character of the *pando* self affords an entirely different perspective of the world this vegetal form of life is able to inhabit (Marder 2013), as well as the kind of legal thinking that emerges from this realization. The law might indeed be an entirely different thing from the perspective of the concealed rhizome, rather than the perspective of the visible tree (Kohn 2022).

5. Expanding agency to nonpersons in the court of justice

The Anthropocene has become a buzzword in today's parlance about climate change, biodiversity loss and related socio-ecological impacts of differentiated human agency. Critical legal studies have recently approached the complicated dynamics of multispecies relations in the production of the law, while situating the human within larger assemblages of living and nonliving agencies (Grear 2017; Philippopoulos-Mihalopoulos 2017; Vermeylen 2017).

As a system of norms and procedures, the law is almost exclusively depicted as an all-too-human institution. This legal ontology achieves the double task of undermining the material and nonhuman dimensions of the legal field, while reinforcing a paradigm that separates humans from the larger community of life (Brown and Timmerman 2015). Does more-than-human life express other kinds of legalities (Braverman 2016)?

As a positional legal fiction, the notion of personhood conjures certain entities at the expense of others in the legal field. For instance, corporations are considered legal persons, yet persons are not always of the human type. What is left outside the person-making legal apparatus? This chapter expanded the notion of legal agency beyond the human and the person, while suggesting that plants and forests are not only rights-bearing entities but sources of legal meaning as well.

The law is almost exclusively conceived as a lettered practice. Can the plant speak *law*? Does the forest always need the mediation of the botanist, for example, in a court of law?

I draw from Eduardo Kohn's work with the Runa of the Ecuadorian Amazon. "Life thinks," he claims as an ontological premise of his work, thus extending the notion of representation to nonhuman selves such as animals, plants and spirits. This chapter expanded the legal framework of agency to engage with the law both as a particular kind of symbolic representation—for example, as a set of positive norms produced by humans—as well as a non-symbolic form of representation vis-à-vis images, processes of materialization, sounds and experience involving other-than-human selves.

Read as a proposal on legal philosophy, *How Forests Think* (2013) also offers an analytically sophisticated methodology to explore instances of legal meaning—that is, sonic images of the forest, shamanistic chants and ecological relations—as sources of legal principles and procedures. Such an effort, however, involves a particular mode of attunement to the social worlds plants and humans co-create through sowing, commensality and ritual, among other practices. An attempt to expand the notion of the law beyond the symbolic (the legal norm), I consider these practices as sources of legal meaning in their own right.

In fact, forests' legal agencies might be better expressed in terms of alliance or partnership between inter-dependent humans and forests. This move problematizes languages of personhood and legal guardianship that separate humans from the larger community of life. Inter-being alliance thus recognizes the human mind as part and parcel of the larger mind of the forest (Kohn 2013).

If the human can engage with the forest through science, the human can also learn how to think with forests in a court of law. While this methodological question requires an independent treatment, appropriate cultural engagement with plants may be one such mode of learning with forests' minds and the legal protocols they harness for post-extractivist transitions in Amazonia. While botanists and anthropologists may be summoned to render testimony on behalf of forests and cultures—respectively—it remains an important challenge to explore whether judges should engage with other-than-human beings as they do with humans as expert witnesses.

How far-off are we from asking judges and legislators to interact with other-than-humans such as forests and rivers as they decide cases involving these kinds of beings? Should a judge, for example, ingest, in some cases, a ritual plant to understand what the forest *wants* when it comes to a mining license in Amazonia? Could this be considered an appropriate methodology for adjudicating justice in certain cases? Could a judge walk the *angua* (a fragile ecosystem of the Andes), let it speak the language it speaks best and then consider this experience a form of witness testimony? Should we elect legislators with proven commitment to listening to forests? How about forest literacy as a requirement for licensing lawyers and adjudicating justice? These are some questions for potential engagements on this thorny issue.

Notes

1 An earlier version published as Vargas Roncancio, I.D. 2020. "Forest on Trial: Towards a Relational Theory of Legal Agency for Transitions into the Ecozoic." In Orr, Christopher, Kish, Kaitlin, and Jennings, Bruce (eds.). *Liberty and the Ecological Crisis: Freedom on a Finite Planet.* New York: Routledge.

2 In the Latin American context we have, among others, the following judicial decisions: Protective Action issued by the Provincial Court of Loja, Sentence No. 1121–2011–001, 30 March 2011; Constitution of the Republic of Ecuador 2008, Legislative Decree No. 0, Official Registration 449 October 20 2008; Colombian Constitutional Court, Sentence C-035 2016; Colombian Constitutional Court, Sentence T-622 2016; Justice Supreme Tribunal STC 4390–2018.

3 Wohlleben writes "plants are perfectly capable of distinguishing their own roots from the roots of other species and even from the roots of related individual." (2015, 17).

4 See Sierra Club Vs. Rogers Clark Ballard Morton, Secretary of the Interior, et al. 405 U.S. 727 (more) 92 S.Ct 1361, 31 L. Ed. 2nd 636.

5 See https://pandopopulus.com/about/pando-the-tree/ (Accessed 27 June 2019).

6 See De la Cadena (2015), Kohn (2013), and Viveiros de Castro (1998). On plant science and anthropological takes on the matter see Myers (2015). On cognition and life see Ingold (2011), Varela (1999).

7 On plant communication and memory see Mancuso and Viola (2015), Trewavas (2016).

References

Acosta, Alberto, and Martínez, Esperanza. 2011. *Naturaleza Con Derechos: De La Filosofía a La Política* (1st ed.). Quito, Ecuador: Ediciones Abya-Yala.

Anker, Kirsten. 2017. "Law as . . . Forest: Eco-logic, Stories and Spirits in Indigenous Jurisprudence." *Law Text Culture*, 21: 191–213.

Atleo, Richard (Umeek). 2011. *Principles of Tsawalk. An Indigenous Approach to Global Crisis.* Vancouver: University of British Columbia.

Barad, Karen. 2007. *Meeting the Universe Halfway. Quantum Physics and the Entanglement of Matter and Meaning.* Duham: Duke University Press.

Berry, Thomas. 1999. *The Great Work. Our Way into the Future.* New York: Bell Tower.

Berry, Thomas, and Swimme, Brian. 1992. *The Universe Story. From the Primordial Flaring to the Ecozoic Era—A Celebration of the Unfolding of the Cosmos.* San Francisco: Harper.

Borrows, John. 2016. *Freedom and Indigenous Constitutionalism.* Toronto: University of Toronto Press.

Braverman, Irus. 2016. "Introduction. Lively Legalities." In Braverman, Irus (ed.). *Animals, Biopolitics, Law. Lively Legalities.* New York: Routledge.

Braverman, Irus. 2018. "Law's Underdog: A Call for More-Than-Human Legalities." *Annual Review of Law and Social Science*, 14: 127–144.

Brown, Peter G., and Timmerman, Peter. 2015. *Ecological Economics for the Anthropocene.* New York: Columbia University Press.

Burdon, Peter. 2010. "The Rights of Nature: Reconsidered." *Australian Humanities Review*, 49: 69.

Burdon, Peter. 2012. "A Theory of Earth Jurisprudence." *Australian Journal of Legal Philosophy*, 37: 28.

Capra, Frijoft, and Mattei, Ugo. 2015. *The Ecology of Law: Towards a Legal System in Tune with Nature and Community.* Oakland: Berrett-Koehler Publishers.

Cullinan, Cormac. 2011. *Wild Law. A Manifesto for Earth Justice* (2nd ed.). Vermont: Chesea Green Publishing.

Davies, Margaret. 2017. *Law Unlimited. Materialism, Pluralism, and Legal Theory.* London: Routledge.

De la Cadena, Marisol. 2015. *Earth Beings: Ecologies of Practice across Andean Worlds.* Durham: Duke University Press.

Descola, Philippe. 2013. *Beyond Nature and Culture.* Chicago: University of Chicago Press.

Dewey, John. 1926. "The Historic Background of Corporate Legal Personality." *Yale Law Journal*, 35(6): 655–673.

Escobar, Arturo. 2016. "Sentipensar con la Tierra: Las Luchas Territoriales y la Dimensión Ontológica de las Epistemologías del Sur." *Revista de Antropologia Iberoamericana*, 11(1): 11–32.

Escobar, Arturo. 2018. *Designs for the Pluriverse: Radical Interdependence, Autonomy, and the Making of Worlds.* Durham: Duke University Press.

Esposito, Roberto. 2010. "For a Philosophy of the Impersonal." *CR: The New Centennial Review*, 10(2): 121–134.

Few, Martha, and Tortorici, Zeb. 2013. *Centering Animals in Latin American History.* Durham: Duke University Press.

Foucault, Michel. 1978. *The Will to Knowledge: The History of Sexuality* (vol. 1). London: Penguin.

Gagliano, Monica. 2013. "Persons as Plants: Ecopsychology and the Return to the Dream of Nature." *Landscapes: The Journal of the International Centre for Landscape and Language*, 5(2): 1–11.

Gagliano, Monica. 2018. *Thus Spoke the Plant. A Remarkable Journey of Groundbreaking Scientific Discoveries and Personal Encounters with Plants.* Berkeley: North Atlantic Books.

Gagliano, Monica, Grimonprez, Mayra, Depczynski, Martial, and Renton, Michael. 2017. "Turn in: Plant Roots Use Sound to Locate Water." *Oecologia*, 184(1): 151–160.

Gagliano, Monica, Renton, M., Depczynski, M., and Mancuso, S. 2014. "Experience Teaches Plants to Learn Faster and Forget Slower in Environments Where It Matters." *Oecologia*, 175: 63–72.

Garver, Geoffrey. 2013. "The Rule of Ecological Law: The Legal Complement to Degrowth Economics." *Sustainability*, 5: 316–337.

Garver, Geoffrey. 2019. "A Systems-based Tool for Transitioning to Law for a Mutually Enhancing Human-Earth Relationship." *Ecological Economics*, 157: 165–174.

Graham, Laura. 2011. *Lawscape: Property, Environment, Law.* New York: Routledge.

Grear, Anna. 2017. "Anthropocene, Capitalocene, Chthulucene': Re-encountering Environmental Law and Its 'Subject' with Haraway and New Materialism." In Kotzé, Louis (ed.). *Environmental Law and Governance for the Anthropocene.* Oregon: Hart Publishing.

Gudynas, Eduardo. 2009. "La Ecología política del giro biocéntrico en la nueva Constitución del Ecuador." *Revista de Estudio Sociales*, 34: 34–47.

Haraway, Donna. 2007. *When Species Meet.* Minneapolis: University of Minnesota Press.

Harris, Angela. 2014. "Vulnerability and Power in the Age of the Anthropocene." *Washington and Lee Journal of Energy, Climate, and the Environment*, 6: 98–160.

Ingold, Tim. 2011. *Being Alive. Essays on Movement, Knowledge, and Description.* New York: Routledge.

Kimmerer, Robin Wall. 2013. *Braiding Sweetgrass. Indigenous Wisdom, Scientific Knowledge and the Teching of Plants.* Minneapolis: Milkweed Editors.

Kohn, Eduardo. 2013. *How Forests Think. Toward an Anthropology Beyond the Human.* Berkeley: University of California Press.

Kohn, Eduardo. 2022. "Forest Forms and Ethical Life." *Environmental Humanities*, 14(2): 401–418.

Lopez Medina, Diego Eduardo. 2018 (2004). *Teoría Impura del Derecho. La Transformacion de la Cultura jurídiica latinoamericana.* Bogotá: Legis.

Mancuso, Stephano, and Viola, Alessandra. 2015. *Brilliant Green. The Surprising History and Science of Plant Intelligence.* Washington, DC: Island Press.

Marder, Michael. 2013. *Plant-thinking. A Philosophy of Vegetal Life.* New York: Columbia University Press.

Marder, Michael. 2016. *Grafts.* Minneapolis: University of Minnesota Press.

Margulis, Lynn, and Sagan, Dorian. 2003. *Acquiring Genomes. A Theory of the Origins of Species.* New York: Basic Books.

Mesa Cuadros, Gregorio. 2008. "De la ética del consume a la ética del cuidado: de cómo otro mundo sí es anguage desde otra manera de anguage y consumer." *Pensamiento Juridico*, 22: 333–345.

Myers, Natasha. 2015. "Conversations on Plant Sensing: Notes from the Field." *Nature Culture*, 3: 35–66.

Pelizzon, Alessandro. 2014. "Transitional Justice and Ecological Jurisprudence in the Midst of an Ever-Changing Climate." In Szablewska, N., and Bachmann, S.D. (eds.). *Current Issues in Transitional Justice. Springer Series in Transitional Justice* (vol. 4). New York: Springer.

Philippopoulos-Mihalopoulos, Andreas. 2017. "Critical Environmental Law in the Anthropocene." In Kotzé, Louis (ed.). *Environmental Law and Governance for the Anthropocene*. Oregon: Hart Publishing.

Posner, Eric. 2014. "The Case Against Human Rights." *The Guardian*.

Rodríguez, Abel. 2014. "Así es como se empezó a enseñar." *Mundo Amazónico*, 5.

Stephens, Piers H.G. 2019. "Why Nature Experience Still Exists and Matters in the Anthropocene." In Orr, Christopher, Kish, Kaitlin, and Jennings, Bruce (eds.). *Liberty and the Ecological Crisis: Freedom on a Finite Planet*. London and New York: Routledge.

Stone, Christopher. 1972. "Should Trees Have Standing? Toward Legal Rights for Natural Object." *Southern California Law Review*, 45: 450–501.

Strathern, Marilyn. 2005. *Kinship, Law and the Unexpected. Relatives Are Always a Surprise*. Cambridge: Cambridge University Press.

Teubner, Gunther. 1987. *Juridification of Social Spheres: A Comparative Analysis in the Areas of Labor, Corporate, Antitrust and Social Welfare Law*. Berlin, W. de Gruyter, European University Institute, Series A—Law, 6.

Trewavas, Anthony. 2016. "Plant Intelligence: An Overview." *BioScience*, 66(7): 542–551.

Varela, Francisco. 1999. *Ethical Know-How. Action, Wisdom and Cognition*. Stanford: Stanford University Press.

Vargas Roncancio, I., Temper, L., Sterlin, J., Smolyar, N.L., Sellers, S., Moore, M., Melgar-Melgar, R., Larson, J., Horner, C., Erickson, J.D., Egler, M., Brown, P.G., Boulot, E., Beigi, T., and Babcock, M. 2019. "From the Anthropocene to Mutual Thriving: An Agenda for Higher Education in the Ecozoic." *Sustainability*, 11: 3312.

Vermeylen, Saskia. 2017. "Materiality and the Ontological Turn in the Anthropocene: Establishing a Dialogue between Law, Anthropology, and Eco-philosphy." In Kotzé, Louis (ed.). *Environmental Law and Governance for the Anthropocene*. Oregon: Hart Publishing.

Vieira, Mónica Britto, and Runciman, David. 2008. *Representation*. Cambridge: Polity Press.

Viveiros de Castro, Eduardo. 1998. "Cosmological Diexis and Amerindian Perspectivism." *Journal of the Royal Anthropological Institute*, 4(3): 469–489.

Viveiros de Castro, Eduardo. 2014. *Cannibal Metaphysics*. Minneapolis: Univocal.

Westermann, Gert, and Mareschal, Denis. 2014. "From Perceptual to Language-Mediated Categorization." *Philosophical Transactions of the Royal Society of London. Series B, Biological Sciences*, 369: 1634.

Winter, Steven. 2001. *A Clearing in the Forest. Law, Life, and Mind*. Chicago: The University of Chicago Press.

Wolfe, Cary. 2016. "Foreword. 'Life' and 'the Living,' Law and Norm." In Braverman, Irus (ed.). *Animals, Biopolitics, Law. Lively Legalities*. New York: Routledge.

Wohlleben, Peter. 2015. *The Hidden Life of Trees: What They Feel, How the Communicate—Discoveries from a Secret World*. Vancouver: Greystone Books.

Youatt, Rafi. 2017. "Personhood and the Rights of Nature: The New Subjects of Contemporary Earth Politics." *International Political Sociology*, 11: 39–54.

Chapter 9

Concluding, opening

Abstract

Climate change and COVID-19 have revealed the limited response capacity of conventional environmental law and governance models that insist on the separation between law, society and Earth systems of sorts. A paradigm shift based on epistemic plurality, relational thinking and decolonial praxis is needed. How are Indigenous cosmologies and legal systems contributing to this paradigm shift in law? What kind of theoretical and methodological tools does an Earth-oriented law offer us? Beyond the rights of nature approach, how does a law that is entangled with local territorial practices challenge anthropocentric and colonial concepts of justice, agency and value in times of socio-ecological transitions? At the intersection between Indigenous legal epistemologies, Earth jurisprudence, plant studies and post-humanist anthropology, *Law, Humans and Plants* probed these and similar questions as a way to contribute to the "ecologization" of legal theory and practice in Latin America and beyond.

1. The legal narrative of other-than-human beings: a methodological consideration

The law is conventionally defined as a system of normative statements (Kelsen 1991), that is, as language, or a form of symbolic representation. However, the law can also be defined as a non-symbolic system comprising ecological relations, lived experience, artifacts and dreams, among other sources (Anker 2017; Boulot and Sterlin 2021; Borrows 2016; Davies 2017; Mills 2016, 2019; Pelizzon and Gagliano 2015; Vargas Roncancio 2017, 2020, 2021, 2023; Vargas Roncancio et al. 2022). This expanded definition is based on a bold ontological and methodological assumption, namely humans are not the only thinking selves in the world (Kohn 2013). More broadly, this means that "life thinks," or that "life is semiotic" (2013, 9), that is, beetles, plants, fungi, fish and tapirs . . . are not only sentient but cognitive and meaning-making selves (Gagliano 2018; Mikhalevich and Powell 2020). They represent the world in one way or another.

Extending the notion of 'representation' to other beings therefore has profound implications for legal thought and practice globally. If, at a fundamental

DOI: 10.4324/9781003349426-15

level, the law is defined as a system of representations, that is, as a system of signs that includes language and other sign modalities, then, fungi, jaguars, and forests can teach us something crucial about how the law comes into being, how it changes over time, and how it can contribute to restore Earth's life-support systems (Anker et al 2021). This is particularly relevant today when we face the interrelated crises of climate, socio-ecological justice and meaning at a global scale. (Borrows 2016; Anker et al. 2021).

Nevertheless, such a broad definition of law would be untenable unless we, *humans*, open ourselves to the possibility of a mode of socio-legal agency that exceeds *us*; that is, a mode of doing things in the world, for example, making decisions about the "environment" or adjudicating justice, whereby human perspectives are considered one among *many* in a larger cosmological meshwork of forces and lifeways (Ingold 2011; Viveiros de Castro 1998). And contrary to modernist views that separate nature and culture, this suggests a form of "continuity" (and cultural interiority) between humans and other beings (Descola 2013) that invite us to reimagine law for times of ecological crisis (Anker et al. 2021). Plants such as the Yage, the Yoco and the coca leaf are masters, partners and sources of an "ancestral" yet emergent and rapidly evolving legal practice in Amazonia and beyond (Luna 1984; Caicedo 2015).

An Earth-oriented legal thinking implies a post-anthropocentric analytical framework and methodology. Working with the Runa people of the Ecuadorian Amazon, post-humanist anthropologist Eduardo Kohn develops a biosemiotic framework to reimagine our relationships with the more-than-human world—thus laying the groundwork for another kind of legal imagination in times of climate disturbances. Besides symbolic signs such as human language, there're two other sign modalities: icons and indexes. An icon is a type of sign that indicates similarity to that which it represents, for example, a drawing of a macaw is not the bird, but it indicates a relation of similarity between the icon (the drawing) and its referent (the macaw). An index, on the other hand, signals a relation of spatial or temporal contiguity with what it points to, for example, sea-level rise is an index of climate change. These representational modalities "have to be brought into the anthropological [and legal] agenda . . . because icons and indexes are the signs that nonhuman organisms use to represent the world and communicate between life forms" (Descola 2014, 269).

"Life-forms represent the world in some way or another, and these representations are intrinsic to their beings' (Kohn 2013, 9), and this means humans and not share "the fact that [they] live with and through signs . . . signs make what we are" (9). Attributes such as 'perception', 'intelligence' and 'communication' are therefore distributed across all life-forms. They are not the exclusive domain of human animals endowed with a central nervous system. If signs make what we are, a continuity across humans and other beings exceeds our mere shared physicality.

For animist societies in Amazonia all beings harbor a form of interiority concealed under the mask of the body (Descola 2013). In other words, all beings are 'persons' and 'culture', as a changing expression of this form of shared interiority is a common attribute of life. If the law belongs to the realm of culture—an expanded form of culture, to be sure—can we say that there is a sort of *lawness* of life? Or is the law human value imprinted upon agentless life instead? This ontological shift—the lawness of life—may also offer a compelling methodological guidance for an Earth Law praxis today (Zelle et al. 2021). For instance, learning the law from the vantage point of a territory involves thinking *with* this territory as a relational field full of meaning (human and not), rather than an object of scientific description: in Amazonia, thinking with medicinal plants or learning what plants can teach us about territorial governance necessitates what we may call "embodied methodologies" insofar as they emerge from direct experience, ritual, dreaming, commensality, among others—which are mostly marginalized from anthropocentric legal theory (Burdon 2010, 2011) or relegated to the status of "cultural belief" (De la Cadena 2010).

For the Inga communities of Southwestern Colombia, for example, law and justice are based on four main pillars or mandates, namely "do not steal, do not lie, do not be lazy, and live with dignity" (*Taita H*, Inga Community, Nariño). For centuries, the Inga of the Caquetá, Putumayo, Cauca and Nariño regions have designed different social institutions to resolve conflicts arising from noncompliance with these mandates. This book has focused on one of these institutions, namely the ingestion of the Yage or ambihuasca (*Banisteriopsis caapi)* brew and other plants in ritualized and everyday settings. When humans encounter the plant, they reflect on the sources and consequences of their actions and learn how to correct course, guided by the traditional medic and the plant itself (UMIYAC 2000).[1]

As a way of resolving conflicts, repairing cosmological relations and restoring harmony between human people, and between human people and other-than-human people—including "*las cosas invisibles*" (UMIYAC 2000)—the ambihuasca-*consejo* or advise enact one form of non-symbolic justice (or not only symbolic!) at the margins of the state. What can the current Colombian state model of transitional justice, for example, based primarily on liberal/modern notions of reparation and accountability learn from these forms of embodied justice?

Therefore, learning with territories, plants, animals and other beings surpasses symbolic analysis, that is, it requires different forms of embodied engagement with these beings insofar as they "suspend" symbolic representation and critique, as we usually understand those terms in the social sciences. Based on ethnographic engagement in Amazonia, the following ius-philosophical argument concerning the rights of nature (see Chapter 7) can illustrate the ontological and methodological shift *Law, Humans and Plants* advocates for:

1 *Basic assumption*: Normative systems such as the law are usually defined in terms of their all-too-human qualities (i.e., language). This means, among other things, that they are fundamentally separated from ecological relations. However, a global "legal revolution" is taking place: the rights of nature (Boyd 2017).
2 In a sense, the rights of nature challenge this premise of separation between human norms and life, or between culture and nature. Yet the rights of nature approach seems to take the word "law" for granted.

3 The law is conventionally understood as a system of norms made by humans to regulate human societies and the relationship between them and the environment. Thus, it is considered a human system. An all-too-human system.

4 Taking the rights of nature seriously may require an entirely different understanding of what the law could become. *Law, Humans and Plants* suggests that attention be paid to what legal scholar Christopher Stone (1972) has called our "ontological choices" or commitments to the law in times of crisis and socio-ecological transitions. Here, we define "ontology" as engagement with the real as multiple (Escobar 2018): a world where many worlds fit, or the pluriverse (Zapatistas 1996. See Introduction: "Law and the Pluriverse").

5 *Law, Humans and Plants* aimed at showing how we can imagine the law *differently* and with analytical precision, that is, how we can situate the law within the pluriverse as a hypothesis of the *real* and the *law* (Zapatistas 1996; Kothari et al. 2019; Escobar 2018). To contribute to this novel understanding of the law, the book ethnographically followed legal scholars, Indigenous practitioners, biologists and ritual plants across legal documents, conversations, territories and courts of justice.

6 The rights of nature are concrete instruments for socio-ecological transformation. Yet our ontological commitments to either i) a form of law as a system of norms *only* or ii) a form of law as pluriversal possibilities (Escobar 2020) may lead to different orientations for the rights of nature.

7 One of these ontological commitments emphasizes the attribution of rights to natural entities such as rivers, forests and animals through the state (i.e., constitutions, statutes, case law). And this orientation suggests that, contrary to commonly held anthropocentric views of life and social systems, **nature has value in itself.** Much like other historically marginalized groups, the intrinsic value of nature as a legal principle has a place in the current state apparatus. However, this normative orientation is closer to a multicultural interpretation of nature's rights. A multicultural interpretation creates "nature" as a constitutional subject or person (see Chapters 6 and 7) that is recognized by the rule of law, often at the expense of practices of legal difference based on local legal cosmologies. Such legal local differences are therefore considered myth, cultural belief (De la Cadena 2010) or local custom. According to this view, law = state (i.e., norms, power, decisions, frameworks, values).

8 On the other hand, a pluriversal orientation for the rights of nature goes beyond the multicultural recognition of nature's intrinsic value vis-à-vis the state's constitution. According to this second ontological commitment, "nature" is an active social force rather than the backdrop of human action and the state's normative recognition. Moreover, "nature" is also the locus of legal meaning rather than the recipient of state-sanctioned rights alone.

9 In other words, "nature" is not just the object of legal meaning vis-à-vis the allocation of rights, insofar as the relations that make up "nature" are themselves law-producing relations. This is consistent with Indigenous legal cosmologies from the Boreal to the Amazonian forests (Mills

2019; Borrows 2016; UMIYAC 2020). Yet the word "nature" is not an adequate description of cosmological interdependencies.

10 This does not mean that there is *a singular* nature out there and *multiple* representations over this common "nature." On the contrary, "nature" is *multiple*, and cultural representations are *singular*; or, better yet, the capacity to represent and create the world is distributed across different kinds of beings (Viveiros de Castro 1998; Kohn 2013). This means that plants, animals, humans and other beings share similar attributes, for example, cognitive abilities, moral standing and decision-making capacities of sorts. This idea has solid backing in anthropology, cognitive science, plant studies, among other fields (see Descola 2013; Franks et al. 2020; Gagliano et al. 2014, 2018; Kimmerer 2013; Wohlleben 2015).

11 Therefore, what matters for a pluriversal orientation of law is not so much the existence of cultural representations of a common nature that is external to us (humans), but the possibility of multiple "natures" with human-like perspectives from which different worlds and possibilities can emerge: a "multi-naturalist" interpretation of the rights of nature is only possible in a world of multiple worlds (Viveiros de Castro 1998. See Chapter 6 of this book). And this implies a different legal ontology beyond multiculturalism.

There are several limits to this kind of approach, however. I will signal some of them in what follows.

2. Rights of nature: limits and possibilities

The rights of nature in Colombia: Ranging from rivers to entire ecosystems, the increasing recognition of legal personhood for natural beings has been, in terms of legal scholar David Boyd, a legal revolution. The Colombian legal system is a case in point. Between 2016 and 2020, our courts have recognized the rights of ten different rivers (2016, 2018, 2019); one moor (2018); the Colombian Amazon as a whole (2018); two Afro-Colombian collective territories; the collective territory of the Eperara Euya Indigenous nation (2020); three national parks; and numerous animals including bees and other pollinators (2018). What is all this telling us? What are the limits and possibilities of affording legal personhood to natural entities amid exponentially increasing neo-extractivist economies in the region?

Context: Since 1970, the Southwestern region of Colombia, territory of the Cofán and Inga Indigenous communities and many others, has been affected by indiscriminate deforestation, the presence of guerrilla groups, drug traffickers and paramilitaries. In 1991, for example, poppy crops (*Papaver somniferum*) began to be planted in this territory up until they reached more than 2,500 hectares by the end of the decade. The indiscriminate logging and soil sterilization caused by these plantations was further aggravated by the implementation of the *Plan Colombia*—a bilateral agreement between the governments of Colombia and the United States in 1999 to defeat the guerrillas and drug traffickers in the country. While the country's internal armed conflict intensified, glyphosate spraying of illicit poppy crops left deeply negative traces on the Indigenous and peasant inhabitants of this area: the Cofán and Inga peoples have suffered unimaginable losses in Southern Colombia, while seeing how their school-age children and youth are increasingly involved in the "illicit crops" production chain and no effort has been made to overcome this situation, as environmental and social leaders are increasingly targeted, forcibly displaced and assassinated (H. Chindoy, interview, 2021).

As this region has become an epicenter of the Colombian (neo-)extractivist boom, it has also become the recipient of important internationally designed forest conservation programs. Ranging from the extraction of hydrocarbons and rare minerals to bioprospection initiatives and infrastructural projects, today's extractivist-based economies in this region seem to run parallel with powerful environmental narratives as well. A multifaceted phenomenon, (neo-)extractivism is coupled with participatory and land-oriented reconstruction plans in war-torn rural areas of the country. Simultaneously, recent legislations and court decisions foreground the collective rights to a safe environment, while declaring the legal standing of natural beings.

For example, the Colombian Constitutional Court has granted rights to a mercury-polluted river in the Pacific rainforest (2016), as the Supreme Court recognized the personhood of the Amazon in the face of exponentially increasing socio-ecological pressures in this region. Moreover, a celebrated set of regulations, the 2016 Peace Agreement (PA), between the Colombian government and the largest guerrilla group in the country enlists the "preservation of the environment" as a crucial element of a long-awaited—and still pending—rural reform in Colombia. An impressive catalogue of rights, procedures and institutional arrangements, this impressive legal artifact remains, however, mostly aligned with the extractive-based development model just described.

In the Colombian Amazon alone, for example, deforestation doubled between 2016–2018,[2] and nearly 10 percent of the deforested area overlaps with Indigenous territories as international conservation efforts steadily increase in the region: there seems to be a productive tension between eco-centric legal narratives, such as the rights of nature, and anthropocentric economic practices, which poses serious questions not only to the effectiveness of the command and control approaches of environmental governance models in the Andean-Amazonian region but also Earth-oriented legislation and case law.

Interrogating a legal revolution? What are some of the barriers to realize the eco-centric orientation of the rights of nature and other measures in our context? As impressive and meaningful as this legal revolution is, *Law, Humans and Plants* argued that recognizing nature as subject of rights might fall short if the law is understood as a matter of language *only*, and nature as an adequate conception of ecological and cosmological interdependencies. The thesis of law as language *only* seems to reinforce a much-contested rift between culture and nature and other boundary-making concepts at the root of modern legal thought and practice. How can Indigenous legal traditions contribute to this eco-centric project? Can the law become an emancipatory tool for these communities? Could reckoning with other-than-human beings as agents of legal meaning, rather than mere recipients of state-sanctioned rights, transform what we mean by the rights of nature (RON) and the law more broadly? These are pressing questions.

Some of the challenges: As discussed in this book (Chapters 6, 7 and 8), modern legal theory is mostly based upon the primacy of separation between social facts and ecological interdependencies; norms and values; positive law and local customs, among others. And it is precisely because of this separation that it is possible to speak of rights for *external* natural beings. It is challenging, however, if one takes a rights approach, to say that nature should be *in* law without radically transforming what we mean both by nature and law. The difficulty of a legal embeddedness of "nature" speaks to the limits of using categories of a legal framework based on "nature," and of the concept of rights as trump-style claims conferred by the state on nonhumans, giving them legal meaning that they would otherwise lack. There are several conceptual, but also deeply political, challenges for the realization of the RON today in our country (see Chapter 7 for a detailed analysis):

1 *Diffuse nature*: Since nature is pervasive in human life, and human impacts are pervasive in nature, they cannot be separated. The notion of nature is diffuse because it may refer to humans and nonhumans, or to nonhuman beings only.
2 *Discreteness*: Nature is composed of millions of species, and "each aspect of nature involves a different (socio-legal) interest." As a result, it is impossible to articulate legal claims for each component of nature. This may lead to a sort of multinaturalist identity politics with challenges that are similar to those already faced by multicultural politics. Extractives, to be sure, target this compartmentalized nature.
3 *Human mediation and collision of legal cosmologies*: The self-standing of nonhumans, as it were, is impossible within a legal system based on a conception of law as a human-only system of meaning. The difference in modes of communication between human and nonhuman selves should not foreclose other forms of speaking and listening in the legal field.

Some questions remain: These conceptual and political challenges raise at least three crucial questions for the theory and practice of the rights of nature and other Earth-centered tools: 1) What should be considered as existent in concrete scenarios of adjudication? 2) What kind of people should act on whose behalf? 3) What is the procedure for adjudicating rights in contexts of neo-extractivism and war such as Colombia? The preceding assessment calls for a radical transformation of RON's legal imagination. As RON highlight substantial territorial and cultural claims by Indigenous and peasant communities in Colombia, established critique has underlined the dangers of reducing those rights to a mere icon of the state's "environmental politics." The gap between aspirational legal propositions, on the one hand, and increasing neo-extractivist practices, on the other, is but a symptom of a deeper rift between the co-emergent logic of life and the mechanistic logic of the law in modern societies.

A way forward? Inga intellectual and political leader Hernando Chindoy says the following:

> Inga law is recognized in daily life as the existence of the infinite interrelations between human and nonhuman beings in their material and spiritual dimensions. Inga law is also found in the Inga language as one of its most important sources (but not the only one) where the ancestral knowledge of our community is revitalized. . . . Inga law is samai, or a point of joyful encounter and resting of all beings, and it is a pillar for every lively encounter with these other worlds (invisible worlds). . . . The methodology to recognize and study the law is the return to ancestral knowledge from a decolonized perspective and through our own language. And this requires a journey of connection [with all beings of the forest].
>
> (Personal communication, February 2020)

Indigenous legal traditions in Colombia and Latin America raise a crucial question in times of planetary crisis. In a world where animals, plants and other beings hold "human features" such as the ability to communicate, make decisions and transmit knowledge to humans, words such as "society" and "law" seem to take on an entirely different meaning. What would happen to conventional knowledge and legal systems when—in the words of Indigenous legal scholar Hernando Chindoy—we leave room for "the time when plants and animals transmitted their powers and knowledge to people in dreams"? What if we imagine a form of law beyond human modes of representation? This possesses a serious methodological challenge as well: how can we seriously engage with legal traditions—in research, teaching and social life at large—that go beyond "symbolic language," when predominant research methodologies seem mostly aligned with anthropocentric narratives? The book was an attempt to answer some of these questions. In the next and final section, I summarize some of the main conclusions I reached.

3. Onto-epistemic and methodological openings

Part I: Law and its ontological itineraries: a legal herbarium

Part I ethnographically explored connections between humans, other-than-humans and the law and why these connections matter today. This part was comprised of four interconnected chapters: the first three focused on plant-human relations, and the fourth concerned the making of an ethnobotanical research agreement in southwestern Colombian Amazon. Thus, Part I can be considered as one larger ethnographic and conceptual argument around the socio-legal agency of plants and non-visible peoples in Southwestern Colombia (Andes-Amazon) and their potential contributions to expand normative systems such as law and ethics beyond anthropocentric views and practices. I present subsequently the conclusions I have reached in each of these chapters.

Chapter 1—Yoco

Chapter 1 told a story of Yoco (*Paullinia Yoco*) and how this Amazonian vine prepares humans to work with and learn about anything in the forest and the invisible worlds that sustain it. Expanding the idea of learning beyond the human, the chapter surveyed a relational approach to cognition in the work of Chilean neurobiologist Francisco Varela (1999). Varela's approach was crucial to understanding how normative systems such as ethics and law are indeed grounded in the everyday experience of an organism (Varela 1991), and how we can expand these normative systems beyond abstract and disembodied norms, principles and values sanctioned by a state (Winter 2001). Therefore, the chapter concluded, among others, that a non-dualist and post-anthropocentric narrative of environmental decision-making in Amazonia involves learning with plants as persons of sorts.

Chapter 2—Yagé

The book then turned to another crucial plant teacher in the Andean-Amazonian slopes. This plant person was central to the argument about learning law where the *law* is not named as such. Here, the focus was on the disruption of linear time as a pre-analytical category of Western (legal) epistemologies. Chapter 2 was based on ethnographic encounters with the Yagé vine (*Banisteriopsis caapi*) in Upper Putumayo, Colombian Amazon (Caicedo 2015; Weiskopf 2002) and investigated different modes of learning and practicing time in this region as well as the potential normative consequences of this disruption. A snapshot of recent experiences with the Yagé concoction with the guidance of several practitioners from the regions of Sibundoy (Upper Putumayo region) and the Guamuez Valley (Lower Putumayo), it discussed whether a non-modern approach to the idea of time can contribute to a post-anthropocentric view of legal institutions and decision-making practices in Amazonia. The chapter posed, among others, the following question: how is the juridical imagination transformed in response to the entangled temporalities of the Amazon, that is, to the different ways of practicing time beyond the linear temporalities of modernity? (Mignolo 2011) The altered temporalities of vegetal epistemologies not only disrupt the linear temporalities of modernity, but also the linearity of the modern legal process.

Chapter 3—Coca

Chapter 3 offered further ethnographic analysis to illustrate the emergence of what the book calls a "relational protocol" or the "law of the place," that is, a way to participate in the entangled lives of law and ecology in this region. Chapter 1 addressed how we can *learn to learn* law with the emetic Yoco vine (Paullinia Yoco), while Chapter 2 explored the altered temporalities of the Yagé liana (Banisteriopsis caapi) and how they trouble the linear legal temporalities of prior consultation as a modern legal process (Chapter 2). Similarly, Chapter 3 followed plants and humans as they co-create knowledge and place to conclude that daily encounters between humans and a local preparation of the coca leaf (*Erythroxylon coca*) among the Murui of Putumayo can broaden legal theory and practice beyond anthropocentric views.

This chapter engaged with *vibrations* as active material events taking place in the skin and through the incorporation of *mambe* (the Amazonian coca leaf preparation). This conceptualization of the skin as a knowledge interface can open the evocative notion of *sentipensar* to other senses (Escobar 2015). The event of *vibration* is conflated with the event of *thought*, thus making it almost impossible to distinguish between the two. The skin, so to speak, is itself thinking. This relationship between thinking and feeling with the skin that the plant capacitates disrupts the division between knowledge practices and bodily perception. Perception—as the act of engaging the world with the senses—and thinking—as the act of signifying the world—are thus intertwined. Engaging with the skin in decolonial practices raises the question of what it means to engage with other ways of being in the world and not only how knowledge is produced as a function of symbolic representation. Working with the *mambia* involves the task of critically (and carnally) confronting our own habits of thought and practice, as well as how we are in (and as) place with other beings.

Chapter 4—The making of an ethnobotanical research agreement

With this discussion on embodied methodologies at hand, and after analyzing various aspects of the entangled lives of law and ecology in Amazonia (Chapters 1–3), Chapter 4 used a different format: it invited ethnobotanist David Rodríguez Mora to the conversation. The chapter discussed several aspects of our year-long conversations about plants, law, the politics of naming nature; the invisible people and the ethical and conceptual dilemmas we both faced as we engaged with "law" and "ecology" with the guidance of humans and plants in Southern Colombia. The chapter told the story of a collaborative learning with *Yagé* (*Banisteriopsis caapi* (Spruce ex Griseb.) Morton, a.k.a. Ayahuasca) and members of the A'i (a.k.a. Cofán or Kofán) Indigenous people of Nariño in Southwestern Colombia, with whom David has been closely working since 2019.

This chapter probed the entangled lives of law and ecology in Amazonia and focused on two main aspects of this assemblage: (1) how plants as persons may become part of a larger conversation about knowledge and world-making in this region, and (2) how may we come to learn the legal mandates that emerge from encounters with different beings of the forest. To probe this relationship between law and ecology, we focused on the making of an ethnobotanical research agreement concerning wild varieties of the *Yagé* vine in the Cofán ancestral territory. This protocol or agreement involved the contested participation of human and other-than-human agencies, including the plant as person.

There were, however, multiple epistemological, ethical and methodological challenges in the process of creating this legal artifact, for example, how may "*los Invisibles*" mediate norms for doing or not doing something in the forest? How can we know (or not) this? Rather than answering this difficult set of questions—which confronts us with the limits of our own knowledge "as long as we dare to ask the question"—this chapter has suggested, among other things, that the ingestion of plants as people may be a form of participation in the making of science and law (i.e., an ethnobotanical protocol) in one Cofán community of Nariño. This participation is widely distributed and may involve other-than-human beings, and thus may challenge the epistemic and ontological closure of symbolic forms of representation.

Part II: On the rights of nature: limits, possibilities and challenges in neo-extractivist worlds

Part II dealt with some of the conceptual limits and possibilities of the rights of nature clause in Latin America in the context of an emergent regional and global Earth Law movement. By attending to the social and legal worlds of other-than-human beings introduced in the first part of the book, *Rights of Nature* invited us to reimagine core premises of social and legal sciences at present, for example, the idea that the law is primarily linguistic or propositional; the notion that rights and responsibilities are commensurable across all legal cultures and cosmologies (Chapter 7, "Conjuring"), or that "personhood" is fundamental for legal redress (Chapter 8, "Forest on trial"). Thus, as a contribution to a relational theory of legal agency, Part II critically assessed core notions of Western law such as legal personhood, standing and rights. Part II starts off with a detailed critical literature review.

Chapter 5—Sowing concepts

The chapter was divided into four parts: 1) post-humanist theory and material agency; 2) plant studies and plant-human relations; 3) Earth Law and the rights of nature; and 4) Indigenous legal traditions and decoloniality. A central claim, *Sowing Concepts* suggests that while multicultural notions such as "traditional knowledge," "traditional ecological knowledge," "Indigenous know-how" and "Indigenous science" populate important scholarly conversations around local ways of dealing with non-humans, they are insufficiently capable to address the sentient, cognitive and even political capacities of plants, animals, soils, mountains and other beings and relations. In one way or another, the heuristic potentials and political capaciousness of these concepts have been the object of critique in the anthropology of knowledge, post-humanist anthropology, political ontology and decolonial studies, among others.

The chapter argued that the place-based and relational character of local "knowledge practices" in the Andean-Amazonian region concerning the "natural world" require relational idioms able to convey the highly asymmetrical character of environmental knowledge practices in colonial contexts, as well as the limits of human representation of forest life. Notions such as cultural translation (Buden et al. 2009), re-appropriation and re-signification (Rappaport and Cummins 2011), other-than-human agencies (De la Cadena 2015) and perspectivism and multi-naturalism, among others (Viveiros de Castro 1998), are paramount to an epistemology and ontology of Amerindian forest practices and territorial governance models in the Andean-Amazonian region today.

Moreover, the relentless multiplicity of "Indigenous conceptual worlds" (Viveiros de Castro 2014, 2015) around "natural systems" can hardly be confined to concepts whose fundamental ontological premise is the modern separation between knowledge and life, culture and nature and body and mind (Escobar 2018; Agrawal 2002). This chapter thus reviewed some streams of post-humanist and relational approaches in social theory to start framing legal themes in a post-anthropocentric key, in particular, the rights of nature.

Chapter 6—Plants and the law

The chapter proposed two anthropological readings and textual methodologies concerning the rights of nature in Latin American constitutionalism. Taking cues from the science of plant sensing and intelligence, *Plants and the law* probed how plants can serve as a prototype of constitutional analysis that fully asserts Amazonian principles of relationality and interdependency between all entities. It concluded with an invitation to take seriously interspecies encounters and forms of agency and to pay close ethnographic attention to how they unfold in Indigenous law and constitutional analysis and practice in neo-extractivist contexts.

Chapter 7—Conjuring

Recent norms and judicial decisions on the rights of nature (RON) place life at the center of legal discourse in Latin America. This "legal revolution" thus purports to upend the paradigm of solely human legal subjectivity in recognizing the personhood of nature. Nevertheless, the RON approach seems to depend on an assumption that the form of law is primarily linguistic and propositional. In this way, it reveals another critical assumption: that law is a system of norms made by humans to regulate human conduct in relation to an externally existing natural world, thereby insisting on a separation between law and life processes. This chapter argued that recognizing nature as a legal person and subject of rights falls short if law is understood as a matter of human language only and nature is understood as an adequate conception of cosmological interdependencies between "all that exists." The thesis of law as language seems to reinforce a much-contested rift between mind and body, culture and nature, among other boundary-making notions at the root of modern thought and practice. In what sense, then, could conjuring other-than-human beings as agents of legal meaning, rather than mere recipients of state-sanctioned rights, transform what we mean by law and RON in Latin America?

This chapter dealt with two different legal projects. The first, *RON as text*, is based upon the ontological assumption that the real is divided into nature and culture and other cascading divisions. This ontology leads to seeing what positive law calls "nature" as a legal person, often at the expense of the relations behind the mask of legal subjectivity. The second, *RON as teks*, is based upon another pre-analytical assumption, which, following Escobar (2018, 2020), I have termed the Principle of Radical Interdependence. Translated into a legal principle, this cosmological premise suggests that the project of the law is also about discerning (legal) meaning in relationships beyond the human, language and the state (Davies 2017), and I have proposed a methodology to encounter such relations in the law: a tectonic reading. Chapter 8 follows a similar line of analysis, exploring the ius-philosophical foundations of the notion of personhood and its relevance in adjudication scenarios.

Chapter 8—Forest on trial

"Persons" such as human beings and corporations can seek redress before a court of law. The notion of legal personhood, however, actualizes the contested modern tension between nature and culture in most of social and legal theory at present. More than discontinuous and self-contained beings, Amazonian forests embody sentient and mind-bearing relations involving humans and other-than-human beings such as plants, animals and spirits, as amply demonstrated in preceding chapters. Can the forest speak law? Do forests endlessly require the mediation of human modes of legal representation? Overflowing the ontological stability of the person, forests teach a rhizomatic notion of legal agency beyond the human, the state and the norm.

An opening

There is a long way before state-oriented legal frameworks incorporate more-than-human vegetal legalities in theory and practice (Pelizzon and Gagliano 2015; Braverman 2018; Davies 2017). Although this emergent legal frame may benefit from Indigenous cosmologies and plant science alike, symbolic representation distinguishes the law from other fields of practice and experience. The law is almost exclusively conceived as a symbolic (language-based) practice. Can the plant speak *law*? Does the forest always need the mediation of the botanist, for example, in a court of law? How far removed should judges and decision-makers be from direct experience with these beings in legal proceedings and decisions involving them?

"Life thinks," says anthropologist Eduardo Kohn (2013), describing an ontological premise that goes beyond the notion of representation to include nonhuman beings, such as animals, plants and spirits, as creators of meaning. This book expanded the legal framework of agency to engage with the law both as a particular kind of symbolic representation—for example, as a set of positive norms produced by humans—as well as a non-symbolic form of representation vis-à-vis images, processes of materialization, sounds and experience involving other-than-human selves.

Read as a proposal on legal philosophy, *Law, Humans and Plants* offered a methodology to explore instances of legal meaning—that is, sonic images of the forest, shamanistic chants and ecological relations—as sources of legal practices. Such an effort, however, involves a particular mode of attunement to the social worlds plants and humans co-create through sowing, commensality and ritual, among other practices. An attempt to expand the notion of the law beyond the symbolic (the legal norm), I consider these practices as sources of legal meaning in and of themselves. In fact, forests' legal agencies might be better expressed in terms of alliance or partnership between inter-dependent humans and forests. This move problematizes languages of personhood and legal guardianship that separate humans from the larger community of life. Inter-being alliance thus recognizes the human mind as part and parcel of the larger mind of the forest (Kohn 2013).

If the human can engage with the forest through science, the human can also learn how to think with forests in a court of law. While this methodological question requires an independent treatment, appropriate cultural engagement with plants may be one such mode of learning with forests' minds and the legal protocols they harness for post-extractivist transitions in Amazonia. While botanists and anthropologists may be summoned to render testimony on behalf of forests and cultures—respectively—it remains an important challenge to explore whether judges should engage with other-than-human beings as they do with humans as expert witnesses.

How far-off are we from asking judges and legislators to interact with other-than-humans such as forests and rivers as they decide cases involving these kinds of beings? Should a judge, for example, ingest, in some cases, a ritual plant to understand what the forest *wants* when it comes to a mining license in Amazonia? Could this be considered an appropriate methodology for adjudicating justice in certain cases? Could a judge walk the *páramo* (a fragile ecosystem of the Andes), let it speak the language it speaks best and then consider this experience a form of witness testimony? Should we elect legislators with proven commitment to listening to forests? How about forest literacy as a requirement for licensing lawyers and adjudicating environmental justice?

Notes

1 Another institution is the *Atun Puncha*. The *Atun Puncha*—the Great Day—or Carnival of Forgiveness is when the Inga communities commemorate the legacy of Carlos Tamabioy, unite in thought, song, and spirit to celebrate the beginning of a new year of life, forgive each other and start a new cycle (Interview with H. Chindoy, Jan. 2021).

2 In the span of one year, from 2021 to 2022, however, deforestation in Colombia dropped from 174,103 hectares (672sq miles) to 123,517 hectares (477sq miles), marking a nearly 30-percent decrease. See www.aljazeera.com/news/2023/7/12/deforestation-in-colombia-dropped-by-29-percent-a-milestone

Bibliography

Agrawal, Arun. 2002. "Indigenous Knowledge and the Politics of Classification." In *UNESCO*. Oxford: Blackwell Publishers.

Anker, Kirsten. 2017. "Law as . . . Forest: Eco-logic, Stories and Spirits in Indigenous Jurisprudence." *Law Text Culture*, 21: 191–213.

Anker, Kirsten, Burdon, Peter, Garver, Geoffrey, Maloney, Michele, and Sbert, Carla (eds.). 2021. *From Environmental to Ecological Law*. London and New York: Routledge.

Borrows, John. 2010. *Canada's Indigenous Constitution*. Toronto: University of Toronto Press.

Borrows, John. 2016. *Freedom and Indigenous Constitutionalism*. Toronto: University of Toronto Press.

Boulot, E., and Sterlin, J. 2021. "Steps Towards a Legal Ontological Turn: Proposals for Law's Place Beyond the Human." *Transnational Environmental Law*: 1–26.

Boyd, David. 2017. *The Rights of Nature. A Legal Revolution that Could Save the World*. Toronto: ECW Press.

Braverman, Irus. 2018. "Law's Underdog: A Call for More-Than-Human Legalities." *Annual Review of Law and Social Science*, 14: 127–144.

Buden, Boris, Nawotny, Stefan, Simon, Sherry, Bery, Ashok, and Cronin, Michael. 2009. "Cultural Translation: An Introduction to the Problem, and Responses." *Journal of Tranlation Studies*, 2(2): 196–219.

Burdon, Peter. 2010. "The Rights of Nature: Reconsidered." *Australian Humanities Review*, 49: 69.

Burdon, Peter. 2011. *Exploring Wild Law: The Philosophy of Earth Jurisprudence*. Cambridge: Wakefield Press.

Caicedo, Alhena. 2015. *La Alteridad Radical que Cura. Neo-chamanismos yageceros en Colombia*. Bogotá: Universidad de los Andes.

Capra, Fritjof, and Ugo, Mattei. 2015. *The Ecology of Law: Toward a Legal System in Tune with Nature and Community*. Oakland: Berrett-Koehler Publishers, Incorporated.

Davies, Margaret. 2017. *Law Unlimited. Materialism, Pluralism, and Legal Theory*. London: Routledge.

De la Cadena, Marisol. 2010. "Indigenous Cosmopolitics in the Andes: Conceptual Reflections Beyond 'Politics'." *Cultural Anthropology*, 24(2): 334–370.

De la Cadena, Marisol. 2015. *Earth Beings. Ecologies of Practice Across Andean Worlds*. Durham: Duke University Press.

Descola, Philippe. 2013. *Beyond Nature and Culture*. Chicago: University of Chicago Press.

Descola, Philippe. 2014. "All to human (still). A comment on Eduardo Kohn' How Forest Think." *HAU: Journal of Ethnographic Theory*, 4(2): 268.

Escobar, Arturo. 2015. *Sentipensar con la Tierra. Nuevas lecturas sobre desarrollo, territorio y Diferencia*. Medellin, Colombia: Ediciones UNIAULA (Universidad Autonoma Latinoamericana).

Escobar, Arturo. 2018. *Designs for the Pluriverse: Radical Interdependence, Autonomy and the Making of Worlds*. Durham: Duke University Press.

Escobar, Arturo. 2020. *Pluriversal Politics. The Real and the Possible*. Durham: Duke University Press.

Franks, B., Webb, C., Gagliano, M., and Smuts, B. 2020. "Conventional Science Will Not Do Justice to Nonhuman Interests: A Fresh Approach Is Required. Commentary on Treves et al. on 'Just Preservation'." *Animal Sentience*, 27(17): 1–5.

Gagliano, Monica. 2018. *Thus Spoke the Plant: A Remarkable Journey of Groundbreaking Scientific Discoveries and Personal Encounters with Plants*. Berkeley: North Atlantic Books.

Gagliano, Monica, Abramson, C.I., and Depczynski, M. 2018. "Plants Learn and Remember: Lets Get Used to It." *Oecologia*, 186: 29–31.

Gagliano, Monica, Renton, M., Depczynski, M., and Mancuso, S. 2014. "Experience Teaches Plants to Learn Faster and Forget Slower in Environments Where It Matters." *Oecologia*, 175: 63–72.

Garver, Geoffrey. 2021. *Ecological Law and the Planetary Crisis. A Legal Guide for Harmony on Earth*. London and New York: Routledge.

Ingold, Tim. 2011. *Being Alive: Essays on Movement, Knowledge, and Description*. New York: Routledge.

Kelsen, Hans. 1991. *General Theory of Norms* (M. Hartney, trans.). Oxford: Oxford University Press.

Kimmerer, Robin Wall. 2013. *Braiding Sweetgrass. Indigenous Wisdom, Scientific Knowledge and the Teching of Plants*. Minneapolis: Milkweed Editors.

Kohn, Eduardo. 2013. *How Forests Think. Toward an Anthropology Beyond the Human*. Berkeley: University of California Press.

Kothari, Ashish, Salleh, Ariel, Escobar, Arturo, Demaria, Federico, and Acosta, Alberto. 2019. *Pluriverse. A Post-Development Dictionary*. New Delhi: Tulika Books.

Luna, Luis Eduardo. 1984. "The Concept of Plants as Teachers Among Four Mestizo Shamans in Iquitos, Northeaster Peru." *Journal of Ethnopharmacology*, 11(2): 135–156.

Mignolo, Walter. 2011. *The Darker Side of Western Modernity. Global Futures, Decolonial Options*. Durham: Duke University Press.

Mikhalevich, I., and Powell, R. 2020. "Minds Without Spines: Evolutionarily Inclusive Animal Ethics." *Animal Sentience*, 29(1): 1–25.

Mills, Aaron. 2016. "The Lifeworlds of Law: On Revitalizing Indigenous Legal Orders Today." *McGill Law Journal*, 61(4): 847–884.

Mills, Aaron. 2019. *Miinigowiziwin: All that Has Been Given for Living Well Together: One Vision of Anishinaabe Constitutionalism*. University of Victoria Dissertation, iii. https://dspace.library.uvic.ca/bitstream/handle/1828/10985/Mills_Aaron_PhD_2019.pdf?sequence=1&isAllowed=y.

Pelizzon, Alessandro, and Gagliano, Monica. 2015. "The Sentience of Plants: Animal Rights and Rights of Nature Intersecting?" *Australian Animal Protection Law Journal*, 11: 5–13.

Rappaport, J., and Cummins, T. 2011. *Beyond the Lettered City. Indigenous Literacies in the Andes*. Durham: Duke University Press.
Stone, Christopher. 1972. "Should Trees Have Standing? Toward Legal Rights for Natural Object." *Southern California Law Review*, 45: 450–501.
Strathern, Marilyn. 2010. *Kinship, Law and the Unexpected. Relatives Are Always a Surprise*. Cambridge: Cambridge University Press.
UMIYAC. 2000. *Pensamiento de los Mayores: Código de ética de la medicina indígena del piedemonte Amazónico colombiano*. Putumayo: UMIYAC.
Varela, Francisco. 1991. "Organism: A Meshwork of Selfless Selves." In Tauber, A.I. (ed.). *Organism and the Origins of Self. Boston Studies in the Philosophy of Science* (vol. 129). Dordrecht: Springer. https://doi.org/10.1007/978-94-011-3406-4_5
Varela, Francisco. 1999. *Ethical Know-How. Action, Wisdom and Cognition*. Stanford: Stanford University Press.
Vargas Roncancio, I.D. 2017. "Plants and the Law: Vegetal Ontologies and the Rights of Nature. A Perspective from Latin America." *Australian Feminist Law Journal*, 43(1): 67–87 (Reprinted for special edition in Gustafsson, R., Hill, R., and Ngo, H. (eds.). 2018. *Philosophies of Difference: Nature, Racism, and Sexuate Difference*, first edition. London and New York: Routledge).
Vargas Roncancio, I.D. 2020. "Forest on Trial: Towards a Relational Theory of Legal Agency for Transitions into the Ecozoic." Orr, C., Kish, K., and Jennings, B. (eds.). *Liberty and the Ecological Crisis: Freedom on a Finite Planet*. London and New York: Routledge.
Vargas Roncancio, I.D. 2021. "Conjuring Sentient Beings and Relations in the Law: Rights of Nature and a Comparative Praxis of Legal Cosmologies." In Anker, K., Burdon, P., Garver, G., Maloney, M., and Sbert, C. (eds.). *From Environmental to Ecological Law*. London and New York: Routledge.
Vargas Roncancio, I.D. 2023. "Law as Relation and the Co-emergence of Beings: Towards a Paradigm Shift in Legal Education for Socioecological Transitions." In Giddens, Thomas, and Siliquini-Cinelli, Dundee Luca (eds.). *Life and the Structures of the Law School: The Biopolitics of Legal Education. Vol. 2 (Resisting the Law School)*. London and New York: Routledge.
Vargas-Roncancio, I.D., Boulot, E., Grear, A., and Sterlin, J. (eds.). 2022. *Posthuman Legalities: New Materialism and Law Beyond the Human*. Cheltenham: Edward Elgar Publishing.
Viveiros de Castro, Eduardo. 1998. "Cosmological Diexis and Amerindian Perspectivism." *Journal of the Royal Anthropological Institute*, 4(3): 469–489.
Viveiros de Castro, Eduardo. 2014. *Cannibal Metaphysics*. Minneapolis: Univocal.
Viveiros de Castro, Eduardo. 2015. *The Relative Native. Essays on Indigenous Conceptual Worlds*. Chicago: HAU Books.
Weiskopf, Jimmy. 2002. *Yagé: El Nuevo Purgatorio*. Bogotá: Villegas Editores.
Winter, Steven. 2001. *A Clearing in the Forest. Law, Life, and Mind*. Chicago: University of Chicago Press.
Wohlleben, Peter. 2015. *The Hidden Life of Trees: What They Feel, How the Communicate—Discoveries from a Secret World*. Vancouver: Greystone Books.
Zapatistas. 1996. "Cuarta Declaración de la Selva Lacandona." *Enlace Zapatista*. https://enlacezapatista.ezln.org.mx/1996/01/01/cuarta-declaracion-de-la-selva-lacandona/
Zelle, Anthony, Wilson, Graham, Adam, Rachel, and Greene, Hermann (eds.). 2021. *Earth Law: Emerging Ecocentric Law. A Practitioner's Guide. Aspen Coursebook Series*. New York: Wolters Kluwer.

Index

Milton Keynes UK
Ingram Content Group UK Ltd.
UKHW051906230624
444477UK00005B/97

9 781032 393674